RUSSIAN ETYMOLOGICAL DICTIONARY

Also available in the Russian Language series:

Modern Russian: an advanced grammar course, D. Offord
First Russian Vocabulary, P. Waddington

RUSSIAN ETYMOLOGICAL DICTIONARY

Terence Wade

Bristol Classical Press

This impression 2002
This edition published in 1996 by
Bristol Classical Press
an imprint of
Gerald Duckworth & Co. Ltd.
61 Frith Street, London W1D 3JL
Tel: 020 7434 4242
Fax: 020 7434 4420
inquiries@duckworth-publishers.co.uk
www.ducknet.co.uk

© 1996 by Terence Wade

All rights reserved. No part of this publication
may be reproduced, stored in a retrieval system, or
transmitted, in any form or by any means, electronic,
mechanical, photocopying, recording or otherwise,
without the prior permission of the publisher.

A catalogue record for this book is available
from the British Library

ISBN 1 85399 414 X

Typeset by Terence Wade
Printed in Great Britain by
Antony Rowe Ltd, Eastbourne

CONTENTS

Introduction	1
Glossary	11
Abbreviations	13
RUSSIAN ETYMOLOGICAL DICTIONARY	15
Bibliography	262

INTRODUCTION

Aims and method

The *Russian Etymological Dictionary* gives the derivations of some 1, 500 Russian words, chosen for their frequency or intrinsic interest. A typical entry includes present meaning, time of first appearance in the language, and subsequent meaning changes, as well as orthographical, phonetic or social factors that have affected lexical development. Cognate words help to place each item in its linguistic context. The dictionary is designed to show the factors that affect word derivation and inter-action with other languages. It also aims to facilitate the learning of vocabulary and raise language awareness.

Sources consulted

Entries in the dictionary draw on information contained in Russian etymological dictionaries and other works on lexis, checked against Sreznevskij's source materials (see bibliography), standard and etymological dictionaries of other languages, language histories, Mann's comparative dictionary of Indo-European, and primary sources. Dal''s four-volume dictionary has been used as an invaluable source of archaic and dialect words.

HISTORICAL DEVELOPMENT FROM INDO-EUROPEAN TO RUSSIAN

Indo-European

The 18th-century discovery that many languages in Europe and Northern India share common linguistic features (for example, similar words for the lower numerals, natural phenomena, domestic animals, parts of the body and close relations) led scholars to assume the existence of an ancient speech community of pastoral nomads or agriculturists, speaking related dialects from which a number of European and Asian languages subsequently evolved. Much research was devoted in the 19th century to establishing the original homeland of this speech community and to reconstructing its language, which was given the name 'Indo-European' (IE).

In the face of opposing claims that the IE community originally inhabited the shores of the Baltic, Central Turkey or India itself, a general consensus eventually placed its homeland somewhere in South Russia, perhaps in the middle reaches of the Volga. However, IE linguistic unity began to disintegrate in the third millennium BC, towards the end of the Neolithic period, as whole peoples began moving out in the direction of Hindustan and across the expanses of Europe. These migrations continued for some 3, 000 years, culminating in the Norman conquests of the eleventh century.

As the migrations progressed, linguistic and cultural differences intensified and new languages evolved from IE dialects. Twelve sub-groups of IE languages can be distinguished: Albanian, Armenian, Baltic, Celtic, Germanic, Greek, Hittite (a language spoken in Anatolia or Asia Minor up until the 13th century BC, evidence of which is based on cuneiform texts excavated in Turkey), Indian (in particular Sanskrit, the classical Indian literary language of the period from the 5th century BC to the 7th century AD, and still the sacred language of the Hindus), Iranian, Italic (in particular Latin), Slavonic, and Tocharian (evidence of which is based on Buddhist writings dating from the 6th-8th centuries and discovered in Chinese Turkestan).

Western and Eastern branches of the IE languages may be differentiated by their treatment of the IE palatal plosive *k̂ in *k̂m̥tóm, the word for 'hundred'. It appears as a velar in the **Western** branch (Greek, Italic, Celtic and Germanic, the so-called *centum* languages, after the Latin for *hundred*) but as a sibilant in the Eastern branch (Indo-Iranian, Armenian and Balto-Slavonic, the so-called *satem* languages, after the Avestan for *hundred*, cf. Russian сто 'hundred').

Some of the groups sub-divided further, for example, the Romance languages (French, Italian, Portuguese, Romanian, Romansh, Spanish, etc.) derived from Vulgar Latin (the spoken form of the language that had spread throughout the Roman Empire prior to its disintegration in the 5th century AD), while Slavonic languages derive from Common Slavonic, a hypothetical parent language which has been reconstructed on the basis of the evidence of individual Slavonic languages.

Common Slavonic

Common Slavonic is assumed to have existed for more than three thousand years before breaking up into individual languages over the period from the 6th to the 9th centuries AD. As the Slavs expanded from their putative homeland (which is thought to have stretched from the Pripet to the Carpathians, the middle reaches of the Vistula and the Dniester) and moved West, East and subsequently South, three groups of languages evolved:

East Slavonic: Russian, Ukrainian, Belorussian
South Slavonic: Serbian, Croatian, Bulgarian, Slovene, Church Slavonic
West Slavonic: Czech, Slovak, Polish, Sorbian, Cassubian and (extinct) Polabian

Russian

Russian developed as follows:

(1) *Early E. Slavonic. The Kievan period* (up to about 1250 AD). A major event in this period was the adoption of Greek Orthodoxy in 988, together with the Cyrillic alphabet and Old Church Slavonic, the language of early religious literature, which introduced South Slavonic features into Russian such as non-'pleophonic' forms (cf. pleophonic город 'town' and non-pleophonic град, as in Волгогра́д 'Volgograd') and the reflexes жд and щ for *dj* and *tj*, alongside Russian ж and ч (cf. надёжный 'reliable' but наде́жда 'hope', свеча́ 'candle' but освеще́ние 'illumination').

(2) *Muscovite Russian* (c. 1250-1700). Following the Mongol invasion (1237-1240), Russian, Ukrainian and Belorussian (all deriving from Old Russian) began, in due course, to develop

separately. This period in the development of Russian lasted until the seventeenth century, when Western influences began to affect the language of Muscovy.

(3) *The modern period*, from about 1700 to the present day.

The distinctive features of Russian

The distinctive features of Russian include:

(1) 'Free' stress (initial, as in кры́ша 'roof', medial, as in доро́га 'road', final, as in семья́ 'family').

(2) Absence of nasal vowels, replaced in Russian by я (e.g. пять 'five') and у (e.g. у́гол 'angle').

(3) Pleophony (inter-consonantal flanking vowels, e.g. голова́ 'head', cf. non-pleophonic глава́ 'chapter'). See glossary, under 'Pleophony (полногла́сие)'.

(4) The development of Common Slavonic short vowels ь and ъ to e and o in 'strong' position (i.e. either stressed or followed by unstressed ь or ъ, e.g. день 'day' from *дьнь*, сон 'sleep' from *сънъ*).

(5) Initial o- before a soft consonant, e.g. оди́н 'one'.

(6) The palatalization (softening) of consonants, as follows:

(a) the palatalization of velar consonants (к, г, х) followed by or sometimes preceded by front vowels has produced the mutations г:ж (e.g. у́жин 'dinner'), к:ч (e.g. мяч 'ball'), х:ш (e.g. у́ши 'ears'), г:з (e.g. состяза́ние 'contest'), к:ц (e.g. лицо́ 'face')
(b) the palatalization of dental consonants (д, т) before *j* has produced the reflexes ж and ч (e.g. ви́жу 'I see', лечу́ 'I fly').
(c) the palatalization of labials (б, п, в, м) before *j* has produced the consonant groups бл, пл, вл, мл (e.g. люблю́ 'I love', куплю́ 'I will buy', ловлю́ 'I catch', дремлю́ 'I doze')
(d) the groups ск and ст palatalize to щ (ищу́ 'I seek' from infinitive иска́ть, чи́щу 'I clean' from infinitive чи́стить), з

palatalizes to ж (ла́жу 'I climb' from infinitive ла́зить), с to ш (ве́шу 'I weigh' from infinitive ве́сить) and ц to ч (у́личный 'street', adj. from у́лица).

Influence of Church Slavonic

The effect of Church Slavonic on Russian is analogous to that of Latin on English, but less obvious, since both languages are Slavonic. Some of the principal Church Slavonic elements in Russian may be summarized thus (contrasted with following East Slavonic forms):

(1) lack of pleophony, as in град 'town', cf. East Slavonic го́род 'town' (2) stressed e before a hard consonant, as in не́бо 'sky', cf. нёбо 'palate' (3) жд/щ as reflexes of д/т, as in граждани́н 'citizen', освеще́ние 'illumination', cf. горожа́нин 'city-dweller', свеча́ 'candle' (4) the prefixes со-, из-/ис- and воз-/вос-, as in собо́р 'cathedral', излага́ть 'to expound', восто́к 'east', cf. сбор 'collection', вы́ложить 'to lay out', всходи́ть 'to rise' (5) the endings -ение, -ание, -тие, as in уче́ние 'learning', зна́ние 'knowledge', разви́тие 'development', cf. гла́женье 'ironing', бритьё 'shaving' (6) initial а-, as in а́гнец (eccles.) 'lamb', cf. ягнёнок 'lamb' (7) initial ю-, as in юг 'south', cf. у́жин 'dinner' (8) initial е-, as in еди́ный 'one', cf. оди́н 'one' (9) ра́зный 'different', ра́вный 'equal', ладья́ 'boat', etc. (initial ра-/ла- + consonant), cf. ро́зничный 'retail', ро́вный 'level', ло́дка 'boat'

The vocabulary of Russian

The IE provenance of Common Slavonic vocabulary is clear from an examination of Russian words: брат 'brother', гусь 'goose', вода́ 'water', нос 'nose', но́вый 'new', сиде́ть 'to sit', etc. Many words are shared with other Slavonic languages (дождь 'rain', Polish *deszcz*, id., по́ле 'field', Polish *pole*, id., etc.), some are unique to East Slavonic (e.g. се́лезень 'drake'), others are exclusively Russian (e.g. ру́хлядь 'lumber', крестья́нин 'peasant').

The Russian vocabulary developed through expansion of meaning (e.g. ру́чка 'small hand', then 'handle, knob, pen'), compounding (e.g. самова́р 'samovar', from сам 'self' and вар- 'boiling') and derivation (e.g. приземля́ться 'to land', from земля́ 'land'). Some words changed their meaning (see ружьё 'gun'), new words emerged during times of social or technical change (see царь 'tsar', рубль 'rouble').

Concentration on Slavonic roots means that many words in a semantic field often derive from a single source, thus боль 'pain', бо́лен 'is sick', боле́ть 'to hurt', больни́ца 'hospital', больно́й 'patient', болеутоля́ющий 'analgesic'. The last-named word, based on боль 'pain' and утоля́ть 'to alleviate', also illustrates the 'transparency' of Russian vocabulary, that is to say, the meaning of a word is often apparent from the meanings of its component parts (cf. пылесо́с 'vacuum-cleaner', from пыль 'dust' and сос- 'sucking'). This is partly explained by the language's predilection for loan-translations, e.g. небоскрёб, from English 'skyscraper'.

Borrowing has been another fruitful source of new lexis. The type of word borrowed at a particular time can help to throw light on the development of the society and its language. Main sources of loans are:

Iranian. A number of words, mainly of a religious nature, entered Common Slavonic from Iranian languages from c. 700 BC to c. 200 AD, perhaps as the result of links with Scythians and other semi-nomadic pastoralists in the Southern steppes (see бог 'God', мир 'peace, world', рай 'paradise').

Gothic. In the 3rd to the 4th centuries Goths from Southern Sweden invaded the area between the Vistula and Dnieper. Resultant loans included some of Mediterranean provenance (see купи́ть 'to buy', осёл 'ass', as well as loans military (see меч 'sword'), everyday (see хлеб 'bread') and medical (see лечи́ть 'to cure').

West Germanic (the 'parent' of English, Frisian, High and Low German). After the collapse of Gothic power the Slavs came into contact with West Germanic influences in Central Europe over the period 400-800 AD (see князь 'prince').

Baltic. The loosening of Gothic power also led to a resumption of earlier contacts with the Balts (Baltic and Slavonic share about 300 common words and are closer to each other than to any other IE language sub-group). See дёготь 'tar', янтáрь 'amber'.

Finnic. Finnic loans in Russian describe the natural world of the Far North: морж 'walrus', тюлéнь 'seal', пургá 'blizzard' (probably also Москвá 'Moscow', the river, then the town).

Scandinavian. In the 9th century Scandinavians opened up a trade route from the Baltic down the Dnieper and across the Black Sea to Byzantium, imposing political control over the East Slavs in the 9th-10th centuries. The term Русь 'Rus'' (cf. Finnish *Ruotsi* 'Swedes') was eventually applied to the country as a whole. Apart from personal names (Óльга 'Olga', etc.), main Scandinavian loans related to the sea (якорь 'anchor', акýла 'shark').

Greek. Trade with Byzantium and missionary activities in Kiev led to an influx of Greek loans from the 10th to the 15th centuries, reflecting advances in trade, craftsmanship, literacy and material culture (see и́звесть 'lime', сáхар 'sugar', тетрáдь 'exercise book', фонáрь 'lantern'). Byzantine Greek β was pronounced [v], hence, e.g., кровáть 'bed' from $\kappa\rho\alpha\beta\beta\alpha\tau\iota o\nu$.

Church Slavonic. Church Slavonic, brought from Bulgaria in the 10th century, provided ESl. with Christian terminology, mostly of Gk. provenance (евáнгелие 'gospel', etc.), some of it translated (e.g. всéнощная 'night service'), as well as the names of months and certain affixes (e.g. благо- in благодари́ть 'to thank').

Turkic languages. After the downfall of the Goths the Southern steppes were occupied by a succession of peoples speaking languages of the Turkic family. The administration of the Mongol Empire was carried on mainly in Turkic, whence an influx of loans into Russian following the destruction of Kiev in 1240 and the subjugation of most of Russia to Tatar rule. Loans included clothing (see башма́к 'shoe'), adornment (see изумру́д 'emeralds'), implements (see карандаш 'pencil'), military terms (see карау́л 'guard'), administration (see тамо́жня 'customs'). Borrowing resumed in the 16th century and grew with Russian expansion to East and South from the 17th century. Turkic languages are subject to 'vowel harmony' (if a word's root vowel is frontal or back, the other vowels in the word will follow suit, see, for example, бараба́н 'drum').

Low German. Low German (Saxon and Franconian) was important as the *lingua franca* of the Baltic Hanseatic League (and its capital Lübeck), with which Novgorod and Pskov continued to trade during the period of the Tatar yoke. See, for example, ба́рхат 'velvet'.

Polish. The influence of Turkic slackened after Ivan III shook off the Tatar yoke in the 15th century, and the impact of Polish grew as Muscovy expanded at the expense of Poland/Lithuania and the Golden Horde. Polish influence was especially strong from the 17th century onwards, partly due to translations of tales and learned texts. Many loans related to the military, administration, the professions, arts and learning (see апте́ка 'chemist's', полко́вник 'colonel', канцеля́рия 'office').

Eighteenth century. The advent of Peter I unleashed a flood of loans from Western Europe, both written and oral, through the translation of technical manuals, the development of printing, the presence of foreign specialists, new ways of reckoning the time and date, the founding of the Academy of Sciences. German and Latin dominated technical fields until the 1730s, when French asserted its primacy in diplomacy, culture and the theatre (аплоди́ровать 'to applaud', суфлёр 'prompter'). Italian contributed lexis such as о́пера 'opera' and а́рия 'aria', while Dutch and English were confined mainly to nautical terminology (cf. пиджа́к 'jacket', трюм 'hold'). Calques from French were particularly common, e.g. впечатле́ние from French *impression*.

Nineteenth century. The abstract vocabulary of German philosophy made its mark in calques such as мировоззре́ние 'Weltanschauung', while an interest in sciences, social and economic matters gave rise to alien vocabulary such as акклиматизáция 'acclimatisation' and альтруи́зм 'altruism', despite the efforts of purists to stem the tide.

Twentieth century Borrowing peaked in the late 1920s and early 1930s, with the introduction of scientific and industrial terms from English, French and German (e.g. тáнкер 'tanker', стенд 'stand', метрó 'underground'), and again in the late 1950s and early 1960s, following the conclusion of economic and cultural agreements with Western countries (джи́нсы 'jeans', хóбби 'hobby', моторóллер 'motor-scooter'). The period of liberalization in Russia since the mid-1980s has occasioned a flood of loans, mainly from American English, especially in commerce (би́знес 'business'), computing (компью́тер 'computer'), politics (плюлари́зм 'pluralism'), new technology (факс 'fax') and other spheres, including fashion and music.

Transcription

Cyrillic is used for Bulgarian, Russian, Serbian, Ukrainian. Church Slavonic and Old Russian (including ѣ, the letter *jat'* -- see glossary under 'Front vowel' -- but excluding the major *jus* and minor *jus*, which had symbolized the old Slavonic nasal vowels ϱ and φ and are represented here, respectively, by Russian у and я, as well as the vowel usually transliterated as *je*, which is rendered here as e, see Matthews, pp. 72, 77-78).

Each Russian headword is transliterated, in *square* brackets, using the ISO (International Organization for Standardization) system of transliteration. ISO symbols include č (as *ch* in *cheese*), š (as *s* in *sure*), ž (as *s* in *treasure*), c (as *ts* in *tsar*), j (as *y* in *yes* or *boy*), ch (as *ch* in *loch*), ë (as *ya* in *yacht*). An apostrophe (') denotes the soft sign (ь), a double apostrophe ('') the hard sign (ъ).

The ISO system is also used to indicate phonetic change and to transcribe Common Slavonic, representing the Common Slavonic nasal vowels as φ, pronounced approximately as French *in*, and ϱ, pronounced approximately as French *on*. The letter *jat'* is transcribed as ě.

The transcription of Arabic, Armenian, Georgian, Greek, Mongolian, Persian, Sanskrit and Turkic languages (e.g. Karačaj-Balkar, Kirghiz, Tadžik, Uzbek) accords with accepted convention. All non-Russian illustrative material (including Old Russian) is rendered in *italic*.

Acknowledgements

The generous assistance given by specialists in many languages, ranging from Arabic, Persian, Dutch, Sanskrit, Albanian and Mongolian to Lithuanian, Latvian, Old English, Latin, Greek, Hebrew, and Turkic languages has been invaluable, and the author wishes to thank the following for their assistance with difficult points: Dr R. Sobel (Beaconsfield), Mr. C. Bissell (Bedford), Dr V.N. Nersessian (British Library), Dr. J. Caney (Cheltenham), Mrs M. Wade (Glasgow), Mr A. Fenton, Dr. D. Guild, Dr A. Hood, Dr R. McCail (University of Edinburgh), Professor G.D. Caie, Mr B. Ettaouchi, Professor J. Mattock, Mr G. Whitaker (University of Glasgow), Dr I. Bellèr-Hann (University of Kent), Mr V. Filipov (University of Leeds), Mr A. Sanders (School of Oriental and African Studies, University of London), Professor C. Drage, Dr. J. Dingley, Dr F. Wigzell (School of Slavonic and East European Studies, University of London), Dr P. Mayo (University of Sheffield), Mr C. Dixon, Dr K. Foley, Professor A.J. Harper, Dr G. Martin, Mrs M. Montgomery, Mrs N. White (University of Strathclyde). I also wish to thank Dr J. White (University of Glasgow) and Mr N. Wagstaffe (University of Strathclyde) for their technical assistance with the *Nota Bene* package which was used to prepare this book.

Any errors are, of course, entirely the responsibility of the author.

GLOSSARY

Akan'je (áканье) The articulation of 'a' or the substitution of 'a' (sometimes ə) for unstressed 'o'. See стакáн 'tumbler'.

Assimilation The process by which two sounds adjacent or close to each other acquire common characteristics or become identical. See плестú 'to braid'.

Back formation The creation by analogy of a new word from an existing word in the mistaken assumption that the existing word is a derivative of the new word. See зóнтик 'umbrella'.

Calque (loan-translation) A loan created by translating a word from another language, either by a word-formatory (see правописáние 'orthography') or a semantic process (see ýтка 'duck, newspaper lie').

Cognate A word related to another by derivation from the same root. See дóмна 'furnace'.

Contamination. The process by which the form of a word changes under the influence of another close to it in sound or meaning. See хрустáль 'cut glass'.

Devoicing The pronunciation or spelling of a voiced consonant (e.g., б, г, з, д, в, ж) as its unvoiced counterpart (e.g., п, к, с, т, ф, ш). See пчелá 'bee'.

Dissimilation A process by which like sounds are made unlike each other. See феврáль 'February'.

Dual number A grammatical number used to designate two objects or objects combined with the numeral '2'. See воóчию 'with one's own eyes'.

False ('popular' or 'folk') etymology The interpretation of the meaning, or change in the written form or pronunciation of a word, on the basis of its chance phonetic or semantic similarity to a familiar word. See верблю́д 'camel'.

Front vowels In the context of the palatalization of velar consonants (г, к, х): е, ь, и, ę (a nasal vowel) and ѣ (*jat'*, a letter replaced by е in the orthographic reform of 1918).

Haplology The loss of one of two consecutive identical sounds or groups of sounds in a structure. See бу́дни 'weekdays'.

Homonym A word identical in form with another word but from a different root. See лук 'bow, onions'.

Ikan'je (и́канье) The pronunciation of 'е' or 'я' as 'и'.

Metathesis The transposition of letters within a word or between two words. See таре́лка 'plate'.

Onomatopoeia The formation of words through the imitation of natural sounds. See грач 'rook'

Pleophony (полногла́сие) A feature of East Slavonic whereby -оро-, -оло-, -ере- (from early *or, *ol, *er, *el) appear between consonants. See бе́рег 'shore', го́род 'town', молоко́ 'milk'.

Prosthesis The addition of a consonantal sound or letter (normally в or *j*) before a vowel sound. See во́семь 'eight', ягнёнок 'lamb'.

Reduplication Repetition of a syllable or letter in word formation. See ко́локол 'bell'.

Taboo The avoidance of the use of certain words, and their replacement by euphemistic expressions, for superstitious, moral, social, etc., reasons. See медве́дь 'bear'

Voicing The pronunciation or spelling of an unvoiced consonant as its voiced counterpart. See сва́дьба 'wedding' and compare **Devoicing** above.

ABBREVIATIONS

acc. accusative
act. active
adj. adjective, adjectival
adv. adverb, adverbial
Amer. American
Ar. Arabic
arch. archaic (not in ordinary use, but retained for special purposes)
Arm. Armenian
Balk. Balkar
Balt. Baltic
BR Belorussian
Bulg. Bulgarian
Byz. Byzantine
c. (*circa*) approximate(ly) (of dates)
C. Central
cf. compare
ChSl. Church Slavonic
coll. colloquial
Croat. Croatian
CSl. Common Slavonic
Cz. Czech
D. Dutch
Dan. Danish
dat. dative
dial. dialect(al)
dim. dimunitive
E. East(ern)
eccles. ecclesiastical
e.g. for example
Eng. English
ESl. East Slavonic
esp. especially
Est. Estonian
Eur. European
fem. feminine
fig. figurative(ly)
Finn. Finnish
Fr. French
Gael. Gaelic
gen. genitive
Georg. Georgian
Ger. German
Gk. Greek
Gmc. Germanic
Goth. Gothic
hist. historical
Hung. Hungarian
Icel. Icelandic
id. (*idem*) the same word, meaning
i.e. that is to say
IE Indo-European
imper. imperative
impf. imperfective
infin. infinitive
instr. instrumental
Ir. Irish
Iran. Iranian
Ital. Italian
Kar.-Balk. Karačaj-Balkar
Kirgh. Kirghiz
Lat. Latin
Latv. Latvian
LG Low German
lit. literal(ly)
Lith. Lithuanian
masc. masculine
MD Middle Dutch
ME Middle English
MHG Middle High German
MidE. Middle Eastern
mil. military
MLat. Medieval Latin

MLG Middle Low German
Mong. Mongolian
N. North(ern)
neut. neuter
Norw. Norwegian
NS New Style (following replacement of the Julian by the Gregorian calendar, February 1918)
obs. obsolete
OE Old English
OFr. Old French
OHG Old High German
OIr. Old Irish
ON Old Norse
OPers. Old Persian
OPol. Old Polish
OPr. Old Prussian
OR Old Russian
orn. ornithological
OS Old Style (see NS)
OSc. Old Scandinavian
OSw. Old Swedish
part. participle, participial
pass. passive
pers. person
Pers. Persian
pf. perfective
pl. plural
poet. poetic
Pol. Polish
pop. popular
Port. Portuguese
prep. preposition(al)
pres. present
prov. provincial
R. Russian
ref. reference
reg. regional

rel. religious
rhet. rhetorical
Rom. Romanian
S. South(ern)
sc. (*scilicet*) understand or supply
Sc. Scandinavian
Scot. Scottish
Serb. Serbian
sing. singular
Skr. Sanskrit
Slav. Slavonic
Sp. Spanish
SSl. South Slavonic
Sw. Swedish
Tadž. Tadžik
tech. technical
theatr. theatrical
Tkc. Turkic
Turk. Turkish
Ukr. Ukrainian
Uzb. Uzbek
voc. vocative
Vulg. Lat. Vulgar Latin
W. West(ern)
WSl. West Slavonic
zool. zoological

* = form not recorded but merely inferred

A

АБРИКОС [abrikós] 'apricot'. Early 18th century, from D. *abrikoos*, id. (the first apricots came to Russia from Holland, which had had the lion's share in carrying trade to Russia's Baltic outlets since the 16th century). The word entered Europe from Ar. *al-barqūq*, via Sp. *albar(i)coque* 'apricot', the primary source (via Gk.) being Lat. *praecoquus*, a variant of *praecox* 'ripe before its time, precocious' (apricots ripen earlier than another soft fruit, the peach) or possibly Lat. *aprīcō* 'I warm in the sun', cf. Lat. *aprīcus* 'warmed by sunshine, exposed to the sun, sunny'.

АВГУСТ [ávgust] 'August'. 11th century *аугустъ*, from Lat. *augustus* 'august, majestic', cognate with Lat. *augur* 'soothsayer' and possibly with *augeō* 'I augment, enrich' (whence false etymological interpretation of the month as 'time of increase, harvest time'), via Byz. Gk. *Aúgoustos* and ChSl. Named after the first Roman emperor Octavius Caesar, to whom the Senate awarded the title Augustus after he attained to undivided authority, and after him to all Roman emperors. Август replaced *заревъ* (cf. ревéть 'to roar') as the eighth month of the year after the adoption of Christianity.

АВОСЬКА [avós'ka] 'string shopping bag' (lit. 'bag carried on the off-chance'). Early 19th century 'future good fortune', 1920s (a time of privation in Russia) 'string bag' (symbolizing the opportunism required of would-be shoppers), from авóсь 'perhaps', cf. на авóсь 'on the off-chance'.

АД [ad] 'hell'. 11th century, via ChSl., from Gk. *hadēs* or *Háidēs* 'Pluto, god of the lower world', later 'Hades', lit. 'the unseen, the invisible' (Gk. *a* 'not', *ideīn* 'to see', aorist infin. of *horáō* 'I see').

АЗБУКА [ázbuka] 'alphabet'. 13th century *азбука, азъбукы*, based on the first two letters of the Cyrillic alphabet: *азъ* ('I') and *букы* ('letter') -- every letter of the alphabet was given a name, as an aid to memory. *Азъбукы* (later ázбука), an amalgam of these two letters, was calqued from Gk. *alphábētos* 'alphabet', from the first two letters of the Gk. alphabet, *álpha* and *bēta*.

АЗОТ [azót] 'nitrogen'. Recorded in dictionaries since 1803, from Fr. *azote*, id., a term coined in 1787 on the basis of Gk. *a* 'not' and *zōé* 'life', so called from the element's inability to support life.

АКУЛА [akúla] 'shark'. Recorded in dictionaries (originally with -kk-) since 1789, but known earlier, probably from Sc. languages, cf. OSc. *hākarl* (with -a in R. perhaps by analogy with рыба 'fish'), alternatively from a Norw. dial. source, cf. also Farøese *hákallur* 'basking shark', *hákelling* 'Greenland shark', Icel. *hakka* 'to eat like a beast'.

АЛМАЗ [almáz] 'diamond'. 15th century, ultimately from Gk., via Tkc. (cf. Turk. *elmas*, id.) and Ar., a modified form of Gk. *adámas*, gen. *adámantos* 'indestructible' (from Gk. *a* 'not', *damáō* 'I conquer', cf. Lat. *adamās* 'adamant, hardest iron, steel'), referring to the supposed indestructibility of the diamond as the hardest of the precious stones. Cf. Eng. *adamant* (arch.) 'diamond or other hard substance' (now normally an adj. meaning 'unyielding').

АЛФАВИТ [alfavít] 'alphabet'. 16th-century Russification of Gk. *alphábētos*, Late Lat. *alphabētum*, an amalgam of the first two letters of the Gk. alphabet, *álpha* and *bēta* (adopted during the Byz. period, hence pronunciation of Gk. -β- as [v]). Cf. also áзбука 'alphabet'.

АМБАР [ambár] 'barn'. 16th century *анбар, онбар*, from Tkc. (cf. Turk. *ambar* 'granary, storehouse'), ultimately Ar. or Pers. *ambar* 'storehouse'.

АНКЕТА [ankéta] 'questionnaire'. Late 19th-/early 20th centuries, from Fr. *enquête* 'investigation, questionnaire', itself from Lat. *inquisita*, a substantivized fem. past part. form from *inquirō* 'I investigate'.

АПЕЛЬСИН [apel'sín] 'orange'. Early 18th century, from D.

appelsien (obs.), id. (now predominantly South D., cf. standard *sinaasappel*, id.), whence Ger. *Apfelsine*, id., lit. 'Chinese apple' (oranges were first brought from China by the Portuguese in the 16th century and were imported from Holland into Russia, where they were enjoyed as a delicacy by Moscow magnates).

АПЛОДИРОВАТЬ [aplodírovat'] 'to applaud'. 1760s. Like many theatrical terms (e.g. кулисы 'wings', суфлёр 'prompter'), of Fr. origin, from Fr. *applaudir* 'to applaud', Lat. *applaudō* 'I applaud'. Pl. аплодисменты 'applause' is from Fr. *applaudissements*, id.

АПРЕЛЬ [aprél'] 'April'. 11th century *априль*, via Gk. *aprili(o)s* from Lat. *Aprīlis*, id., with -и- to -е- in the early 15th century, perhaps by association with преть 'to go damp' (of the ground in spring, from the warmth of the atmosphere, cf. also прель 'mould'). The Lat. word was popularly interpreted as 'the month when the earth opens and softens', cf. Lat. *aperiō* 'I uncover, lay bare', but is more probably cognate with *aprīcor* 'I bask in the sun', *aprīcus* 'warmed by the sunshine, exposed to the sun, sunny'.

АПТЕКА [aptéka] 'chemist's shop'. Known since the mid-16th century (apothecaries were referred to in the 15th century, but the first chemist's shop in Moscow, serving the royal court, opened in 1581, the first general chemist's in 1672). Via Pol. *apteka*, id., Ger. *Apotheke*, id., Lat. *apothēca* 'warehouse', from Gk. *apothḗkē* 'storehouse' (cf. Gk. *thḗkē* 'chest, place for storing'), interpreted more specifically, in borrowing languages, as a 'storehouse' for *medicines*, cf. библиотека 'library' (lit. 'storehouse for books').

АРБУЗ [arbúz] 'water-melon'. 15th century, via Tkc. (cf. Turk. *karpuz*, id.), from Pers. *kharbúzah*, id., lit. 'cucumber the size of a mule' (in Pers. *khar* 'mule' may have an augmentative function, cf. *kharmush* 'rat', lit. 'mule-mouse', *kharbaṭṭah* 'goose', lit. 'mule-duck').

АСБЕСТ [asbést] 'asbestos'. 19th century, from Gk. *ásbestos* 'unquenched, inextinguishable, unslaked lime', based on Gk. *a* 'not' and *sbestós* 'quenched', from *sbénnumi* 'I quench'. See известь 'lime'.

АТЕЛЬЕ [atel'jé] 'workshop, artist's studio'. 1880s 'artist's studio', 1930s 'sewing workshop', from Fr. *atelier* 'workshop, studio', itself from OFr. *astelier*, originally 'pile of wood, place where there are many shavings' (cf. OFr. *astelle* 'splinter, thin board', Late Lat. *astella*, id.), then 'workshop, work area' (initially for joiners and masons).

АТЛАС I [átlas] 'atlas'. Late 17th-/early 18th centuries (the first R. atlas, I.K. Kirillov's *Атлас Всероссійской Имперіи* 'Atlas of the Russian Empire', came out in 1734). From Ger., based ultimately on Atlas, a Titan in Gk. mythology, often depicted with the terrestrial globe on his shoulders (his punishment for having rebelled with the other Titans against Zeus), hence the application of the name to a collection of maps. The word had became generic following the publication in Duisburg of G. Krämer's (Mercator's) *Atlas* in 1595, with a depiction of Atlas on the cover (Ger. edition 1727). Атлантический 'Atlantic' derives ultimately from Gk. *Atlantikós* via Lat. (*oceanus*) *Ātlanticus* (or W. Eur. languages), after the Atlas mountains in W. Africa, which were thought to support heaven and all its stars, hence the application of the adj. to the sea near the W. African coast, subsequently to the present Atlantic Ocean.

АТЛАС II [atlás] 'satin'. 15th-16th centuries, from Ar. *'atlas* 'smooth', via Pol. *atłas* 'satin', Ger. *Atlas*, id. or Tkc. (cf. Turk. *atlas*, id.).

АТОМ [átom] 'atom'. Early 18th century, via Lat. and W. Eur. languages, from Gk. *átomos* 'indivisible', from *a* 'not', and *tomē* 'a cutting', *témnō* 'I cut' (the atom was regarded as an indivisible particle of matter, a concept which survived until the 19th century).

Б

БАБА [bába] 'grandmother, old woman'. OR 'married woman, grandmother, old woman, midwife, sorceress', from IE/CSl. *baba, a reduplicated form based on the prattling of small children (cf. мáма 'mummy', дя́дя 'uncle', etc.).

БАБОЧКА [bábočka] 'butterfly'. Early 18th century in this meaning, dim. of бáба/бáбка 'grandmother' (according to popular belief, the butterfly was the incarnation of the soul of an ancestor of the owners of a house, cf. analogous dial. *ду́шечка* 'butterfly', from душá 'soul'). Alternatively, from root -бава (cf. dial. *бавýшка* 'plaything', also rendered as *бабýшка*, which in dial. also means 'butterfly'), with -в- to -б- under the influence of бáба and derivatives.

БАБУШКА [bábuška] 'grandmother'. 17th century (also дéдушка 'grandfather'), dim. of бáба 'old woman'.

БАКЛАЖАН [baklažán] 'aubergine'. Recorded in dictionaries from 19th century, via Tkc., from Ar./Pers. *bădinjăn* or *bădiljăn*, id. (cf. Turk. *patlican*, id.).

БАЛАЛАЙКА [balalájka] 'balalaika'. First ref. 1688, onomatopoeic, possibly from the reshaping of dial. *балабáйка* through assimilation (-лала- for -лаба-). Comprises dial. *бáлы* 'idle chatter, jokes' and бáйка 'story, lullaby', also associated with dial. *балáкать* 'to chatter' and perhaps dial. *лáйка* 'grumbling, grumbler'. Less plausibly from Kirgh. *bala* 'child' + pl. *lar* + suffix -ka.

БАЛЕТ [balét] 'ballet'. 18th century (regular performances were staged in Russia from the mid-1730s), from Fr. *ballet*, id., ultimately Ital. *balletto*, id., cf. Ital. *ballo* 'dance, dancing', Ital. and MLat. *ballare* 'to dance'. Балетмéйстер 'ballet master' derived from Ger. in the 1760s, балери́на 'ballerina' in the 1890s from Ital., via Fr.

БАЛЛ [ball] 'school mark, unit of measure'. 18th century, from

Ger. *Ball* or Fr. *balle* 'ball, sphere', the meaning progressing in R. from 'ball, ballot' (in voting, time of Peter I, cf. Fr. *ballotte* 'small ball, ball used in voting', баллотировать 'to ballot') to 'assessment mark' (19th century), finally 'unit of measurement' (e.g. in measuring wind-strength).

БАЛОВАТЬ [balovát'] 'to spoil, pamper'. 12th century 'to cure' (by incantation), then 'to say pleasant things' (to indulge a patient), finally 'to pander to', the verb deriving from OR *балии* 'sorcerer, doctor', OR *баяти* 'to tell stories, cast spells' (cf. dial. *баить*, id.).

БАНК [bank] 'bank'. Early 18th century, from Ital. *banco/banca* 'bench, bank' (via MHG *banc* or Fr. *banque* 'bank'), ultimately from MLat. *bancus/banca* 'bench, counter, money-changer's table' (as medieval trade developed, money-changers expanded their activities, eventually becoming bankers in the modern sense of the word).

БАНТ [bant] 'ribbon'. 18th century in modern form and meaning, from Ger. *Band*, id., cf. cognate Ger. *binden* 'to bind', бинт 'bandage' (Ger. *Binde*, id.), alternatively via Ger. from Fr. *bande* 'band, strip, ribbon'.

БАНЯ [bánja] 'bath-house'. 11th century, possibly from Vulg. Lat. **baneum*, pl. **banea*, cf. Lat. *bal(i)neum* 'bath, bathing-place', Gk. *balaneĩon*, id. (Byz. Gk. *baneion*, pl. *baneia*), whence also Fr. *bain* 'bath', Ital. *bagno*, id. 17th-century банка 'jar' (initially 'receptacle for blood-letting') is probably a derivative of баня, perhaps via Pol. *bania* 'dome, big-bellied bottle, vapour bath', dim. *bańka*, whence originally банька, then банка, with hard -н- possibly by dissimilation from банька 'small bath', or by analogy with склянка 'phial', etc.

БАРАБАН [barabán] 'drum'. 17th century, probably via Tkc. (cf. Crimean Tatar *balaban* 'big drum'), ultimately from Pers.

БАРАК [barák] 'wooden hut'. Early 18th century, from Fr. *baraque* 'hut', ultimately Ital. *baracca* or Sp./Catalan *barraca*, id. (possibly initially of clay, cf. Sp. *barro* 'clay').

БАРИН [bárin] 'barin, landowner'. Mid-18th century, a contraction of боя́рин 'bojar' (perhaps originally as a form of address, cf. allegro truncation of госуда́рь to су́дарь 'sir', also with initial stress). The title боя́рин arose due to changes in social terminology occasioned by the fall of Kiev and is possibly a derivative of бой 'battle', thus initially 'warrior', alternatively from Tkc. *bajar* 'magnate'. Ба́рыня (from боя́рыня) 'mistress, bojar's wife' and ба́рышня (from боя́рышня), 'bojar's daughter', then 'girl from a gentry family', subsequently 'young lady', are derivatives.

БАРСУК [barsúk] 'badger'. 15th century, from Tkc. (cf. Turk. *porsuk*, id.), seemingly originally 'grey animal', from the colour of the animal's fur, cf. *gray*, an early Eng. name for a badger.

БАРХАТ [bárchat] 'velvet'. Late 14th century, seemingly, via Novgorod, from LG or MHG *barchant* (cf. Ger. *Barchent* 'fustian'), as shown in writs between Germans in Riga and Dorpat and the Russians of Novgorod/Pskov. Ultimately from Ar. via MLat. *barraccanus.*, cf. reg. барака́н/барка́н 'thick upholstery material'.

БАСНЯ [básnja] 'fable'. 11th century баснь 'tale', 17th century ба́сня (cf. песнь (obs.)/пе́сня 'song') from CSl. *basnja/*basnь, based on OR *баяти* 'to narrate', cf. dial. *ба́ять/ба́ить* 'to speak'.

БАСТОВАТЬ [bastovát'] 'to (be on) strike'. 18th-19th centuries, based on Ital. *basta!* 'enough!', initially used only in games of chance, in particular *ombre* (a game for three, popular at Catherine II's court, in which one player tried to scoop the pool, from Sp. *hombre* 'man', cf. Fr. *baste* 'ace of clubs in *ombre*'), subsequently extended, e.g., to stopping a horse in riding school. The meaning 'to strike' evolved in the 1880s-1890s and забасто́вка 'strike' is recorded from the end of the 19th century, with the rise of the working-class movement.

БАШМАК [bašmák] 'shoe'. 16th century, from Tkc. *bašmaq* 'footwear, sandal, shoe', based on *baš* 'head', cf. analogous

голо́вки 'small heads', also 'shoe uppers' and other Tkc. loans in
баш-: башка́ (coll.) 'head', башлы́к 'hood' (cf. Turk. *başlik*
'headgear').

БАШНЯ [bášnja] 'tower'. Mid-16th century, via Pol. *baszta*,
id., Ukr. *башта*, id., from Cz. *bašta* 'bastion', ultimately Ital.
bastia 'fortress, rampart' (MLat. *bastire* 'to build'), reshaped by
adding the locational suffix -ня (cf. карау́льня 'guardroom').
Alternatively, from the putative adj. **баштьна(я)* (sc. оборо́на
'defence'), back-formed to ба́шня.

БЕЗДНА [bézdna] 'abyss'. From ChSl., an imprecise calque of
Gk. *atérmōn* 'without bound or end' or *abyssos* 'bottomless,
unfathomable' (from *a* 'not', *byssós* 'depth of sea').

БЕЛКА [bélka] 'squirrel'. Especially common from the 14th
century, from OR *бѣла* 'squirrel skin, monetary unit' (for the
payment of tax, quitrent, for land purchase, etc.). A substantivized adj. (sc. *вѣверица* 'squirrel, squirrel skin as monetary
unit'), referring to a skin with a high-quality white inner hide
(мездра́), subsequently to the animal itself, ultimately replacing
вѣверица and *вѣкша/векша* 'species of squirrel', which had been
adopted in early Novgorod as a unit of exchange in the fur trade,
and in some dials. denoted the summer squirrel or low-quality
yellow summer fur. Squirrel fur was one of the commonest cur-
rencies in Old Russia, and the white pelts of animals caught in
winter, and their white inner hide -- hence бе́лка, from бе́лый
'white' -- were particularly prized.

БЕЛЫЙ [bélyj] 'white'. 11th century, from CSl. (cf. IE **bhēlos*
'bright, white'), with cognate in Lith. *balti* 'to become white'.
Бельё 'linen, table-linen, underwear', etc., initially only of white
articles, subsequently of all colours.

БЕРЕГ [béreg] 'shore'. From CSl. **bergъ* 'hill' (IE **bhergh-*
'high, height'), with ESl. inter-consonantal -ере-, subsequently
'high bank near a water surface', then 'strip of land adjacent to
water, bank', cf. Serb. *брег* 'hill', Ger. *Berg*, id., Eng. *barrow*
'mountain (obs.), grave mound', and note, as a reverse
phenomenon, dial. *гора́* 'high river bank, high right bank, espe-

cially of the Volga', *горóй* 'along the bank', beside standard горá 'hill'.

БЕРЕЗА [berëza] 'birch'. CSl. *berza, id., with ESl. inter-consonantal -ере-, ultimately from IE *bhergos 'birch, the bright tree', thus named for the silveriness of birch bark, with cognates in берёста 'birch bark', whence берестянь́іе грáмоты (birch-bark writs, mainly from the 13th-/14th centuries, found near Novgorod from 1951), Lith. *beržas* 'birch', Ger. *Birke*, id., etc.

БЕРЕЧЬ [beréč'] 'to take care of'. CSl. *bergti (IE *bherghō 'to protect, save'), cf. Goth. *(ga)bairgan*, Ger. *bergen* 'to conceal, secure', with inter-consonantal -ере- in ESl. and -gti changing to -kti, subsequently -čь.

БЕСЕДА [beséda] 'chat'. CSl. *besěda, originally 'sitting outside' (*bez-/*bes- 'outside', *sěda 'sitting'), subsequently used for all relaxed conversation, with derivative бесéдка 'summer-house' retaining the meaning 'outside' (cf. Icel. *utiseta* 'sitting outside', used in antiquity of wizards practising nocturnal sorcery or prophesy).

БЛАГО [blágo] 'good, blessing'. From CSl. *bolgo (possibly IE *bhleĝ- 'to shine'), based on the short-form neut. adj. *блáго* 'good', a component of many words of ChSl. origin, e.g. благодарить 'to thank', calqued from Gk *eucharízō* 'I render thanks' (*eû* 'good', *charízō* 'I oblige', cf. Eng. *Eucharist* 'an act of giving thanks'). However, благосостоя́ние 'well-being' is a late 18th-century calque of Fr. *bien-être*, id.

БЛИЗОРУКИЙ [blizorúkij] 'short-sighted'. First third of 18th century, based on earlier *близозорокий*, id., then близорýкий after the reduction, resulting from haplology, of -зозо- to -зо- and through false analogy with adjs. in -рукий (e.g., однорýкий 'one-armed'). For retention of зор-, cf. Ukr. *короткозорий* 'short-sighted' (where there was no potential for haplology), reg. *близорóчный*, id., cf. also дальнозóркий 'long-sighted'.

БЛИН [blin] 'pancake'. Apparently 15th century, cf. 14th-century *млинъ*, from CSl. *mъlinъ 'windmill' (seemingly then 'millstone', subsequently 'round object', cf. Pol. *młyn* 'mill', Late Lat. *molinum*, id., whence Fr. *moulin*, id.), cognate with молóть 'to grind', thus lit. 'something ground', with м- to б- by dissimilation of nasals: м-н to б-н, thus блин (cf. analogous dissimilation of m-m to б-м in Turk. *Müslüman* 'Moslem', R. басурмáн (obs.) 'infidel' (esp. Mohammedan, cf. standard мусульмáнин 'Moslem').

БЛЮДО [bljúdo] 'dish'. 11th century, from CSl. *bljudo, Goth. *biuds* 'dish' (from *-biudan* 'to offer', cf. OHG *biotan*, id., Ger. *bieten*, id.), with *biu-* changing to блю-. Alternatively, both forms from IE *bheudh- 'make conscious of' and (according to Černych) 'preserve', cf. IE *bheudhos 'bowl, offertory'.

БОБР [bobr] 'beaver' (cf. бобёр 'beaver fur'). From CSl. *bobrъ/*bebrъ, IE *bhebros 'red-brown, beaver' (cf. Lith. *bebras* 'beaver'), the animal thus being named for the colour of its fur.

БОГАТЫЙ [bogátyj] 'rich'. 11th century, from CSl. *bogatъ, comprising *bogъ (probably of Iran. provenance) 'prosperity' (later 'god', cf. бог, id.) + -at- 'endowed with' (cf. рогáтый 'horned'), thus initially 'endowed with prosperity', subsequently 'rich', cf. cognate убóгий 'poverty-stricken' (lit. 'deprived of prosperity') and analogous negative meaning of у- in урóд 'monster'.

БОГАТЫРЬ [bogatýr'] 'Russian epic hero'. From Tkc. (with cognates in languages of the Iran. and Indian groups, e.g. Pers. *bahādur*, possibly the direct source of богатырь, whose shape was influenced by богáтый 'rich'). Cf. also Mong. *bagatur* (modern Mong. Cyrillic *баатар*) 'brave warrior'. Originally *богатур*, subsequently богатырь by analogy with nouns such as поводы́рь (coll.) 'leader'.

БОЛЬШЕВИК [bol'ševík] 'Bolshevik'. Coined in 1903 at the II Congress of the Russian Social Democratic Workers' Party, denoting the supporters of V.I. Lenin, who advocated a maximalist socialist programme, later reinterpreted as those who received the majority of votes in elections to the central organs of the Party, from бо́льше 'more' + -(ев)ик (denoting membership of a group, cf. строеви́к 'combatant'), whence большеви́зм 'Bolshevism', большеви́сткий 'Bolshevik' (adj., from former большеви́ст 'Bolshevik'), cf. большинство́ 'majority' and see меньшеви́к 'Menshevik'.

БОРЗА́Я [borzája] 'borzoj'. Adj. noun based on fem. adj. бо́рзая (obs. or poet.) 'swift' (sc. соба́ка 'dog'), with stress change possibly indicating functional shift from adj. to noun (cf. stress change in functional shift from gerund судя́ 'when judging' to prep. су́дя по 'judging by').

БОРМОТА́ТЬ [bormotát'] 'to mutter'. Seemingly from dial. борбота́ть, id., with -б- to -м- by dissimilation (for reverse process, see блин 'pancake'). Cf. repeated 'b' in Slovene *brbljati* 'to mutter', Gk. *barbarízō* 'I speak gibberish, like a barbarian, a foreign tongue', Fr. *balbutier* 'to stammer', Lith. *burbėti* 'to mumble', and repeated 'm' in Fr. *marmotter* 'to mumble', Ger. *murmeln*, id. For б-м mutation, cf. му́сор 'rubbish', a transformation of dial. бу́сор, id.

БОРОДА́ [borodá] 'beard'. OR 'beard, chin', from CSl. *borda (IE *bhardhā, id.), with inter-consonantal -оро- in ESl. (cf. Cz. *brada* 'beard, chin', Pol. *broda* 'beard', Ger. *Bart*, id.). Purportedly linked to бор 'coniferous forest' (IE *bhorus 'pine, pine-needle') and бо́ров 'hog, castrated boar' by the shared meaning of 'sharp, cutting' (cf. IE *bher- 'to strike', possibly 'to cut', CSl. *bordъ 'sharp, prickly').

БРАК I [brak] 'marriage'. 11th century 'marriage, feast', from CSl. *borkъ, based on *bьrati 'to take' (cf. брать, id.) + suffix -к (cf. знать 'to know', знак 'sign'), a reference to 'taking a bride' from another tribe in pagan Slav communities, a custom refined by 'taking for a bride-price' with the advent of Christianity. Cf. брать в жёны 'to take a wife'.

БРАК II [brak] 'defective products'. Late 17th-/early 18th centuries, from LG, possibly via Pol. *brak* 'lack' (cf. MLG *brack* 'refuse', lit. 'break, fracture', *bracken* 'to reject', Ger. *Brack* 'refuse', *bracken* 'to sort out refuse', *Bracker* 'sorter', *Brackgut* 'article of poor quality'). Бракова́ть 'to reject' (manufactured articles) somewhat later, possibly from Pol. *brakować* 'to be wanting'.

БРАТ [brat] 'brother'. 11th century, from IE **bhrātēr-*, CSl. **bratrъ*, with cognates in Lat. *frater*, id., Ger. *Bruder*, id., etc., loss of suffix -r- possibly by dissimilation from initial (b)r-. Pl. бра́тья 'brothers' from a reinterpretation of a former fem. collective, cf. extant collective семья́ 'family'.

БРЕЗЕНТ [brezént] 'tarpaulin'. Early 18th century, originally *презенинг*, from D. *presenning*, id. (now also *geteerd zeildoek*), cf. Ger. *Persenning/Presenning*, id., ultimately from Fr. *préceinte* 'covering, casing, broad thick timber along a ship's side', Lat. *praecincta* (fem. part. of *praecingō* 'I encircle').

БРЕМЯ [brémja] 'burden'. 11th century, based on CSl. **bermę*, id., ultimately from IE **bher-* 'to carry', with ChSl. -pe- and with -mę changing to -мя, cf. cognate Gk. *phérma* 'burden, fruit of the womb' and, with ESl. -ере-, бере́менная 'pregnant'.

БРОНЯ [bronjá] 'armour, armour plating'. 11th century, from CSl. **brъnja*, itself probably from Goth. *brunjo*, OHG *brunia* 'coat of mail', Gmc. **brunjōn*, id. (cf. Ger. *Brünne*, id.). The Goth. is probably from Celtic, cf. OIr. *bruinne* 'breast', perhaps also 'breast covering' (cf. Gael. *bruinne* 'breast', correlate with Goth. *brunjo*). Бро́ня (на биле́т) 'ticket reservation' is based on броня́, sharing with it an element of protection, change in meaning marked by stress change, cf. борза́я 'borzoj'.

БРЮКИ [brjúki] 'trousers'. Second half of 18th century, little used till second quarter of 19th century, superseding штаны́, id., from LG, or D. *broek*, ultimately Lat. *brācae* 'breeches' (e.g., as worn by the Gauls), with -рю- perhaps under the influence of *брю́киш* 'a woollen fabric', from Ger. *brüggisch* 'Bruges' (adj.). Brought to Russia from Holland by sailors during the reign of Peter I, originally denoting sailors' trousers only, subsequently all trousers.

БУДКА [búdka] 'booth'. 18th century, dim. of OR *буда* 'small wicker hut, wattle hut', a loan, via Pol. *buda* 'shed, stall', Cz. *bouda* 'cabin', from MHG *buode*, id., MLG *bode*, cognate with Ger. *bauen* 'to build', Eng. (Scot.) *bothy* 'one-roomed building in which labourers are lodged' (OIr./Gael. *both* 'hut'). Seemingly, via Slav., a component of Budapest (there were Slav settlements in the area until the 10th century AD), implying earlier smelting or charcoal-burning in the vicinity of the city, which arose in its present form in 1872 from the fusion of left-bank Pest (lit. 'lime kiln'), right-bank Buda (cf. Ger. name *Ofen* 'furnace, kiln') and Obuda.

БУДНИ [búdni] 'weekdays'. 18th century, pl. of *будень* (arch., demotic), from *буденъ день* (*будьнъ дьнь*) 'working day', as the result of haplology (-ден- for -ден- ден-), ultimately from OR *будити* 'to awaken' (cf. будить, id.), thus lit. 'days on which people are wide awake, active'. Alternatively, будни could be a short-form substantivized pl. adj. (sc. дни 'days').

БУКВА [búkva] 'letter of alphabet'. 11th century (apparently replacing *pismę, cf. письмена 'letters'), based on OR *букъ* 'beech' and oblique cases of OR *букы* 'second letter of the alphabet', both probably deriving from Goth. *bōka* 'letter', Gmc. *bōkō* 'beech' (in antiquity runes were inscribed on beechwood tablets, cf. similar correlations in OHG *buohha* 'beech', *buoh* 'book', Ger. *Buche* 'beech', *Buch* 'book', *Buchstabe* 'letter' -- OHG *buohstap* denotes Lat. letters used in a book, as opposed to carved runes). Буква in due course replaced букы (cf. тыква 'pumpkin' from *тыкы*). The beech tree and its habitat W. of a line extending approximately from Danzig to the Crimea have played a part in the research of scholars concerned to establish the whereabouts of the IE homeland (cf. also лосось 'salmon').

БУЛАВКА [bulávka] 'pin'. Early 17th century, dim. of 15th-century булава 'mace', probably via Ukr. from Pol., where *buława* 'baton, staff' was based on Slav. *bula 'sphere, lump, knob', with augmentative suffix -ava (cf. держава 'orb'), perhaps originally 'round object', then 'cudgel with rounded bulge', in Old Russia used as a weapon, and in the Middle Ages symbolizing the power of the hetman in Ukraine and Poland. Possibly also associated with Ger. *Beule* 'lump, tumour'.

БУЛКА [búlka] 'roll'. First third of 18th century, possibly from the same root ('something round') as булавá 'mace', alternatively from Pol. *bułka* 'roll', cf. *buła* 'large roll', ultimately from Romance languages, cf. Fr. *boulanger* 'baker', from Picardy dial. *boulenc* 'someone who makes rounded bread' -- *pain en boule*, Fr. *boule* 'ball', from Lat. *bulla* 'bubble'. Arguably, an alternative source is Sw. *bulle* 'bun, roll, loaf'.

БУМАГА [bumága] 'paper'. Early 15th century, from Italy, maybe via Black Sea trade, earlier 'cotton products, yarn', assumed to derive from Ital. *bombagia/bombagina* 'cotton', MLat. *bombāx* 'silk, cotton', rather than from Gk. *bombýkion* 'silkworm cocoon', *bómbyx* 'silkworm, silk', ultimately from Iran. (perhaps via Arm. *pambag* 'cotton'). Бумáга evolved by dissimilation of b-b to б-м and the transformation of -am-/-om- to -у-, later (15th century) acquiring the meaning 'paper', made from shreds of flaxen and cotton fabrics, imported from Byzantium and Italy since the 14th century but not made in Russia until the mid-16th century. Fr. *bombasin* 'bombasine' derives from MLat. *bombacīnum*, and бумазéя 'fustian' from the Fr.

БУНТ [bunt] 'revolt, rebellion'. Early 17th century, from MHG/MLG *bunt* 'union, federation' (cf. Ger. *Bund* 'league'), via Ukr. *бунт* 'riot, rebellion' or Pol. *bunt* 'conspiracy, rebellion', the change in meaning attributable to a medieval assumption that groupings were likely to be conspiratorial, cf. Pol. *urządzić bunt* 'to conspire'.

БУРЯ [búrja] 'storm'. 11th century, from CSl. *burja, perhaps based on IE onomatopoeic *bhur- 'to roar', cf. Lat. *furor* 'rage', Icel. *byrr* 'fair wind', Lith. *biaurus* 'hideous', and associated with dial. *бýрить* 'to cast down' or *бурúть* 'to pour in excess'.

БУТЫЛКА [butýlka] 'bottle'. Late 17th century, probably a loan, perhaps via Pol. *butelka*, id., with -e- to -ы- possibly under the influence of *бýтель* 'large bottle' (the unstressed -e- pronounced as -ы-, according to Cyganenko), from Fr. *bouteille* 'bottle', ultimately from Vulg. Lat. *butticella* 'keg', dim. of *buttis* 'cask'.

БЫК [byk] 'bull'. 11th century, based on IE onomatopoeic *bhuki̯ō 'roar, bellow', from OR *бучати/бучити* 'to roar', the bull being named for its bellow, cf. букáшка 'small insect', пчелá 'bee' (OR *бъчела*, id.), both emitting a buzzing noise (cf. also IE *bhouqu̯os 'buzzing insect', *bhūkos 'hummer, roarer').

БЫСТРЫЙ [býstryj] 'quick'. 11th century, from IE *bhūsteros 'raging, wild', CSl. *bystrъ, initially *bysrъ (for -t- infix, cf. струя́ 'stream'), seemingly cognate with the river Бы́стрица (Rom. Bistriţa) in the Danube basin, cf. Bulg. *бистър* 'clear, limpid, transparent' (fast-flowing water is often the purest). Fr. *bistro(t)* 'small bar or restaurant' is said to derive from cries of Бы́стро! 'Hurry up!' by R. officers in Paris cafés following the defeat of Napoleon in 1812 (alternatively, from Fr. (N. region) *bistouille* 'bad alcohol, coffee mixed with alcohol').

БЮСТГАЛЬТЕР [bjustgál'ter] 'brassière'. From Ger. *Büstenhalter*, id.

В

ВАГОН [vagón] 'railway carriage'. Evolved in this meaning in the 1830s (originally in the form *ваггон*), at a time of intense railway building in Russia, later superseding synonyms повозка 'conveyance' and телега 'waggon'. From Ger. *Waggon* 'carriage, goods truck' or Fr. *wagon* 'carriage', both from Eng. *waggon*, ultimately IE *u̯eĝh 'transport', *u̯oĝhos 'conveying, cart' (whence also везу́ 'I convey').

ВАЖНЫЙ [vážnyj] 'important'. From Pol. *ważny*, id., a derivative of Pol. *waga* 'scales, weight, significance', itself from OHG *waga* 'scales' (cf. Ger. *Waage*, id.), thus lit. 'of weight, significance'.

ВАКСА [váksa] 'shoe polish'. 18th century, from Ger. *Wachs* 'wax' (cf. IE *u̯oksos, id.). See also воск, id.

ВАННА [vánna] 'bath'. Early 18th century, via Ger. *Wanne* 'winnowing fan, bath', from Lat. *vannus* (associated with Lat. *ventilō* 'I toss in the air, fan') 'winnowing machine, fan' (whence also OE *fann* 'winnowing machine', cf. Fr. *vanner* 'to winnow', from Vulg. Lat. *vannare*). The meaning broadens subsequently to denote means of freshening up in general, thus 'bath'.

ВАРЯГИ [varjági] 'Varangians' (Norsemen who penetrated Russia in the 9th-10th centuries). Equivalent of Byz. Gk. *Baraggoi*, a body of mercenaries forming part of the Byz. emperor's palace guard, MLat. *Varangus*, id., from OSc., cf. ON/Icel. *vaeringi*, from *varar* (obs.) 'pledge' (with -in- replaced by ESl. -я-), thus properly 'bound by oath, confederates'. Alternatively, a link has been suggested with OR *варити* 'to warn, prevent'.

ВАСИЛЕК [vasilëk] 'cornflower'. 17th-century reshaping of базили́к 'basil' (*Ocymum basilicum*), an aromatic herb, from Gk. *basilikón* ('royal', a neut. adj., sc. *phytón* 'plant'), id., MLat. *basilicum*, id., в- possibly under the influence of Василий 'Basil' or василиск 'basilisk', with -ik misinterpreted as a dim. ending, following the reduction of -ón, and rendered as dim. -ëк.

ВАТА [váta] 'cotton wool'. Mid-18th century, from Ger. *Watte*, id., itself from Fr. *ouate*, id., probably ultimately from Ar., via D. *watten*, id. and MLat. *wadda*, id., cf. also Ital. *ovatta*, id., Eng. *wad*.

ВДОВА [vdová] 'widow'. 11th century, from CSl. short fem. adj. *vьdova, lit. 'deprived', cognate with Lat. *vidua* 'unmarried woman, widow', cf. Lat. *viduus* 'deprived' (*viduō* 'I deprive'), IE *u̯idheu̯os 'separate, set aside'.

ВЕДЬМА [véd'ma] 'witch'. From CSl. *věděti 'to know' (cf. вéдать 'to know', IE *u̯idmi 'know, see'), originally 'she who knows', then 'witch' (cf. знáхарь 'sorcerer', from знать 'to know').

ВЕЕР [véer] 'fan'. Early 18th century, either a reshaping of Ger. *Fächer*, id., from *fächeln* 'to fan gently', on the basis of вéять 'to blow' (probably through a false etymology), or from D. *waaier* 'fan'.

ВЕЗДЕ [vezdé] 'everywhere'. 11th century *вьсьде*, id., from CSl. *vьs(ь)de, comprising *vьs- (cf. весь 'all') and the adv. suffix *-de (cf. где 'where'), with -s- voicing to -z- before voiced -d-.

ВЕРБЛЮД [verbljúd] 'camel'. CSl. *velьbǫdъ, from Goth. *ulbandus*, id., itself based on Lat. *elephantus* 'elephant', Gk. *eléfas*, gen. *eléfantos*, id. (seemingly a case of mistaken identity on the part of travellers encountering an exotic species, cf. OE *olfend* 'camel' and, for an analogous misunderstanding, see слон 'elephant'). *Ulbandus* developed to CSl. *velьbǫdъ through the addition of prosthetic v-, the replacement of -an- by -ǫ- and the loss of final -us. Subsequently -бл- evolved, possibly from a false etymology based on блудѝть/блуждáть 'to wander', thus 11th-13th centuries OR *вельблудъ* 'camel', lit. 'great wanderer' (cf. *velьjь 'great'). 14th century *верблудъ/верблюдъ*, id., resulted from dissimilation of л-л to р-л (cf. l-ł in Pol. wielbłąd 'camel').

ВЕСЛО [vesló] 'oar'. 11th century, comprising the root of

31

везти́ 'to transport' (cf. IE *u̯eĝh 'convey, transport') and agent suffix -сл(о) (cf. ма́сло 'butter'), thus 'what you transport (row) with', i.e. 'oar'.

ВЕТЕР [véter] 'wind'. 11th century (IE *(a)u̯e- 'to blow'), with cognates in Lith. *vėjas* 'wind', Goth. *wajan* 'to blow' (cf. Ger. *wehen*, id.), Lat. *ventus* 'wind'. Cognate with ве́ять 'to blow', perhaps originally a personification, thus 'he who blows, wind-god'.

ВЕТЧИНА [vetčiná] 'ham'. Late 15th century, possibly based on ве́тхий 'old' and deriving from 11th-century *ветъшина* 'something old' (for -ш- to -ч-, cf. ма́чта 'mast' from *машта*), originally 'old, stale pork', later 'smoked and salted gammon' (cf. dial. *свежина́* 'fresh, recently-slaughtered meat', from све́жий 'fresh'), less plausibly from Pol. *wędlina* 'smoked meats'. For ending -ина 'meat', cf. говя́дина 'beef', etc. (however, final stress in ветчина́ suggests an abstract source, cf. ширина́ 'breadth', etc.).

ВЗРОСЛЫЙ [vzróslyj] 'grown-up'. First half of 18th century, from a part. in -л- meaning 'who has grown up' (cf. вз- 'up', расти́ 'to grow'), later reinterpreted as an adj. and noun.

ВИНО [vinó] 'wine'. 11th century 'wine, grapes', from CSl. *vino, probably borrowed early AD from Lat. *vīnum* 'wine' (or Vulg. Lat. *vīno), or even, plausibly, Pontic *voino (since the development of viticulture by the Romans began in Pontus, the region round the Black Sea, particularly a district in Asia Minor between Bithynia and Armenia, subsequently a Roman province). Possibly cognate with ви́ться 'to twine' and ветвь 'branch'.

ВИНОГРАД [vinográd] 'grapes'. 11th century 'vineyard', then 'vine, grapes', ultimately CSl. *vinogordъ, probably from ChSl. (cf. *град-* 'enclosed place') or Gmc., and calqued from Goth. *weinagards* 'vineyard', cf. OHG *wingarto*, id., whence (in the Rhine provinces and Switzerland) *Wingert*, id., and Ger. *Weingarten*, id.

ВИНТ [vint] 'screw'. Pre-17th century, via Pol. *gwint* 'worm (spiral part) of a screw' and Ukr. *гвинт* 'screw', a reshaping of Ger. *Gewinde* 'worm of a screw', from *winden* 'to wind, twist'. Loss of initial g- possibly by false etymological association with виться 'to wind' (and later juxtaposition with Fr. *vis* 'screw').

ВИНТОВКА [vintóvka] 'rifle'. 17th century, from a compound based on винтовой 'spiral' (e.g., мелкое винтовое ружьё 'small rifled gun') + -ка, denoting a firearm with a rifled barrel (i.e. with spiral grooves that impart rotatory motion to a projectile), by contrast with the smooth bore of a shotgun (ружьё). See винт 'screw'.

ВЛАГА [vlága] 'moisture'. From IE *u̯elgos 'damp', CSl. *volg- (whence also Волга 'Volga'), of ChSl. origin, cognate with dial. *волглый* 'damp', *волгнуть* 'to become damp', Ger. *Wolke* 'cloud'.

ВЛАСТЬ [vlast'] 'power, authority'. From IE *u̯oldh- 'rule, control, possess', CSl. *voldtь/*volstъ, cognate with владеть 'to own', cf. OHG *waltan*, Ger. *walten* 'to govern', область (originally об- + власть) 'province', Eng. *wield*. Of ChSl. origin, cf. волость (hist., with ESl. inter-consonantal -оло-) 'smallest administrative division in tsarist Russia'.

ВЛИЯНИЕ [vlijánije] 'influence'. Semantic calque (earlier meaning 'pouring in') of Fr. *influence* (в = *in* 'in', and -лияние = *-fluence* 'flowing'), from MLat. *influentia* 'influence' (initially in an astronomical/astrological sense), cf. Ger. *Einfluß*, id., Pol. *wpływ*, id.

ВОДОРОД [vodoród] 'hydrogen'. First half of the 19th century, calqued from Lat. *hydrogenium*, id. (from Gk. *hydōr* 'water', *gennáō* 'I produce' -- hydrogen was considered to be the generator of water). The term was introduced in 1824 by the chemist M.V. Solov'ëv, replacing earlier *водотвор* (cf. творить 'to create'). Cf. also Fr. *hydrogène*, the term proposed by the chemist G. de Morveau in 1787.

ВОКЗАЛ [vokzál] 'mainline station'. From Eng. *Vauxhall*, a pleasure garden opened in 1661 and a favourite resort of the

English metropolis until its closure in 1859. Similar gardens appeared in 1770s in St. Petersburg and Moscow (as *фоксал/воксал*, with subsequent replacement of -с- by -з-, by analogy with зал 'hall'), described as 'illuminated garden[s] with pleasure pavilions, buffets, music, plays and comic operas', and later in the provinces. With the advent of railways the Pavlovsk terminus (вокзáл) of the St. Petersburg-Pavlovsk line (opened in 1837) combined the functions of passenger hall and concert hall (with orchestra and gipsy singing and, from 1840, symphony concerts). As the prestige of вокзáлы as leisure centres declined, the meaning 'railway station' (recorded in dictionaries late 19th century) emerged as the sole connotation of the word.

ВОЛК [volk] 'wolf'. 11th century, from CSl. *vьlkъ, possibly from an IE root (*ul̯quos) meaning both 'rend' and 'wolf', thus 'animal that rends'. Alternatively, cognate with волочи́ть 'to drag' (i.e. sheep and cattle), cf. Lith. *vilkas* 'wolf', *vilkti* 'to drag'.

ВООЧИЮ [voóčiju] 'with one's own eyes'. Lit. 'in the eyes', from OR *въ* 'in' and the prep. dual of *око* 'eye'.

ВОР [vor] 'thief'. Originally (16th century) 'rogue, deceiver', probably connected with врать (coll.) 'to speak, lie', subsequently (17th century) 'thief'.

ВОРОН [vóron] 'raven'. From CSl. *vornъ, with ESl. interconsonantal -opo-, from the bird's colour (cf. вороно́й 'black', now, however, normally of horses), possibly an adj. noun. Likewise воро́на 'crow'.

ВОСЕМЬ [vósem'] 'eight'. 11th century OR *осмь*, id., from CSl. *os(ь)mь, id., ultimately IE *oktō(u), id. (cf. Lat. *octō*, id.), which has been interpreted as the dual of *okĕtis/*okitis 'harrow', lit. 'four-toothed' (thus 'eight' is properly 'two harrows, twice four'), alternatively as 'twice four *fingers*' (in practical terms, enough to pick up an object, cf. analogous Goth. *taihun* 'ten', taken to comprise *twai* 'two' + *handus* 'hand' and, for an example of numerical abstraction, со́рок 'forty'). A prosthetic v- has developed in R. (as in во́тчина 'patrimony', alongside отéц 'father'), cf., without v-, осьминóг 'octopus', Pol. *osiem* 'eight', Cz. *osm*, id.

ВОСК [vosk] 'wax'. 11th century, with cognates only in Balto-Slav. (e.g. Lith. *vaškas*, id.) and Gmc. (OHG *wahs*, id., Ger. *Wachs*, id., also borrowed as вáкса 'shoe polish'), ultimately IE *u̯oksos 'wax' (воск thus displays ks-sk metathesis).

ВОСКРЕСЕНЬЕ [voskresén'je] 'Sunday'. Originally 'Easter Sunday, feast of the resurrection' (cf., with ChSl. -ие ending, воскресéние 'resurrection'), subsequently '(any) Sunday', replacing 11th-century *недѣля* 'Sunday' in this meaning (see понедéльник 'Monday', lit. 'day after Sunday', and cf. Pol. *niedziela* 'Sunday'). *Недѣля* replaced OR *седмица* in the meaning 'week', see недéля 'week'.

ВОСТОК [vostók] 'east'. 11th century, from ChSl., calqued from Gk. *anatolḗ* 'rising, especially of the sun or moon' (cf. Gk. *anatéllō* 'I rise up'), thus the place where the sun rises (вос-/ *ana-* 'upward' + ток, cognate with течь 'to flow', CSl *tekti* 'flow, run'), cf. Lat. *oriēns* 'rising sun, east'.

ВПЕЧАТЛЕНИЕ [vpečaténije] 'impression'. Calque based on Fr. *impression*, id. (*in/im* = в, *presse* = печать, *-ion* = -ение), alternatively calqued from Ger. *Eindruck*, id.

ВРАГ [vrag] 'enemy'. 11th century, from ChSl., hence interconsonantal -pa- (cf. Ukr. *ворог* 'enemy', Pol. *wróg*, id.), perhaps associated with Lat. *urgeō* 'force, drive, impel' (IE *u̯ergō 'force'), thus lit. 'forced, driven out'.

ВРАТАРЬ [vratár'] 'gate-keeper, goal-keeper'. 11th century 'gate-keeper', from ChSl. *врата* 'gate' + agent suffix *-арь*, adopted as a 'puristic' synonym of голкúпер 'goal-keeper' in the mid-20th century, as a calque of Ger. *Torwart*, id.

ВРАТЬ [vrat'] 'to lie'. First recorded in dictionaries 1704, from CSl. *vьrati*, id., a narrowing of the original meaning 'to speak' (cf. 'Полнó *врать* пустякú' 'Stop *talking* nonsense' in Pushkin's *Капитáнская дóчка*). Possibly cognate with Lat. *verbum* 'word', Gk. *rhḗtōr* 'orator', *eírōn* 'a dissembler'.

ВРАЧ [vrač] 'doctor'. 11th century, ultimately from IE *u̯er- 'to speak', via ChSl., cognate with врать 'to lie, talk gibberish', thus 'he who speaks, cures by spell, sorcerer', then 'doctor' (cf. Serb. *врач* 'sorcerer', Bulg. *врач* 'wizard, healer, quack'). Врачéбный 'medicinal' derives from OR *врачьба* 'medicine'.

ВРЕМЯ [vrémja] 'time'. 11th century, from CSl. *vertmen 'rotation' (i.e. of days and months, cf. вертéться 'to rotate', Lat. *annus vertens* 'the course of a year', ultimately from IE radical *u̯ert- 'turn'). Of ChSl. origin, -pe- developing from -er-, -я replacing -en and inter-consonantal -t- being discarded. Cognate with Skr. *vartman* 'track, road', possibly Lat. *Vertumnus*, originally an Etruscan deity, god of the changing year.

ВСЕЛЕННАЯ [vselénnaja] 'universe'. From a ChSl. calque of Gk. *oikouménē* 'the civilized world, habitable globe', pass. part. of *oikéō* 'I inhabit', thus 'inhabited (territory)', then 'the whole world', with ChSl. -é- (cf. R. -ё- in вселённый 'installed').

ВЧЕРА [včerá] 'yesterday'. 11th century, from CSl. *vьčera, old instr. sing. of *večerъ 'evening' (with reduction of first -e-), thus lit. 'on the eve of today', cf. analogous development of зáвтра 'tomorrow'.

ВЫДРА [výdra] 'otter'. Late 14th century, lit. 'water animal', cf. Skr. *uda* 'water' (at beginning or end of compounds), *udra* 'kind of aquatic animal', Gk. *hydōr* 'water', *hydros/hydra* 'water snake', Lith. *ūdra* 'otter', etc. For Slav. prosthetic v-, cf. Pol. *wydra*, id., Cz. *vydra*, id. Cognates include ведрó 'bucket', related to водá 'water' (cf. IE *u̯odōr, id.), and perhaps originally meaning 'something connected with water', then 'receptacle for water'.

Г

ГАВАНЬ [gávan'] 'harbour'. Late 17th-/early 18th centuries (sometimes *гаван*), from D. *haven*, id., with D. -n softening to R. -нь either under the influence of preceding -е- or by analogy with пристань 'landing-stage'.

ГАЗ I [gaz] 'gas'. Late 18th-/early 19th centuries (originally *гас*), probably from Fr. *gaz* 'gas', a term originated by Dutchman J.B. van Helmont (1577-1644), with the words *Halitum illud gas vocavi, non longe a Chao veterum* 'I called these fumes gas as being not far removed from the chaos of the ancients', on the basis of Lat. *chaos*/Gk. *cháos* 'chaos, space', with ch- changing to g- possibly under the influence of D. *geest* 'spirit' (cf. D. *gas* 'gas').

ГАЗ II [gaz] 'gauze'. Second half of the 18th century, from Fr. *gaze*, id., possibly deriving from Gaza, the harbour town and region in Palestine on the E. coast of the Mediterranean where the fabric is thought to have originated. Alternatively, from Ar. *ghizzī* 'gauze'.

ГАЗЕТА [gazéta] 'newspaper'. Early 18th century, succeeding *Вѣсти-Кураńты*, lit. 'News Chimes' (digests of foreign news prepared for Tsar Aleksej Michajlovič 1629-76) and Peter I's *Вѣдомости* 'Gazette', from Ital. *gazzetta*, possibly via Fr. *gazette* 'newspaper', the first newspaper having come out in Venice in 1563 under the title *gazeta de la novitá* 'a pennyworth of news', so called because sold for a *gazeta*, a low-denomination Venetian coin. Газéта became a familiar word in Russia thanks to Kurakin, Peter I's ambassador in Venice.

ГАЛАКТИКА [galáktika] 'galaxy'. 1920s (replacing *галаксия*), based on Gk. *galaxías* (sc. *kýklos* 'circle') 'Milky Way' (cf. Млéчный путь, id.), from *gála*, gen. *gálaktos* 'milk', so called from the milky-white light emanating from vast agglomerations of stars on clear nights.

ГАЛСТУК [gálstuk] 'tie'. Early 18th century, from D. *halsdoek* 'scarf' (*hals* 'neck', *doek* 'cloth') or Ger. *Halstuch* 'scarf'.

ГАММА [gámma] 'musical scale'. The third letter of the Gk. alphabet, also originally the lowest note in the musical scale, subsequently used to denote the whole scale. Attributed to Guido d'Arezzo (c. 990-c. 1050), who applied syllables to the notes of the diatonic scale, based on the first six lines of a Lat. hymn to St. John the Baptist, in which the first note of each measure corresponded to a note in the scale. Cf. Ital. *gamma* 'scale', Fr. *gamme*, id.

ГАРДЕРОБ [garderób] 'wardrobe'. Early 18th century (initially гардероба), from Fr. *garde-robe*, id.

ГАРЬ [gar'] 'burning'. 15th century 'forest area cleared by fire', CSl. in origin, deriving by deaffixation from the verb 'to burn' (R. горе́ть), cf. мазь 'ointment' from ма́зать 'to spread'.

ГАСТРОНОМ [gastronóm] 'gastronome, grocer's shop'. 19th century 'gastronome', probably from Fr. *gastronome*, id., based on Archestratus's *gastronomía* 'Gourmands' Almanach' (*gastér* stomach', *nómos* 'law'), whence Eng. *gastronomy* 'the art and science of good eating and drinking'. In the meaning 'grocer's shop' replaced гастрономи́ческий магази́н in the 1930s/1940s.

ГВОЗДИКА [gvozdíka] 'carnation(s), cloves'. 15th century гвозникы/гвозд(ь)никы, 17th century гвозди́ки, *Dianthus caryophyllus*, thought to be of S. Eur. origin, named in R. for the similarity of their leaves or plant-heads to nails (cf. гвоздь 'nail'). A semantic calque of Pol. *gwoździk* 'carnation' (Pol. *gwóźdź* 'nail'), itself calqued from Ger. *Nelke* 'carnation' (or from MLG *negelkīn* 'clove', lit. 'small nail').

ГВОЗДЬ [gvozd'] 'nail'. From CSl. *g(v)ozdь, 11th century 'nail', perhaps deriving from the earlier meaning 'forest' (also 'hills in N. Dalmatia', there being an affinity, due to their adjacence, between forests and hills), cf. Cz. *hvozd* 'forest', with cognates in Goth. *gazds* 'thorn', Lat. *hasta* 'pole, spear'.

ГЕКТАР [gektár] 'hectare' (ten thousand square metres). Early

19th century (in common use following decree of 11 November 1918), from Fr. *hectare*, id. (from Gk. *hekatón* 'hundred', Fr. *are* '100 square metres', based on Lat. *ārea* 'piece of level ground, building plot').

ГЕРБ [gerb] 'coat of arms'. 16th-/17th centuries, from Ger. (cf. Ger. *Erbe* 'inheritance'), via Pol. *herb* 'coat of arms', Cz. *erb*, id., possibly through the medium of Ukr. and BR.

ГИМНАСТИКА [gimnástika] 'gymnastics'. Early 19th century, from Ger. *Gymnastik* 'gymnastics', ultimately Gk. *gymnastikē* (*téchnē* 'art' understood), id., cf. Gk. *gymnázō* 'I train naked, train in gymnastic exercises', from *gymnós* 'naked' (in ancient Greece youths stripped naked for gymnastic exercises). Early-18th century гимна́зия 'high school' derives from Ger. *Gymnasium*, id., ultimately Gk. *gymnásion*, initially (pl. *-ia*) 'bodily exercises', then 'gymnastic school', finally 'school in general'.

ГЛАВА [glavá] 'head, chapter'. 11th century, with ChSl. interconsonantal -ла- (cf. голова́ 'head'), from CSl. *golva, assumed to be cognate with Lith. *galva*, id. and Lat. *calva* 'scalp' (from *calvus* 'bald'). Глава́ 'chapter' is a semantic calque of Gk. *kephálaion* 'the main point', dim. of *kephalḗ* 'head'.

ГЛАГОЛ [glagól] 'word, verb'. 11th century 'word', of ChSl. origin, from reduplicated onomatopoeic *gol- (cognate with CSl. *golsъ 'voice', Eng. *call*), hence CSl. *golgol, with *gol- subsequently changing to ChSl. *гла-*, thus глаго́л 'word' (cf., from A.S. Pushkin's *Пророк*, Глаго́лом жги сердца́ люде́й 'Burn human hearts with the word'). Глаго́л 'verb' (17th century at latest) is a semantic calque of Gk. *rēma* 'word, verb'.

ГЛАСИТЬ [glasít'] 'to read, run' (of a document). In OR 'to utter a sound', from ChSl. *гласъ* 'voice' (cf., with ESl. interconsonantal -оло-, голоси́ть 'to wail, keen').

ГЛАСНЫЙ [glásnyj] 'vowel'. ChSl. calque of Lat. *vōcālis*, id., an adj. noun based on *vōcālis* 'sonorous' (cf. *vox* 'voice'), also 'open, candid', its derivative гла́сность 'openness' enjoying wide currency in the second half of the 1980s.

ГЛОБУС [glóbus] 'globe'. Early 18th century, from Lat. *globus* 'sphere, globe', possibly via Ger. *Globus* '(model) globe'.

ГЛУПЫЙ [glúpyj] 'stupid'. CSl. *glupъ (based on *glu- 'empty') 'empty-headed, stupid', cognate with глухо́й 'deaf' (cf. confusion of disability with stupidity in Slovene *glûp* 'deaf, stupid', OHG *tumb* 'stupid, deaf, dumb', Amer. Eng. *dumb* 'stupid', Ger. *dumm*, id.). Also cognate with глуми́ться 'to mock', which is possibly from IE *ghleu- 'clever, keen'.

ГЛЯНЕЦ [gljánec] 'gloss'. Early 18th century, from Ger. *Glanz* 'lustre', reshaped on the pattern of nouns in -ец.

ГНЕЗДО́ [gnezdó] 'nest'. 11th century, from CSl. *gnězdo, IE *nisdos (*ni- 'down' + *sed 'sit'), -s- voicing to -z- before -d- by regressive assimilation. Cf. Skr. *ni-* (verb or noun prefix) 'down, in, into, within', Eng. *nether*, Lat. *nīdus* 'nest', Fr. *nid*, id., etc.. Initial г- possibly under the influence of other CSl. words in *gně- (cf. гнедо́й 'bay', гнести́ 'to oppress').

ГОВОРИ́ТЬ [govoŕít'] 'to speak'. 11th century 'to make a noise, speak', from OR *говоръ* 'noise' (IE *gou̯ō 'shout'), ultimately onomatopoeic гов- + suffix -оръ, cf. Pol. *gwar* 'hum, noise', Gk *góos* 'lamentation'.

ГОВЯ́ДИНА [govjádina] 'beef'. OR *говядо* 'bull, herd of bulls, cattle' (IE *gu̯ōu̯ēda 'ox, cattle') derives from CSl. *govędo 'large horned cattle' (with -ę- changing to -я- in ESl). For -ина 'meat', cf. бара́нина 'mutton', etc. *Gov- perhaps onomatopoeic, imitating a bull's roar. Cf. cognate Eng. *cow*, OHG *kuo* 'cow', Arm. *gov*, id., Bulg. *говедо* 'cattle'.

ГОЛОВА́ [golová] 'head'. In OR 'head, conscience, soul, mind, murder victim', from IE *galu̯ā 'head' (possibly cognate with CSl. *golъ 'bare, bald', *IE *galuos 'bare'), CSl. *golva (cf. Lith. *galva* 'head'), with ESl. inter-consonantal -оло-. Maybe originally 'bald head' or 'skull'. Has also been associated with желва́к 'tumour', Pol. *żółw* 'tortoise' (from the hardness of the skull/shell, cf. analogous similarity of form in че́реп 'skull' and черепа́ха 'tortoise', Lat. *tēsta* 'skull' and *testūdō* 'tortoise' (also Lat. *calva* 'scalp', *calvus* 'bald').

ГОЛОС [gólos] 'voice'. Ultimately from IE *gholsos 'sound, voice', possibly onomatopoeic (cf. IE *gal̯u̯ō 'call', *gali̯ō 'shout'), via CSl. *golsъ, with ESl. inter-consonantal -оло- and cognates in Eng. *call*, Dan. *kalde* 'to call'.

ГОЛУБОЙ [golubój] 'light blue'. ESl. (cf. Bulg. *светлосин*, id., Pol. *niebieski*, id.), based on го́лубь 'pigeon' (CSl. *golǫbь), from the sky-blue plumage of a pigeon's neck, cognate with Lat. *columba* 'pigeon'. The meaning 'gay, homosexual' (cf. ро́зовая 'pink, lesbian') is attributed to the association of light-blue colours with male children.

ГОЛЫЙ [gólyj] 'bare'. 13th century, from IE *gal̯uos, id., CSl. *golъ, perhaps originally 'bald' (cf. OHG *kalo*, id., Lat *calvus*, id., Eng. *callow* 'bald (obs.), raw, inexperienced'), subsequently 'naked'.

ГОРЕ [góre] 'sorrow'. 11th century 'anguish, distress', from CSl. *gorje, cognate with горе́ть 'to burn', греть 'to heat', thus lit. 'that which burns, torments'. Possibly originally a substantivized adj. first used in exclamations (О го́ре мне! 'Oh, woe is me!'), cf. also го́рький 'bitter'.

ГОРИЗОНТ [gorizónt] 'horizon'. 17th-/18th centuries, possibly from Ger. *Horizont*, id. or D. *horizon(t)*, id., ultimately via Lat. from the Gk. substantivized act. part. *horízōn*, gen. *horízontos* (sc. *kýklos* 'circle'), from *horízō* 'I limit, define' (cf. *hóros* 'boundary'), initially 'restricting, limiting', then 'limiting circle, horizon'.

ГОРЛО [górlo] 'throat'. From IE onomatopoeic *gher- 'to swallow', CSl. *gъrdlo, OR *гърло* 'throat' (11th century), 'neck' (16th century), with agent suffix -(d)lo simplifying to -lo (cf. мы́ло 'soap', etc.), thus lit. 'what you swallow with'. Cf. (with г:ж mutation) жерло́ 'mouth, orifice, gun muzzle', ожере́лье 'necklace' (also Lat. *gurguliō* 'windpipe', whence Ger. *Gurgel* 'gullet').

ГОРОД [górod] 'town'. From IE *ghordos 'fortified place, walled enclosure', CSl. *gordъ, originally 'enclosed place', whence OR *городъ* (with ESl. inter-consonantal -оро-), initially 'enclosure', then 'fortification, fortress', finally 'town'. Cf. городи́ть 'to enclose, fence in' and cognates Lith. *gardas* 'enclosure', Goth. *garda*, id., Eng. *yard* (OE *ġeard* 'enclosure, courtyard').

ГОРЧИЦА [gorčíca] 'mustard'. 11th century *горьчица* 'bitter potion', from CSl. *goгькъjь, whence го́рький 'bitter'. Cognate with горе́ть 'to burn', originally, perhaps, 'that which burns'.

ГОРЮЧЕЕ [gorjúčeje] 'fuel'. Late 19th-/early 20th centuries, from the pres. act. part. of CSl. *gorěti 'to burn', cf. шипу́чий 'fizzy' from шипе́ть 'to hiss' (and горя́щий 'burning', the standard part., of ChSl. origin, from горе́ть 'to burn'). Probably substantivized from горю́чее то́пливо 'combustible fuel'.

ГОРЯЧИЙ [gorjáčij] 'hot'. Originally a part. from горе́ть 'to burn' (see горю́чее 'fuel'), initially 'warm, hot', exclusively 'hot' from the 15th/16th centuries (see тёплый 'warm').

ГОСТЬ [gost'] 'guest'. 10th century 'merchant, foreign merchant' (cf. Гости́ный двор, a multiple store in St. Petersburg, OR *гостити* 'to trade'), 11th century 'guest', from IE *ghostis 'guest, stranger'. The meaning 'stranger, potential enemy' finds parallels in Lat. *hostis* 'stranger, enemy', Goth. *gasts*, OHG *gast* from Gmc. *gastiz 'stranger', with reversal of meaning in Eng. *guest*, Ger. *Gast* 'guest', гость, id.

ГРАД [grad] 'town'. 11th century 'enclosure, town', from CSl. *gordъ, with ChSl. inter-consonantal -ра-. Homonymous град 'hail' is cognate with Lat. *grandō* 'hail, hail storm' (cf. also IE *ghrōdos 'ice, hail').

ГРАДУС [grádus] 'degree'. Late 17th-/early 18th centuries 'degree, rank', 18th century 'degree of temperature or longitude' (e.g. in M. V. Lomonosov's works on physics and chemistry of 1762-63 -- гра́дус also served as a basis for гра́дусник 'thermometer', coined by Lomonosov. Ultimately via Ukr. from Lat. *gradus* 'step, degree', *gradior* 'I step' (which is cognate with CSl. *grędǫ* 'I go', cf. грядущий (rhet.) 'future', грядущее 'the future').

ГРАЖДАНИН [graždanín] 'citizen'. 11th century, with ChSl. inter-consonantal -ра- and -жд- from -dj- (cf. горожанин 'city-dweller', with ESl. -оро- and -ж-). Etymologically 'city-dweller', subsequently, esp. under the influence of A.N. Radiščev (1749-1802) 'citizen'. Гражданский 'civic' is a calque of Gk. *politikós*, id.

ГРАНАТ [granát] 'pomegranate'. Late 18th century (earlier гранатовое дерево), seemingly from Ger. *Granatapfel*, id., ultimately Lat. *mālum grānātum* (MLat. *pōmum grānātum*), lit. 'many-seeded apple', cf. Lat. *grānum* 'seed'. Cognate with mid-17th century граната 'grenade' (which scatters granular-shaped shrapnel on impact) and mid-18th century гранат 'garnet' (whose colour resembles that of the deep-red pulp of the fruit).

ГРАНИЦА [graníca] 'frontier'. 14th century *грань*, denoting two crossed lines in the form of a multiplication sign, placed on trees marking territorial boundaries (and in clerks' ledgers), perhaps originally 'tree with such a mark' (esp. a fir, cf. Dan. *Gran* 'spruce'), subsequently граница 'frontier', whence, via Pol. *granica*, id., Ger. *Grenze*, id. Cf. грань, now 'verge'.

ГРАЧ [grač] 'rook'. 15th century (initially as a nickname), from IE *graik* 'crow, caw', CSl. onomatopoeic *gra-/grak-, whence гра/кра (the cry of a raven), Ukr. *грак* 'rook', OR *граяти* 'to caw', dial. *гракать*, id. For к:ч mutation, cf. плакать 'to weep', плач 'weeping'.

ГРЕМЕТЬ [gremét'] 'to thunder'. 11th century, cognate with Lith. *grumėti*, id., cf. Gk. *chrómados* 'creaking' and cognates гром 'thunder', громкий 'loud' (IE *ghromi̯ō* 'roar').

ГРЕСТИ [grestí] 'to row'. OR *грети* (грести), 11th century 'to dig, row', 14th century 'to comb' (based on the similarity of the actions), from IE *ghrābhō* 'to rake together', CSl. *gresti (earlier *grebti, cf. Lith. *grėbti* 'to rake'). The meaning 'row' (cf. гребе́ц 'oarsman', гре́бля 'rowing') is secondary to 'rake together', etc. Cf. cognates по́греб 'cellar', гроб 'coffin' (originally 'grave'), гре́бень 'comb', гра́бли 'rake'.

ГРИВА [gríva] 'mane'. From IE *grīu̯os 'neck, nape', CSl. *griva. Purportedly cognate with го́рло 'throat', горта́нь 'larynx', with transition of meaning from 'neck, nape', to 'what grows on the neck', i.e. 'mane', and derivative in гри́вна (originally an OR fem. adj. noun) 'necklace, pendant', then 'grivna' (OR unit of currency in the form of a silver ingot, subsequently 'ten-kopeck coin').

ГРОЗА́ [grozá] 'thunderstorm'. 11th century 'horror, the nether world', from CSl. *groza 'something terrifying', cf. грози́ть 'to threaten', Lith. *grasus* 'menacing', *grasinimas* 'threat', also Gk. *gorgós* 'terrible', Ger. *garstig* 'detestable'.

ГРЯЗЬ [grjaz'] 'mud, dirt'. CSl. *gręzь, initially 'boggy, silted area', cognate with CSl. *grǫz-, whence груз 'weight', cf. погрузи́ться 'to sink into', погря́знуть 'to be stuck in'. Грязь is formed by verbal deaffixation, its meaning probably evolving from 'sinking into' and 'swampy place' to 'mud'.

ГУСЕНИЦА [gúsenica] 'caterpillar, (1930s) caterpillar track', from CSl. *(g)ǫsenica, probably from *ǫsъ (ус 'whisker'), thus, perhaps 'hairy creature, insect with feelers' (for -ица 'living being', cf. сини́ца 'bluebird'), cf. also Pol. *wąs* 'whisker', *wąsienica* 'caterpillar'. Initial г- is attributed to the influence of ChSl. *гоуштерица* 'lizard' (cf. Bulg. *гущер*, id.) or to false etymology involving гусь 'goose' (for y:гу correlation, cf. also OR *ужь* 'rope' and гуж 'tug', the leather loop that attaches the shafts of a carriage to the harness).

ГУСЬ [gus'] 'goose'. CSl. *gǫsь/*zǫsь, cf. Lith. *žąsis* 'goose', possibly from a root meaning 'to yawn, open wide', cf. Gk. *chaínō* 'I yawn', *chḗn* 'goose' ('named for its wide bill'). Initial г- possibly under the influence of onomatopoeic га́га 'cackling, eider duck', dial. гага́кать 'to cackle', OHG *gans* 'goose' (cf. IE *ghansis, id.), or by dissimilation of z- from -s- (g-s for z-s).

Д

ДАТЬ [dat'] 'to give'. 11th century *дати*, with derivatives in дань 'tribute', дар 'gift', also дача 'country cottage', lit. 'that which is given' (cf. сдача 'change'), then 'land bestowed', the meaning 'country cottage' being exclusive to R.

ДВА/ДВЕ [dva/dve] 'two'. 11th century, with cognates in Lith. *du, dvi*, id., Gk. *dúō*, id., Lat. *duo*, id., etc., the basis of двенáдцать 'twelve' and двáдцать 'twenty' (cf. -дцать and non-reduced forms in Pol. *dwadzieścia*, id., Bulg. *двадесет*, id.), двéсти 'two hundred' (from CSl. nom./acc. dual *dъvě sьtě). Двáжды 'twice' (16th century) is thought to derive from *дъва + шьды*, lit. 'two moves, steps', with -ш- voicing to -ж- before -д- following the reduction of -ь- (cf. analogous correlation in Pol. *krok* 'step', *dwakroć* 'twice', Dan. *Gang* 'walk', also 'time').

ДВОР [dvor] 'yard, court'. 11th century, cognate with IE *dhu̯er- 'door', дверь, id., Goth. *daur* (Ger. *Tor* 'gate'), Skr. *dvāram*, id., with probable semantic progression from 'gate' to 'area shut off by gates, courtyard', finally 'estate', and derivatives in late 12th-century дворянúн 'nobleman', 16th-century дворéц 'palace', 15th-century двóрник 'feudal servant', later 'yardman', now also (coll.) 'windscreen-wiper'.

ДВОЮРОДНЫЙ [dvojúrodnyj] 'related through a grandparent'. From OR/ChSl. gen./prep. dual *дъвою родоу*, thus 'related in the second generation' (once removed), hence двоюродный брат/двоюродная сестрá 'cousin'.

ДЕ [de] (coll. particle that attributes an utterance to another speaker). From 14th century *дѣ*, abbreviated form of *дѣетъ* 'says' (OR *дѣти* 'to speak'). Synonymous дéскать is a truncated version of *дѣетъ* 'says' + *съказати*, cf. similar allegro truncation in *так-скать* for так сказáть 'so to speak'.

ДЕВА [déva] 'girl, maiden'. 11th century, from CSl. *děva, cognate with *dětę (whence дитя 'child'), perhaps from IE *dhēi̯ō 'to suck, milk, feed with the breast', thus lit. 'suckling, female child', conversely 'young woman, woman breast-feeding', with cognates in доить 'to milk', Lith. *dėlė* 'leech', and derivatives девочка 'little girl' (15th century), девушка 'girl' (dictionary of 1731). Suffix -v(a) possibly adj. or, as in CSl. *korva 'cow', substantival.

ДЕВЯТЬ [dévjat'] 'nine'. 11th century, from CSl. ordinal *devętъ 'ninth', the cardinal *devętь taking the form of a soft-sign noun, cognate with Lith. *devyni* 'nine'. Probably originally with initial n-, cf. Lat. *novem*, id., Ger. *neun*, id., Fr. *neuf*, id., etc. Slav. d- evolved possibly under the influence of *desętь 'ten', or through dissimilation (n- to d- before subsequent nasal vowel). Initially, perhaps, denoted 'new' -- cf. IE *neuṇ 'nine'/*neuos 'new', whence Lat. *novus*, id., Ger. *neu*, Fr. *neuf/nouveau* (in an ancient system of counting by fours -- see восемь 'eight' -- 'nine' could be seen as 'new', first in the third group of fours).

Девяносто [devjanósto] 'ninety' (14th century), found only in ESl. (cf. Pol. *dziewięćdziesiąt*, id., Bulg. *деветдесет*, id., lit. 'nine tens'), possibly based on IE *nevenədk̥m̥tə '90', lit. 'the ninth ten', reshaped as девяносто by analogy with сто '100' (for formation of numerals by association with round numbers, cf. Lat. *duo-dē-vīgīnti* '18', lit. 'two from twenty', Fr. *quatre-vingts* '80', lit. 'four twenties'). Alternatively, from CSl. *nevę do sъta (lit. 'nine to a hundred', i.e., 'ninety'), then, by assimilation (n-d to n-n) *nevę no sъta, finally *devę no sъta (*devę by analogy with *desę 'ten'), or, implausibly, from *девять до ста*, changing to *девять на сто* by dissimilation (d-d to d-n), thus, finally, девяносто 'ninety'.

ДЕГОТЬ [dëgot'] 'tar'. 17th century, probably of Balt. origin, cf. Lith. *degutas*, id., from *degti* 'to burn' (IE *dheg(h)- 'burn').

ДЕД [ded] 'grandfather'. 11th century, based on childish prattle (de-de), the reduplicated form subsequently truncating to дед, conforming to the pattern of hard-ending masc. nouns.

ДЕЖУРНЫЙ [dežúrnyj] 'duty' (adj.). Early 18th century, from Fr. *de jour*, as in *service de jour* 'day-time service', cf., also based on *jour*, абажу́р 'lamp-shade' (Fr. *abat-jour*, id.), тужу́рка 'military double-breasted jacket' (from Fr. *toujours* 'always').

ДЕКАБРЬ [dekábr'] 'December'. 11th century *декябрь*, 14th century декáбрь and *декемврий*, replacing earlier *студень*, id. Ultimately from Lat. *December* (*december mensis*, lit. 'tenth month' -- December was the tenth month before the reform of the calendar under Caius Julius Caesar), via Gk. *dekémbri(os)*.

ДЕЛЬТА [dél'ta] 'delta'. 1830s, ultimately from Gk. *délta*, id., triangular-shaped fourth letter of the Gk. alphabet, applied by Herodotus to the mouth of the Nile, which branches into two arms below Cairo, remotely resembling a capital delta (Δ), and by Strabo to the Indus, later extended to the mouths of the Danube, Ganges and all other rivers. Дельтаплáн (1974) 'hang-glider', from Fr. *deltaplane*, cf. Fr. *aile delta* 'delta wing' + *planer* 'to glide'.

ДЕМОКРАТИЯ [demokrátija] 'democracy'. Early 18th century, from Gk. *dēmokratía*, id. (*dēmos* 'the common people', *krátos* 'rule'), via Fr. or Ger.

ДЕНЬГИ [dén'gi] 'money'. 14th century *деньгá*, denoting a small metal coin worth about half a kopeck (possibly a variant of *тамга*, but from a different Tkc. dial., see тамо́жня 'customs'). Probably of Tkc. origin, borrowed during the period of Mongol rule, the pl. form де́ньги gaining wide currency and eventually replacing Novgorod *ку́ны* and Pskov *пе́нязи* in the 15th century. Alternatively, the word may have been brought by merchants or travellers from Iran, cf. Pers. *tan(a)kah* 'sheet of metal, gold, money, coin', *dāng* 'coin'. Cf. also Mong. *tengah* 'small silver coin'.

ДЕРЕВНЯ [derévnja] 'village'. 14th century, probably cognate with деру́ 'I tear up, out', thus originally (according to Vasmer) 'ploughed field, area cleared of vegetation' (cf. Lith. *dirva* 'soil, ground, arable land'), then 'peasant holding with plot of land', finally 'village'. Alternatively (perhaps a false etymology) from де́рево 'wood, tree' (since village houses were usually made of wood, cf. stone dwellings in towns).

ДЕРЕВО [dérevo] 'tree'. 12th century, from CSl. *dervo, with ESl. inter-consonantal -epe-, cf. Gk. *dorý* 'stem of felled tree, beam, plank', OR 11th-century *дрѣво*, from ChSl. (whence древéсный 'wood' (adj.), древесина 'wood-pulp, timber'), Lith. *derva* 'resin', Eng. *tree, tar.* Originally, perhaps, 'that which is torn out', cf. деру́ 'I strip', referring to tree clearance to make space for ploughed land. Cf. дерéвня 'village'.

ДЕРЖАВА [deržáva] 'power'. 11th century, id., from CSl. *dьržava/dьržati (cf. держáть 'to hold' and, for suffix -ава, булавá 'mace'), with meaning developing from 'power' (that which holds, supports), 'orb' (the symbol of royal power), to 'state, independent country'.

ДЕСНА [desná] 'gum'. 14th-/15th centuries, from CSl. *dęsna/dęt-, probably from IE *dont- 'tooth', the nasal vowel subsequently changing to ESl. -я- (cf. retention in Pol. *dziąsło* 'gum'), then to -e- in unstressed position. Cognates in Gk. *odốn* 'tooth', Lat. *děns* id., Lith. *dantis*, id. and Latv. *duntas/duntes* 'gum'. Ending -сна possibly adj.

ДЕСЯТЬ [désjat'] 'ten'. 11th century, having developed from CSl. *desętъ 'tenth', with -tъ softening to -tь and nasal -ę- changing to -я- in ESl. (cf. retention in Pol. *dziesięć* 'ten'). From IE *dek̑m̥tos 'tenth', *dek̑m̥ 'ten', whence Skr. *daśan* 'ten' (nom. *daśa*), Gr. *déka*, id., Lat. *decem*, id., Goth. *taihun*, id. (thought to comprise *twai* 'two' + *handus* 'hand', thus '2 x 5 (fingers)' = 'ten').

ДЕШЕВЫЙ [deševyj] 'cheap'. 13th-/14th centuries, possibly connected with OR *десити* 'to find', cf. Serb. *десити* 'to find, meet by chance', *дешавати се* 'to happen, transpire', thus 'turning up' (as a bargain, cf. купи́ть по слу́чаю 'to buy second-hand', Fr. *marchandise d'occasion* 'second-hand goods'). Has also, implausibly, been linked with Eng. *dogcheap, finally with десни́ца (obs., poet.) 'right hand', perhaps by contrast with the pejorative connotations of 'left', cf. OE *lyftādl* 'paralysis' (lit. 'left-disease'), нале́во 'illicitly', левáк 'dishonest worker', Lat.

sinister 'left, adverse' (conversely, also 'favourable'), Fr. *gauche* 'left, awkward', etc. Thus maybe дешёвый meant 'right, correct' (of prices).

ДИВАН [diván] 'divan'. Late 18th-/early 19th centuries, from Fr. *divan* 'divan, lavishly appointed oriental council chamber', Turk. *divan* 'divan, council of state', of Pers. origin, via Ar., with semantic progression from 'state council' to 'important consultation', 'council chamber', 'long divan along wall with cushions for the back'.

ДИПЛОМ [diplóm] 'diploma'. Early 18th century, from Fr. *diplôme*, id., Ger. *Diplom*, id., Lat. *diplōma* 'written document folded in two, letter of authority', Gk. *díplōma* 'anything folded double' (especially a licence, letter of recommendation, passport), cf. Gk. *diplóō* 'I fold'.

ДИРИЖЕР [diriẑër] 'conductor' (musical). Early 19th century (earlier капельмейстер), from дирижи́ровать 'to conduct', based on Fr. *diriger* 'to direct, conduct' + agent suffix -ёр, a reshaping of Fr. -eur, cf., however, Fr. *chef d'orchestre* 'conductor' ('*personne qui dirige l'orchestre*').

ДИТЯ [ditjá] 'child'. CSl. *dětę 'breast-fed, child', of part. origin, from IE *dhēi̯o 'to suckle, suck', with -ę replaced in ESl. by -я (cf. retention of nasal in Pol. *dziecię* 'child'), thus 11th-century дѣтя 'child', -и- subsequently replacing -ѣ-, perhaps through analogy, cf. OR дѣтина 'child, youth' and (with vowel assimilation) Ukr. *дитина* 'child' (cf. also дети́на 'heavily-built chap'). Cognates include дои́ть 'to milk', де́ва 'girl, maiden'.

ДНЕВНИК [dnevník] 'diary'. 18th century, calque of Fr. *journal* 'journal, diary'.

ДНО [dno] 'bottom'. 11th century 'bottom, depth', from CSl. *dъno/*dъbno 'bottom', with -bn- simplifying to -n- (cf. CSl. *sъnъ 'sleep', from *sъpnъ), interpreted by some as a metathesis of *bъdno, which is cognate with Ger. *Boden* 'bottom, floor', cf. also Skr. *budhna* 'depth, bottom', IE *dhoubh 'deep, depth'.

ДОЖДЬ [dožd'] 'rain'. OR *дъждь*, also *дождчь*, from CSl. *dъščь, earlier *duskjos, possibly initially 'cloudy sky, bad weather', cf. Skr. *dus-* (noun, occasionally verb, prefix) 'bad', *div* 'day', *diva* 'heaven, sky, day', Norw. *duskregn* 'drizzle', Lith. *dūzgėti* 'to clatter, patter', *dūzginti* 'to make a rumbling noise'.

ДОЗОР [dozór] 'patrol'. Comprises до- + зор- (whence зо́ркий 'keen-eyed', cognate with зреть (obs.) 'to see').

ДОИТЬ [doít'] 'to milk'. 11th century *доити* 'to breast feed', also 'to milk', ultimately from IE *dhoi̯ō 'to suckle, milk, suck', cognate with дитя́ 'child', де́ва 'girl, maiden'.

ДОЛЛАР [dóllar] 'dollar'. Late 18th century, from LG *Daler*/Ger. *Taler*, an abbreviation of *Joachimstaler*, coins from the silver mines of St. Joachimstal (Cz. Jachymov, a spa to the NE of Karlovy Vary [Karlsbad]), in the Erzgebirge mountain range, along the border between Germany and the Czech Republic, minted in the area since 1518.

ДОЛОЙ [dolój] 'down with'. From OR *долови* 'downwards, away', dat. sing. of OR *долъ* 'bottom, valley', with -*ови* shortened to adverbial ending -ой (cf. домо́й 'homewards'), possibly via dat. variants *доловь/доловъ*. Cognate with доли́на 'valley' (cf. IE *dholos 'hollow, valley').

ДОЛОТО [dolotó] 'chisel'. Recorded mid-16th century (earlier *длато*, cf. also OR *долотити* 'to gouge'), from CSl. *dolbto, with ESl. inter-consonantal -olo- and -bt- simplifying to -t-. Cognate with долби́ть 'to hollow, gouge', cf. Eng. *to delve*. For suffix -то, cf. си́то 'sieve', from се́ять 'to sow'.

ДОЛЯ [dólja] 'portion, share'. 14th century 'part', from 11th-century OR *одѣлити* 'to share', underlying одоле́ть/преодоле́ть 'to overcome' (originally, in all probability, 'to gain the larger share'), with cognates in отде́л 'department', разде́л 'section, partition', обездо́лить 'to deprive of one's share'. Cf. also Lith. *dalis* 'part'.

ДОМ [dom] 'house'. 11th century, from CSl. *domъ, IE *domos 'building, house'/*demro 'to build', cf. Gk. *dómos*, 'house' (*démō* 'I build'), Skr. *dhāman* 'house', Lat. *domus*, id. Cognate also with Eng. *timber*, Ger. *Zimmer* 'room' (OHG *zimbar* 'timber, wooden structure, room'). Possible residual prep. or gen. case survives in дóма 'at home' and dat. case in домóй 'home' (common since 17th century, cf. also долóй). Note Lith. *namai* 'house', through assimilation of d-m to n-m.

ДОМНА [dómna] 'blast furnace'. 17th century *домня*, present form recorded since 1780s (*дóмницы* 'iron foundries' operated in pre-Kievan times), based on root *дъм-*. Cognate with дуть 'to blow' (cf. Pol. *dmę* 'I blow'), дым 'smoke', надмéнный (part. in origin) 'arrogant, puffed up'.

ДОРОГА [doróga] 'road'. 12th century, from CSl. *dorga, cognate with дёргать 'to pull, jerk, drag', with ESl. interconsonantal -оро-. Originally, perhaps, 'up-rooting of plants, clearance of an area', then 'area cleared in a forest', finally 'road' (cf. тракт 'highway', ultimately from Lat. *tractus* 'dragging', *trahō* 'I drag'). Alternatively, though perhaps less plausibly, originally 'valley, gully', then 'track laid through a valley or gully' (cf. Serb. *драга* 'gorge, canyon').

ДОСКА [doská] 'board'. 11th century 'board, table', from CSl. *dъska, perhaps ultimately from Lat. *discus* 'quoit, discus, dish' or Gk. *dískos* 'flat, round plate' (*diskéō* 'I throw'), possibly via Gmc. (cf. OHG *tisc* 'dish, table', Ger. *Tisch* 'table', Eng. *desk*).

ДОСТОПРИМЕЧАТЕЛЬНЫЙ [dostoprimečátel'nyj] 'noteworthy'. A calque of Gk. *axiothéatos*, id. (*axios* 'worthy', *theatós* 'to be seen'). Cf. достопримечáтельности 'the sights', Ger. *Sehenswürdigkeiten*, id.

ДОЧЬ [doč'] 'daughter'. OR *дъчи*, id., from CSl. *dъkti, gen. *dъktere, IE *dhugtēr- (cf. Lith. *duktė* 'daughter'), with retention of -er- in пáдчерица 'stepdaughter' and cognates in Gk. *thugátēr* 'daughter', Ger. *Tochter*, id. Possibly based on IE root *dhoi̯ō 'suckle, milk, suck' (see доúть 'to milk').

ДРАКА [dráka] 'fight'. Based on дра́ться 'to fight' (for -к-suffix, cf. сти́рка 'washing' from стира́ть 'to wash'). Root variants *dr-/*der-/*dir-/*dor- are reflected in драть 'to rend', деру́сь 'I fight', задира́ться 'to pick a quarrel', раздо́р 'discord'.

ДРОБЬ [drob'] 'grapeshot, fraction'. From CSl. *drobь, IE *dhrubh- 'to crush, crumble', common early 17th century, by deaffixation from дроби́ть 'to break up, crush' (cf. сыпь 'rash', deaffixed from сы́пать 'to sprinkle'). Originally 'particle' (hence подро́бный 'detailed', вдре́безги 'to smithereens'), subsequently 'grapeshot, fraction, drum roll'.

ДРОВА [drová] 'firewood'. 11th century, from CSl. *drъva (pl. of *drъvo), with cognates in де́рево 'tree, wood', Gk. *drys* 'any timber tree, oak', *dóry* 'stem of felled tree'.

ДРУГ [drug] 'friend'. 11th century, from CSl. *drugъ, IE *droughos 'comrade', cognate with Lith. *draugas*, id., with derivative in дружи́на 'prince's rctinue' (-г- changing to -ж- before -и-), cf., instituted in 1958, Soviet Доброво́льная наро́дная дружи́на 'Voluntary People's Militia'.

ДРУГО́Й [drugój] 'other'. OR *другыи* 'other, next, second' (cf. Ukr. *другий* 'second'). Based on the use of *drugъ 'friend' in the series друг дру́га, etc. 'each other', with ending -ой by analogy with adjs. such as ино́й 'other'.

ДУБ [dub] 'oak'. 11th century 'tree, oak', from CSl. *dǫbъ, perhaps IE *dhūbhos 'dark' (cf. Ir. *dub*, id.), and thus named after its dark core (possibly initially of the морёный дуб or water-darkened oak, which has dark grey or black wood). Alternatively, if somewhat implausibly, from IE *demō 'to build', thus lit. 'timber' (from the tree's use in construction and shipbuilding).

ДУЛО [dúlo] 'gun muzzle'. First half of 17th century, with agent suffix -л(о), lit. 'what you blow with' (cf. мы́ло 'soap', lit. 'what you wash with'), referring to the aperture through which projectiles are expelled. Perhaps originally *dudlo, -dl-subsequently simplifying to -l-, ultimately from дуть 'to blow'.

ДУМАТЬ [dúmat'] 'to think'. OR *думати* 'to confer, think', *дума* 'thought, counsel', probably from Goth. *doms* 'judgement' (cf. Eng. *doom* 'judgement, fate'). Alternatively cognate with мысль 'thought' (from *myd- + suffix *-slь), Gk. *mythos* 'word, speech, plan', IE *madh- 'thought', with metathesis m:d to d:m (cf. Goth. *ga-maudjan* 'to remind, mention').

ДУРАК [durák] 'fool'. CSl. *dur- (cf. дурь 'stupidity'), IE *dhuor- 'rush, be mad', *dhūrō 'rampage, rave'. Known as a nickname in the 15th century and as 'court jester' in the 17th, дýра 'fool' (fem.) evolving in the early 18th century. Alternatively connected with CSl. *dǫti 'to blow', cf. dial. *дýтик* 'small, tubby, haughty person', дýться 'to pout, play with abandon'.

ДУХ [duch] 'spirit'. OR *духъ* 'breath of wind, soul, mood', from CSl. *duchъ (IE *dhousos 'spirit, breath, creature'), with cognates in Lith. *dvasia* 'breath', Cz. *dychati* 'to breathe', дышáть, id., дохнýть 'to emit a breath' and derivatives in душá 'soul', душúть 'to smother'. Also cognate (through IE *dheusom 'breathing animal') with OE *deór* 'animal', Goth. **dius* 'wild animal', Eng. *deer*, Ger. *Tier* 'animal'. For link between 'spirit' and 'animal', cf. Lat. *animus* 'spirit', *animal* 'animal'.

ДУШ [duš] 'shower'. 1860s, from Fr. *douche*, id., itself from Ital. *doccia* 'water-pipe, gutter, shower', ultimately Lat. *ductio* 'leading off or away, drainage system'.

ДЫМ [dym] 'smoke'. 11th century, from CSl. *dymъ, IE *dhūmos 'smoke, fog'. Cognate with дуть 'to blow', Skr. *dhūma* 'smoke', Lith. *dūmai*, id., Lat. *fumus*, id. (Lat. f- derives from IE *dh-).

ДЫНЯ [dýnja] 'melon'. 14th century, perhaps cognate with дуть 'to blow', thus lit. 'puffed up, plump'. Alternatively from Lat. *mālum Cydōnium* 'Cydonian apple, quince' (from Cydonia in Crete), Gk. *mēlon Kydōnion*, id. (Gk. *Kydōnéa* 'quince tree', *Pyrus Cydonia*).

ДЫРА [dyrá] 'hole'. 11th century *дupa*, lit. 'torn place', from CSl. *dira/*dyra, cf. драть 'to tear', раздирáть 'to lacerate' (CSl. *dьrati, iter. *dirati).

ДЮЖИНА [djúžina] 'dozen'. 17th century, from Fr. *douzaine*, id., possibly introduced to Russia by Ger., D. or Eng. merchants. The form of the word was influenced by дю́жий (coll.) 'robust'.

ДЮЙМ [djujm] 'inch'. Early 18th century, seemingly introduced by Peter I, from D. *duim* 'thumb, unit of measure equal to 25.4 cm., inch' (in use in Russia until introduction of metric system in 1918), cf. Sw. *tum* 'inch', *tumme* 'thumb', Fr. *pouce* 'thumb, big toe, inch'.

ДЯДЯ [djádja] 'uncle'. OR reduplicated form originating in childish prattle (cf. Lith. *dėdė*, id.), with its origins in the formative period of IE languages.

ДЯТЕЛ [djátel] 'woodpecker'. 12th century *дятьлъ*, from CSl. *dętьlъ* (for suffix, cf. *orьlъ 'eagle', орёл, id.), initially *delbtьlъ (cf. долби́ть 'to hollow, gouge'), with -bt- simplifying to -t-, l-l changing to n-l by dissimilation (thus *dentьlъ/*dętьlъ) and -ę- changing to ESl. -я- (cf. retention of nasal in Pol. dzięcioł, id.). Alternatively, originally *tętьlъ from *tęti 'to strike, cut, hack' (OR *мяти* 'to cut, hack', Pol. *ciąć* 'to hew, smite'), with t- changing to d- under the influence of долби́ть 'to hollow, gouge'. Named from its habit of tapping trees to discover insects. Note dial. *дятлина* 'red clover', possibly from the red rump and neck of the woodpecker.

Е/Ё

ЕДИНЫЙ [jedínyj] 'one, single'. 11th century, from ChSl., whence also единица 'unit', единство 'unity', cf. один 'one' (for SSl./WSl. (j)e-/R. o-, cf. Serb. *jeзepo*/Pol. *jezioro*/R. óзеро 'lake').

ЕЖ [jëž] 'hedgehog'. OR *ежь*, id., from IE *eĝhis, id., cf. Ger. *Igel*, id., Lith. *ežys*, id., R. ё- having developed before the hardened consonant after the loss of -ь. Alternatively, associated with Gk. *echis* 'viper' (sharing a potential to sting or prick), *echinos* 'hedgehog'. Cf. derivative ежевика 'blackberries, blackberry bush', from the plant's prickly stem (for -ика 'berries', cf. голубика 'whortleberry', etc.).

ЕЖЕДНЕВНЫЙ [ježednévnyj] 'daily'. Recorded in dictionaries from the first half of the 18th century, based on ChSl. neut. *еже* 'which' (cf. use of что/Pol. *co* 'what' in что ни день/Pol. *co dzień* 'every day') + -дневный 'day'.

ЕЗДА [jezdá] 'ride'. 12th century *ѣздъ* 'journey, crossing' (cf. съезд 'congress', etc.), езда having been recorded in dictionaries since 1704, from CSl. *jezdъ/*jezda, cf. ездить 'to travel'. For -зд(а) suffix, cf. борозда 'furrow'.

ЁМКИЙ [jëmkij] 'capacious'. Recorded in dictionaries from 18th century, based on OR *емлю* 'I take' (from infin. *емати*), cognate with объём 'capacity', приёмлемый 'acceptable', etc.

ЕРУНДА [jerundá] 'nonsense'. 1840s, from the language of church seminarists, based on Lat. *gerundium* 'gerund', possibly out of disrespect/dislike for Latin grammar, or from dial. *ерунда/еранда* 'watery tasteless kvass (rye beer)'. For similar semantic correlations, cf. dial. *буза* 'buza' (fermented beverage made from millet, buckwheat or barley), also 'a row', окрошка 'okroška' (cold kvass soup with chopped vegetables, meat or fish), also 'jumble, hotch-potch', кавардак 'dregs, skilly', also 'a mess, muddle'. Alternatively, if fancifully, from Ger. *hier und da* 'here and there', purportedly used by St. Petersburg Ger.

sausage-makers about poor-quality sausage.

ЕСЛИ [jésli] 'if'. Originally *естъли/есть ли*, comprising есть 'is' and ли (conditional/interrogative particle), with subsequent loss of -т-, cf. Cz. *jestliže* 'if'/Pol. *jeśli*, id. Если recorded first half of 18th century, but not used exclusively as late as early 19th.

ЕСТЕСТВЕННЫЙ [jestéstvennyj] 'natural'. 11th century, ultimately from OR *естъство* 'substance' (есть 'is' + -ство, естество́ after the vocalization of -ъ), itself from ChSl., a calque of Gk. *ousía* 'substance'.

ЕСТЬ [jest'] 'to eat'. 11th century, from CSl. **jedti/*jesti* (IE **ēd-* 'food', **ēdmi* 'eat'), cognate with еда́ 'food', обе́д 'lunch' (cf. Lith. *èsti* 'to eat', Lat. *edō* 'I eat', Eng. *edible*), also е́дкий 'acrid, pungent', cf. OR *ѣдъкыи* 'edible' (now съедо́бный, id.).

ЕФРЕЙТОР [jefréjtor] 'lance-corporal'. Early 18th century, from Ger. *Gefreiter* 'lance-corporal', lit. 'exempted' (from some of a private's duties, from guard duty), calqued from Lat. *exēmptus* 'exempt', *eximō* 'I exempt', cf. Cz. calque *svobodnik* 'lance-corporal' (Cz. *svoboda* 'freedom'). For e- instead of ge-, cf. sub-standard *енерал*, commonly found in the 1650s for генера́л 'general'.

Ж

ЖАВОРОНОК [žávoronok] 'lark'. Probably based on onomatopoeic жа + вóрон 'raven' (cf. OR *гавранъ* 'raven', Ukr. *гайворон* 'rook').

ЖАЛЕТЬ [žalét'] 'to regret'. Cf. 11th-/12th centuries *жаловати* 'to regret', 15th century *желати* 'to regret, wish'. *Жалети* (whence жалéть), recorded in dictionaries from the early 18th century, is from CSl. *žal-, ultimately IE *guel- 'to prick, sting', whence also жаль 'a pity', жáлость 'pity', with cognates in Lith. *gelti* 'to ache, sting', OHG *quala* (Ger. *Qual)* 'torment', OHG *quelan* 'to feel pain, suffer'.

ЖАР [žar] 'heat'. 12th century *жаръ* 'fire, intense heat', from CSl. *gērъ/*žarъ. Cognate with горéть 'to burn', греть 'to heat', горя́чий 'hot', жа́ркий 'hot' (of climate), Gk. *thermós* 'hot'.

ЖЕЛЕЗО [želézo] 'iron'. From IE *ghelĝh-, id., cognate with Lith. *geležis*, id., with g(h)- palatalizing to ž- before -e-, and with ESl. inter-consonantal -еле-.

ЖЕЛТЫЙ [žëltyj] 'yellow'. Ultimately from IE *ghel- 'yellow, green'/*gheltos 'yellow', with g(h)- palatalizing to ž- before -e-, cognate with Ger. *gelb*, id., Ger. *Galle* 'gall', Eng. *gold*, also (with reflex з-) зелёный 'green', зóлото 'gold'. Derivatives in 15th-century жёлчь 'bile', желту́ха 'jaundice' (recorded first half of 18th century) and желтóк 'yolk'.

ЖЕЛУДОК [želúdok] 'stomach'. 15th century, possibly from жёлудь 'acorn', from a supposed similarity in shape to an acorn, a view rejected by some on the grounds of stress and size (however, original comparison may have been with the stomach of a smaller creature, or from the colour of the stomach wall, not its shape, or perhaps original reference was to another organ such as the gall-bladder -- жёлчный пузы́рь). Alternatively, associated with Gk. pl. *choládes* 'bowels, intestines' and OHG *kela*/Ger. *Kehle* 'throat' (the *passage* to the stomach), from Gmc.

*gel- 'to devour', cf. also Lat. *gula* 'throat, gullet'.

ЖЕЛУДЬ [žëlud'] 'acorn'. CSl. *želǫdь, with -ǫ- to -u- in ESl. (cf. retention of nasal in Pol. *żołądź*, id.). Possibly (Cyganenko) from a variant of IE *gu̯er- 'to devour', thus lit. 'what is devoured' (perhaps of acorns as pig fodder), with cognates in Lat. *glāns*, gen. *glandis* 'acorn', Lith. *gilė*, id. Alternatively, associated with Gk. *bálanos*, id., from *bállō* 'I fall' (Gk. β from IE *gu̯, cf. жрать 'to devour'), thus possibly 'that which falls, windfall' (-ǫdь perhaps of part. origin), from the ease with which acorns are dislodged by the wind.

ЖЕМЧУГ [žémčug] 'pearls'. First recorded 1161 on the cross of the Polovcian princess Jefrosinija, ultimately from Chinese via Tkc. *jünčü* (hence original R. -н-, with added final -г perhaps under the influence of -к -- a homophone of -г -- in OR камыкъ 'stone, precious stone'). Possibly introduced by nomadic tribes who settled on the N. Black Sea plains after the defeat of the Huns.

ЖЕНА [žená] 'wife'. 10th century (11th century 'woman'), from CSl. *žena, IE *gu̯nā, id. Cognate with Gk. *gunḗ*, id., Skr. *jani/janī* 'woman, wife, birth, origin', Goth. *qinō* 'woman', Eng. *queen* (cf. also ME *quean* 'hussy'), *gynaecology, misogynist* (from *gunḗ*), etc.

ЖЕНИХ [ženích] 'bridegroom, fiancé'. 11th century, from CSl. *ženichъ, id., *ženiti 'to marry', cf. женить(ся), id.

ЖЕНЩИНА [žénščina] 'woman'. First recorded 16th century, originally apparently a collective which was based on женьск- + suffix -ин(а), with -ск- changing to -щ- before -и-, cf. dial. substantivized adj. *женска* 'woman', Serb. *женска*, id., Cz. *ženska* 'woman, female'.

ЖЕРЛО [žerló] 'gun muzzle'. OR 'river mouth, throat', from CSl. *žerdlo (IE *gu̯er- 'to swallow'), cognate with *gъrdlo (whence го́рло 'throat'), *žerti (cf. жрать 'to devour'), Lith. *gerti* 'to drink', with g:ž mutation and agent suffix -dl- simplifying to -l- (cf. мы́ло 'soap'). Cf. also derivative ожере́лье 'necklace'.

ЖЕРТВА [žértva] 'victim, sacrifice'. 11th century, from CSl. *žьrtva, cognate with Gk. *géras* 'esteemed gift, prize, privilege', Lith. *girti* 'to praise', *geras* 'good', with g- changing to ž- in Slav. Жéртвовать 'to sacrifice' first recorded 1704.

ЖЕЧЬ [žeč'] 'to burn'. CSl. *žegti, from *gegti (with g- palatalizing to ž- before -e- and -g- devoicing to -k- before -t-, subsequently -č-). Perhaps originally *degti (cf. IE *dheguhō 'burn, fire', Lith. *degti* 'to burn', Eng. *day* 'time when the sun is hot'), with d-g changing to g-g through assimilation of velars, possibly under the influence of *gorěti (горéть 'to burn').

ЖИВОТ [živót] 'abdomen'. 11th century 'life, animal', 13th century 'property', with 'abdomen' common from the 17th century. From CSl. *životъ (*živ- 'alive', cf. IE *guis 'life'), cf. also Lith. *gyvas* 'live', Cz. *život* 'life'. Живóтное 'animal' (earliest form recorded 11th century) is a substantivized neut. adj. from живóт (arch.) 'life' (cf. adj. use in живóтный мир 'animal world' and earlier meaning of живóтное 'property, relating to property', reinforcing the association between 'animal' and 'possession', cf. скот 'cattle').

ЖИТЬ [žit'] 'to live'. 11th century 'to live, graze', from CSl. *žiti (IE *guiios 'alive'), cf. Lith. *gyvas* 'live', *gyventi* 'to live', with Slav. initial ž- (cf. живóй 'alive', жи́тель 'inhabitant', жизнь 'life', -знь, of ChSl. provenance, denoting 'state', cf. болéзнь 'sickness', etc.).

ЖРАТЬ [žrat'] 'to devour'. From CSl. *žerti (cf. Lith. *gerti* 'to drink'), IE *guer- 'swallow, food, drink, gulp' (cognate with CSl. *gъrdlo, гóрло 'throat'). Originally 'to swallow' (perhaps greedily and noisily), cf. cognates обжóра 'glutton', прожóрливый 'voracious', also Gk. *borá* 'food' (Gk. β from IE *gu), Lat. *vorō* 'I devour'.

ЖУЖЖАТЬ [žužžát'] 'to buzz'. Based on onomatopoeic жу/жузг (cf. визжáть 'to scream' from визг 'scream'), with cognates in жук 'beetle', жу́желица 'ground beetle' (from the buzzing sound they make).

ЖУРАВЛЬ [žurávl'] 'crane' (orn. and, fig., tech.). CSl. *žeravjь, IE *ger- (perhaps onomatopoeic), cf. Lith. *gervė* 'crane' (cognate with Lith. *garnys* 'heron'), Gk. *géranos* 'crane' (cf. IE *gerənos, id.), Lat. *grūs*, id. Originally *жеравль* (ž- from g- before -e- in Slav.), журавль possibly under the influence of журчать 'to murmur' (of water), dial. *жулькать* 'to squelch'. Cf. also герань 'geranium' (esp. the species *cranebill*, from the plant's resemblance to the bird's long neck).

ЖУРНАЛ [žurnál] 'journal, magazine'. 18th century (known earlier in the meaning 'official records, ship's log'), from Fr. *journal* 'journal, diary' (earlier adj. 'daily', from Vulg. Lat. *diurnalem*), журналист 'journalist' first recorded 1803.

ЖЮРИ [žjurí] 'jury, judges' (at a competition). Used in a judicial sense in the early 19th century (referring to British and Fr. practice, cf. now суд присяжных 'jury'), 'competition jury' from the late 19th century. From Fr. *jury*, Eng. *jury* (itself from OFr. *jurée* 'oath, judicial enquiry, inquest'), ultimately Lat. part. *iūrāta* 'solemn vows, evidence', from *iūrō* 'I swear'.

З

ЗАБОР [zabór] 'fence'. Recorded since the 16th century, possibly a verbal noun from dial. *забрáть* 'enclose, fence in', thus lit. 'enclosing' (cf., from собрáть 'to collect', сбор 'collection'), subsequently 'enclosure'. Alternatively, lit. 'that which is enclosed, plot of land' (cf. Lith. *baras* 'part, section, field' and pass. meaning in dial. *забóр* 'that which has been borrowed'), then 'enclosure'. Cf. analogous connotation of protection in cognate OR *забрало* 'fortification' (now 'visor').

ЗАВЕТ [zavét] 'testament'. 11th century, from CSl. *zavětъ, cognate with отвéт 'answer', привéт 'greeting', совéт 'advice', завещáние 'will', also вéче 'assembly in medieval Russian towns'. Perhaps based on the underlying root 'to speak' (cf. IE *u̯er- 'speak', *u̯equō 'say', OR *вътовати*, id.).

ЗАВИДОВАТЬ [zavídovat'] 'to envy'. 11th century *завидѣти* 'to envy', perhaps originally 'to catch sight of' (cf. завидеть (coll.), id.), then 'to look malevolently, see in distorted fashion' (possibly connected with the concept of the 'evil eye', cf. Lat. *invideō* 'I cast the evil eye on, envy', from *videō* 'I see', *invidia* 'envy'). Завидовать is recorded in dictionaries since 1704, resolving the homonymy. Note зáвисть 'envy', завúстливый 'envious'.

ЗАВОД [zavód] 'works, factory'. From заводúть 'to set up, start' (an enterprise).

ЗАВТРА [závtra] 'tomorrow'. 11th century *за утра* (OR за took gen. case in temporal meaning, cf. Pol. *za króla Jana* 'in the time of King John'), originally 'during the morning', then 'during the morning of the next day, tomorrow' (cf. Ger. *morgen* 'tomorrow', from OHG dat. sing. *morgane* 'on the next day', Ger. *Morgen* 'morning'). Both зáвтра and the more poet. *заутра* were used up to the 19th century. Derivatives зáвтрашний 'tomorrow's' and зáвтрак 'breakfast' (OR *заутрокъ/завтрокъ*, the latter still used in the 16th century, with -окъ eventually changing to -акъ due to *akan'je* and the influence of за́втра 'tomorrow') evolved in the 18th century.

ЗАКОН [zakón] 'law'. 11th century, originally 'divine law', subsequently 'civil law', from *kon- 'beginning' (also 'end', cf. коне́ц, id.), cognate with OR поконъ 'custom, beginning', искони́ 'since time immemorial', испоко́н веко́в, id., thus possibly 'something instituted, established'. Alternatively (or additionally), за- may imply a limit 'beyond which' one may not go (cf. запре́т 'ban', загражде́ние 'barrier').

ЗАКУ́ПОРИТЬ [zakúporit'] 'to cork'. First half of the 18th century, based on купор (obs.) 'cooper', from Eng. *cooper* or D. *kuiper*, id. (D. *kuip* 'barrel'). Cf. бонда́рь 'cooper' (possibly from Ger. *Büttner*, id.).

ЗАЛП [zalp] 'volley'. Early 18th century, originally залв/залф, then залп, with -п replacing the more literary -ф (cf. obs./dial. шкап and шкаф 'cupboard'), from Ger. *Salve* 'volley', rather than Fr. *salve*, id. (since Ger. S- is pronounced [z]). Ultimately from Lat. *salvē*, the 2nd pers. imper. of *salveō* 'I am in good health', thus lit. 'may you enjoy good health'.

ЗА́МОК [zámok] 'castle'. 17th century, from Pol. *zamek* 'lock, castle', via Ukr. or BR, Cz. *zamek*, id. (-ek to -ок probably under the influence of замо́к 'lock', a derivative of замкну́ть 'to lock' of much earlier provenance). Cz. and Pol. are semantic calques of Ger. (cf. MHG *sloz* 'lock', Ger. *Schloß* 'lock, castle'), MHG *sloz* having itself been calqued from Lat. *clūsa/clausa* 'enclosed space', *clausura* 'lock, fastening'.

ЗА́МУЖ (выходи́ть за́муж) [vychodít' zámuž] 'to marry' (a man). CSl., based on за- 'behind' + муж (old acc. case) 'husband' (by the 17th century, acc. = gen. case was the general rule for all masc. sing. animate nouns, hence now acc. му́жа).

ЗА́МША [zámša] 'chamois, suede'. 16th-/17th centuries, from Ger., via Pol. *zamsz*, id., cf. MHG *saemisch leder*, Ger. *Sämischleder*, id. Probably ultimately from Fr. *chamois*, MLat. *camox*, id. The word has also, implausibly, been linked with Turk. *semiz* 'fat, fleshy'.

ЗАПАД [západ] 'west'. 11th century, from западáть 'to sink down' (of the sun), cf. Lat. *occidēns* (originally a pres. part. from *occidō* 'I fall') 'sunset, west'.

ЗАПАНИБРАТА [zapanibráta] 'hail-fellow-well-met'. From за + acc. case of obs. *панибрáт* 'acquaintance, equal, match' (cf. coll. панибрáтский 'familiar', панибрáтство 'familiarity'), based on Pol. *pan* 'master', *i* 'and', *brat* 'brother'.

ЗАПЛАТА [zapláta] 'patch'. Based on за + платáть 'to patch', плат (obs.) 'square of fabric', cf. платóк 'shawl, kerchief', плáтье 'dress' and, with ESl. -оло-, полотнó 'linen'.

ЗАПЯСТЬЕ [zapjást'je] 'wrist'. 11th century, from за + пясть 'metacarpus' (part of hand between wrist and fingers), cognate with Ger. *Faust* 'fist', perhaps linked to пять 'five' (cf. пятернá 'palm with five fingers'). Cf. also IE *pn̥kstis 'fist'.

ЗАПЯТАЯ [zapjatája] 'comma'. 16th-/17th centuries, substantivized pass. part. of *запяти* (obs.) 'to stop' (cf. *запятися* 'to catch oneself on'), perhaps бýква 'letter' understood. Cognate with запи́нка 'hesitation in speech', зáпонка 'cuff-link, stud', also with знак препинáния 'punctuation mark'. In medieval lit. used for various punctuation marks, e.g. the apostrophe.

ЗАРЯ [zarjá] 'dawn'. 11th century, from CSl. *zorja/*zarja (-a- perhaps through assimilation of vowels: a-a for o-a), from IE *ĝōr- 'glow', with Slav. *zer-/*zor-/*zar- reflected in заря́ 'dawn' (pl. зóри), зáрево 'glow', озари́ть 'to illuminate', зéркало 'mirror', зрéние 'sight', cf. also Lith. *žara* 'glow'.

ЗАСТЕНЧИВЫЙ [zasténčivyj] 'shy'. Either from застéнок, earlier 'back room, space between two walls' (now 'torture chamber'), or from dial. *застень* 'shade, shady place', *застенить* 'to shade', cf. тень 'shadow', OR *стѣнь* 'place protected from the light, shade'. Thus lit. 'preferring to be in the shade, avoid attention'.

ЗАТЫЛОК [zatýlok] 'nape of the neck'. Based on за- 'behind'

+ тыл 'rear'.

ЗАЩИТИТЬ [zaščitít'] 'to defend'. Lit. 'to protect with a shield' (за- 'behind + щит 'shield'). See щит 'shield'.

ЗАЯДЛЫЙ [zajádlyj] 'inveterate'. From Pol. *zajadły* 'furious', based on Pol. *zajadać* 'to eat heartily' (cf. еда 'food').

ЗАЯЦ [zájac] 'hare'. 11th century, from CSl. *zajęсь, cf. Lith. *žaisti* 'to play', *zuikis* 'hare', thus perhaps lit. 'animal that jumps, plays' (cf. IE *ghai̯i̯os 'lively'). Possibly cognate with Lat. *haedus* 'kid', Goth. *gaits* 'goat' (Ger. *Geiß* 'wild goat'), or linked to зиять 'to gape' (a reference to the hare's cleft top lip).

ЗВЕЗДА [zvezdá] 'star'. 11th century, from CSl. *gvězda/*zvězda 'star', IE *ghu̯oi̯ĝ- 'to flash, shine' (cf. WSl. gw-/hv- in Pol. *gwiazda*, Cz. *hvězda* 'star'), with cognate in Lith. *žvaigždė* 'star'.

ЗВЕНЕТЬ [zvenét'] 'to ring'. 11th century, from CSl. *zvьněti (cf. IE *su̯en 'sound, echo'), cognate with звон 'ringing' and звук 'sound' (CSl. *zvǫkъ, cf. retention of nasal in Pol. *dźwięk*, id.), Lat. *sonus* 'sound'. R. зв- possibly under the influence of звать 'call' (cf. also Skr. *svan* 'to sound, make any noise', *svana* 'noise, cry').

ЗВЕРЬ [zver'] 'wild animal'. 11th century, from CSl. *zverь, IE *ĝhēr-, id., with cognates in Lat. *ferus* 'wild, untamed' (cf. Eng. *feral*), Lith. *žvėris* 'beast', Gk. *thēríon*, id.

ЗДАНИЕ [zdánije] 'building'. OR зьданиѥ, 10th century 'creation', 11th century 'building'. Originally a verbal noun from CSl. *zьdati, OR зьдати 'to build, create', derived from зьдъ 'structure, clay', cf. Bulg. *зидам* 'I build' (more usually *съдавам*), Serb. *зидати* 'to build', Lith. *žiesti* 'to make clay pots', зодчий (obs.) 'architect' (originally 'potter'). Cognate with создать (со + здать) 'to create', now reinterpreted as a compound of дать 'to give' and conjugated accordingly (создам, создашь).

ЗДЕСЬ [zdes'] 'here'. One of the first adverbs of pronominal origin, CSl. *sьde, id., is based on *sь 'this' (cf. сей, id.) + suffix *-de (cf. где 'where'), subsequently reinforced by particle сь (abbreviated from се) 'behold' (cf. reg. *днесь* 'today', *вчерáсь* 'yesterday', *ночéсь* 'at night'). Thus, OR *сьдесе*, eventually здесь, with с- voicing to з- before -д- after the reduction of -ь-.

ЗДОРОВЫЙ [zdoróvyj] 'healthy'. From CSl. *sъdorvъ, comprising *sъ- 'good' (cognate with sū- in Lith. *sūdrus* 'compact') + *dorvъ, cognate with дéрево 'tree' (IE *doru 'tree'), s- voicing to z- before -d- and inter-consonantal -oro- evolving in ESl. Originally, perhaps, 'as sturdy as a tree', cf. analogous Lat. *rōbustus* 'oaken, sturdy' from *rōbur* 'oak'.

ЗДРАВСТВУЙТЕ [zdrávstvujte] 'how are you?'. Recorded in dictionaries early 18th century, of ChSl. provenance, the imper./optative mood of *здравствовати* 'to prosper, be healthy' (now здрáвствовать, id.), subsequently an autonomous word meaning lit. 'may you prosper'.

ЗЕВАТЬ [zevát'] 'to yawn'. From CSl. *zěvati, recorded in dictionaries since early 18th century, cf. зев 'pharynx', ротозéй 'scatter-brain, gaper', львúный зев 'antirrhinum', зиять 'yawn, gape', зияние 'hiatus', also Lith. *žiovauti* 'to yawn'.

ЗЕЛЕНЫЙ [zelënyj] 'green'. 11th century, from CSl. *zel-, IE *ghel- 'yellow, green'/*gheltos 'yellow' + suffix -en- (cf. червлёный (obs.) 'dark red'). Cognate with злак 'cereal', зóлото 'gold', жёлтый 'yellow', Lat. *gilvus* 'pale yellow'.

ЗЕМЛЯНИКА [zemljaníka] 'wild strawberries'. 18th century (early 17th century *земляница*, id.), from the adj. землянóй 'earth' (for -ика 'berries', cf. бруснúка 'red whortleberry', etc.). So called because the berries are found lying on the ground, thus, lit. 'earth-berries', cf. Ger. *Erdbeere*, id.

ЗЕНИТ [zenít] 'zenith'. 16th/17th centuries *зéниф*, from MLat., early 18th century зенúт, ultimately from Ar. *samt* 'path, direction' (whence also áзимут 'azimuth, arc from zenith to horizon'), as in Ar. *samt arra's* 'zenith', lit. 'path over the head' (*arra's*, by assimilation of liquids, from *al-ra's*, cf. Ar. *ra's* 'head'), wrongly transcribed in MLat. as *cenith/zenith* (with -ni- for -m-), a scribal error transmitted to other Eur. languages, probably initially via Sp. and Ital.

ЗЕРКАЛО [zérkalo] 'mirror'. 11th century зьрьцало, 14th century зéркало, based on the root of CSl. *zьrěti (cf. obs. зреть 'to see'), from *zьrka- (cf. dial. зéркать 'to stare') + agent suffix -dl(o) (simplified to -l(o)). Thus lit. 'what you look at yourself in', possibly an adaptation/calque of Lat. *speculum* 'mirror' (cf. Lat. *speciō/spiciō* 'I look').

ЗЕРНО [zernó] 'grain'. 11th century, from CSl. *zerno, IE *ĝr̥nom 'cultivated grain', cognate with зреть 'to ripen', perhaps lit. 'that which has ripened'. Also related to Lat. *grānum* 'grain', Lith. *žirnis* 'pea', Ger. *Korn* 'grain' (hence, perhaps, Vasmer's interpretation as растёртое 'something ground up').

ЗИМА [zimá] 'winter'. 11th century 'winter, cold', from CSl. *zima, IE *ĝhim- 'winter', with cognates in Lith. *žiema*, id., Skr. *hima*, id., Gk. *cheima* 'winter weather, cold, frost', *chiōn* 'snow', Lat. *hiems* 'wintertime, rainy season'. Originally, perhaps, 'time of rains', cf. Gk. *chéō* 'I pour'.

ЗЛАК [zlak] 'cereal'. 11th century, probably ultimately from CSl. *zolkъ (*zol- = *zel- 'green'), via ChSl. (hence SSl. -ла-). For suffix -к, cf. знак 'sign', etc.

ЗЛОБОДНЕВНЫЙ [zlobodnévnyj] 'topical'. Second half of the 19th century, on the basis of the Biblical Довлеетъ дневи злоба его 'Sufficient unto the day is the evil thereof' (*Matthew* 6:34), cf. злоба дня 'topic of the hour, latest news'.

ЗМЕЯ [zmejá] 'snake'. 11th century змья, from CSl. *zmьja, lit. 'earth reptile', cognate with земля 'earth', thus 'of the earth, crawling along the ground'. May have replaced an earlier word as the result of taboo.

ЗНАК [znak] 'sign'. Based ultimately on знать 'to know, distinguish', with derivatives in значить 'to mean', значéние 'significance'. For suffix -к, cf. брак 'marriage'.

ЗНАМЯ [známja] 'banner'. 14th century 'distinction', perhaps 'distinctive mark', 16th century 'military banner', replacing стяг, id. (rhet.) in this meaning by the end of the 17th century. Based on CSl. *znati 'to know, distinguish' + suffix -men (cf. céмя 'seed, semen' from сéять 'to sow'), thus 'that which distinguishes', i.e., 'banner', with derivatives in знаменáтель 'denominator', знамéние врéмени sign of the times'.

ЗНАТЬ [znat'] 'to know'. 11th century 'to know, acknowledge', from CSl. *znati, IE *ĝn̥- 'knowledge', cognate with Lith. *žinoti* 'to know', Gk. *gnōsis* 'knowledge', Lat. *cōgnōscō* 'I understand', Ger. *kennen* 'to know'.

ЗОДЧИЙ [zódčij] (obs.) 'architect'. 12th century зьдъчии 'builder, potter', based on OR зьдъ 'clay', зьдати 'to build'. For professional suffix -чий, cf. стряпчий (hist.) 'scrivener'. Зóдчий was supplanted by архитéктор 'architect' in the 1620s. See здáние 'building'.

ЗОЛОТО [zóloto] 'gold'. 10th century, from CSl. *zolto, IE *gheltos 'yellow', with ESl. inter-consonantal -оло- and cognates in жёлтый 'yellow', Latv. *zelts* 'gold', Ger. *Gold*, id., thus named for its colour by the Balto-Slav./Gmc. group.

ЗОНТИК [zóntik] 'umbrella'. 18th century, from D. (cf. D. *zonnedek* 'awning, canopy'), lit. 'sun-cover' (D. *zon* 'sun', *dek* 'cover'). Initially зондек 'sun-canopy stretched across a deck', later зóнтик (recorded 1834 as 'parasol, umbrella'), under the influence of dim. ending -ик, with зонт 'umbrella, awning' evolving in the 19th century as a back formation.

ЗОРКИЙ [zórkij] 'keen-eyed'. ESl., cognate with зреть (obs.) 'to see', зрéние 'sight', дальнозóркий 'long-sighted', etc.

ЗРАЧОК [zračók] 'pupil of the eye'. Dim. of OR зракъ 'image, form', of ChSl. provenance, based on CSl. *zorkъ 'image', found in present form since the 18th century, seemingly calqued from Lat. *pūpula* 'pupil of the eye', dim. of *pūpa* 'girl, doll' (sometimes confused with Lat. *pūpilla* 'orphan girl, female ward'), referring to the reduced image of a person reflected in another's eye (cf. dial. *зрачёк*, defined as человечек в глазу́ 'small person in the eye, pupil'). Cognate with прозра́чный 'transparent', невзра́чный 'unprepossessing', etc.

ЗРЕТЬ [zret'] (obs.) 'to see'. 11th century, from CSl. *zьrěti, with many cognates/derivatives: зря́чий 'seeing', зри́тельный 'visual', etc., cf. also Lith. *žiūrėti* 'to look' and homonym зреть 'to ripen', which is cognate with зерно́ 'grain' and also, possibly, with Gk. *geraiós* 'old, venerable', *gérōn* 'old man'.

ЗРЯ [zrja] 'to no purpose'. Initially an adv. part. from OR *зьрѣти* 'to see', originally (15th/16th centuries) 'looking around, looking idly', entering the standard language from popular speech in the new meaning 'at random' in the 1830s.

ЗУБ [zub] 'tooth'. 11th century, from CSl. *zǫbъ 'tooth' (cf. Latv. *zobs*, id., Pol. *ząb*, id.), ultimately IE *gombhos 'spike', possibly 'tooth' (cf. IE *gembh- 'to bite, crush'), with cognates in Gk. *gomphíos* 'grinder-tooth, molar', Skr. *jambha* 'tooth' (from *jabh/jambh* 'crush, destroy'), OHG *kamb* 'comb', Ger. *Kamm*, id. (lit. 'teeth', then 'toothed implement'). Possibly with a derivative in зубр 'bison', which may originally have been a name for an extinct 'sharp-toothed' predator (maybe an example of taboo, cf. OPol. *ząbrz* 'tiger').

ЗУБРИ́ТЬ [zubrít'] 'to notch, serrate; to swot'. The meaning 'to swot' (19th century) is secondary to 'to notch', both perhaps ultimately from зуб 'tooth, cog' (cf. учи́ть на зубо́к 'to learn by heart'), and is usually interpreted as a semantic calque of Ger. *büffeln* 'to swot', lit. 'work like a buffalo' (Ger. *Büffel* 'buffalo', зубр 'bison') or Ger. *ochsen* 'to swot' (*Ochse* 'ox').

ЗЯТЬ [zjat'] 'son-in-law, brother-in-law'. 11th century, from CSl. *zętь, ultimately from IE *gen- 'to give birth', thus 'one who continues the line', cf. Lith. *žentas* 'son-in-law', Gk. *génesis* 'birth, descent', Lat. *genitor* 'begetter, parent'. Alternatively (if less plausibly), cognate with знать 'to know' and originally meaning 'acquaintance'. See неве́ста 'bride'.

68

И

ИГО [ígo] 'yoke'. 11th century 'yoke, oppression', from CSl. *jьgo, IE radical *i̯ug- 'join', *i̯ugom 'yoke, pair' (cf. Gk. *zugóō* 'I join, together, yoke, subdue', *zugón* 'yoke', Lat. *iungō* 'I join, yoke', *iugum* 'yoke', Lith. *jungas*, id., Ger. *Joch*, id., Skr. *yugam*, id.). Originally 'yoke' (part of harness), then 'yoke' in the fig. sense (purportedly from a Roman habit of making prisoners of war pass under a yoke fashioned from spears). Cognate with ижица (possibly a dim.), the last letter of the ChSl. and pre-1918 R. alphabet, representing the Gk. letter *v* (U-psīlon), with г:ж mutation before -и-, from the letter's yoke-shaped appearance. Possibly also cognate with 11th-/12th-century иглá 'needle' (perhaps originally the thin sharpened pin which fastened the yoke on the animal's neck).

ИДОЛ [ídol] 'idol'. 11th century, via ChSl., from Gk. *eídōlon* 'image, spectre, portrait', a derivative of Gk. *eidos* 'form'.

ИДТИ [idtí] 'to go'. 11th century, from CSl. *iti (IE *eimi 'to go'), cf. Lith. *eiti*, id., Skr. *eti* 'goes', Lat. *īre* 'to go', -д- by analogy with идý 'I go', *ити* appearing only in compounds (зайти́ 'to call in', etc.).

ИЕРОГЛИФ [ieróglif] 'hieroglyph, character'. 18th century adj. *гиероглифический*, early 19th century adj. and noun without г-. From Fr. *hiéroglyphe* 'hieroglyph', ultimately Gk. *hieroglyphiká* (sc. *grámmata* 'letters') 'hieroglyphics', from *hierós* 'sacred', *glýphō* 'I carve, engrave, write on a tablet', thus lit. 'sacred carvings'.

ИЗБА [izbá] 'peasant hut'. CSl. *jьstъba/*istъba 'bath-house', then 'room heated by a stove', OR *истъба* 'dwelling', from OHG *stuba* 'heated room, bathhouse', Ger. *Stube* 'room' (possibly based on Ger. *stieben* 'to fly about', of sparks from the stove). *Истъба* possibly merged with OR *истопька* 'warm room with a stove' (from топи́ть 'to heat', cf. dial. *истóпка* 'hut, heating, amount of firewood needed to heat the stove', *истóбка* 'hut'), with contamination from Vulg. Lat. *extūfāre* 'to heat with coals' (*extūfa* 'stove, heated room'), whence Fr. *étouffer* 'to stifle', cf. Fr. *étuve* 'steam room', Sp. *estufa* 'stove, sweating room', Ital. *stufa* 'stove'. Истьба was transformed into изба through the loss of inter-consonantal -т- and the subsequent voicing of -с- to -з- before -б-. Initial и- is either from Romance influence or a sporadic phenomenon, cf. analogous изумру́д 'emeralds'.

ИЗВЕРГ [ízverg] 'monster'. From ChSl., known since the 14th century in the meaning 'abortion', probably, by deaffixation, from изверга́ть 'to expel' (cf. IE *u̯ergō 'to force', OR вьргнути 'to throw'), cf. изверже́ние 'eruption', Gk. *éktrōma* 'abortion' *(ek* 'from out of', *trōma/trauma* 'wound, damage').

ИЗВЕСТЬ [ízvest'] 'lime'. 12th century, adapted from Gk. *ásbestos* 'inextinguishable' (β pronounced [v] 9th to 11th centuries), from *a-* 'not' + *sbestós* 'quenched'. Из- results from an erroneous division of the Gk. word as *as + bestos*, perhaps under the influence of извести́ 'to exterminate' or изъе́сть 'to corrode' (due to the latter verb's implications for the effect of asbestos). The Gk. was reborrowed in the 19th century as асбе́ст 'asbestos'. Cf. also изве́стка 'slaked lime', известня́к 'limestone'.

ИЗВИНИТЬ [izvinít'] 'to excuse'. Possibly a calque of MLat. *exculpāre* 'to get rid of' (cf. ex-/из- 'out of', *culpa*/вина́ 'guilt'). Cf. also 13th century OR *извинитися*, initially 'to commit an offence' (cf. провини́ться, id.), then 'to be exonerated'.

ИЗГОРОДЬ [ízgorod'] 'hedge'. Through deaffixation from *изгороди́ть* (obs.) 'to partition off', cf. городи́ть 'to enclose, fence'.

ИЗДЕВАТЬСЯ [izdevát'sja] 'to mock'. 15th century, based on OR *дѣти* 'to speak' (see also де, де́скать), originally (according to Vasmer) 'to give a name, nickname' or (according to Šanskij) 'to mock in conversation'. Less probably from a semantic identification with раздева́ться 'to undress', with the meaning 'to mock by baring a certain part of the body'.

ИЗЛАГАТЬ [izlagát'] 'to expound'. 11th century, from ChSl., comprising из- + -лагать 'to place' (pf. изложи́ть, with -г- changing to -ж- before -и-).

ИЗОБЛИЧИТЬ [izobličít'] 'to expose, unmask'. 12th century, from ChSl., based ultimately on о́блик 'look, aspect', from лик (obs.) 'face', thus 'to reveal the appearance of, unmask'. See лик (obs.) 'face', лицо́, id.

ИЗОБРАЗИТЬ [izobrazít'] 'to depict'. From ChSl., based ultimately on о́браз 'image'.

ИЗОБРЕСТИ [izobrestí] 'to invent'. 11th century, from ChSl., based on обрести́ (rhet.) 'to find', conjugated обря́щу, обря́щешь (arch.). See *Matthew* 7:7 (R. version): Проси́те, и дано́ бу́дет вам; ищи́те, и найдёте (ChSl. *ищите да обрящете*) 'Ask, and it shall be given you; seek, and ye shall find'. Cf. приобрести́ 'to acquire'.

ИЗОЛИРОВАТЬ [izolírovat'] 'to isolate, insulate'. 19th century, modelled on Fr. *isoler* 'to isolate, insulate', itself a back formation from *isolé* 'isolated', from Ital. *isolato* 'separated like an island, isolated', Ital. *isola* 'island'.

ИЗУМИТЬ [izumít'] 'to amaze'. 11th century *изумити* 'to drive mad, make someone swoon', *изумитися* 'to go mad' (cf. dial. *изуми́ться*, id.). From ChSl. The meaning 'to amaze' established itself during the 18th century, cf., however, изумле́ние 'madness' (1704) and L. Rakovskij's 18th-century tale *Изумлённый капитан* 'The Deranged Captain'. Cf. also ум 'mind', сходи́ть с ума́ 'to go mad', своди́ть с ума́ 'to drive mad'.

ИЗУМРУД [izumrúd] 'emerald'. Second half of the 15th century, ultimately from a MidE. source, via Gk. *smáragdos*, id. (whence OR *смарагдъ*, id., cf. Ger. *Smaragd*, id., Ital. *smeraldo* 'emerald, green') and Tkc. (cf. Turk. *zümrüt* 'emerald'). Из- possibly from a misinterpretation of the word as a prefixed compound (cf. и́звесть 'lime', also изъя́н 'defect', wrongly associated with изъя́ть 'to remove').

ИЗЫСКАННЫЙ [izýskannyj] 'refined, recherché'. 18th century, calqued from Fr. part. adj. *recherché* 'refined, exquisite' (cf. *rechercher*/изыскáть 'to seek out').

ИЗЮМ [izjúm] 'raisins'. At latest early 17th century, from Tkc. (cf. Turk. *üzüm* 'grape(s)'), with narrowing of meaning perhaps under the influence of trade practices involving the sale of *dried* grapes from the S. (cf. Turk. *kuru* ['dried'] *üzüm* ['grapes'] 'raisins').

ИЗЯЩНЫЙ [izjáščnyj] 'elegant, graceful'. Based on *jьzętjьnъ 'selected' (CSl. *jьzęti 'to select'), a pass. part. of ChSl. provenance (cf. изъя́ть 'to withdraw, remove'), with -tj- to -šč- before adj. suffix -ьn-, thus, 'taken out of, selected', then 'best, splendid', finally (19th century) 'artistically fine'. Perhaps modelled on Fr. *élégant* 'elegant, stylish', ultimately from Lat. *ēligō* 'I select' (cf. also Lat. *eximius* 'distinguished', from *eximō* 'I take out').

ИКОНА [ikóna] 'icon'. 11th century, from Gk. *eikṓn* 'likeness, image', then (from early centuries AD) 'icon'. Иконостáс 'iconostasis' derives from Byz. Gk. *eikonostásion* 'icon screen' (Gk. *stásis* 'position, station').

ИКРА [ikrá] I 'fish roe, caviar'. 12th-/13th centuries, from CSl. *jьkra, cognate with Lith. *ikrai* 'roe', possibly associated with IE *i̯equər 'liver' (cf. Lat. *iecur*, id., Lith. substandard *jeknos*, id., alongside standard Lith. *kepenys*, id.). The two meanings seem to be linked by some concept such as 'mass, lump'.

ИКРА [ikrá] II 'calf of the leg'. 17th century, possibly cognate with икрá I 'caviar' (linked by some concept such as 'thick mass, tuber, swelling'), though an association has also been suggested with Gk. *íkria* 'platform, scaffolding' (cf. similar link between Lat. *sūra* 'calf' and *sūrus* 'branch, stake, stick'). D. *kuit* 'spawn, roe', 'calf of leg' suggests the two meanings are somehow connected.

ИЛИ [íli] 'or'. OR *или* 'if, or, than', from ChSl., comprising и 'and' + particle ли 'whether'.

ИМЕНИНЫ [imeníny] 'name-day'. Based on root имен- (cf. и́мя 'first name') + suffix -ин(ы), cf. -ины 'ceremony' in кристи́ны 'christening, christening party', смотри́ны (hist.) 'inspection of prospective bride'.

ИМУЩЕСТВО [imúščestvo] 'property'. Recorded in 18th-century dictionaries, based on the part. adj. иму́щий 'well-off', thus lit. 'what a wealthy man has' (namely 'property'). Cf. име́ть 'to have', also власть иму́щие 'the powers that be'.

ИМЯ [ímja] 'first name'. 11th century 'name, word', from CSl. *jьmę, gen. *jьmene, with -ę to -я in R. (cf. final nasal in Pol. *imię* 'name'), and -en- retained in oblique cases (и́мени, и́менем, etc.). Cognate with Gk. *ónoma*, id., Lat. *nomen*, id., Goth. *namo*, id., etc., with derivatives including безымя́нный 'anonymous'. Possibly ultimately based on an IE root meaning 'to distinguish'.

ИНАЧЕ [ináče] 'otherwise'. Based on OR *инако*, id., neut. sing. of *инакъ* (short form of *инакыи* 'other') + -je, with -к- palatalizing to -ч- before suffix -j-. Cf. инакомы́слящий 'heterodox', resurrected in the 1960s to refer to dissidents, pejorative nuance lost during period of 'glasnost'' from the mid-1980s.

ИНДЮК [indjúk] 'turkey'. Mid-19th century (pre-dated in late 18th century by инде́йка 'turkey-hen', whence by back-formation *индей* 'turkey-cock'), from Pol. *indyk* 'turkey', itself from Lat. (*pāvō*) *indicus*, lit. 'Indian peacock' (cf. инде́йский пету́х 'turkey-cock', Fr. *dinde*, originally *coq/poule d'Inde*, initially of the Abyssinian guinea-fowl, subsequently 'turkey'). A bird discovered in Mexico by the Spaniards, the confusion possibly resulting from Columbus's mistaken belief that in landing in S. America he had in fact reached his original goal, the W. part of India (hence 'Indians', инде́йцы, of indigenous Americans). Eng. *turkey* possibly because the bird was originally brought from New Guinea by the Portuguese through Turk. dominions.

ИНЖЕНЕР [inženér] 'engineer'. Late 17th century (originally 'mechanic, technician'), via Ger. *Ingenieur* or D. *ingenieur*, or directly from Fr. *ingénieur* 'engineer' (OFr. *engeigneur* is from 12th-century *engin* 'engine of war'-- denoting all missile launchers except for cannon). Ultimately based on MLat. *engenium* 'military engine' (perhaps influenced by MLat. *ingenium* 'high intellectual capacity').

ИНТЕЛЛИГЕНЦИЯ [intelligéncija] 'intelligentsia'. 1860s in meaning 'mental capabilities' (from Fr. *intelligence*), then (e.g., in *Война и мир* 'War and Peace' 1865-69) 'the intelligentsia' ('that part of educated [Russian] society which held radical left-wing views'), passing subsequently into W. Eur. languages (e.g. Fr. *intelligentsia/-zia* 1920). Ultimately from Lat. *intellegentia* 'understanding'. Интеллигéнт 'intellectual, member of intelligentsia' appeared in the 1870s.

ИППОДРОМ [ippodróm] 'racecourse'. 17th century (cf., however, OR *иподрумие* 1073), from Gk. *hippódromos* 'race course for chariots' (Gk. *híppos* 'horse', *drómos* 'course, race').

ИРОНИЯ [irónija] 'irony'. 18th century, possibly via Pol. *ironia*, id. or, more probably, Fr. *ironie*, Ger. *Ironie* from Lat. *īrōnīa*, id., of Gk. origin (*eirōneía* 'simulated ignorance, ignorance purposely affected to provoke an antagonist', from Gk. *eírōn* 'a dissembler', *eírō* 'I say'). First said to have been used by Socrates, who would pretend ignorance during disputation in order to expose the threadbare nature of his opponents' argument, hence 'Socratic irony'.

ИСКЛЮЧИТЬ [isključít'] 'to exclude, expel'. Based on *ключити* (obs.) 'to lock' (cf. ключ 'key'), with the ChSl. prefix ис-, originally 'to release', subsequently 'to exclude', with derivatives in исключéние 'exclusion, exception', исключи́тельный 'exclusive, exceptional'.

ИСКРА [ískra] 'spark'. 11th century, cognate with dial. *яска* 'bright star', ясный 'clear', Pol. *jaskrawy* 'glaring', probably also with Lith. *aiškus* 'clear', Gk. *eschára* 'hearth, brazier'.

ИСКУССТВО [iskússtvo] 'art'. Recorded in dictionaries since the 17th century, based on ChSl., comprising *искусъ* 'test, temptation' (cf. CSl. *kusiti 'to taste, try', from Goth. *kausjan* 'to prove, examine', whence also Fr. *choisir* 'to choose') + abstract suffix -ств(о). Perhaps originally 'test', then 'skill developed by experience', finally 'creative craftsmanship, art'.

ИСПОЛИН [ispolín] 'giant'. 11th century, thought to have derived from the tribal name of the Spoli, who in antiquity lived between the Don and the Volga and were defeated by the Goths in S. Russia in the 2nd century AD. И- possibly from a scribal error (исполи́н for и споли́н 'and the Spolin'), alternatively a sporadic phenomenon, cf. изумру́д 'emerald'.

ИСТЕЦ [istéc] 'plaintiff'. OR *истьць* 'litigant' ('plaintiff' *or* 'defendant', cf. отве́тчик 'defendant'), from и́стый 'genuine', thus 'the genuine person, real owner'. Often wrongly associated, through false etymology, with иск 'law suit', иска́ть 'to seek'.

ИСТИНА [ístina] 'truth'. 10th century, from ChSl., meaning 'truth, loyalty', from и́стый 'genuine, real' (cf. commercial meaning 'capital' in 15th-century Novgorod).

ИСТОК [istók] 'source' (of river). 11th century, based on ChSl. *истещи* 'to flow out'. Cf., with R. вы-, вы́течь, id., also исто́чник 'source' (of information, etc.).

ИСТУКАН [istukán] 'idol, statue'. Substantivized masc. short-form pass. part. from *истукати* 'to sculpt, cast', from the onomatopoeic root тук-, cognate with ткать (from *тъкати*) 'to weave', ты́кать 'to jab'. For у:ы mutation, cf. дух 'spirit', дыша́ть 'to breathe'. Lit., истука́н means 'sculpted'.

ИТОГ [itóg] 'sum, total'. 18th century, from и того́/итого́ 'in total, altogether', a term seemingly used in business correspondence and documentation since 1584.

ИЩЕЙКА [iščéjka] 'bloodhound'. Based on иск 'search', with mutation from -sk- to -šč- (cf. иска́ть 'to look for', ищу́ 'I look for').

ИЮЛЬ [ijúl'] 'July'. 11th century, ultimately from Lat. *Iūlius (mensis)* 'July', from ChSl. via Byz. Gk. *ioúli(o)s,* fifth month in the Roman calendar, dedicated to Caius Julius Caesar, who is said to have been born on 12 July 102 BC. Cf. OR *ли́пец* 'July', the month in which the lime tree (ли́па) blossoms, thus Pol. *lipiec* 'July'.

ИЮНЬ [ijún'] 'June'. 11th century, ultimately from Lat. *Iūnius (mensis)* 'June', from ChSl. via Byz. Gk. *iouni(o)s,* fourth month in the Roman calendar, named in honour of the goddess Juno, Jupiter's counterpart, queen of heaven, and protector of women (the month of June was considered to be the most favourable period for marrying). According to some accounts, but less plausibly, from Jūnius Brutus, first consul. Cf. OR *че́рвень* 'June', the time for gathering cocheneal (черве́ц, whence a dye of the same name) in the W. provinces (cf. Pol. *czerwiec* 'June').

К

КАБАН [kabán] 'wild boar'. Early 18th century, from Tkc.

КАБИНЕТ [kabinét] 'study, consulting-room, surgery'. Early 18th century (also spelt г-, an Italianism), from Fr. *cabinet* or Ger. *Kabinett*, ultimately Ital. *gabinetto* 'study, consulting-room'. Note кабина 'cabin', now also 'cockpit, voting-booth', from Fr. *cabine* 'cabin'.

КАДЕТ [kadét] 'cadet'. Early 18th century, from Fr. *cadet* 'elder (in family), cadet', possibly via Ger. *Kadett* 'cadet', later also used as an abbreviation for конституциóнный демокрáт 'Constitutional Democrat', member of the Конституциóнно-демократи́ческая пáртия 'Constitutional Democratic Party', formed by left-wing liberals on 31 October 1905, replacing original *кадéк* (from the initials КД) under the influence of кадéт, disbanded in 1918.

КАДКА [kádka] 'tub, vat'. 12th century, ultimately from Gk. *kádos* 'jar, vessel for water or wine' or Byz. Gk. *kádos* 'tub, bucket', via Lat. *cadus* 'wine jar, earthenware or stone jug', said to have originated in Hebrew. Cf. IE *kādhis 'vessel, container'.

КАДЫК [kadýk] 'Adam's apple'. Early 18th century, possibly from a Tkc. root (cf. Tatar *kadyk*) meaning 'firm, strong', cf. закадычный друг 'bosom (firm) friend'. Alternatively, if somewhat fancifully, originally *кадых (cf. dial. *кадышить* 'to cough violently'), perhaps based on dial. *дыхи* 'nostrils, organs of breathing' (of a horse), with -х changing to -к under the influence of dial. *кадук* 'epilepsy'. Unlikely to derive from Pol. *grdyka* 'Adam's apple', seemingly a blend of *gardło* 'throat' and *krtań* 'wind-pipe'.

КАЗАК [kazák] 'Cossack'. 1395 in meaning 'hired labourer', 1444 in hist. meaning. From a Tkc. word meaning 'free man, adventure seeker', based on *qaz* 'to roam, wander about', perhaps via Ukr. *козак* 'Cossack', from Pol. *kozak* (whence also Eng. *Cossack*, Fr. *cosaque*), cognate with казáх 'a Kazach'. Pl.

казáки with penultimate stress, alongside standard казакú, may owe something to Pol. influence (Vasmer).

Cossacks arose as irregular frontier troops of the Crimean Khanate in the 15th century, and in the following century formed communities along the banks of the Dnieper and Don, their numbers swollen by refugees from serfdom. The word has been reinterpreted in Turk. *kazak* to mean 'dominating, despotic', of a husband.

КАЗАРМА [kazárma] 'barracks'. Early 18th century, seemingly based on Ital. *caserma*, id., a coalescence of *casa* 'house' and *arma* 'weapon'. Purportedly via Pol. (now *koszary* 'barracks') and Ger. *Kaserne*, id. (Grimm also cites Swabian *Kasarme*, id.), from Fr. *caserne*, id. (originally, 16th century, 'accommodation for four soldiers of the guard'), Provençal *cazerna* 'group of four', Late Lat. *quaterna*, id., Lat. *quaternī* 'four each'.

КАЗНА [kazná] 'treasury'. 14th-/15th centuries 'store room, property', via Tkc., ultimately from Ar. *khazīna* 'treasury, treasure house' (cf. Turk. *hazine* 'treasury, exchequer'), brought to Russia by the Tatars. Cf. also казначéй 'treasurer'.

КАЗНЬ [kazn'] 'execution'. 10th-/11th centuries, from ChSl., originally 'punishment' (cf. казнь (fig.) 'torture, punishment'), perhaps from or cognate with OR *каяти* 'to censure' (for -знь 'state', cf. жизнь 'life'). Alternatively from or contaminated by the root каз- 'to say' (for -нь, cf. дань 'tribute' from дать 'to give'). The meaning 'capital punishment' was established by the second half of the 19th century, before which смéртная казнь 'death penalty' was specified in judicial practice.

КАЛЕКА [kaléka] 'cripple'. 14th century as nickname, probably connected with OR *калика* 'vagrant', via Tkc., perhaps ultimately from Ar. *kālih* 'adverse'. Alternatively based on OR лѣкъ 'remainder', a reference to amputated limbs. For rare prefix ка-, cf. кáверза 'intrigue'.

КАЛЕНДАРЬ [kalendár'] 'calendar'. Late 17th-/early 18th centuries, probably via Pol. *kalendarz*, from Lat.

calendārium/kalendārium 'account-book, interest-book of a money-lender', lit. 'list of calends', from Lat. *calendae/kalendae* 'first day of the month' (on which accounts were due) + *-ārium* 'receptacle, aggregate'. Cognate with earlier коляда́ 'house-to-house Christmas carol singing' (also from Lat. *calendae*).

КАЛО́ША/ГАЛО́ША [kalóša/galóša] 'galosh'. 18th-/19th centuries, from Fr. *galoche*, id., or Ger. *Galosche*, id., cf. Ital. *galoscia*, id. Not from кал 'excrement', though some are said to associate the two at a phonetic level.

КА́ЛЬКА [kál'ka] 'tracing paper, tracing paper copy, calque, loan translation'. 19th century, from Fr. *calque* 'tracing, copy, calque', *calquer* 'to trace, copy' (from Ital. *calcare* 'to press down', cf. Ital. *calco* 'drawing, tracing', Lat. *calcō* 'I tread upon, press close together').

КАЛЬКУЛЯ́ЦИЯ [kal'kuljácija] 'calculation'. 19th century, ultimately from Lat. *calculātio*, id., based on *calculus* 'pebble, stone used in counting' (in antiquity calculations were carried out with pebbles). Cf. микрокалькуля́тор 'pocket calculator'.

КАЛЬСО́НЫ [kal'sóny] 'underpants'. 1860s at latest, from Fr. *caleçon(s)*, id., an adaptation of Ital. *calzoni* 'trousers'.

КА́МЕРА [kámera] 'prison cell, camera, inner tube'. Early 18th century, cf. OR *камара/камора* 'vault' (камо́рка (coll.) 'closet, box-room'), late 17th century 'room, hotel room'. From Gk. *kamára* 'vault, anything with a vaulted or arched covering', via Ger. *Kammer* 'chamber', D. *kamer*, id. or Sw. *kammare*, id. Alternatively, directly from Lat. *camera* 'vault, arched roof'.

КАМПА́НИЯ [kampánija] 'campaign'. Early 18th century, from Fr. *campagne* via Ger. *Kampagne* or Pol. *kampania*, id., ultimately from Ital. *campagna*, id., MLat. *campania* 'unenclosed land', Lat. *campus* 'field, place of action, arena'.

КАМЫ́Ш [kamýš] 'reeds'. First half of 18th century, a Tkc. loan, cf. Turk. *kamiş* 'reed, bamboo'.

КАНАРЕЙКА [kanaréjka] 'canary'. Late 17th century, based on Fr. *canari*, id. (for suffix -ейка, cf. индейка 'turkey'), ultimately Sp. *canario* 'of the Canary Isles, canary', from the home of these birds.

Canaria Insula, one of the Fortunate Isles, from where the canary was brought to mainland Europe in the 16th century, literally 'Isle of Dogs' (so called because of its large dogs -- Lat. *canārius* 'appertaining to dogs').

КАНДИДАТ [kandidát] 'candidate'. Early 18th century, from Lat. *candidātus* 'candidate for office' (lit. 'dressed in white' -- candidates for office in ancient Rome would present themselves to the people dressed in a *toga candida* 'white toga'), possibly via Ger. *Kandidat*, id. D. *kandidaat*, id. or Fr. *candidat*, id. The meaning 'kandidat' (holder of a higher degree) is of Ger. origin (cf. Ger. *Kandidat* 'degree candidate') and became established in R. in the early 19th century.

КАНИКУЛЫ [kaníkuly] 'holidays'. Late 18th century loan, possibly via Pol. *kanikuła* (also *psianka*, from *pies* 'dog') 'dog star, Cirius', from Lat. *Canīcula* (dim. of *canis* 'dog') 'dog-star', also known as *Canis* or *Sirius*, regarded by the Romans as Orion's hunting dog, the most important star in the 20-star constellation *Canis Major* (lit. *Great Dog*, созвéздие (Большóго) Пса). In the Roman calendar the Sun was in the constellation *Canis*, and *Sirius* was in the ascendant, between 22 July and 23 August, the hottest period of the year, when all activities would be suspended. Каникулы appears in R. in 18th-/early 19th centuries as 'school, academic holidays' (lit. 'days of the constellation *Canis*'). Cf. Eng. *dog days*, the hottest period of the year ('reckoned in antiquity from the helical rising of the dog-star'), Lat. *diĕs canīculāres*, id., Fr. *jours* (also *chaleurs*) *caniculaires*, Ger. *Hundestage*, Pol. *dni kanikularne* or *psie dni* 'dog days'. In R. horoscopes the period 22 July to 23 August is associated with the constellation Leo (Лев), the ruby stone, the colour red, the symbol fire, and the Sun.

КАНИТЕЛЬ [kanitél'] 'gold thread, red tape'. 16th century (used in describing Boris Godunov's clothing 1589), from Fr.

cannetille 'gold thread, gold wire', itself from Sp. *cañutillo* 'small tube or pipe, gold or silver quill for embroidery', from *caña* 'reed', rather than Ital. *canutiglia* 'tinsel', from Lat. *canna* 'reed'. The change to -итель from Fr. *-etille* perhaps by vowel dissimilation, end stress possibly under the influence of Fr. The meaning 'bureaucratic red tape' evolved in the 19th century.

КАНУН [kanún] 'eve'. 12th century, from Gk. *kanón* 'ruler, straight stick', then 'model, norm', further 'church rule, canticle'. Канон 'established order, church rule, church service' also developed from the Gk., but through written sources, while канун evolved through oral sources (hence not uncommon verbal transfer of Gk. *ō* to R. y). The meaning 'eve' derived from the practice of reading canons at vespers on the eve of a church festival, subsequently 'eve' was extended to non-eccles. contexts (cf. накануне 'on the eve'). Канон survives in the meaning 'canon', reinforced by analogous lexis in Eur. languages in which the word derived from Gk., via Lat.

КАНЦЕЛЯРИЯ [kanceljárija] 'office'. First half of 17th century, from Pol. *kancelaria* 'office, chancery', via MLat. *cancelleria* 'chancery', from Lat. *cancellī* 'grating, bars, bar in a court of justice'. Thus *cancellārii* 'secretaries, scribes', lit. those who worked at the bars of a court (*ad cancellos*).

КАПИТАЛ [kapitál] 'capital'. Recorded in dictionaries from 1731, based ultimately on MLat. *capitāle* (substantivized neut. adj. from *capitālis* 'main') 'movable goods' (1114), 'capital' (1200), possibly via Fr. *capital* or Ger. *Kapital* 'capital, stock'.

КАПУСТА [kapústa] 'cabbage'. 11th century, a hybrid, probably deriving from a contamination of two MLat. words: *caputium* 'white cabbage' (lit. 'small head', dim. of *caput* 'head') and *composita* 'compounded, compound', fem. part. from *componō* 'I compose, compound, mix' (cf. also Ital. *composto* 'compound', *composta* 'stewed fruit').

КАПЮШОН [kapjušón] 'hood, cowl'. 18th century, via Fr. *capuchon*, id., from Ital. *capuccio*, id., Late Lat. *cappa* 'cap, cowl'. Cf. Ital. *cappucino* 'cappucino, white coffee, esp. made with espresso coffee', so called from its white 'head', Eng. *Capuchin* 'Franciscan friar', *capuchin* monkey, pigeon (with head hair, head and neck feathers reminiscent of a cowl).

КАРАКУЛЬ [karákul'] 'caracul, astrachan fleece'. Recorded in dictionaries from late 19th century, from Tkc. or, arguably, Fr. *caracul*, a reference to the Karakul oasis near Buchara (Uzbekistan), where caracul sheep were bred, from Tkc. *qara* 'black', *qul* 'lake'. Caracul lambs have dark curly fleece similar to astrachan (the fleece of lambs bred at Astrachan' in the mouth of the Volga).

КАРАКУЛЯ [karákulja] 'scrawl, scribble' (usually pl. каракули). Late 17th century, from Tkc., lit. 'bad hand' (*qara* 'bad', *qul/qol* 'arm, hand', cf. Turk. *kol* 'arm'). Alternatively, from Fr. *caracole* 'half turn executed by a horse', Sp. *caracol* 'prancing, cochlea', the various words sharing the meaning of convoluted shape or movement.

КАРАНДАШ [karandáš] 'pencil'. 17th century, from Tkc., cf. Turk. *qara* 'black', *taş* 'stone', perhaps a reference to graphite shales or the gnesses from which graphite is mined (for increscent -н-, cf. каланчá 'watch-tower', also a Tkc. loan). *Caran d'ache* is used as a brand name by the well-known Swiss manufacturers of high-quality writing implements.

КАРАНТИН [karantín] 'quarantine'. 18th century (sometimes also spelt *карантен*), from Fr. *quarantaine* 'about forty, forty days, forty (of age), quarantine' (originally forty days' isolation, from Fr. *quarante* 'forty'), based on Ital. *quarantena* 'quarantine', *quaranta* '40' (Lat. *quadrāgintā*, id.). Quarantine is said to have originated in Italy in the 14th century, first denoting institutions for the isolation of people, ships and goods from infected areas for a period of 40 days, subsequently isolation in general.

КАРАПУЗ [karapúz] 'small child'. Early 19th century карапýзик, карапýз recorded 1865, from a Tkc. word meaning 'melon', cf. арбýз, id., Turk. *karpuz*, id., recalling small children's 'melon-like' chubbiness. Alternatively based on Fr.

crapoussin 'small person, urchin', from *crapaud* 'toad' and influenced by *poussin* 'chick', contaminated by association with коротышка 'tubby person' and пу́зо 'belly', or from Gk. *kárabos* 'kind of beetle', cf. Lat. *scarabaeus* 'beetle, scarab'.

КАРАУЛ [karaúl] 'guard'. 14th century Tkc. loan (cf. Turk. *karakol* 'police station'), ultimately from Mong. *карагул* (classical script), *харуул* (modern Mong.), cf. Mong. suffix in еса́ул 'Cossack captain'.

КАРИЙ [kárij] 'dark brown (of eye colour), chestnut (of horses)'. Late 14th-/early 15th centuries *карый* (of horses), 16th century ка́рий 'dark brown', from Tkc. *qara* 'black'.

КАРИКАТУРА [karikatúra] 'caricature'. 17th-/18th centuries, from Ital. *caricatura*, id., lit. 'loading' (possibly via Fr. *caricature* 'caricature' or Ger. *Karikatur*, id.), from *caricare* 'to load, burden, exaggerate'. Cf. шарж 'caricature', from Fr. *charge* 'load, caricature'.

КАРЛИК [kárlik] 'dwarf'. 18th century, from Pol. (cf. Pol. *karzeł*, gen. *karła*, id. -- however, *Карло* was known as a proper name in the 15th century). Alternatively from MHG *karl* 'man, husband', ultimately Gmc. *kerla-, cf. Ger. *Kerl* 'fellow', MLG *kerla* 'free man not of knightly station, coarse person' (Eng. *churl*). Perhaps a hybrid formation.

КАРМАН [karmán] 'pocket'. 16th-/17th centuries *корман*, then карма́н through *akan'je*. Originally 'purse' (as late as early 19th century), probably from a N. Tkc. word meaning 'purse, moneybag' (early 'pockets' appear not to have been sewn to clothing). Lat. *crumēna* 'purse' has also been suggested as a possible source.

КАРНАВАЛ [karnavál] 'carnival'. 18th century, from Fr. *carnaval*, id., ultimately Ital. *carnevale*, id., purportedly comprising *carne* 'meat' and *vale* 'farewell', a reference to fasting during Lent. Alternatively, *-vale* has been associated (through l:v metathesis) with Ital. *levare* 'to raise, remove' (cf. MLat. *carnelevāmen* 'Shrovetide', also *carnilevaria, carnislevamen,* *carnelevarium*, referring to the removal of meat during Lent). Ital. *carnescialare* 'to carnival' has been linked with *carne* 'meat' + *lasciare* 'to renounce'.

КАРТА [kárta] 'map, playing card'. 16th century ка́рты 'playing cards', 18th century ка́рта 'map' (apparently 17th century карти́на, id., now 'picture'). Ultimately from Gk. *chártēs* 'papyrus, roll made therefrom, sheet of paper, charter', whence Lat. *charta* 'a leaf of the Egyptian papyrus, paper', Ital. *carta* 'paper, charter, map, playing-card', possibly via Pol. *karta* 'card' (cf., however, Pol. *mapa* 'map').

КАРТОН [kartón] 'cardboard'. Early 18th century, via Fr. *carton* 'pasteboard', D. *karton* 'cardboard' or Ger. *Karton*, id., from Ital. *cartone* 'cardboard' (comprising *carta* + augmentative suffix *-one*).

КАРТОФЕЛЬ [kartófel'] 'potatoes'. Late 18th century, based on early 18th-century Ger. *Tartüffel/Tartoffel*, from Ital. *tartufo, tartufolo* 'truffle', itself from Late Lat. *terrae tuber*, id. (potatoes shipped into Italy from America in the 16th century grew under the soil, had truffle-like tubers, and were thus named after them). Ger. *Kartoffel* perhaps through dissimilation of plosives (t-t changing to k-t). Карто́шка 'potatoes, potato' derived from dial. *карто́ха*, entered the literary language in the 1830s and also became synonymous with карто́фелина 'potato' in the 1860s.

КАССА [kássa] 'cash-box, booking-office'. 17th-/18th centuries, from Ital. *cassa* 'cash-box, cash', probably via Pol. *kasa* 'cash-box' or Ger. *Kasse* 'till, safe, booking office, cash'. Ultimately from Lat. *capsa* 'repository, box' (mainly for manuscripts), whence also Eng. *case, cash*.

КАСТРЮЛЯ [kastrjúlja] 'sauce-pan'. Early 18th century, originally *кастрол* (cf. D. *kastrol* 'casserole'), probably from Ger. *Kasserolle* 'saucepan' (Grimm also cites popular Ger. *Kastrol(le)*, as well as NE Fr. *castrole*), itself from Fr. *casserole*, id., dim. of *casse* 'pan', from Late Lat. *cattia* 'spoon', Gk. *kyáthion* (dim. of *kýathos* 'cup, ladle'). Ending -юля by analogy with nouns such as пилю́ля 'pill'.

КАТАСТРОФА [katastrófa] 'catastrophe'. At the latest early 19th century, from Fr. via Ger., ultimately Gk *katastrophḗ* 'an overturning, catastrophe' (in drama, the catastrophe or turn of the plot), from *katá* 'over, down', *strophḗ* 'a turning', *stréphō* 'I turn'.

КАТОРГА [kátorga] 'penal servitude'. 15th century *катарга* 'trireme, galley', from Byz. Gk. 14th-century *káterga* 'the hulks', pl. of *kátergon*, properly 'work in the lower tiers of oar-driven vessels', from *katá* 'down, below', *érgon* 'work'. The meaning 'penal servitude' evolved from 18th-century сослáть на кáторги 'to consign to the galleys'. Cf. classical Gk. *kátergon* (substantivized neut. adj.) 'wages, labour costs'.

КАФЕДРА [káfedra] 'rostrum, chair, university department'. 18th century *катедра* 'rostrum, pulpit', with -т- under W. Eur. influence (e.g. Ital. *cattedra* 'desk, professorship, pulpit'). Ultimately from Gk. *kathédra* 'seat, bench, seat of authority' (*katá/kath'* 'down', *hédra* 'seat'), with initial stress in R. possibly under the influence of Lat. *cáthedra* 'chair, stool, professor's chair'. Cf. Eng. *cathedral* 'principal church in a diocese, containing the bishop's seat or throne'.

КАЧЕСТВО [káčestvo] 'quality'. 11th century *качьство*, from ChSl., initially как- + ьство, with -к- changing to -ч- before -ь- and -ь- vocalizing to -е-. Calqued from Gk. *poiótēs* 'quality' (*poiós* 'of a certain kind'), cf. Eng. *quality* from Lat. *quālitās* (*quālis* 'of what kind').

КАШЕЛЬ [kášel'] 'cough'. CSl. *kašьlь, based on onomatopoeic *кахи-кахи*, cognate with Lith. *kosulys*, id.

КАШТАН [kaštán] 'chestnut, chestnut-tree'. 17th century, via Pol. *kasztan*, id., from Ger. *Kastanie* 'chestnut', itself from Lat. *castanea*, id., Gk. *kastanéa*, id. or *káruon* ('nut') *kastanaïkón* (*kastáneion káruon*, according to Onions), after Castanæa in Asia Minor or Castana in Thessaly.

КАЯТЬСЯ [kájat'sja] 'to repent'. 11th century, id. (cf. IE *kāi̯ō, id., Skr. *cayate* 'punishes'), cognate with цена́ 'price', Lith. *kaina*, id., Gk. *poinḗ* 'ransom, vengeance, penalty'. Cf. also казнь 'execution'.

КВАДРАТ [kvadrát] 'square'. Early 18th century (cf. *квадратум* 1499), from Lat. *quadrătum* 'square, rectangle', via Ger. *Quadrat* 'square' or D. *kwadraat*, id.

КВАРТИРА [kvartíra] 'lodging'. Early 18th century (also *квартера/кватера*), from Ger. *Quartier* 'lodging, billet' or D. *kwartier* 'quarter, fourth part', possibly via Pol. *kwatera* 'lodging, quarters'. Ultimately Fr. *quartier(s)* 'sector, quarter(s) allocated for billeting the military' (e.g. *quartiers d'hiver* 'winter quarters'), based on Lat. *quartărius* 'a fourth part', *quaterni* 'four at a time, four from each legion, four together'. (Billeting regulations in many Eur. states obliged local populations to set aside part of their accommodation for troops on campaign, cf. Eng. 16th-century *quarters* 'soldiers' lodgings'. Subsequently the word extended beyond the military to all lodgings.)

КВАС [kvas] 'kvass'. 11th century, cognate with ки́слый 'sour', cf. ква́сить 'to pickle, make sour', Pol. *kwas* 'acid', Lat. *căseus* 'cheese'.

КВИТАНЦИЯ [kvitáncija] 'receipt'. 18th century, from D. *kwitantie*, id., reshaped on the pattern of nouns in -ция. Ultimately from Lat. *quiētus* 'at rest, calm, quiet', *quiēscō* 'I am calm' (whence also coll. квит 'quits', via Ger. *quitt*, id.), via OFr. *quite* 'free' (cf. Fr. *quitte* 'free of a juridicial obligation, of a debt'), MLat. *quitus*, fundamentally 'a sanguine person, with whom accounts have been settled'.

КЕФАЛЬ [kefál'] 'grey mullet'. Recorded in dictionaries in the second half of the 19th century, possibly from Gk. *kephalinos* 'a sea fish' (cf. *kephalís*, dim. of *kephalḗ* 'head' -- the fish's elongated and compressed body may have concentrated attention on its head) or from Cephallenia (Cephalonia), now Kefallinia, the largest island in the Ionian Sea, where these fish are found.

КИБЕРНЕТИКА [kibernétika] 'cybernetics'. Coined in 1948-9 by the American N. Wiener, found in R. dictionaries 1956, ultimately from Gk. *kybernētikē (sc. téchnē* 'skill') 'the art of steering'. Cf. *kybernētikós* 'skilled in steering or governing', *kybernētēs* 'helmsman', cognate with Eng. *govern.*

КИЛОГРАММ [kilográmm] 'kilogram'. Early 19th century (originally with reference to the Fr. measure), in general use following the decree on the metric system of 11 September 1918. Via Ger. *Kilo(gramm)* from Gk. *chílioi* 'thousand' + *grámma* (Late Lat. *grámma*) 'a small weight'.

КИНО [kinó] 'cinema'. An abbreviation of early 20th-century *кинематограф*, from Ger. *Kinematograph* 'film camera' (Gk. *kínēma* 'movement, motion', *gráphō* 'I write', cf. Fr. *cinéma* from *cinématographe*, Ger. *Kino*), replacing *биоскоп, иллюзион, синематограф* (к- maybe under the influence of already-extant words such as кинемáтика 'kinematics').

КИРПИЧ [kirpíč] 'brick'. 14th century, from Pers. *kirpij* 'sun-dried brick', cf. Turk. *kerpiç* 'adobe'.

КИСЛОРОД [kisloród] 'oxygen'. Recorded in dictionaries 1847 (replacing *кислотвор*, devised by the chemist V.M. Severgin in 1810), calqued from Lat. *oxygenium* (cf. Fr. *oxigène*, replacing the now-standard *oxygène* 1786 -- short for *principe oxygène* 1785-86 -- in de Morveau and Lavoisier's *Nomenclature Chimique* 1787, on the basis of Gk. *oxýs* 'sharp, keen' + *gennáō* 'I produce'). Кислорóд seemingly by analogy with *водорóд* 'hydrogen', from *hydrogenium*, id.

КИТ [kit] 'whale'. 11th century, from Gk. *kētos* 'sea monster' (cf. OR *китосъ* 'whale' 1073), subsequently 'whale', cf. Lat. *cetos* 'sea monster' for standard Lat. *bālaena* 'whale', Gk. *phálaina*, id., Fr. *baleine*, id.

КЛАДБИЩЕ [kládbišče] 'cemetery'. From *кладьба 'stowing away' (cf. кладý 'I place') + locational suffix -ище, cf. стрéльбище 'firing range' from стрельбá 'shooting'. Possibly tabooistic for an earlier form, perhaps погребéние 'burial'.

КЛАСС [klass] 'class'. Early 18th century, via Fr. *classe*, from Lat. *classis* 'army, fleet', then 'category, social class', from Servius Tullius's 6th-century BC division of the Roman people into five classes according to wealth (in the Servian Constitution).

КЛАСТЬ [klast'] 'to place'. CSl. *klasti from *kladti (IE *kla- 'to spread out, pile up') with -dt- changing to -tt- by assimilation, -tt- to -st- by dissimilation (cf. retention of -д- in кладу́ 'I place'). Cognate with Lith. *kloti* 'to cover, make a bed', Ger. *laden* 'to load' (OHG *(h)ladan*), *Last* 'a burden'.

КЛЕВЕТА [klevetá] 'slander'. 11th century 'false accusation, misrepresentation', from ChSl., possibly based on OR *клъвати* 'to peck, strike' (cf. клева́ть 'to peck'). Alternatively associated with dial. *клеви́ть* 'to tease mercilessly' or, less plausibly, with Gk. *chleuasía* 'mockery' or Lat. *calumnia* 'misrepresentation'.

КЛЕЙ [klej] 'glue'. 12th century, from CSl., possibly cognate with Gk. *kólla*, id. Alternatively of Gmc. origin, cf. Ger. *Klei* 'clay, loam', D. *klei* 'clay', from IE *gleibh- 'to stick', cognate with Ger. *kleben*, id.

КЛИНИКА [klínika] 'clinic'. Second quarter of the 19th century (recorded 1804 also in pl., as 'bed-ridden patients, mausolea'). Probably from Ger. *Klinik* 'clinic', ultimately Lat. *clīnicē*, Gk. *kliniké téchnē* 'doctoring', based on *klinikós* 'of, for a bed, physician who visits patients in their beds', from *klínē* 'couch, bed'. Final -a possibly under the influence of больни́ца 'hospital', лече́бница 'clinic'.

КЛИНОК [klinók] 'blade'. Early 18th century at latest, from D. *kling*, id., cf. Ger. *Klinge*, id. (cognate with *klingen* 'to sound, ring'). Developed, possibly under the false etymological influence of клин 'wedge' + -ок (cf., however, кли́нышек 'small wedge'), from *kling* to клино́к (final -g devoiced to homophonous -k). See зо́нтик 'umbrella' and cf. analogous мунди́р 'uniform' from Ger. *Montierung* 'military clothing, equipment' via assumed dim. *мундиро́к*.

КЛУМБА [klúmba] 'flowerbed'. 19th century, from Eng.

clump, -a possibly by analogy with гря́дка 'bed'. Cf. Ger. *Klumpen* 'clod, lump', Pol. *kląb/klomb* 'flowerbed'.

КЛЫК [klyk] 'tusk, fang'. Based on CSl. **kolti* (коло́ть 'to prick, stab'). For -ык, cf. OR *камыкъ* 'stone'.

КЛЮЧ [ključ] 'key'. 11th century 'bolt, key', from CSl. **ključь/*kljukjь* (IE **klāu̯is*, id.), cognate with клюка́ 'walking stick', Lat. *clāvis* 'key', *claudō/clūdō* 'I lock', Gk. *klēís* 'key'. Cf. derivative ключи́ца 'clavicle, collar-bone', from the key-shaped appearance of the bone, perhaps calqued from Lat. *clāvicula*, id., Ger. *Schlüsselbein*, id. (*Schlüssel* 'key', *Bein* 'leg', properly 'bone'). Homonym ключ 'source, spring' is from onomatopoeic клю-клю, cf. dial. клю́кать 'to drink, get drunk' and analogous плач 'weeping', from пла́кать 'to weep'.

КЛЯКСА [kljáksa] 'blot'. 1860s, from Ger. *Klecks* 'blot', *klecksen* 'to blot'.

КНИГА [kníga] 'book'. 11th century, from OSc. *kenning* 'teaching doctrine', thus perhaps 'that which one learns', or from Tkc. *küin* 'scroll' (possibly from Chinese *küan*), Arm. *knik'* 'seal, stamp, sign', or Assyrian *kunukku* 'seal, sealed clay tablet, seal impression'. A derivation has also been suggested from Chinese *Ših-čing* 'Book of Odes' (10th to 7th centuries BC), an early poetic masterpiece possibly brought to Europe by the Huns.

КНОПКА [knópka] 'drawing-pin, press-button'. 19th century, perhaps reshaped from D. *knoop* 'button, stud', *knop* 'knob, button', cf. Ger. *Knopf*, id.

КНЯЗЬ [knjaz'] 'prince'. 11th century, based ultimately on W. Gmc. **kuninga-* 'king' (whence OHG *kuni(n)g* 'tribal leader, leader of a military retinue'), Goth. *kuni* 'family, kin, clan', itself from **kunja* 'noble line' (cf. Gk. *gennikós* 'noble' from *génna* 'birth, origin'). CSl. -ę- (in **kъnędzь*) and subsequently R. -я- evolved from Gmc. -in-, and Gmc. -g- changed to R. -з- in accordance with the third palatalization of velars. Pl. *княжья*, originally a collective, subsequently *князья* 'princes' under the influence of князь, derivatives in *княжна́* 'prince's daughter' and княги́ня 'prince's wife'.

КОВЕР [kovër] 'carpet'. Possibly from Tkc. Not from Ital. *coperchio* 'lid, cover', *coperta* 'blanket, coverlet' or Eng. *cover*.

КОЖА [kóža] 'leather, skin'. 11th century, from коза́ 'goat' + *-ja (cf. ко́зья шку́ра 'goat-skin'), with -z- to -ž- before -j. Subsequently of any skin or leather.

КОЗЫРЕК [kozyrëk] 'peak of cap'. Based either on *козырь* (obs.) 'tall standing collar' or (according to Šanskij) on *козъ 'leather cap-band'. Cf. homonymous ко́зырь 'trump', from Tkc. (thus Turk. *koz*, id.), via Pol. *kozera*, id. (Card-playing terminology in R. developed under W. influence, esp. that of W. Poland.) For ending and initial stress, cf. пла́стырь 'plaster'.

КОЙКА [kójka] 'bunk'. Widely used from 1740s-50s, from D. *kooi* 'berth, bunk' or LG *koje* 'partition' (cf. Ger. *Koje* 'cabin'), ultimately Lat. *cavea* 'cage' (whence Ger. *Käfig* 'cage'), from *cavus* 'hollow'. Ending -ка perhaps in dissimilation from кой (obs.) 'which'.

КОЛБАСА [kolbasá] 'sausage'. 13th century, probably from Tkc., cf. Turk. *külbasti* 'grilled cutlet', with -t- lost initially, perhaps, in inter-consonantal position in adj. *колбас(т)ный (now колба́сный). Alternatively from колобо́к 'small round loaf', from their shared roundness, or, dubiously, from Fr. *calebasse* 'gourd', also through their similarity in appearance, from Pol. *kiełbasa* 'sausage' (perhaps originally a fish delicacy, cf. Pol. *kiełb* 'gudgeon', ко́лбень 'goby'), or finally from Hebrew *kolbasar* 'all kinds of meat'.

КОЛИЧЕСТВО [kolíčestvo] 'quantity'. 11th century *количьство*, from ChSl./OR *колико* 'how much' + -ьство, with -к- palatalizing to -ч- before -ь- (subsequently vocalized to -е-). Calqued from Gk. *posótēs* 'quantity' (*pósos* 'how much'), cf. Lat. *quantitas* 'quantity', from *quantus* 'how much'.

КОЛОДЕЦ [kolódec] 'well'. 16th century, from CSl. *koldęzь, 10th-/11th centuries *колодязь*, id., -ец probably by analogy with ChSl. *стоуденецъ*, id., a calque (cf. студёный 'cold') based on Goth. *kalding-, *kalds* 'cold'. *Колодязъ* evolved through the emergence of inter-consonantal ESl. -оло- and the development of -я- from -in- via CSl. -ę-, further through g:z mutation (third palatalization of velars). For semantic correlation between 'cold' and 'source', cf. Lith. *šaltas* 'cold', *šaltinis* 'spring'. Alternatively, колодец may derive from колода 'water-trough, block, log', the usual mounting for a Slav. well, often hollowed into a groove at a well-spring or above a watering-hole.

КОЛОКОЛ [kólokol] 'bell'. 11th century, from CSl. onomatopoeic *kolkolъ 'ringing', with ESl. -оло- between consonants, cognate with Skr. *calācala* 'moving to and fro, unsteady', Gk. *kaléō* 'I call', *kélados* 'noise of wind, din of battle', Lat. *cālō* 'I summon'. See глагол 'verb'.

КОЛОС [kólos] 'ear of corn'. From CSl. *kolsъ, with ESl. inter-consonantal -оло-, perhaps cognate with *kolti (колоть) 'to prick' (a reference to the prickly nature of an ear of corn, or to corn after threshing) or with колотить 'to beat' (referring to the process of shelling ['beating'] the seeds from the ear). Cf. also Ger. *Hülse* 'shell, husk', *hehlen* 'to conceal' (implying the ear as container of flowers or seeds).

КОЛПАК [kolpák] 'cap'. 15th century, from Tkc. *kalpak* 'type of headgear, cap of felt or other material', cf. клобук 'Orthodox monk's cowl', from the same source. Note каракалпаки 'Karakalpaks', lit. 'Black Caps', an ethnic group living in the W. of the Kyzylkum desert, in the delta of the river Amudarja.

КОЛЧАН [kolčán] 'quiver'. 16th century, from Tkc.

КОЛЫБЕЛЬ [kolybél'] 'cradle'. 15th century, from dial. *колыбáть* 'to rock' (possibly a blend of колебáть 'to shake' and колыхáть 'to sway') + -ель (cf. купéль 'font' from купáть 'to bathe').

КОЛЬЦО [kol'có] 'ring'. 14th century, originally *кольце* (cf. лицó 'face'), dim. based on CSl. *kolo 'circle', cf. other derivatives колесó 'wheel', колея́ 'railway track', óколо 'near', коля́ска 'carriage'.

КОЛЯ́СКА [koljáska] 'carriage, brougham, perambulator'. Late 17th century, from Pol. *kolaska* 'chaise' or Cz. *kolesa* 'carriage' (or they from R.), cf. Ital. *calesse* 'cabriolet', Eng. *calash* 'light low-wheeled carriage', Fr. *calèche* 'open carriage', etc., all of Slav. origin. Ultimately based on OR *коло* 'circle, arc, wheel'. See колесó 'wheel', кольцó 'ring'.

КОМА́Р [komár] 'gnat'. Seemingly based on an IE root meaning 'buzz' (cf. IE *kemelos 'bumble bee') and related to шмель (from *чмель), id., Ger. *Hummel*, D. *hommel*, id., Eng. *hum* (note that Eng. *humble-bee* preceded *bumble-bee*).

КОМЕ́ДИЯ [komédija] 'comedy'. 17th century, from Pol. *komedia*, id., ultimately Lat. *cōmoedia*, Gk. *kōmo(i)día*, id. (*kṓmos* 'revel, band of revellers', *aoidḗ* 'song, legend, tale'). Association with Gk. *kṓmē* 'village, country town' is disputed.

КО́МКАТЬ [kómkat'] 'to crumple'. From комóк (dim. of ком 'lump'), gen. комкá.

КО́МНАТА [kómnata] 'room'. 15th century, originally with penultimate stress, perhaps under the influence of Pol. *komnáta* (obs.) 'hall with a fire-place'. Subsequent initial stress may be due to Gmc. mediation, cf. MHG *kómmet*, a possible direct source (alternatively directly from Lat.), cf. also Ger. *Kemenate* 'women's room', OHG *kemināta*, MHG *kemenāte*, from MLat. *(camera) camīnāta* 'heated room' (whence also Fr. *cheminée* 'chimney'), *camīnāta* being the fem. pass. part. of *camīnāre* 'to build up in the form of a stove' (Lat. *caminus* 'furnace, stove', from Gk. *káminos*, id., cognate with Ger. *Kamin* 'fire-place').

КО́МПАС [kómpas] 'compass'. 18th century, from Ger. *Kómpass* 'compass' or (as компáс, recorded in 18th-century dictionaries and still used with this stress by sailors, cf. lexical nature of most professionalisms, e.g. ёж lit. 'hedgehog', additionally, among meteorologists, 'a type of snow-flake') from Ital. *compasso* 'compasses, compass' (the magnetic compass was perfected in 14th-century Italy). *Compasso* lit. means 'even pace', from *compassare* 'to measure with compasses, pace out' (the magnetic needle was suspended in a freely-rotating round box whose circular shape may account for the extension of meaning in Ital. *compasso* from 'compasses' to 'compass', cf. Eng. *encompass* 'to circle around'). In view of the final stress in D. *kompás* and early R. компа́с, the R. is possibly from D., esp. since the word was introduced after Peter I's visit to Holland and was included, opposite a parallel D. text, in the maritime statutes of 1720.

КОМПОТ [kompót] 'stewed fruit'. 18th century, from Fr. *compote* 'fruit salad' or Ger. *Kompott* 'stewed fruit', probably ultimately Lat. *composita/composta* 'compound', past pass. part. of *compŏnō* 'I compose, aggregate'.

КОНВЕЙЕР [konvéjer] 'conveyor belt'. Recorded in dictionaries since 1933, from Eng. *conveyer*.

КОНВЕРТ [konvért] 'envelope'. Early 18th century (however *куверт*, id., was also current, especially from the mid-18th century, конве́рт dominating from the first half of the 19th century). From Fr. *couvert* (possibly via Ger. *Kuvert* 'envelope, place at table'), a part. adj. meaning 'covered, cover, set place at table', formerly 'envelope' (cf. Fr. *enveloppe* 'envelope', but *sous* **couvert** *séparé* 'under separate cover'), from *couvrir* 'to cover', ultimately Lat. *cooperiō* 'I cover'. Medial -н- possibly from a confusion between written Fr. -u- and -n-, the influence of Lat. *convertō* 'I convert', the avoidance of homonymy with *куверт* 'envelope, wrapper, place at table', or the influence of, e.g., Dan./Sw. *Konvolut/konvolut* 'envelope'.

КОНЕЦ [konéc] 'end'. 11th century, from CSl. *kon- 'end', cognate (due to the similarity of the concepts 'beginning' and 'end') with нача́ло 'beginning', OR *поконъ*, id., иско́нный primordial, immemorial', also Lat. *recēns* 'fresh, young', Gk. *kainós* 'new, fresh'.

КОНСЕРВЫ [konsérvy] 'tinned goods'. 18th century, from Fr. *conserve* 'preserve, pickle', *conserver* 'to preserve', Lat.

cōnservō 'I preserve'.

КОНФЕТА [konféta] 'sweet'. 18th century, from Ger. *Konfekt* 'sweetmeats', originally конфекты (recorded 1780), later конфéты (1847) under the influence of Ital. *confetto* 'sweet' (cf. Late Lat. *cōnfectum* 'confection, mixed drug, comfit', from *conficiō* 'I prepare'), hence also конфеттй 'confetti', from Ital. *confetti* 'small sweets thrown as missiles at carnival time' (subsequently small paper discs thrown at weddings -- cf. Ital. *mangiare i confetti* 'to celebrate a wedding').

КОНЬ [kon'] 'horse' (esp. male). 11th century, from CSl. *konjь, perhaps based on *komnь/*kobnь, cf. OR *комонь*, id., with cognate кобы́ла 'mare', Lith. *kumelė* 'mare', *kumelys* 'stallion', Lat. *caballus* 'nag' (whence Fr. *cheval* 'horse'), a Gallic word, supplanting Lat. *equus* 'horse'. Alternatively from *skopnь, thus initially 'castrated stallion', cf. скопéц 'eunuch'. In either case with simplification of the final consonant cluster mn/bn/pn to n (cf. сон 'sleep'). See ло́шадь 'horse'.

КОПЕЙКА [kopéjka] 'kopeck'. End 15th-/early 16th centuries (esp. after the monetary reform of 1535, in the reign of Ivan IV), originally the name of a silver coin which is said to have appeared in Moscow after the conquest of Novgorod in 1478 and from 1535-1719 depicted the tsar on horseback carrying a spear, replacing the earlier illustration of a fur-bearing animal, with a value of two *деньга́* (see де́ньги 'money'), thus lit. 'spear-coin' (see копьё 'spear'), with final -a possibly under the influence of *гривна* (obs.) 'mark', полти́на 'two roubles fifty kopecks'. Alternatively, копéйка is perhaps a contraction based on *копейные деньги* 'spear coins' (cf. modern электри́чка 'suburban commuter train' from электри́ческий по́езд 'electric train'). Finally, and dubiously, it may derive from the Tkc. word for a dog (cf. Turk. *köpek* 'dog'), since a dog was said to have been depicted on one of the Tatar coins, and lions -- possibly mistaken for dogs -- on coins struck by Timur.

КОПЫТО [kopýto] 'hoof'. CSl., cognate with *kopati 'to strike', Pol. *kopać* 'to dig, kick' (for suffix, cf. си́то 'sieve').

КОПЬЕ [kop'ë] 'spear'. 10th century (also 'man with spear', cf. Eng. *gun* 'member of shooting party'), from CSl. *kopьje, cognate with *kopati 'to strike', thus 'what you strike with', cf. Gk. *kopís* 'cleaver'.

КОРАБЛЬ [korábl'] 'ship'. 11th century (also *korabь*), from Byz. Gk. *karábion*, dim. of *kárabos* 'ship', with -bj- to -бл- in ESl. Possibly an early or oral loan, maybe through interpreters, since written Byz. Gk. -β- would have given R. -в- (cf. амвóн 'pulpit'), or perhaps via Late Lat. *carabus* (itself from Gk. *kárabos* 'light wicker boat'), whence also Ital. *caravella*, Fr. *caravelle* 'caravel'. Possibly influenced by CSl. *korbъ (cf. кóроб 'box, chest').

КОРЗИНА [korzína] 'basket'. ESl., cf. Ukr. *корзати* 'to weave', but also Latv. *kurza* 'basket of wickerwork for collecting berries', from IE *(s)ker- 'to turn, twist, bend'.

КОРИЧНЕВЫЙ [koríčnevyj] 'brown'. 18th century, from корúца 'cinnamon' (with ц:ч mutation before suffix -(ь)н-), the aromatic inner bark of the SE Asian cinnamon tree, used as spice. Probably ultimately based on корá 'bark', from the IE root *ker- 'to cut', with likely cognates in шкýра 'pelt', скорлупá 'shell', скорнЯк 'furrier'. (Note that many of the newer colours derive from plant-names, e.g. сирéневый 'lilac', орáнжевый 'orange', рóзовый 'pink'.)

КОРОБКА [koróbka] 'box'. Recorded since the 14th century, based on кóроб 'box, basket', with cognates in Lat. *corbis* 'basket', whence also Ger. *Korb*, id. OHG *chorp* (from Lat. *corbis*) is possibly the direct source of кóроб.

КОРОВА [koróva] 'cow'. From CSl. *korva, with ESl. interconsonantal -opo-, lit. 'horned animal', cf. Gk. *kéras* 'horn', *keraós* 'horned', Lat. *cornū* 'horn', Lith. *karvė* 'cow' (also Skr. *carv* 'grind with the teeth').

КОРОЛЬ [koról'] 'king'. 12th century, from CSl. *korl-, based on Карл Велúкий (Charlemagne), the Frankish king 742-814 (cf. царь 'tsar', ultimately based on Caius Julius Caesar), with

ESl. inter-consonantal -opo-. An alternative, somewhat dubious, association has also been made with Gmc. *kerla-/*karlja- 'free man'. Короле́ва 'queen' appeared in the early 18th century (with one reference, however, in the early 15th-century Hypatian Chronicle), replacing 16th-century короле́вна, id., later 'princess'. Короле́ва was perhaps originally an adj. noun from коро́ль, based on analogous Pol. *królowa* 'queen' (cf. Pol. *król* 'king').

КОРО́ТКИЙ [korótkij] 'short'. From CSl. *kortъ, with ESl. inter-consonantal -opo-, probably ultimately from IE *ker- 'to cut', cf. Gk. *keírō* 'I cut', Lat. *curtus* 'short(ened)', whence Fr. *court* 'short' (cf. Eng. *curt*). Possibly cognate with ко́рточки, as in сиде́ть на ко́рточках 'to squat'. Cf. also, of ChSl. provenance (hence inter-consonantal -pa-), кра́ткий 'brief, concise'.

КОРЫ́ТО [korýto] 'trough'. Perhaps based on кора́ 'bark' and thus originally 'article made of bark', cf. корм 'fodder', dial. коре́ц 'scoop' (usually of metal, perhaps originally of bark), Gk. *kóros* 'surfeit'. For suffix, cf. копы́то 'hoof'.

КОРЬ [kor'] 'measles'. 18th century, probably cognate with кора́ 'bark' (cf. 12th century корь, id.), from the rash which forms on, then peels from, the patient's skin. For similar correlations, cf. Pol. *odra* 'measles', *odzreć* 'to tear off, flay', and note analogous designation of ailments through appearance in Fr. *rougeole* 'measles' (*rouge* 'red'), Ger. *Masern*, id. (*Maser* 'knot, excrescence on a tree'). Alternatively associated with хворь (coll.) 'illness, ailment'.

КОСА́ I [kosá] 'scythe'. 14th century, perhaps cognate with Skr. *śasati* 'cuts', *śastram* 'knife', Gk. *keázō* 'I split, cleave', Lat. *castrō* 'I castrate'. Alternatively, from its curved shape, perhaps cognate with косо́й 'slanting, curved', cf. also Lat. *coxa* 'hip'.

КОСА́ II [kosá] 'plait'. 15th century, cognate with Lith. *kasa* 'tress', from the same root as чеса́ть 'to scratch, comb', cf. ко́смы (coll.) 'tousled strands of hair, locks', косма́тый 'shaggy'. Associated with коса́ 'scythe', perhaps, through IE *kesō 'cut, chop, comb'.

КОСМОНАВТ [kosmonávt] 'spaceman'. Based on Gk. *kósmos* 'space', *naútēs* 'sailor', widely known after the first manned space flight by Jurij Gagarin on 12 April 1961 (космонáвтика 'outer space exploration' is recorded in dictionaries from 1958). Cf. астронáвт 'astronaut', used mainly of US spacemen, and occasionalism àстрокосмонáвты, used in 1975 during the joint Apollo-Sojuz flight (ЭПАС -- Экспериментáльный полёт Аполлóн-Союз 'Apollo-Sojuz Experimental Flight').

КОСМОС [kósmos] 'space'. Second quarter of the 19th century, supplanting 18th-century система света (мира) 'world system', созвездие 'constellation'. Ultimately from Gk. *kósmos* 'order, arrangement', then 'universe' (from its supposedly perfect order), a usage first attributed to Pythagoras (582-500 BC), A. Humboldt (1769-1859) giving it European currency in his work *Kosmos*. Cognates include космодрóм 'space-vehicle launching site' and космéтика 'cosmetics', an 18th-century loan from Fr. *cosmétique* 'cosmetic', Gk. *kosmētikḗ (téchnē)* 'the art of adornment', *kosméō* 'I order, arrange, adorn'.

КОСТЫЛЬ [kostýl'] 'crutch'. 18th century, based on кость 'bone', possibly referring to the substance of which the handles are made. For ending, cf. мотыль 'mosquito grub'.

КОТ [kot] 'tom cat'. OR *котъ*, id. (*котъка* 'female cat'), CSl. *kotъ, seemingly from 4th-century Lat. *cattus* 'cat' (which superseded *fēlēs*, id., on the introduction of the domestic cat into Rome), rather than from Goth. *katts. Ultimately, perhaps, from Nubian *kadīs* (ancient Nubia and Egypt are regarded as the home of the cat, cf. the genus *Felis libyca*, thought to be the ancestor of the domestic cat and wide-spread in Africa and Arabia). Кóшка 'cat, female cat' may derive from dim. *коша (cf. Мáша, Грúша, etc.) or from OR *кочка* (cf. Cz. *kočka* 'cat'), perhaps by analogy with собáчка 'small dog', etc., cf. analogous -шка for -чка in клюшка (coll.) 'hockey-stick, walking-stick' (for anticipated *клю́чка), from клюкá 'walking-stick'. A possible connection between Finn. *kissa* 'cat' and кúса/кúска 'pussy cat' is unexplained.

КОТЛЕТА [kotléta] 'cutlet, chop'. Early 18th century, from Fr. *côtelette* 'cutlet' (Lat. *costa* 'rib', Fr. *côte*, id.).

КОФЕ [kófe] 'coffee'. 18th century, originally also *кофий*, *кофей* (whence кофе́йник 'coffee-pot', кофе́йница 'coffee-grinder', кофеёк 'coffee' [coll.]), probably from Eng. *coffee* or D. *koffie*, id., ultimately Ar. *qahwah*, id. (whence Turk. *kahve*, id., then Ital. *caffe*, id., Fr. *café*, id., etc.). Associated etymologically with Kaffa, Ethiopian home of the coffee plant, whence it was transported to Arabia. Masc. gender, implicit in the ending of earlier *кофей/кофий*, is retained in ко́фе.

КОЧЕРГА [kočergá] 'poker'. 17th century, possibly from dial. *кочера́* 'gnarled tree', cf. also cognate коко́ра 'tree with stick-shaped root', maybe also related to ко́рень 'root'. Ending -га perhaps through contamination with клюка́ 'walking-stick' (for mutation to -рг- from -рк-, cf. четве́рг 'Thursday').

КОШМАР [košmár] 'nightmare'. Second quarter of 19th century, from Fr. *cauchemar*, id., 15th century *quauquemaire*, id., based on Picardian *cauquer* 'to press, crush', from Lat. *calcō* 'I trample upon, suppress', and D. *mare* 'phantom, asphyxia'. Cf. Ger. *Mahr* 'phantom, nightmare' (alongside standard Ger. *Alp* 'nightmare').

КРАЙ [kraj] 'edge, territory'. 11th century, from CSl. *krajь, IE *(s)ker- 'cut', by deaffixation from OR *краяти*, iterative of an earlier form of кройть 'to cut (out)', thus, seemingly, 'place of separation, division'.

КРАСНЫЙ [krásnyj] 'red'. 11th century 'magnificent, beautiful' (cf. кра́сная де́вица 'a fair damsel', прекра́сный 'magnificent'), also 'decorated, ceremonial', as in кра́сный у́гол, the front, best, corner of a peasant hut, where guests were entertained. The meaning 'red' developed at the latest in the 15th century, replacing OR *чьрвленьи* 'red' (cf. червлёный (obs.) 'dark-red', чёрмный (obs.) 'crimson', and see червь 'worm'), perhaps because of a perception of red as the 'best, most beautiful' colour.

КРАХМАЛ [krachmál] 'starch'. 18th century, possibly via Pol. *krochmal*, id. (cf. earlier *крохмал*, -o- later changing to -a- through *akan'je*). Seemingly based on Gmc. roots, cf. Ger. *Kraft* 'strength', D. *kracht*, id., Ger. *mahlen* 'to grind', D. *malen*, id. (alongside Ger. *Stärke* 'starch', D. *stijfsel*, id.).

КРЕМЛЬ [kreml'] 'kremlin'. First recorded 15th century, probably related to OR *крома* 'side, edge' (cf., in Pskov area, *кром* 'kremlin'), thus initially, perhaps, 'safe area enclosed round the perimeter', then 'fortress inside a town' (cf. укро́мный 'sheltered, secluded', кро́мка 'edge'). Possibly also cognate with креме́нь 'flint'. Alternatively, from Mong. *kerem* (classical script), cf. *khèrèm* (modern Mong.) 'kremlin'.

КРЕСТЬЯНИН [krest'jánin] 'peasant'. 14th century 'Christian', also 'peasant' (replacing OR *смьрдъ* 'freeman'), from Lat. *christianus* 'Christian', initial *chr*- modifying to кр-, thus крестья́нин, under the influence of крест 'cross'. Christianity, introduced into Rus' in 988-89 and the name 'Christian' -- now христиани́н (cf. Gk. *Christianós*, id.) -- distinguished R. farmers from their nomadic Moslem neighbours (не́христи [obs.] 'unbelievers'), hence semantic link between 'Christian' and 'peasant'. Cf. Sp. *cristiano* 'Christian', a term adopted by Argentinian gauchos to distinguish them from the native Indians (*los Indios*), also (coll.) 'the Spanish language'.

КРОВАТЬ [krovát'] 'bed'. Late 12th century, from Byz. Gk. *krábattos*, id., dim. *krab(b)átion*, -a- in the first syllable changing to -o- possibly under the false etymological influence of кров 'roof, shelter', покро́в 'covering'. The ESls., used to sleeping on benches covered with pelts or outer clothing, were impressed by Byz. luxury and brought samples of their bedding to Kiev.

КРОВЬ [krov'] 'blood'. 11th century, from CSl. **kry*, gen. **krъve* (IE **kruu̯os*, id.), originally the acc. of OR *кры*, id., subsequently also adopted as its nom. (cf. бровь 'brow' from CSl. **bry*). Cognates in Gk. *kréas* 'flesh, meat', Lith. *kraujas* 'blood', *kruvinas* 'bloody', Skr. *kravis* 'raw flesh', Lat. *cruor* 'blood, stream of blood'.

КРОЛИК [królik] 'rabbit'. 17th century (hitherto the rabbit, indigenous in SW Eur., was hardly known in Russia), from Pol. *królik*, id. (lit. 'little king', cf. Pol. *król* 'king'), a calque of MHG *küniclîn* 'rabbit', itself from Lat. *cunīculus*, id., also 'passage underground' (thus perhaps lit. 'animal digging burrows'), and wrongly interpreted as the dim. of MHG *künic* 'king' (cf. S. Ger. *Königlhase* 'rabbit', lit. 'little king hare'). The sequence is thus Lat. *cunīculus* 'rabbit', MHG *küniclîn* 'little king, rabbit', Pol. calque *królik*, id., кролик 'rabbit'. Note that Ger. *Kaninchen* 'rabbit', from *Kanin* 'rabbit skin', derives from MLG/OFr. *conin* 'rabbit' (cf. Eng. *con(e)y* 'rabbit, rabbit fur'), ultimately also from Lat. *cunīculus*. Pol. *królik* possibly from Cz. *kralik* 'rabbit', *kral* 'king'.

КРОМЕ [króme] 'except for, apart from'. 11th century, from CSl. *kroma, initially the prep. sing. of OR *крома* 'edge' (cf. stress in early 18th-century *кромé*, and note кромка 'edge'), thus lit. 'aside, on the periphery'. Subsequently, as a prep., 'outside', then 'apart from'. Cf. also кремль 'kremlin', скромный 'modest', укромный 'secluded'.

КРУГ [krug] 'circle'. 11th century 'circle, gathering, province', from CSl. *krǫgъ 'circle' IE *gringho, id., cf. Gmc. *hringa-, id., OHG *(h)ring* 'ring', with CSl. -ǫ- changing to ESl. -у-. Derivatives include 13th-century кружево 'lace' (seemingly from кружить 'to circle, spin round', alternatively and less plausibly linked with Ger. *Krause* 'frill'). Кругозор, used as a gloss of горизонт 'horizon' in the 18th century, subsequently acquired the fig. meaning 'range of interests' in the 1830s. Кружок 'small circle' acquired the additional meaning 'social, political study group' in the 1830s/40s, possibly through the calquing of Fr. *cercle* or Ger. *Zirkel* 'circle, society'.

КРЫЖОВНИК [kryžóvnik] 'gooseberries'. 17th century at earliest, possibly calqued from Pol. *krzyżewnik (cf. now Pol. *agrest*, id.), on the basis of obs. крыж 'Catholic cross', from Lat. *crux*, id. (cf. Pol. *krzyż*, id., OR крыжь, id.). Ultimately a rendering of Ger. dial. *Christdorn* 'sharp-spined hawthorn', lit. 'Christ's thorns', associated or confused with the gooseberry plant through its prickles (cf. Ger. *Stachelbeere* 'gooseberry', lit. 'prickly berry').

КРЫЛО [kryló] 'wing'. 11th century, from IE root *skrīdh- 'go, dash, fly' (cf. Lith. *skristi* 'to fly', Pol. *skrzydło* 'wing') + agent suffix -l(o), thus lit. 'what you fly with'. Alternatively from крыть 'to cover', thus, 'what you cover with' (namely fledgelings). Cf. derivative крыльцо́ 'porch'.

КРЫСА [krýsa] 'rat'. 17th century, possibly a reworking of a cognate of грызть 'to gnaw' (кр- for гр- maybe through contamination with крот 'mole'). Alternatively (Černych) from OPers. dial. *gerzū* 'mouse' (given the rat's route into Eur. from SE Asia via the Near East) or, implausibly, from *krysъsa (*krysos), lit. 'blood-sucker' (*кры* 'blood', cf. кровь, id. + сос 'sucker', cf. also кровосо́с 'vampire bat, (coll.) blood-sucker').

КРЫША [krýša] 'roof'. ESl., based on the root of крыть 'to cover', thus 'that which covers'.

КУКЛА [kúkla] 'doll'. 15th century, from Lat. *cucullus* 'hood, cowl, cloak', via Byz. Gk. *koukoúllion*, id., whence also (12th-13th centuries) ку́коль 'cowl'. The meaning progresses from 'cowl' to 'mask' to 'puppet' (cf. modern Gk. *koukla* 'doll, dummy'). Derivatives include ку́колка 'dolly, chrysalis', cf. Cz. *kukla* 'cowl, chrysalis'.

КУКУРУЗА [kukurúza] 'maize'. First half of 19th century, possibly of Slav. origin (cf. names of other plants, e.g., Pol. *kokoryczka* 'Salomon's seal', Bulg. *кукуряк* 'hellebore'), or from Rom. *cucuruz* 'maize', Turk. *kokoroz* 'maize stalk' (cf. reg. туре́цкая пшени́ца 'maize', lit. 'Turkish wheat', Cz. *turecka pšenice*, id., analogous to Eng. *Indian corn* 'maize' -- maize was brought to Eur. from C. and S. America by the Spaniards, hence the problem of Turk. provenance for the R. word). A somewhat fanciful suggestion identifies the word with the summoning call кукуру! when feeding corn to chickens (see ку́рица 'chicken').

КУЛАК [kulák] 'fist, rich peasant'. 13th century at latest, possibly from Tkc. (cf. Tkc. *qul* 'hand') or, since the original meaning is said to have denoted a weapon of defence and offence (cf. Lat. *pūgnus* 'fist' alongside *pūgnō* 'I fight'), lit. 'strike force' (cf. IE *kaud- 'strike'). For suffix, cf. желвáк 'tumour'.

КУЛИЧ [kulíč] 'Easter cake' (a wheat-flour cake blessed at the end of the Easter liturgy). No earlier than 17th century, possibly from Byz. Gk. *kollíkion* 'small roll of bread', dim. of *kóllix* 'long roll of coarse bread'.

КУМИР [kumír] 'idol'. 11th century, from ChSl., ultimately, perhaps, via Georg. *gmiri* 'hero, heroine', said to come from the tribal name of the Cymmerians.

КУПИТЬ [kupít'] 'to buy'. 11th century, from CSl. *kupiti, probably a very early loan from Goth. *kaupōn* 'to trade', OHG *koufon* 'to buy' (Ger. *kaufen*, id.), *koufo* 'dealer', from Lat. *caupō* 'huckster, innkeeper', *caupōna* 'retail shop, tavern'. Cf. also Dan. *købe* 'to buy', whence *København* 'Copenhagen', lit. 'trading harbour'.

КУРГАН [kurgán] 'burial mound'. 13th century, etymologically 'fortress', present meaning 16th century, from Tkc., cf. Turk. *kurgan* 'fortress'.

КУРИТЬ [kurít'] 'to smoke'. OR *курити* 'to steam, emit smoke', cf. 17th century *табак пити* 'to smoke' (lit. 'drink tobacco'), from Turk. *içmek* 'to drink, smoke' (perhaps originally a hookah or hubble-bubble, in which smoke is drawn through water). Курить табáк early 18th century, ultimately based on CSl. *kurъ 'smoke' (IE *kur- 'heat, fire, fuel, burning'), cf. Lith. *kurti* 'to kindle a fire', possibly from Gmc. (Sw. *rök* 'smoke', Ger. *Rauch*, id.), with metathesis r-k to k-r.

КУРИЦА [kúrica] 'hen'. 12th century, from 11th-century *куръ* 'cockerel' (*куря* 'chick'), based on CSl. *kurъ 'cockerel', *kura 'hen' (cf. кýры 'hens'). Perhaps onomatopoeic, cf. кукарéкать 'to crow', кудáхтать 'to cluck', Bulg. *кокошка* 'hen', Fr. *coq* 'cockerel', etc. Derivative курóк 'cocking-piece' (lever in gun raised ready to be released by trigger) is from Pol. *kurek*, id., a semantic calque of Ger. *Hahn* 'cockerel, cocking-piece' (cf. analogous собáчка 'small dog, trigger', calqued from Fr. *chien* 'dog, cocking-piece').

КУРОЛЕСИТЬ [kurolésit'] 'to get up to mischief'. Recorded late 18th century, from Gk. *Kýrie eléēson* 'Lord, have mercy', a petition sung in the R. Church, the change in meaning probably from choral disharmony, cf. the saying Поёт куролéсу, а несёт аллилу́ю 'Sings "Lord, have mercy" but talks balderdash'.

КУСАТЬ [kusát'] 'to bite'. From CSl. *$k\varrho s\breve{u}$ 'bit', OR *кусъ*, id., *кусати* 'to bite', with -ǫ- to ESl. -у-. Cf. Eng. *bit/to bite*, Fr. *morceau* 'bit'/*mordre* 'to bite'.

КУСТАРЬ [kustár'] 'handicraftsman'. Mid-19th century, originally *куста́рник*, then куста́рь (perhaps to avoid homonymy with куста́рник 'bushes'), -арь under the influence of бонда́рь 'cooper', etc. Purportedly from 15th-/16th century Ger. *kunst(n)er* 'expert craftsman, artist' (cited by Grimm, subsequently Ger. *Künstler* 'artist'), alternatively from куста́рный 'hand-made, amateurish', cf. dial. *куста́рник* 'weaver or other industrial worker working from home', also (Siberian dial.) 'vagrant hiding in the forest among the shrubs'.

КУХНЯ [kúchnja] 'kitchen'. 18th century, replacing *поварня*, id. (cf. по́вар 'cook'), probably via Pol. *kuchnia*, id. and Cz. *kuchyně*, id., from Ger. *Küche*, id. (OHG *chuhhina*, id., from Late Lat. *coquina*, id., cf. *coquō* 'I cook').

КУШАК [kušák] 'sash'. 16th-century Tkc. loan, cf. Turk. *kuşak*, id.

КУШАТЬ [kúšat'] 'to eat'. 14th-century OR *кушати*, id., probably a variant of *кусити* 'to taste', an early Gmc. loan, cf. Goth. *kausjan* 'to try, taste', whence also Fr. *choisir* 'to choose'.

Л

ЛАВИНА [lavína] 'avalanche'. Recorded in dictionaries since 1845 (cf. 18th-century óползень 'landslide', обвáл 'landslip'), from Ger. *Lawine* 'avalanche', via Romansh (a Romance dial. of SE Switzerland) *lavina*, id., ultimately from MLat. *labina*, id., Lat. *labor* 'I fall, glide', *lābēs* 'subsidence, fall'.

ЛАГЕРЬ [láger'] 'camp'. Early 18th century, from Ger. *Lager*, id., cognate with *liegen* 'to lie'.

ЛАДАН [ládan] 'incense'. 12th century, from Gk. *ládanon* 'ladanum' (a gum resin used in perfumery), ultimately Ar. *lādan* 'laudanum'.

ЛАДОНЬ [ladón'] 'palm of the hand'. A reshaping, through metathesis (д-л to л-д), of pre-18th-century OR *долонь*, id., cognate with Lith. *delnas*, id. Ultimately from CSl. *dolnь, perhaps lit. 'the part of the hand that faces down' (cf. IE *dol- 'bottom, hollow', долина 'valley'). Ладонь developed from initial *лодонь*, with ло- to ла- perhaps through *akan'je*.

ЛАК [lak] 'lacquer, varnish'. Early 18th century (15th-17th centuries as *лек*, seemingly from Pers. dial.), from Ger. *Lack*, id. or D. *lak*, id., cf. Ital. *lacca*, id., MLat. (*coccus*) *lacca* 'plant otherwise unknown' (Lat. *coccum* 'berry yielding a scarlet dye'), *lacca* 'lacquer'. Ultimately, via Ar./Pers., from Skr. *laksha* 'mark'.

ЛАКОМЫЙ [lákomyj] 'tasty'. 11th century, through metathesis from CSl. *olkomъ, deriving, as a pass. part. in -омый (cf. несóмый 'which is carried'), from OR *лакати* 'to hunger for'. Cf. cognates алкáть 'to hunger', áлчный 'greedy', Lith. *alkti*, 'to hunger'.

ЛАМПА [lámpa] 'lamp'. Early 18th century (лампáда, now 'icon-lamp', from Gk. dim. *lampádion* 'small torch', was still commoner in the meaning 'lamp' in the 18th century), from Fr. *lampe*, id. or Ger. *Lampe*, id. Ultimately, via Lat. *lampas* 'light, torch', from Gk. *lampás* 'light, torch, lamp'.

ЛАНДЫШ [lándyš] 'lily-of-the-valley'. 17th century, possibly from a variant of ла́дан 'incense' (with metathesis дн-нд), or from OPol. *łanie uszko*, lit. 'doe's ear', calqued from MLat. *auricula cervi*, id. (cf. standard Pol. *konwalia* 'lily-of-the-valley'), from the plant's ear-shaped leaves, increscent -д- perhaps by popular association with гла́дкий 'smooth', or from ла́да (folk/poet.) 'beloved', ла́данка *Origanum vulgare* (also known as души́ца, from души́стый 'fragrant'). Alternatively, from S. dial. *лан* 'field', thus lit. 'flower of the field' (for -ыш, cf. the plant гла́дыш *Origanum trilobum*). Finally, the name was perhaps transferred from some other plant, cf. dial. *ла́ндушка* 'swede'.

ЛАНЬ [lan'] 'doe'. First recorded in dictionaries 1771, replacing 11th-century *ланья* and 17th-century *ланъ*, ultimately from CSl. *olnь/*olni and cognate with оле́нь 'deer' and лось 'elk', Lith. *elnė* 'doe', Gk. *élaphos* 'deer', *ellós* 'fawn'.

ЛАПА [lápa] 'paw'. 17th century, from CSl. *lapa, earlier *lopa 'something flat' (cf. IE *lāpos 'paw, palm, hand'), with cognates in ла́поть 'bast shoe', лопу́х 'burdock' (perhaps from its broad leaves), лопа́та 'spade' (from its broad blade). Cf. also dial. *ла́пать* 'to seek, grope for', *ла́пить* 'to seize'.

ЛАСКА I [láska] 'caress'. 11th century 'flattery', then 'affection', perhaps from dial. *ла́сить* 'to flatter, fawn on'. Cf. ла́ститься 'to fawn on', Lat. *lascīvus* 'wanton'.

ЛАСКА II [láska] 'weasel'. Mid-18th century (cf. earlier *ласица* 'ferret'), probably from dial. *ла́са* 'gourmand', or from the animal's colour, cf. Latv. *loss* 'dun, light bay' (normally, however, of a horse). Alternatively a tabooistic euphemism based on ла́ска 'caress'.

ЛАСТ [last] 'flipper'. Recorded in dictionaries 1847, possibly via NR dial., from the Finnic group (according to Vasmer, Saami dial. for a back flipper), or from CSl. *lapstъ (cognate with ла́па 'paw'), with -pst simplifying to -st.

ЛАСТОЧКА [lástočka] 'swallow'. 1730s/40s (cf. earlier *ластка*, id.), from *ласта (cf. Serb. *ласта*, id.). Probably cognate with Lith. *lakstyti* 'to fly about' (cf. IE *lek- 'to fly'), and with -kst- simplifying to -st-, thus, perhaps, lit. 'flyer'. An association with *ласти́ться* 'to caress' arises from false etymology.

ЛАЧУГА [lačúga] 'hovel'. OR *алачуга* 'marquee', from Tkc. *ala(n)čyk* 'nomad's tent made of bark'. For discarded Tkc. a-, cf. *ло́шадь* 'horse'.

ЛАЯТЬ [lájat'] 'to bark'. 11th century *лаяти*, id., from CSl. *lajati, onomatopoeic IE *lāi̯ō 'roar, bark', cognate with Lat. *lātrō* 'I bark', Lith. *loti* 'to bark'.

ЛГАТЬ [lgat'] 'to lie'. 11th century *льгати*, ultimately from IE *leugh, id. (cf. Goth. *liugan*, id., OHG *liogan*, id., Ger. *lügen*, id., also *leugnen* 'to deny'), with derivatives in *ложь* 'lie' (-г- palatalizing to -ж- before -ь), *ло́жный* 'false', *лжи́вый* 'mendacious'.

ЛЕБЕДЬ [lébed'] 'swan'. 11th century, from CSl. *lebedь (IE *albhedis, id.), evolving from earlier *olbedь by inter-syllabic assimilation, lit. 'white (bird)', cf. IE *albhi̯s 'white', Lat. *albus*, id., OHG *elbiz* 'swan', 'Elbe', lit. 'white (river)'. Purportedly cognate with *лебеда́* 'goosefoot' (named for the shape of its leaves in Eng., and for the silvery deposit on its leaves in R.).

ЛЕВ [lev] 'lion'. 11th century, apparently a written loan, since an oral loan would have given *лёвъ*, cf. hypocoristic first name *Лёвушка*. The version with -e- was also in use as the name of Byz. emperors, popes, princes and boyars. From Lat. *leo*, id., possibly via OHG *lewo*, id. (Ger. *Löwe*, id.), ultimately from Gk. *léōn*, id., itself probably from an African language.

ЛЕГКОЕ [lëgkoje] 'lung'. Neut. adj. noun, lit. 'light'. As originally observed by hunters and persons offering up sacrifices, the lung is lighter than water and does not sink, unlike other organs such as heart and liver, cf. Eng. *lights* (lungs of sheep, etc., used as food), Gk. *pleúmōn* 'lung' alongside *pléō* 'I float'

(IE *pleu- 'to float'), Ger. *Lunge* 'lung', from IE *le(u)guh 'light', Ir. *scaman* 'light, lungs', etc.

ЛЕД [led] 'ice'. 11th century, with Balt. cognates, cf. Lith. *ledas*, id.

ЛЕЖАТЬ [ležát'] 'to lie'. 11th century, from CSl. *ležati (earlier *legěti, with -g- palatalizing to -ž- before -ě- and subsequently -ě- changing to -a- after -ž-). Cognate with Gk. *léchomai* 'I lie down', Lat. *lectus* 'bed', Goth. *ligan* 'to lie', Ger. *liegen*, id.

ЛЕНТА [lénta] 'ribbon'. 17th-/early 18th centuries (cf. 11th-century *лентии* 'towel, linen cloth', IE *līntos 'flaxen'), with final -a possibly under the influence of тесьмá 'ribbon for tying'. From Late Gk. *léntion* 'cloth, napkin, towel', Lat. *linteum* 'linen cloth', *linum* 'flax', alternatively from Ger. dial. *Linte* 'ribbon' (Vasmer) or D. *lint/lintje*, id. Cf. also Eng. *lint* (perhaps from Fr. *linette* 'linseed', cf. Fr. *lin* 'flax').

ЛЕНЬ [len'] 'laziness'. Through deaffixation from OR *лѣнивыи* 'lazy' (cf. зéлень 'greenery' from зелёный 'green'), possibly cognate with Lat. *lēnis* 'tender, soft', Eng. *lenient*.

ЛЕС [les] 'forest'. 11th-/12th centuries 'forest, timber', from CSl. *lěsъ 'trees as source of building material, fuel or wooden artefacts', then 'forest, timber' (cf. Serb. *лес* 'building material'). Cognate with OE *læs* 'pasture'.

ЛЕСТНИЦА [léstnica] 'staircase, ladder'. 14th century (earlier *лѣствица*, id., from CSl. *lěstva, cf. *lezti 'to climb', with -z- devoicing to -s- before -t-, or from the influence of лесá 'scaffolding', cf. also лéсенка 'step-ladder'). Subsequently лéстница by analogy with nouns in -ница, e.g. кýзница 'smithy'.

ЛЕСТЬ [lest'] 'flattery'. 11th century *льсть* 'cunning' (cf. IE *list- 'guile'), then 'flattery', from Gmc. *listi- (originally 'skill, adroitness'), Goth. acc. pl. *lists*, OHG/MHG *list* 'cunning'. Wrongly associated with лизáть 'to lick' (cf. подлизáться 'to suck up to').

ЛЕТЕТЬ [letét'] 'to fly'. From CSl. *lektěti/*letěti 'to fly' (-kt- perhaps from a contamination of IE *lēk- 'fly' and *pet-, id., cf. Gk. *pétomai* 'I fly'), with -kt- simplifying to -t- (cf. analogous correlation in Lat. *plectō* and плету́ 'I braid'). Cognates in Lith. *lėkti* 'to fly', *lakstyti* 'to fly about'.

ЛЕТО [léto] 'summer'. 11th century 'time, summer', subsequently 'year' (i.e. 'from one summer to the next'). Possibly from an early form of лить 'to pour', thus 'time of rains' (cf. Lith. *lietus* 'rain'), or connected with Lat. *laetus* 'joyful', more controversially with Celtic words meaning 'festival', cf. also Ir. *la* 'day' (pl. *laethanta*). Based on an IE root perhaps meaning 'time when the sun shines and warms'.

ЛЕЧИТЬ [lečít'] 'to treat' (medically). From Gmc., cf. Goth *lēkeis* 'doctor', *lēkinōn* 'to cure', Norw. *laege* 'physician'. Perhaps initially of Celtic origin (cf. Ir. *leigheas* 'medicine', Gael. *leigh* 'physician', *leighus* 'cure'). Comprises CSl. *lěkъ 'medicine' + -iti, with -k- palatalizing to -č- before -i-. Cognates include лече́бный 'medicinal' (from *лечьба* 'treatment') and лека́рство 'medicine'. Alternatively, if less plausibly, linked with IE *leĝō 'gather, read', in which case originally of the gathering of herbs, or words, to cast a spell.

ЛЕЧЬ [leč'] 'to lie down'. From CSl. *legti, id., -gt- changing to -kt-, then -č-, before -i, cf. Gk. *léktron* 'couch', Lat. *lectus* 'bed', Ger. *liegen* 'to lie', *legen* 'to lay'. Possibly also cognate with Lat. *lex* 'law', lit. 'what is laid down' (alternatively from Lat. *ligō* 'I bind', thus 'what is binding'), cf. analogous semantic correlations in Ger. *Gesetz* 'law', *setzen* 'to place', Lat. *statūtum* 'statute', *statuō* 'I cause to stand', etc.

ЛИКОВАТЬ [likovát'] 'to rejoice'. Based on OR *ликъ* 'singing, choir', from Goth. *laiks* 'dance', *laikan* 'to jump' (IE *lāĝō, id.) and cognate with Lith. *laigyti* 'to caper'.

ЛИЛОВЫЙ [lilóvyj] 'lilac'. 18th-/early 19th centuries, based on Fr. *lilas*, id., perhaps via Ger. *lila* 'lilac-coloured', ultimately from Skr. *nīlaḥ* 'dark blue', Pers. *lailak* 'lilac', *nīl* 'blue, indigo', *līlak*, a variant of *nīlak* 'bluish' (with assimilation of n-l to l-l), from the bluish tinge of the flowers.

ЛИМОН [limón] 'lemon'. 16th century, from Byz. Gk. *lemóni*, id., or directly from Ital. *limone*, id., ultimately, via Ar. *laimūn*, id., from Pers. *līmūn* id. Лимонáд 'lemonade' is an early 18th-century loan, via Fr. *limonade*, id., from Ital. *limonata*, id.

ЛИНЕЙКА [linéjka] 'ruler'. Early 18th century, from *линея* (later лúния) 'line', via Ger. *Linie*, id. or Pol. *linia* 'line, ruler', ultimately Lat. *līnea* 'linen thread, plumb-line', *linum* 'flax'.

ЛИПА [lípa] 'lime-tree'. Balto-Slav. (cf. Lith. *liepa*, id., IE *lipō 'stick, glue'), cognate with лúпнуть 'to stick', лúпкий 'sticky', Lith. *lipti* 'to stick to', from the tree's sticky sap, or the sticky deposit left on its leaves by the aphis fly. Лúпа 'forgery' is from card-sharpers' jargon, cf. *липóк* 'fixative that sticks two cards so that the player can reveal either', *липкóвое очкó* 'detachable pip on a playing card'.

ЛИСА [lisá] 'fox'. 11th century *лисица*, 12th century *лисъ*, лисá in dictionaries from 1792, with Balt. cognate in Latv. *lapsa*, id., and -ps- simplifying to Slav. -s-. Cf. p and p + s in Lith. *lapė* 'fox', Fr. *loup* 'wolf', Skr. *lopāśa* 'jackal, fox or similar animal', Gk. *alṓpēs* 'fox', Lat. *volpēs/vulpēs*, id. (there appears to be no unified IE root, cf. IE *alōu̯-pēḱs 'fox').

ЛИХОРАДКА [lichorádka] 'fever'. From лихорáдить 'to be feverish', originally 'to wish evil', from лúхо (poet.) 'evil', dial. *радúть* 'to desire', possibly tabooistic in origin, cf. ни пýху ни перá 'good luck', lit. 'neither fur nor feather'. (In popular tradition, fevers assumed the form of sister-temptresses, ugly hags or the daughters of Herod, the king who executed John the Baptist.)

ЛИЦЕМЕР [licemér] 'hypocrite'. From ChSl., possibly calqued from Gk. *prosōpolḗptēs* 'respecter of persons' (*prósōpon* 'face, mask, person', *lḗptēs* 'one who accepts, receives'), based on *lice 'face' + *měriti (мéрить) 'to measure, try on', thus lit. 'one who tries on a face'. Alternatively, based on root *-měnъ

109

'change', dissimilating (m-n to m-r) to *měra/*měriti 'measure', thus, lit. 'face-changer', cf. Lith. *veidmainys* 'hypocrite' (*veidas* 'face', *mainytis* 'change').

ЛИЦО [licó] 'face'. 11th century *лице*, id., CSl. *lice, from *lik- (cf. лик 'representation of a face on an ikon'), with -k- changing to -c- after -i- (third palatalization of velars), then -e changing to -o following the hardening of OR -ц-.

ЛОБ [lob] 'forehead'. CSl. *lъbъ 'skull, cranium', OR *лъбъ/лобъ* 'skull, head' (cf. Pol. *łeb* 'animal's head', derogatorily used of a human head, Gk *lófos* 'back of head, brow of hill', also reg. *взлóбок* 'low rise'). Meaning later narrows to 'forehead'. Лóбное мéсто 'a raised central area for executions and other punishments and the proclamation of royal decrees' is said to be a translation of Gk. *kraníou tópos*, lit. 'place of the skull'.

ЛОВКИЙ [lóvkij] 'adroit, cunning'. From ловѝть 'to catch', лов 'hunting, catching'. Initially 'skilled in hunting', then 'physically adroit', finally 'cunning'.

ЛОДКА [lódka] 'boat'. Ultimately from CSl. *oldī 'dug-out canoe, boat', with ol- to lo- through metathesis. Cf., from ChSl., ладья́ (poet.) 'boat' (the meaning 'rook' in chess is recorded in dictionaries from 1762), Lith. *eldija* 'canoe'.

ЛОДЫЖКА [lodýžka] 'ankle'. Ultimately, with metathesis from д-л to л-д, from *долъ* 'bottom' (cf. ладóнь 'palm of the hand'). Alternatively, from Pol. *łodyga*, dim. *łodyżka* 'stalk', cf. also OR *лодыга* 'base, foot of hill'.

ЛОЖА [lóža] 'box in theatre'. First half of 18th century, replacing earlier чула́н (now 'store-room'), from Fr. *loge* 'box', via Ger. *Loge*, id. (cf. Ital. *loggia* 'lodge, terrace', alongside *palco* 'box in theatre').

ЛОЖКА [lóžka] 'spoon'. 12th century, from CSl. *lъžьka, ultimately IE *loug̑- 'to break', or perhaps directly from Alb. *lugë* 'spoon'. Initial meaning was probably 'splinter, chip', then 'implement for ladling liquids', cf. Eng. *spoon*, originally 'chip, splinter', then 'spoon', cognate with Ger. *Span* 'splinter, chip'. Alternatively from IE *lūĝ- 'to bend', also 'groove, spoon, ladle' (the prototype of a spoon being a hand bent in the form of a scoop), cf. Gk. *lygízō* 'I bend or twist as one does a withe' (tough flexible branch used for binding bundles, etc.).

ЛОЗУНГ [lózung] 'slogan'. Early 18th century, from Ger. *Losung* 'daily scripture, slogan, motto'.

ЛОКОН [lókon] 'lock, curl'. Early 18th century, based on Ger. pl. *Locken* 'curls', assumed to be a sing. noun, hence лóкон 'curl'. Cf. набáт 'tocsin', etc.

ЛОКОТЬ [lókot'] 'elbow, cubit, ell'. From CSl. *olkъt-, IE *el̯nā 'ell, elbow', with ol- to lo- through metathesis, cognate with Lat. *ūlna* 'elbow', Lith. *alkūnė*, id., Eng. *elbow* (ell from Gmc. *alino, IE *olena 'forearm' + bow 'to bend'). The form of the word was possibly affected by нóготь 'finger-nail' (since лóкоть 'ell' was measured from the elbow to the tip of the middle finger).

ЛОМОТЬ [lomót'] 'slice'. Comprises OR *ломъ* 'breaking' (cf. IE *lomei̯ō 'cut, break', ломáть 'to break') + suffix -оть, cf. кусóк 'bit', from кусáть 'to bite'.

ЛОПАСТЬ [lópast'] 'blade' (of oar, etc.). Recorded in 18th-century dictionaries, based on CSl. *lopa 'something flat', IE *lop- 'flat piece, shovel', through deaffixation from dial. *лопáстый* 'broad-ended, flat-ended'. Cognate with лопáта 'spade' (an implement with a flat blade).

ЛОСК [losk] 'gloss'. First recorded in dictionaries 1704, ultimately from IE *leuk- 'bright, light'. Cognate with лосни́ться 'to shine' (-н- a verbal suffix), лунá 'moon', луч 'ray', лы́сый 'bald', Lith. *lūšis* 'lynx', Ger. *Luchs*, id. (from the animal's light-grey fur or keen sight, cf. IE *lukˆsnis 'lynx').

ЛОСОСЬ [losós'] 'salmon'. 1500 (fem., now masc.), from CSl., cognate with Pol. *łosoś*, id., Lith. *lašiša*, id., Ger. *Lachs*, id., IE *laksos, id. The word root purportedly contains the meaning 'speckle', thus the salmon may be named from the black dots on its sides. Scholars studying fish names in the hope of identifying the region where the IE community lived have paid particular attention to the word-family represented by Ger. *Lachs*/лосось 'salmon' (apparently not, for example, found in rivers emptying into the Black Sea or Mediterranean, Atlantic and Pacific constituting the two major families of salmon). See also бук 'beech'.

ЛОСЬ [los'] 'elk'. From CSl. *olsь (IE *elk-), with ol- to lo- through metathesis and cognates in олень 'deer', лань 'doe', Gk. *álkē* 'elk', Lat. *alcēs*, id., Ger. *Elch*, id.

ЛОШАДЬ [lóšad'] 'horse'. 12th/13th centuries, perhaps originally denoting a breed of steppe horse (recorded Kiev 1103, already with suffix -дь, possibly a collective ending -- cf. челядь 'retainers' -- while конь, maybe originally the *Eur.* horse, was still used in Moscow in the 12th century). From Tkc. *(a)laša (perhaps from Mong.), cf. also Tkc. *alatsa at* 'skewbald' and Kazach *at* 'horse of any kind, specifically a gelding'. For discarded Tkc. a-, cf. лачуга 'hovel'. Cognates include 13th-century лошак 'hinny' (off-spring of she-ass and stallion, -ак perhaps by association with ишак 'ass, hinny'), Ukr. *лоша* 'foal' (but *кінь* 'horse'), Pol. *loszę/loszak* (reg.) 'foal'. Final -адь, if not collective, possibly derives from earlier gen. *лошате, or is a rendering of Tkc. *at* 'horse'.

ЛУЖА [lúža] 'puddle'. 13th century, from CSl. *luža/*lougiā (with -g- palatalizing to -ž- before -i-), perhaps related to IE *louk-/*luk- 'shining', less likely to be connected with луг 'meadow'.

ЛУК I [luk] 'bow'. 11th century 'bow, saddle bow', from CSl. *lǫkъ, id. (IE *lonquos 'bent, crooked', cf. Lith. *lenkti* 'bend', *lankas* 'bow'), with -ǫ- changing to -у- in ESl. and cognates in лука 'bend in river, saddle pommel', излучина 'bend', облучок 'coachman's seat' (originally curved front sections of sledge runners), лукавый 'cunning'.

ЛУК II [luk] 'onions'. 11th century, ultimately Gmc., cf. Ger.

Lauch 'leek'.

ЛУНА [luná] 'moon'. 11th century, from IE *louksna (-ksn- simplifying to -n-), cf. Gk. *leukós* 'light, bright, clear', Lat. *luna* 'moon', *lux* 'light'. Maybe directly from Lat. *luna*, cf. also Gk. *lúchnos*, pl. *lúchna* 'light, lamp'. Synonymous месяц 'moon, month' is held by some to refer to the moon only in sickle shape, i.e. in one of its quarters.

ЛУЧ [luč] 'ray'. 11th century, based on IE *leuk- 'to shine' + suffix -jь-, with -k to -č before -j- by first palatalization of velars, lit. 'light, something shining'. Cf. лучи́на 'torch' (for lighting a peasant hut), Lat. *lūceō* 'I shine'.

ЛУЧШИЙ [lúčšij] 'better, best'. 11th century лучии 'better, distinguished', perhaps from *lučiti, the basis of случи́ться 'to happen'. Alternatively, the comparative of *лукьıи 'designated by fate' (cf. OR лучаи 'chance'), thus lit. 'more suitable', or from IE *leuk- 'to shine', thus originally perhaps 'brighter'.

ЛЫСЫЙ [lýsyj] 'bald'. 15th century, based on IE *leuk- 'to shine', thus perhaps properly 'with a shining scalp'.

ЛЮБОВЬ [ljubóv'] 'love'. 11th century, based on the oblique cases of любы, acc. любъвь, the acc. being subsequently adopted as the nom./acc. Cognate with любо́й 'any', from OR любьıи 'beloved', then 'chosen', finally 'anyone you choose'.

ЛЮДИ [ljúdi] 'people'. 11th century, pl. of *ljudь 'person, people', then of челове́к 'person' (cf. earlier singulative люди́н). Ultimately from IE *leudhō 'grow, thrive', *leudhis 'tribe, people' and cognate with Ger. *Leute* 'people' (cf. OHG *liut*, pl. *liuti* 'members of the alliance eligible for military service and attendance at the assembly'), Lith. *liaudis* 'people, nation'.

ЛЯГУШКА [ljagúška] 'frog'. Early 17th century at latest, based on dial. ля́га 'leg, hip' (hence ляга́ть 'to kick', ля́жка 'thigh, haunch') + -ух(а) + -(ь)ка (cf. dial. лягу́ха 'large frog'), -ch- palatalizing to -š- before -ь-. The frog is thus named for its long back legs.

M

МАЗУРКА [mazúrka] 'mazurka'. Early 19th century, from Pol. *mazurek*, id. (cf. masc. names of dances *krakowiak* and *kujawiak*). Named after the Mazurians (Pol. *Mazurzy*, sing. *Mazur*, fem. *Mazurka*), the inhabitants of Mazovia (Pol. *Mazowsze*) in Warsaw province, where the dance -- originally a folk dance -- came from. Ending -ка by analogy with венгéрка 'Hungarian dance', etc.

МАЙ [maj] 'May'. 11th century, via Byz. Gk. *Máïos* and ChSl., from Lat. *Māius* 'May' (after Maya, Roman goddess of the spring, mother of Hermes, wife of Vulcan), cognate with *māior* 'greater', thus perhaps lit. 'fostering growth'. False etymological association with мáяться 'to toil, pine, suffer' is said to have made May weddings unpopular in Russia, cf. saying В мáе женúться -- век промáяться 'Marry in May, suffer a lifetime.'

МАЙКА [májka] 'T-shirt, sports vest'. First recorded in Ušakov, from Fr. *maillot* 'sports vest'. Alternatively from май 'May' (there are no analogous derivations of clothing from the names of months, but cf. веснýшка 'freckle', from веснá 'spring'). Ending -ка possibly by analogy with рубáшка 'shirt', etc. Мáйка most convincingly derives, via Serb. *maja* 'sports vest', from Ital. *maglia* 'stitch', then, probably under the influence of Fr. *maillot*, 'sports vest', of the pink or yellow jerseys awarded to the winners of stages in the *Coppa d'Italia* cycle race (probably from N. Ital. dials. bordering on SSl. territories).

МАЛЕВАТЬ [malevát'] 'to paint'. From Pol. *malować*, id., itself a reshaping of Ger. *malen*, id.

МАЛИНА [malína] 'raspberries'. 17th century, associated, from the colour of the berries, with IE *mēl- 'blue, dark, stained', cf. Lith. *mėlynas* 'blue', *mėlynė* 'bilberry', Gk. *mélas* 'black, murky', MLat. *mulleolus* 'reddish', Lat. *mōrum* 'mulberry', Ger. *Mal* 'sign, stain, spot', alternatively with мáлый 'small' (since the raspberry is faceted into small sections). For -ина 'berries', cf. сморóдина 'currants', etc.

МАЛОДУШИЕ [malodúšije] 'faint-heartedness'. 11th century, from a ChSl. calque of Gk. *oligopsychía*, id., from *olígos* 'small', *psyché* 'soul, spirit'.

МАЛЫЙ [mályj] 'small'. 11th century 'small, undistinguished' (маленький 'small' 17th century), with cognates in m-/sm-: Lat. *macer* 'lean, meagre' (alongside *malus* 'bad'), Gk. *mēlon* 'small cattle', Lith. *mažas* 'small', Goth. *smals, id. (cf. Ger. *schmal* 'narrow'). Cf. p- in Romance words for small: Lat. *parvus*, Fr. *petit*, Sp. *pequeño*, Ital. *piccolo*.

МАЛЬЧИК [mál'čik] 'boy'. Recorded in dictionaries 1731, from OR assumed *малыць (cf. coll. малец/малéц) 'lad' + dim. suffix -ик, with -ц- to -ч- before -и-. Based on малый 'small'.

МАЛЯР [maljár] 'painter' (domestic). 17th century, from Pol. *malarz*, id. (domestic and artistic), possibly via Ukr., a reshaping of Ger. *Maler*, id. Cf. малевáть (coll.) 'to paint' (beside писáть for artistic, крáсить for domestic painting).

МАЛЯРИЯ [maljaríja] 'malaria'. 19th century (1861 малáрия), from Ital. *malaria*, id. (*mala* 'bad', *aria* 'air' -- malaria was thought to be caused by bad air).

МАМОНТ [mámont] 'mammoth'. 17th century (for some time in the 19th century also *мамут*, cf. Pol./Cz. *mamut*, id.), possibly from a Jakut or Tungus word meaning 'living in the ground' (the mammoth was thought to be a burrowing animal, cf. Tatar *mama* 'earth' and 17th-century accounts of a 'sea elephant' that lived underground). Alternatively, from Gk. *mammoúth*, with phonetic shape affected, perhaps, by the OR name Мамонть, cf. absence of -n- in Eng., and in Fr. *mammouth*, id., Ger. *Mammut*, id., explained, perhaps, by a misreading of -on- as -ou-, or by derivation from an earlier form. Finally, the name could have been transferred from some other exotic animal, based on the *мамоны* (nocturnal predators said to live in hills or rocks) described in travellers' tales from India, perhaps wild cats or lynxes, or, perhaps most logically in view of the burrowing legends, mole-like creatures (cf., however, OR *мамоны* 'monkeys').

МАНИ́ТЬ [manít'] 'to beckon, lure'. Recorded in dictionaries since 1731, cognate with Skr. *māya* 'creating illusions', маха́ть 'to wave', possibly мани́шка 'false shirt-front', with derogatory suffix -ишк(а). See also обма́н 'deception', мая́к 'beacon'.

МАРГАРИ́ТКА [margarítka] 'daisy'. 18th century, from Ger. *Margerite*, id. or Fr. *marguerite*, id., ultimately Lat. *margarīta* 'pearl', Gk. *margarítēs*, id., from the flower's resemblance to a pearl (cf. маргари́н 'margarine', from its similarity to the *colour* of pearl or the pearly lustre of the crystals of 'margaric acid' -- Fr. *margarique* -- that margarine was thought to contain).

МА́РКА [márka] 'stamp'. Recorded in dictionaries 1861 (the first, ten-kopeck, stamp was introduced in Russia 1857-58), from Ger. *Marke*, id. In the meaning 'make, brand', late 19th century from Fr. *marque* 'mark, trade-mark'.

МА́РЛЯ [márlja] 'gauze'. Recorded in dictionaries of the 1860s (as *ма́рли* and ма́рля), from Fr. *marli*, a type of gauze in use during the 18th century, seemingly manufactured in Marly-la-Machine (section of Bougival (Yvelines) commune, better known for the hydraulic machine constructed by Rennequin under Louis XIV to supply the Marly acqueduct, which conveyed the waters of the Seine to Versailles and functioned 1682-1818), -я back-formed on the assumption that -и was a gen. sing. ending.

МАРТ [mart] 'March'. 11th century, from Lat. *Mārtius*, id., via Gk. *Márti(o)s* and ChSl., ultimately from Mars, the god of war, whose festival was celebrated in this, the first month of the Roman year.

МА́СКА [máska] 'mask'. Late 17th-/18th centuries (originally *машкара*, *машка*, replacing earlier ха́ря, id., now 'mug' (= 'face')), from Ital. *maschera* 'mask', via Ger. *Maske*, id. or Fr. *masque*, id., ultimately Ar. *maskhara* 'buffoonery' (cf., from Ital. *maschera*, Eng. *mascara* 'cosmetic for darkening eyebrows, eyelashes'). Derivative маскара́д 'masked ball' was adopted in the 18th century.

МАСЛИНА [maslína] 'olive'. 11th century, from a ChSl. calque of Gk. *elaía* 'olive-tree, olive' (cf. *élaion* 'olive-oil'), on the basis of масло 'butter, oil'.

МАСЛО [máslo] 'butter, oil'. 11th century, from CSl. *mazslo, comprising the root of *mazati (мáзать) 'to grease, smear' (whence deaffixed мазь 'ointment') + agent suffix -slo, and with resultant -zsl- simplifying to -sl-. Lit. 'what you smear with' (cf. мы́ло 'soap', 'what you wash with'), said to come originally from the habit of smearing the body as a protection against cold and insects, and for hygiene.

МАСТЕР [máster] 'foreman, master craftsman'. No later than the 10th century, from Byz. Gk. *mástoras* 'master craftsman', final -er possibly under the influence of Pol. *majster* 'foreman'. Alternatively, from Lat. *magister* via MHG *meistar*. Мáстер was also used to denote the Grand Master of the German Knights 1229, later the Bishop of Riga (Russia, esp. Novgorod, Pskov and Smolensk, maintained relations with Riga through Baltic trade), also, from the 16th century, master gunsmiths, armourers, printers, etc.

МАСШТАБ [masštáb] 'scale'. First half of the 18th century, from Ger. *Maßstab* 'ruler, scale', lit. 'measuring stick' (Ger. *Maß* 'measure', *Stab* 'staff, stick').

МАТЕРИК [materík] 'mainland'. 17th century, based on матёрый (coll.) 'experienced, strong, practised', also (obs., provincial) 'relating to the mainland', cf. матёрая земля 'terra firma', cognate with мать 'mother'.

МАТРАС/МАТРАЦ [matrás]/[matrác] 'mattress'. 18th century (cf. 1731 *мадрац*), contemporary forms recorded 1804, матрáс from D. *matras*, id., матрáц from Ger. *Matratze*, id., both ultimately from Ar. *al-maṭrah* 'cushion, pillow' (from a root meaning 'to lay, throw down'), via Ital. *materasso* 'mattress'.

МАТРОС [matrós] 'sailor'. Late 17th century, originally commoner in the form *мамроз*, from D. *matroos*, id., seemingly

16th century from Fr. pl. *matelots* 'sailors', OFr. *matenot*, itself from MD *mattennoot*, lit. 'bed mate' (a reference to the original need for sailors to share their hammocks), alternatively 'table companion' (*maat* 'companion', *genoot* = *genoten* from *genieten* 'to enjoy', cf. *genot* 'enjoyment').

МАТЬ [mat'] 'mother'. 11th century, from CSl. *mati, gen. *matere, IE *mātē/*mātēr-, id., based on onomatopoeic *mā, cf. Skr. *mā̆tri̯*, id., Gk. *mḗtēr*, id., Lat. *mā̆ter*, id. Loss of -r- is characteristic of Balto-Slav., cf. Lith. *motina*, id., Latv. *mā̆te*, id. Cognates include мáчеха 'step-mother' (with pejorative suffix -еха, cf. дурёха 'stupid woman').

МАЯК [maják] 'lighthouse, beacon'. Recorded in dictionaries from 1771, originally 'beacon', but known earlier (beacons were lit on the steppe during nomad invasions), based on OR *маяти* 'to wave, sway', thus lit. 'that which looms' (cf. мая́чит 'looms'), whence also мáятник 'pendulum'. See too мани́ть 'to entice', махáть 'to wave' (cf. IE *mā̄i̯ō 'sign, wave').

МЕБЕЛЬ [mébel'] 'furniture'. Early 18th century (mainly in pl. until end of century), from Fr. *meuble* 'movable', also 'piece of furniture', *meubles* 'furniture', possibly via Ger. *Möbel*, id. or Pol. *mebel* 'piece of furniture', pl. *meble* 'furniture'. Ultimately from Vulg. Lat. *mōbilis* 'movable', *mōbile* (coll.) 'movable goods'.

МЕД [mëd] 'honey'. 11th century (IE *medhu, id.), with cognates in Lith. *medus*, id., Eng. *mead*, Gk. *méthy* 'wine' (cf. *methyl* -- whence *methylated spirit* -- 'hypothetical radical of wood spirit', from Gk. *méthy* + *húlē* 'wood'), Dan. *Mjød* 'mead' (alongside *Honning* 'honey').

МЕДВЕДЬ [medvéd'] 'bear'. 11th century, from CSl. *medvědь/*meduedis, lit. 'honey eater' (*medv- + *ědь), a euphemism for an original taboo form probably similar to Gk. *árktos* 'bear' (from IE onomatopoeic *r̥kts- 'bear'). The interpretation 'honey *knower*' is a false etymology based on confusion with вéдать 'to know'.

МЕЖДОМЕТИЕ [meždométije] 'interjection'. 17th century, calqued from MLat. *interjectiō*, id., lit. 'throwing between' (*inter*/между 'between', *ject*-/мет- 'throw'), with -у- replaced by connective -о-.

МЕЛ [mel] 'chalk'. OR мѣлъ 'lime', from CSl. *melъ 'small, finely ground' (cf. молóть 'to grind', IE *mel-, id.), later substantivized as 'fine limestone, chalk', whence мéлкий 'small, fine', also 'shallow', cf. мель 'shoal, the shallows', which derived by reaffixation from мелъ (cf. also IE *mēlos 'shallow'). Cognates of мел include Lith. *miltai* 'flour', Ger. *Mehl*, id., cf. also 14th-century derivative мéльница 'mill'.

МЕНЬШЕВИК [men'ševík] 'Menshevik'. Arose after the second congress of the Russian Social Democratic Workers' Party in 1903 to denote the more moderate section of the party, on the basis of мéньше 'less' + suffix -(ев)ик (cf. большевúк 'Bolshevik'), later interpreted as 'one in the minority'. Variant *меньшевист* survives only in the adj. меньшевúстский 'Menshevik'. Меньшинствó 'minority' is calqued from Fr. *minorité*, id., cf. Ger. *Minderheit*, id.

МЕРА [méra] 'measure'. 11th century (IE *mēros 'measure, division, share'). For commoner suffix -р, cf. дар 'gift', etc.

МЕСТИ [mestí] 'to sweep'. 11th century 'to throw' (cf. Lith. *mesti*, id., метáть, id., IE *metō, id.). First recorded in present meaning in dictionaries 1704. From CSl. *metti (-st- following dissimilation), with cognates in метлá 'broom', метéль 'snowstorm' and сметáна 'soured cream', a fem. short-form part. (perhaps часть 'part' understood) from сметáть 'to sweep away, together', thus lit. 'what is skimmed from the milk'.

МЕСТО [mésto] 'place'. 11th century 'place, container, post', from CSl., with Balt. cognates (Latv. *mist* 'to live', Lith. *misti* 'to feed oneself'). The meaning 'town' (cf. Ukr. *мicmo*, id.) is of WSl. provenance (cf. Pol. *miasto* 'town', *miejsce* 'place', Cz. *město* 'town', *misto* 'place'), calqued from OHG *stat* 'place, town', cf. Ger. *Stadt* 'town'.

119

МЕСТЬ [mest'] 'revenge'. 11th century 'retribution', subsequently also 'punishment', from CSl. *мьтть (cf. IE *moit 'turn, change'), with -tt- dissimilating to -st- and medial -ь- vocalizing to -e-, originally (Cyganenko) 'substitution', subsequently 'evil for evil, revenge'. There are cognates in Sicilian Gk. *moitos* 'thanks, favour', Lat. *mūtuus* 'reciprocal', and a possible connection with мзда (now facetious) 'recompense'. Cf. мстить 'to avenge'.

МЕСЯЦ [mésjac] 'month, moon'. 11th century, id., from CSl. *měsęcь, IE *mēns/*mēnes/*mēnō, id., *menot, id., also 'moon change' (cf. Gk. *mḗn* 'month', *mḗnē* 'moon', Lat. *mēnsis* 'month', Lith. *mènuo* 'month, moon', *mènulis* 'moon', Ger. *Mond* 'moon', *Monat* 'month', etc.), with -ę- changing to R. -я-. The practice in antiquity of measuring time by the phases of the moon links the meanings 'month' and 'moon', cf. also a link with the root *mē- 'measure', e.g. Lat. *mēnsis* 'month', *mēnsūra* 'measurement'. See луна́ 'moon'.

МЕТАФОРА [metáfora] 'metaphor'. 18th century, originally as a rhet. device, ultimately, via Lat. *metaphora*, id., from Gk. *metaphorá*, lit. meaning 'carrying from one place to another', fig. 'transferring to one word the sense of another'. Cf. Gk. *metá* 'change of place, condition', *phorá* 'carrying', also перено́сный 'portable, figurative'.

МЕТЕЛЬ [metél'] 'snow-storm'. From the root of мести́ 'to sweep' (cf. на дворе́ метёт 'there is a snow-storm outside'), with suffix -ель (cf. купе́ль 'font' from купа́ть 'to bathe'). Less plausibly from мета́ть 'to throw'.

МЕЧ [meč] 'sword'. CSl. *мьčь, probably from Goth. *mēkeis, id. (found in acc. sing. *mēki*), with -k- changing to -č- before a front vowel, alternatively borrowed by Gmc. and Slav. from a third source.

МЕЧТА [mečtá] 'dream'. 11th century, from CSl. *мьčta, IE *mīk 'shine, flash, twinkle', seemingly (Šanskij) initially 'phantom, vision'. Possibly cognate with Lat. *micō* 'I dart to and fro'.

МЕШОК [mešók] 'bag, sack'. Dim. from OR мѣхъ 'hide, bag, sack' (cf. Pushkin's Ко́зий мех, вино́м нали́тый 'A goatskin bag filled with wine'), later 'fur', with -х palatalizing to -ш- in мешо́к (cf. пастушо́к, dim. of пасту́х 'shepherd'). Cognate with Lith. *maišas* 'bag'.

МИГ [mig] 'instant'. Recorded in dictionaries since 1731, from CSl. *migti, IE *meigh- 'to wink, sleep'/*mīg 'wink, blink' (cf. Lith. *migti* 'to fall asleep'), seemingly first 'blinking', subsequently 'instant'. Cognate with мига́ть 'to blink', мгнове́ние 'instant'. Note that the МиГ fighter plane was named after its designers, A.I. Mikoján and M.I. Gurévič.

МИГРЕНЬ [migrén'] 'migraine'. Early 19th century, from Fr. *migraine*, id., MLat. *hemicrania*, id., from Gk. *hēmikranía*, lit. 'half the skull' (the ailment affects one side of the head only).

МИЗИНЕЦ [mizínec] 'little finger'. OR мѣзиньць 'younger son, little finger', from мѣзиньш 'smaller, younger', ме- changing to ми- through assimilation to medial -и- or through *ikan'je*. Alternatively said to be a pet name cognate with Pol. *umizgać się* 'to pay court'.

МИЛИЦИЯ [milícija] 'police'. 17th-/18th centuries 'militia, levy', probably via Pol. *milicja* 'militia' and Fr. *milice* (earlier *milicie*), id., from Lat. *mīlitia* 'military service, warfare, soldiery'. Ultimately from Lat. *mīles* 'soldier'. Name given to the Soviet police force by a decree of 28 October (10 November NS) 1917.

МИЛОСЕРДИЕ [milosérdije] 'mercy, charity'. From a ChSl. calque of Lat. *misericordia* 'compassion, mercy' (*miser* 'wretched', *cor* 'heart') or OHG *armiherzida* 'compassion'. OHG *armherzi* (cf. Ger. *barmherzig* 'compassionate', b- from *erbarmen* 'to move to pity') is a calque of Lat. *misericors*, lit. 'who has a heart for the poor'. Милосе́рдие, out of favour due to the brutalizing effect of Stalinism, was restored post-1985.

МИНДАЛЬ [mindál'] 'almond-tree, almonds'. 16th century at latest (also *мигдаль*), from Gk. *amygdálē/amýgdalon* 'almonds', possibly via Lat. *amygdalum*/Late Lat. *amandula* and Pol. *migdał* 'almond', with m-g to m-n through secondary nasalization, possibly influenced by OHG *mandala* 'almond'. Ultimately, миндáль perhaps results from the contamination of Gk. *amygdálē*, Late Lat. *amandula* and OHG *mandala*.

МИНУТА [minúta] 'minute'. Late 17th century or early 18th century (originally 'one sixtieth of a degree', then 'one sixtieth of an hour'), from Lat. *minūta* (via Ger. *Minute* 'minute' or Fr. *minute*, id.), fem. pass. part. of *minuō* 'I diminish, reduce to small pieces', an ellipsis of *pars minūta prima* 'first small part' (of the hour), i.e. 'minute' (cf. *pars minūta secunda* 'second small part' (of an hour), i.e. 'second', see секу́нда, id.). Until the 18th century in Russia time was counted without minutes and seconds. Half hours were first to be marked within an hour, and, by the end of the 16th century, quarters. There were also 10-minute sections. Minutes and seconds came with the invention of the pendulum, the sexagesimal system, hitherto used in astronomy to measure angles, being transferred to chronometry. Pendulum clocks were introduced from Holland in the early 18th century, and минýта and секýнда were established by the 1730s.

МИР [mir] 'peace, world'. 11th century 'peace' (IE *mīr- 'fair, fine'), perhaps of Iran. provenance, cognate with ми́лый 'nice' (IE *meilos 'dear, kind'), Skr. *mitra* 'friend', Lat. *mītis* 'mild, gentle'. Subsequently, by metaphoric transfer, 'peasant commune' (properly 'peaceful community'), finally extended to mean 'world' (before the 1918 orthographic reform миръ 'peace' was distinguished orthographically from міръ 'world').

МИШЕНЬ [mišén'] 'target'. 14th century 'seal, stamp', 16th century 'round disc', of near-E. origin, cf. (ultimately from Pers.) Turk. *nişan* 'sign, mark, target', with n-n to m-n by dissimilation, and note retention of n- in Serb. *нишан* 'target'.

МЛАДШИЙ [mládšij] 'younger, junior'. Based on ChSl. *младъ* 'young' (cf. молодóй, id.) + comparative suffix -(ь)ш-.

МНЕНИЕ [mnénije] 'opinion'. From a ChSl. calque of Gk.

dókēsis 'opinion, suspicion' (*dokéō* 'I think, suppose, imagine'), based ultimately on IE *menā 'thought, desire', *menō 'remember, think', *mentis 'thought, remembrance'. Cognate with Lith. *mintis* 'thought', *miñti* 'to remember', Lat. *meminī* 'I remember', *mens* 'mind', Ger. *meinen* 'to suppose', Eng. *to mean*, and with a derivative in сомнéние 'doubt' (original form was in су- 'incomplete, indefinite', as in сýмрак 'dusk', со- by analogy, perhaps, with nouns of the type сóвесть 'conscience').

МОГИЛА [mogíla] 'grave'. 10th century, from CSl., perhaps based on IE *mogh- 'large, powerful, heavy', *moghtis 'power' (cf. CSl. *mogti 'to be able'), thus either 'dominant place' or 'where the powerful (the Slav. élite) are buried' (cf., in Dal', the explanation 'burial-mound where by tradition giants and heroes -- могýтники, богатырú -- are buried'). Alternatively, from Ar. *maghārah* 'cavern'. Cf. also Alb. *gamulë* 'hill' (with m-g/g-m metathesis), Rom. *magura*, id. (conversely, these may be from Slav.), Serb. *гомила* 'heap, crowd' (also metathetic), and a more dubious source in Gk. *mégaron*, originally 'sacred chamber in the temple at Delphi, shrine, tomb'. Cf. also OIr. *mag* 'plain, field', Gael. *magh*, id.

МОГУЧИЙ [mogúčij] 'powerful'. Based on CSl. *mogti 'to be able', originally a pres. act. part. (cf., of ChSl. origin, standard part. могýщий 'who is able', from мочь 'to be able'), a formation analogous to горя́чий 'hot', etc. Closest cognates are in Goth. *magan* 'to be able', Ger. *Macht* 'power'. Ultimately from IE *magh- 'to be able'.

МОЛ [mol] 'he says/they say, said', etc. (used in conveying someone else's words). An allegro form of мóлвил (obs.) 'he said' or мóлвит (obs.) 'he says' (cf. dial. *грыт/грит/гьıт* for говорúт 'he says'), with cognate молвá (obs.) 'rumour, talk'. Homonymous мол 'mole, pier' is probably from Ital. *molo*, id.

МОЛНИЯ [mólnija] 'lightning'. 11th century, linked with OPr. *mealde*, id. and Icel. *myln* 'fire', less probably with *malleus* and other Lat. words for hammer, cf., however, Latv. *milna* 'thunderbolt, hammer of Thor', Icel. *Mjölnir* 'the hammer of Thor, the Thunderer'.

МОЛОДОЙ [molodój] 'young'. 11th century *молодыи*, id., from CSl. **moldъ*, id., IE **meldhos* 'soft, tender' (cf. Lat. *mollis* 'tender', as in *mollibus annis* 'in tender years, youth'). Root *молод-* forms the basis of молодец 'fine fellow, well done' and молодёжь 'young people', cf., from ChSl., стар и млад (obs. and poet.) 'one and all', младенец 'infant'. Possible cognates include Gk. *málthōn* 'weakling', Eng. *mild*, OPr. voc. pl. *maldai!* 'youngsters, lads!'.

МОЛОКО [molokó] 'milk'. CSl. **melko*, perhaps originally 'moisture, liquid' (possibly from Gmc. **meluk-*, cf. also IE **melĝos/*molĝ-* 'milk'). Gmc. cognates include Ger. *Milch* 'milk', *melken* 'to milk', Balt. include Latv. *malks* 'a swallow'. In ESl., -e- changes to -o- before -л- and inter-consonantal -оло- evolves, cf. ChSl. *млѣко* 'milk', whence млекопитающее 'mammal' and Млечный путь 'Milky Way', calqued via Lat. *via lactea*, id., from Gk. *(kýklos) galaxías*, id., *gála* 'milk'.

МОЛОТ [mólot] 'hammer'. CSl. **moltъ*, id., IE **mel-* 'to crush', with ESl. inter-consonantal -оло-, associated with молоть 'to grind', thus lit. 'grinder'. Cognate with MLat. *martulus* 'small hammer' (r-t for l-t by dissimilation from -l- in dim. -ulus). Cf. also 16th-century молоток 'hammer'.

МОЛОТЬ [molót'] 'to grind'. 11th century, from CSl. **melti* 'to crush', IE **mel-*, id., with -e- to -o- before -л- and subsequent inter-consonantal -оло- in ESl., cf. Lat. *molō* 'I grind', Lith. *malti* 'to grind', Goth./OHG *malan*, id., Ger. *mahlen*, id., Gk. *mýlē* 'handmill'.

МОНАСТЫРЬ [monastýr'] 'monastery, convent'. 11th century *манастырь*, subsequently монастырь, possibly via Ger. *Monasterium* 'monastery' (cf. standard Ger. *Kloster*, id.), from Byz. Gk. *monastḗrion*, id. (lit. 'house for living alone', cf. Gk. *mónos* 'alone', *monachós* 'solitary'). Suffix by analogy with other nouns in -ырь.

МОНАХ [monách] 'monk'. Recorded in dictionaries 1704, from Gk. *monachós* 'solitary, monk' (lit. 'one who lives alone', from *mónos* 'alone'), cf. монáшка/монáхиня 'nun' (replacing earlier *мнишица* 'nun', cf. also earlier *мнихъ* 'monk').

МОНЕТА [monéta] 'coin'. 18th century, from Lat. *monēta* 'mint, money', based on the epithet 'Monēta' ('the Warner') given to the Roman goddess Juno, at whose temple (Juno Monēta) on the Arx (N. summit of the Capitoline Hill) a mint was established. Monēta is connected with *moneō* 'I warn' (according to legend Juno received the epithet after warning the Romans of an earthquake next to the temple that housed the mint). Cognate with Eng. *money*.

МОРЕ [móre] 'sea'. 11th century, with cognates in Lat. *mare*, id., Ger. *Meer*, id., Fr. *mer*, id., Eng. *mere* 'lake, pond, sea' (as in *Windermere*), the IE root *mari 'sea' having been associated with the meaning 'to twinkle, glint', cf. мерцáть 'to twinkle', Gk. *marmaírō* 'I glisten', thus lit., maybe, 'the shining element'.

МОРЖ [morž] 'walrus'. 16th-/17th centuries, from Finnic, cf. Finn. *mursu*, id., from Lapp. *moršša*, id., cf. also Fr. *morse*, id. (borrowed 1540), Eng. 16th-century *morsse* 'walrus'.

МОРКОВЬ [morkóv'] 'carrots'. Recorded no earlier than the 17th century, from the oblique cases of CSl. *mърky (gen. *mърkъve) 'carrots', perhaps ultimately from Gmc., cf. OHG *mor(a)ha* 'carrot', Ger. *Möhre*, id. Cf. also OE *more* 'root' (IE *mrk 'edible root').

МОРОЗ [moróz] 'frost'. CSl. *morzъ, id., with ESl. interconsonantal -оро- and derivatives in морóженое 'ice-cream', úзморозь 'hoar-frost'. Cognate with мёрзнуть 'to freeze'.

МОРФОЛОГИЯ [morfológija] 'morphology'. Lit. 'study of forms', from Gk. *morphḗ* 'form, shape', *lógos* 'an account, science'.

МОСТ [most] 'bridge'. CSl., possibly from IE *meto 'fling, cast' (cf. метáть 'to throw') + -тъ (cf. concrete-noun suffix in мóлот 'hammer'), thus *mettъ, then (through e:o mutation) *mottъ, lit. 'something thrown across' (sc. a river), with subsequent dissimilation of -tt- to -st-. Alternatively from IE *mazdo, cf. Ger. *Mast* 'mast', and possibly originally 'structure of crossbeams or on piles'.

МОТОР [motór] 'motor, engine'. Lit. 'mover', via Ger. *Motor*, id., or Fr. *moteur*, id., from Lat. *mōtor* 'mover', *moveō* 'I set in motion', cf. calque двигатель 'engine' from двигать 'to move'.

МОЧА [močá] 'urine'. OR 'rain, rainy weather, urine' (cf. Serb. *моча* 'dampness, rainy weather, swampy area', R. dial. *мочажинина* 'swamp grass'). Based on CSl. *mok-, as in мокрый 'wet', мокнуть 'to get wet', with -k- palatalizing to -č- before suffix -j-.

МОЧЬ [moč'] 'to be able'. 11th century *мочи* (= *мощи*), from CSl. *mogti 'to have strength, be able' (IE *mogh- 'large, powerful, heavy'), with -gt- to -kt-, subsequently -č-, before -i, unstressed -i subsequently reducing to -ь. Cognates include могучий 'mighty', мощь 'might', Goth. *magan* 'to be able', Ger. *Macht* 'might'.

МОШЕННИК [mošénnik] 'scoundrel'. 16th century, seemingly originally 'purse-maker', then, perhaps initially in the professional speech of craftsmen, 'cutpurse, scoundrel', from OR *мошьна* 'pocket, purse', cf. Cz. *taška* 'bag', *taškař* 'scoundrel' and reverse process, from general to specific, in вор (originally 'rogue', subsequently 'thief').

МРАМОР [mrámor] 'marble'. 13th century, from ChSl., ultimately, via Lat. *marmor/marmur*, id. (cf. Pol. *marmur*, id.), from Gk. *mármaros* 'sparkling', substantivized as 'sparkling crystalline rock' (cf. Gk. *marmaírō* 'I shine'), then 'marble'. Note metathesis from -ar- to R. -pa-.

МУЖ [muž] 'husband, (obs.) man'. 11th century *мужь* 'person, man, husband', from CSl. *mǫžь/*mongjos 'man, husband' (IE *man-/*manus, id., possibly connected with IE *men- 'to think'), with -g- to -ž- before -j- and -ǫ- to -u- in ESl. In 18th century the meaning 'man' was already high-flown (cf. also 11th-century meaning 'man of renown'), as in великий муж 'great man', cf. also госуда́рственный муж 'statesman'. Derivatives include мужчи́на 'man', from мужско́й 'male' + suffix -(ч)ина (formed by analogy with же́нщина 'woman'), му́жество 'courage', a ChSl. calque of Gk. *andreía* 'manliness, courage', from *anḗr*, gen. *andrós* 'man', also (mid-16th century) мужи́к 'mužik, peasant', used of underprivileged individuals, esp. serfs, designated as minors from their lack of legal rights, subsequently (sub-standard) 'man, husband'.

МУЗЫКА [múzyka] 'music'. No later than the 18th century, via Ukr. from Pol. *muzyka*, id., a reshaping of Lat. *musica/musice* 'the art of music, music (including poetry)', Gk. *mousikḗ (téchnē)* 'any art over which the Muses presided, esp. poetry set to music'. Originally with penultimate stress (seemingly a Polonism, cf. Pol. coll. *muzýka* 'orchestra', alongside *múzyka* 'music', with subsequent initial stress possibly under the counter-influence of substandard Austrian Ger. *Músik*, cf. standard Ger. *Musík*). Cognates include музыка́нт 'musician', from Ger. *Musikant* (sometimes derogatory), cf. *Musikus* (arch. or facetious), alongside standard *Musiker* 'musician', from Lat. *mūsicus* 'musical, musician'.

МУКА [muká] 'flour'. From CSl. *mǫka 'kneaded, easy to knead', cf. Lith. *minkyti* 'to knead', мять, id., Ger. *mengen* 'to mix', cognate with *mękъkъ 'soft', cf. мя́гкий, id., Lith. *minkštas*, id. Possibly cognate with му́ка 'torment' and its derivatives in му́чить 'to torment', муче́ние 'torture'.

МУРАВЕЙ [muravéj] 'ant'. A reshaping of OR *мравии*, id., under the influence of мурава́ (poet.) 'grass, sward', with cognates in Skr. *vamraḥ* 'ant', Gk. *mýrmex*, id. (cf. also IE *meur-/mour-, id.).

МУХА [múcha] 'fly'. 11th century, from CSl. *mucha, IE *mu- (possibly onomatopoeic), with cognates in Lith. *musė*, id., Lat. *musca*, id., Fr. *mouche*, id., мо́шка 'midge', Ger. *Mücke*, id.

МЫЛО [mýlo] 'soap'. 11th century, from CSl. *mydlo, comprising the root of *myti 'to bathe, wash' + agent suffix *dl(o), with -dl- simplifying to -l- in ESl. (cf. Pol. *mydło* 'soap'), lit.

'what you wash with'.

МЫС [mys] 'cape, promontory'. 17th century, possibly from the root мык- (cf. размыкáть 'to disconnect'), thus perhaps lit. 'separating'. Alternatively, if dubiously, from Gk. *mychós* 'nook, bay, creek'.

МЫШЬ [myš'] 'mouse'. IE *mūs 'mouse, biceps, muscle', with -s- changing to Slav. -š- before -ь, possibly semantically linked with Skr. *mush* 'to rob' (cf. Skr. *mūṣ* 'mouse'). Derivatives include мы́шца 'muscle' (from the resemblance of a flexed upper-arm muscle to a running mouse, cf. мýскул 'muscle' from Lat. *musculus* 'little mouse, muscle' and analogous meaning transfers in Fr. *souris* 'mouse, knuckle of a leg of mutton', Ger. *Maus* 'mouse, nasal muscle of a horse'). Cf. also подмы́шка 'arm-pit' (hollow under the biceps), and мышья́к 'arsenic' (lit. 'mouse poison', 18th century).

МЯ́ГКИЙ [mjágkij] 'soft'. Cognate with мукá 'flour', cf. derivative мя́коть 'fleshy part, pulp'.

МЯ́МЛИТЬ [mjámlit'] 'to mumble'. Based on onomatopoeic reduplication of м, cf. Eng. *mumble, murmur*, Fr. *marmotter*, id., Cz. *mumlati*, id.

МЯЧ [mjač] 'ball'. Originally (Vasmer) 'that which is squeezed, compressed', possibly from CSl. *mę̌čь 'soft (object)' (*mękъ 'soft' + suffix *-jь, with -kj- palatalizing to -č-, later -ч, and ESl. -я- evolving from -ę-, referring to the resilience of a soft ball, cf. *смякáть, смя́кнуть* 'to get sodden and swell, get soft' (Dal').

Н

НАБАТ [nabát] 'tocsin'. Mid-16th century 'enormous copper drum', from Ar. *nauba*, pl. *-āt* (mistaken by Russians for a sing.) 'guard duty, guard, bugle call' (possibly via Tkc., cf. Turk. *nöbet* 'turn, watch of sentry'). The meaning 'alarm, alarm signal, tocsin' appeared in the first half of the 18th century.

НАВОЛОЧКА [návoločka] 'pillow-slip'. Early 17th century, dim. of наволока, id., cf. *наволочь* (obs.) 'to pull on' (and волочь 'to drag'), thus 'what is pulled on'. Cognate with проволока 'wire', оболочка 'casing, cover' and влечь 'to draw, drag'.

НАГРАДИТЬ [nagradít'] 'to reward'. Originally CSl. *nagorditi 'to bestow a town' (cf. город/град 'town'), a sign of royal favour in feudal times, granted to military commanders for services to the crown. Via ChSl., hence inter-consonantal -pa-.

НАДЕЖДА [nadéžda] 'hope'. OR *надежа* (with ESl. -ж-, cf. надёжный 'reliable'), *надежда* (with SSl. -жд-) 'hope, reliable person' (cf. personification in Eng. 'she is our last hope'), from CSl. *nadědja 'hope' (*na- 'on', *děti 'to put'), via ChSl.

НАДМЕННЫЙ [nadménnyj] 'haughty'. Based on a ChSl. past pass. part. from *надмить* 'to puff up, blow up', thus initially 'puffed up', then 'haughty' (cf. надутый, id., from надуть 'to blow up, puff out'). See домна 'furnace', дуть 'to blow'.

НАДОЕДАТЬ [nadoedát'] 'to bore'. In dictionaries from 18th century, a derivative of доедать 'to finish eating something', fig. 'to annoy' (Cyganenko), with quantitative prefix на-.

НАИЗУСТЬ [naizúst'] 'by heart'. Probably a calque of Gk. *apó stómatos*, id., lit. 'from the mouth' (уста 'mouth, lips').

НАКАНУНЕ [nakanúne] 'on the eve'. In dictionaries from 18th century, based on канун 'eve' from Gk. *kanón*. See канун.

НАОБУМ [naobúm] 'at random'. Comprises на + об + ум 'mind' (cf. dial. *обум* 'without thinking'), lit. 'bypassing the mind, without awaiting the dictates of reason'.

НАПЕРСТОК [napërstok] 'thimble'. From OR *пьрстъ* 'finger', (cf. obs. перст, id.), with stressed -е- to -ё- before a hard consonant, cf. пёрстень 'signet-ring', перчатка 'glove', and see палец 'finger'.

НАПРАСНЫЙ [naprásnyj] 'vain, unfounded'. OR 'quick, irascible, sudden', based on CSl. *prask- (cf. dial. *праск* 'crack'), thus *naprask- 'suddenness' + suffix -n-, with -skn- simplifying to -sn- (cf. лоск 'gloss', лосниться 'to shine'). The meaning 'vain, unfounded' evolved in the early 17th century. Possibly affected by CSl. *porz- (whence порожний 'empty' and праздный 'idle').

НАРЕЧИЕ [narēčije] 'adverb'. A loan from ChSl., calqued from Gk. *epírrēma*, id. (*epí* 'on, ad-' + *rēma* 'word, verb'), rather than Lat. *adverbium* 'adverb' (also calqued from the Gk.).

НАРЗАН [narzán] 'Narzan' (kind of mineral water). Recorded in dictionaries from the second half of the 19th century, from Kabardinian, lit. 'drink of the *narty*, a fabulous tribe of heroes', a name given in the N. Caucasus to all mineral springs, cf. M. Lermontov in *Герой нашего времени* (*Hero of Our Time*): Недаром Нарзан называется богатырским ключом 'It is not for nothing that Narzan is called the spring of heroes.' ('Княжна Мэри', 10 June).

НАРОД [naród] 'people'. 11th century 'people, population of country', based on CSl. *rodъ 'family, kin, clan', closely related to народить 'to bear (many)', народиться 'to come into being, arise', thus properly 'people of the same stock'.

НАРОЧНО [naróčno] 'on purpose'. Recorded in dictionaries from the 18th century, neut. short form of нарочный (= нарочитый) 'deliberate', cf. (obs.) *нарок* 'intention', *нароком* 'on purpose', ненароком (coll.) 'unintentionally'. Cognate with нарекать 'to name'.

НАСЕКОМОЕ [nasekómoje] 'insect'. 18th-century calque (in the form of a pres. pass. part.), via Fr. *insecte*, id., of Lat. *insectum*, id., from *ĭnsecō* 'I cut up, into', Gk. *éntoma* (sc. *zδa* 'animals') 'insects' (*éntomos* 'cut in pieces', *éntomē* 'incision'), thus lit. 'cut into sections' (cf. насекáть 'to make incisions in'), from the segmented nature of insects' bodies.

НАУКА [naúka] 'science, learning'. 18th century, comprising na- + *uka 'learning' (IE *ouk-/*ūk-, id., OR укъ, id.), with four variants: (i) -ук-, e.g. наýка 'science' (ii) -ык-, e.g. обыкновéнный 'ordinary', from a ChSl. pass. part., cf. привыкáть 'to get used to', with prosthetic в-, since ы could not normally appear at the beginning of a root, cf. вы́дра 'otter' (iii) -уч-, with -k- to -č- before front vowels, e.g. учи́ть 'to teach, learn' (iv) -ыч-, with -k- to -č- before front vowels or -j-, e.g. обы́чай 'custom', whence обы́чный 'customary'.

НАХЛОБУЧИТЬ [nachlobúčit'] 'to pull down' (over the head or eyes). From клобýк 'klobuk' (headgear of an Orthodox monk), initial к- changing to -х- possibly under the influence of хлóпать 'to bang, slam'.

НАЧАТЬ [načát'] 'to begin'. 11th century *начати* 'to begin' (also an auxiliary verb for the future tense and conditional mood), from CSl. *načęti, IE *kīn 'start, move', cognate with искони́ 'from time immemorial', почи́н 'initiative, beginning', зачáть 'to conceive', Gk. *kainós* 'new', Lat. *recēns* 'fresh, new'.

НЕБО [nébo] 'sky'. 11th century, from CSl. *nebo, gen. *nebese (IE *nebhos 'sky, cloud, mist', root *nebh- 'moisture'), cf. Skr. *nabhas* 'mist, cloud', Gk. *néphos/nephélē* 'cloud, mass of clouds', Lat. *nebula* 'mist', OHG *nebul*, id. (Ger. *Nebel*, id.). Medial -e- suggests a written loan from ChSl., cf. нёбо 'palate, roof of the mouth', from нéбо 'sky' by metaphorical extension, with stressed -e- to -ё- before a hard consonant. Derivatives of нéбо 'sky' include небéсный 'celestial' (cf. pl. небесá 'skies'). Lith. *debesis* 'cloud' is thought to be a cognate, d- rather than n- possibly under the influence of Lith. *dangus* 'sky'.

НЕБОСКРЁБ [neboskrëb] 'sky-scraper'. Calqued from Eng., cf. нёбо 'sky', скребу́ 'I scrape'.

НЕВЕСТА [nevésta] 'fiancée, bride'. 11th century 'bride, daughter-in-law', from CSl. *nevědta/*nevěsta (cf. Lith. *nevedęs* 'single'), lit. 'unknown' (to her future in-laws), from не 'not' + вёдать 'to know' (cf. OR невѣсть 'ignorance, obscurity, unexpectedness'), possibly a taboo protecting a woman entering a strange house against evil spirits (cf., in wedding songs, analogous *чужени́н* 'bridegroom', from чужо́й 'alien'). Alternatively, comprises *nev- 'new' + *ved- 'lead' (cf. IE *neu̯os 'new', *u̯edh 'lead, bring, carry', *ne-u̯edh 'unmarried') + ta, thus lit. 'newly led', cf. (Novgorod birchbark writ no. 9) reference to 'leading/introducing (*водя́*) a new wife', also *води́ма* (obs.) 'wife, mistress, bride'. Cf. also (based on the root 'new') Lat. *noverca* 'step-mother'. Finally, if dubiously, from *nevě- 'new' + *sthā 'standing', thus 'in a new state'.

НЕДЕЛЯ [nedélja] 'week'. 11th century *недѣля* (from CSl. *nedělja), originally 'rest day', 'Sunday', based on *не дѣлати* 'not to do' and possibly calqued from Gk. *ápraktos (hēméra)* 'idle' (day) or Lat. *feria* 'holiday', *diēs feriātus/feriāta*, id., lit. 'idle day'. Eventually the meaning 'week' (already present in the 11th century) prevailed, with *недѣля* (неде́ля) denoting the seven days *beginning* Sunday, not Sunday itself, and replacing OR *седми́ца* 'week', while воскресе́нье, of ChSl. origin (initially 'Easter Sunday'), came to denote 'Sunday (in general)'. (*Седми́ца* 'week' had been based on Gk. *hebdomás* 'seven' or Late Lat. *septimāna* 'relating to the number seven', itself -- the source of Fr. *semaine* 'week' -- from Gk. *hebdomás*, id.) The semantic changes are partly attributed to the ambiguity of Gk. *Sábbaton* 'Hebrew Sabbath, the seventh day, day of rest', also 'week'. See воскресе́нье 'Sunday', понеде́льник 'Monday'.

НЕДРА [nédra] 'bowels of the earth'. Recorded in dictionaries since 1731. May derive from *vъn jědra 'into the interior', from CSl. *jědra 'entrails, interior', with n- transferring from the preposition *vъn 'in' to the noun (a process facilitated by the practice of continuous script, without gaps between words, or perhaps by analogy with other words in ne-, cf. незри́мый 'invisible', etc.), or through euphemism or taboo. Thought to be cognate with Gk. *nḗduia* 'entrails', *ētor* 'heart', Ger. *Ader* 'vein' and perhaps to imply 'that which is not eaten' (cf. CSl. **jěsti* from **jědti* 'eat'). Cf. also ядро́ 'nucleus' and нутро́ 'interior', and similar n-displacement in a number of Eng. words, e.g. *nickname* from *an + ekename* (*eke* 'addition(al)').

НЕЗАБУ́ДКА [nezabúdka] 'forget-me-not'. Recorded in dictionaries from 1847, based on не забу́дь 'don't forget', perhaps calqued from Ger. *Vergißmeinnicht*, id., cf. Pol. *niezapominajka*, id., or based on a general Eur. pattern, cf. Fr. *ne m'oublie pas*, id. alongside formal *myosotis*, lit. 'mouse ear' (Gk. *mûs*, gen. *muós* 'mouse', *oûs* 'ear', whence also Fr. *oreille de souris* 'forget-me-not', lit. 'mouse ear', from the plant's soft hairy leaves).

НЕЛЕ́ПЫЙ [nelépyj] 'absurd'. 11th century 'indecent', ultimately based on не + OR лѣпыи 'magnificent, good, beautiful' (perhaps originally 'well-modelled', cf. лепи́ть 'to model'), subsequently 'absurd'. Cf. cognate великоле́пный 'magnificent', Pol. *lepszy* 'better'.

НЕЛЬЗЯ́ [nel'zjá] 'it is impossible, not allowed'. OR нельзя (also нѣл(ь)га and нел(ь)зѣ). Comprises ne + CSl. **lьzě* (cf. Cz. *lze* 'it is possible'), the dat./prep. case (third palatalization of velars) of **lьga, perhaps meaning 'freedom, permission'. The final -я (cf. OR льзя 'one may') derives from -ѣ perhaps by analogy with phrases of the type не вре́мя 'this is not the time to'. Cognate with льго́та 'privilege', по́льза 'benefit'.

НЕ́МЕЦ [némec] 'German'. OR нѣмьци 'dumb, speaking indistinctly', нѣмци 'any foreign people, peoples of the German tribe', from CSl. **němьcь 'foreigner', **němъ 'dumb', originally 'speaking indistinctly', cf. *говори́ть не́мо* 'to speak indistinctly' (e.g. of a child, Dal'). Possibly onomatopoeic, **němъ having evolved through dissimilation of nasals (m-m to n-m) from **měmъ 'stammer' (cf. Ger. *mummeln* 'to mumble', мя́млить, id., dial. ня́млить). The meaning developed from 'foreigner, someone not speaking Russian, speaking incomprehensibly' (cf. Gk. *berberízō* 'I stammer', *bárbaros* 'barbarous', i.e. non-Greek, foreign -- 'a word imitative of the confused and meaningless sound of voices, repeating the syllables *bar, bar*'), to 'German'.

НЕНАВИ́ДЕТЬ [nenavídet'] 'to hate'. 11th century, from ne 'not' + *naviděti 'to look willingly, visit', thus lit. 'not to want to see' (cf. Serb. *навидети се* 'to live in harmony', R. dial. *навидеть его не могу́* 'I can't stand him'). Derivatives include 11th-century не́нависть 'hatred' (with original -dt- to -tt-, subsequently -st-) and ненави́стный 'hated, hateful'.

НЕФТЬ [neft'] 'oil'. 17th century, perhaps from Tkc. (cf. Turk. *neft* 'naphtha'), entering Eur. languages via Gk. *náphtha(s)* 'a clear, combustible petroleum' (whence Lat. *naphtha* 'naphtha, flammable oil from coal'). Ultimately from Pers. (whence perhaps directly to R.) or Ar. *naft/naft*, from a root meaning lit. 'to burst into flame'.

НО́ВЫЙ [nóvyj] 'new'. 11th century, ultimately from IE *neu̯os 'new', cognate with Gk. *néos*, id., Lat. *novus*, id., Ger. *neu*, id., etc.

НОГА́ [nogá] 'foot, leg'. 11th century, originally seemingly 'hoof, claw' (IE *onughos 'nail, claw, hoof', cf. Lith. *naga* 'hoof', *nagas* 'nail, claw', Skr. *nakha* 'nail', OHG *nagal*, id., Ger. *Nagel*, id.), perhaps cognate with но́готь 'nail'. Initially facetious, subsequently the standard word for leg or foot (cf. Ital. *testa* 'head', from Lat. *tēsta* 'brick, tile, pot', alongside standard Lat. *caput* 'head'), supplanting the CSl. root *pěšь that survives in пешко́м 'on foot', пехо́та 'infantry', пе́шка 'pawn', etc.

НОЗДРЯ́ [nozdrjá] 'nostril'. 11th century, from CSl. *nozdьra (IE *nãsdr-, id.), comprising nos- 'nose' + suffix -dr-, possibly (arguably a false etymology) associated with деру́ 'I tear', thus lit. 'nose-hole' (cf. дыра́ 'hole' and Eng. *nostril*, lit. 'nose + hole').

НОЛЬ, НУЛЬ [nol', nul'] 'nought'. Нуль late 17th-/early 18th centuries (also *о́никъ* 'nought', from *онъ*, the name of the letter 'o'), from D. *nul*, id. or Ger. *Null*, id. (whence also Sw. *noll*, id., seemingly the source of ноль, -о- perhaps explained by the influence of short Ger. -u-). Ultimately, via Ital. *nulla* 'nothing', from Lat. *nūllus* 'none', substantivized in neut. *nūllum* 'nothing', and acquiring the meaning 'nought, zero' through the dissemination of Ar. number theory (officially adopted in the reign of Peter I, though known in the early 17th century), as the equivalent of Ar. *ṣifr* 'zero, empty'. Нуль/ноль appear in dictionaries from 1847.

НОРА [norá] 'burrow, lair'. OR 'underground passage', from CSl. *nora, possibly from *nerti 'to hide, plunge' (IE *ner-/*nor- 'into, under'), cf. Lith. *nerti* 'to dive, plunge'. Cognate with понурый 'downcast, depressed', нырять 'to dive', probably also with норка 'mink' (for its swimming and diving skill).

НОСОРОГ [nosoróg] 'rhinoceros'. A calque of Gk. *rinókerōs*, id. (*rís*, gen. *rinós* 'nose', *kéras* 'horn'), cf. Ger. *Nashorn*, id., lit. 'nose-horn', also calqued from Gk.

НОЧЬ [noč'] 'night'. 11th century, from CSl. *noktь, id., with -kt- to -č- before -ь, cognate with Lith. *naktis*, id., Ger. *Nacht*, id., Lat. *nox*, gen. *noctis*, id., Sp. *noche*, id., etc.

НОЯБРЬ [nojábr'] 'November'. 11th century, from ChSl., based on Gk. *noémbri(o)s*, id., with -em- changing to -я- in R., ultimately from Lat. *November (mensis)*, id., lit. 'ninth month' -- the Roman year began with March. Cf. Ukr. *листопад* 'November', Pol. *listopad*, id., lit. 'fall of leaves'.

НУТРО [nutró] 'inside, interior'. First half of the 18th century (cf. 11th century *нутрь* 'interior'), from *vъn ǫtrь 'into the interior' (CSl. *ǫtrь 'interior'), reinterpreted, with n-displacement (cf. недра 'depths') as *vъ nǫtrь, with -ǫ- changing to R. -у- and subsequent autonomy for нутро́. Cognates include утроба 'womb', Gk. *éntera* 'entrails', Skr. *antara* 'inner', cf. also внутри́/внутрь 'inside'.

НЯНЯ [njánja] 'nurse'. Recorded in dictionaries 1704 but doubtless in use much earlier, from child's speech, based on reduplicated ня, cf. Gk. *nénnos* 'uncle', *тятя* (dial.) 'dad'.

O

ОБА/ОБЕ [óba/óbe] 'both'. 11th century, with cognates in Gk. *ámphō* 'both of two', Lat. *ambō* 'both', Lith. *abu, abi*, id.

ОБЕД [obéd] 'lunch'. 11th century 'midday meal' (cf. dial. *обед* 'south, midday', see *ýжин* 'supper'), from CSl. *obědъ, comprising ob- in temporal meaning (cf. о сю пóру 'at this time') + *ěd- 'food'.

ОБЕЗЬЯНА [obez'jána] 'monkey'. At the latest 16th century, from Pers. *būzineh*, id. (perhaps ultimately from Ar.), replacing earlier *пифик*, id. (cited by Uspenskij, from Gk. *píthēkos* 'ape'), possibly influenced by forms in о- (esp. OR *отица* 'monkey'), in -без-, and adjs. and nouns in -ан-/-ян-, including purportedly (although seemingly of later provenance) изъян 'defect, flaw'.

ОБЕСПЕЧИТЬ [obespéčit'] 'to provide, guarantee'. Based on prefix обес- 'deprivation' (cf. обессилить 'to weaken') + root *pek- 'concern' (cf. опéка 'tutelage'), with -k- palatalizing to -č- before -i-, lit. 'to remove concern'.

ОБИДЕТЬ [obídet'] 'to offend'. Ultimately from CSl., perhaps originally *ob(ь)-viděti, initially 'to inspect, survey' (maybe disdainfully, cf. also осмотрéть 'to inspect'), then 'to offend', with -bv- simplifying to -b-. Cf., also with combined visual and attitudinal connotations, ненавидеть 'to hate', Lat. *invidia* 'envy' and (cf. obs. зреть 'to see'), презрéние 'scorn', подозревáть 'to suspect', сглáзить 'to put the evil eye on', from глаз 'eye'. Less plausibly, from бедá 'trouble' (for е:и mutation, however, cf. лепить/липнуть 'to stick' -- transitive and intransitive).

ОБИЛЬНЫЙ [obíl'nyj] 'abundant'. 11th century *обилие* 'abundance', *обило* 'many' (earlier *обиль* 'standing corn'), from CSl. *obilь/*obvilъ 'abundant' (perhaps cognate with Lat. *vīs* 'you want', *vīs* 'strength'). Alternatively, a derivative of бить 'to beat', lit. 'that which has been beaten, threshed', cf. prefix о(б)- in обмолóченное 'threshed'.

ОБЛАДАТЬ [obladát'] 'to possess'. From CSl. *voldati, via ChSl. (ob- 'encompassing' + *vladati 'to possess', with -bv- simplifying to -b-). Cf. владéть 'to own'.

ОБЛАКО [óblako] 'cloud'. CSl. *obvolkъ, with -bv- simplifying to -b-, 11th century облакъ, id., óблако recorded in dictionaries from 1731. Literally 'that which envelopes', cf. обволáкивать 'to envelope', with cognates in облачáть 'to robe', разоблачáть 'to divest' and (with inter-consonantal -оло- in ESl.) оболóчка 'cover, casing'.

ОБЛАСТЬ [óblast'] 'oblast, province'. 11th century 'power, province', 12th century 'population of province', from CSl. *obvolstь (ob- 'around', *volstь 'possession'), with -bv- simplifying to -b- and -ol- changing to ChSl. -ла-. Meaning develops from 'power' to 'control of country', 'administrative unit of state'. Cf., with ESl. -оло-, вóлость 'volost, smallest administrative unit of tsarist Russia'.

ОБЛИЧАТЬ [obličát'] 'to expose, reveal'. 11th century, id., based ultimately on лик (obs.) 'face', thus 'to reveal, expose' (cf. óблик 'look, aspect, appearance'). First recorded in dictionaries 1731. See also лицó 'face'.

ОБМАН [obmán] 'deception'. From обманýть 'to deceive', through deaffixation. See also манúть 'to entice'.

ОБМОРОК [óbmorok] 'faint'. Recorded in dictionaries from 18th century, possibly based on dial. мóрок 'darkness, dusk' (cf. морóка (coll./fig.) 'darkness, confusion'), from CSl. *merkъ/*morkъ 'darkness', cf. мрак 'gloom', сýмерки 'dusk'. Alternatively, from обмóр 'catalepsy'.

ОБОД [óbod] 'rim'. OR ободъ 'circumference, circle', later 'rim' of a helmet (1589), then of a wheel, from CSl. *obvodъ (cf. обводúть 'to encircle'), with -bv- simplifying to -b-.

ОБОИ [obói] 'wall-paper'. First half of the 18th century, from обúть 'to upholster, cover', originally 'fabric or leather tacked to a wall' (earlier wall-fabrics were tacked, not pasted).

ОБОРОНА [oboróna] 'defence'. From CSl. root *bor-, with derivatives in *borti (sę), *bornь, whence OR *бороти(ся)* 'to do battle', *боронь* 'defence', with inter-consonantal ESl. -оро-. See боро́ться 'to struggle', броня́ 'armour', борьба́ 'struggle' and cf. (from ChSl.) по́ле бра́ни (obs., poet.) 'field of battle'.

ОБОЮДНЫЙ [obojúdnyj] 'mutual, reciprocal'. Recorded in dictionaries since 1704, based on 11th century *обоюду* 'on, from both sides', ultimately CSl. *oboj- 'both' + adv. suffix *-ǫdu (ǫ to (j)u in ESl.), cf. всю́ду 'everywhere', from весь 'all'.

ОБРАЗ [óbraz] 'form, icon'. 11th century 'depiction, icon', cf. OR *образити* 'to depict', from CSl. *obrazъ (ob- + *razъ 'blow'), cognate with рази́ть 'to strike' (cf. OR *образити* 'to strike') and ре́зать 'to cut'. See раз 'time'.

ОБРАЗОВАНИЕ [obrazovánije] 'education'. Considered to be a 19th-century calque of Ger. *Bildung* 'education, culture' (cf. Ger. *Bild*, о́браз 'image'), but seemingly appeared in church texts in this meaning as early as the 16th century.

ОБРУЧ [óbruč] 'hoop'. 11th century 'wrist, bracelet', 12th century 'ring' (whence обручи́ться 'to get engaged'), 15th century 'belt', from CSl. *obrǫčь (with -k- -- cf. *rǫka = рука́ 'hand, arm' -- having palatalized to -č- before -j-), thus lit. 'around the hand, arm', finally 'hoop round a barrel'.

ОБСТОЯТЕЛЬСТВО [obstojátel'stvo] 'circumstance'. First half of 18th century, calqued from Lat. *circumstantia*, id., via Ger. *Umstand*, id. or Fr. *circonstance*, id., cf. *circum-/um-/*об- 'around' + *stō/stehen*/стоя́ть 'stand'.

ОБУТЬ [obút'] 'to put someone's shoes on'. 11th century, from CSl., cf. разу́ть 'to take someone's shoes off', with cognate forms in Lith. *aūti* 'to put on someone's boots', Lat. *exuō* 'I take off', *induō* 'I put on'. Ону́ча 'sock or cloth puttee worn in boot or bast shoe' is from the same Slav. root.

ОБШЛАГ [obšlág] 'cuff'. 17th-/early 18th centuries, from D.

opslag, id. (hence *опшлаг*, id., 1702) or Ger. *Aufschlag*, id.

ОБЩЕСТВО [óbščestvo] 'society'. From ChSl., based on óбщий 'general, common' and calqued from Gk. *koinōnía* 'communion, association, partnership', on the basis of Gk. *koinós* 'common'.

ОБЩИЙ [óbščij] 'common, general, total'. 11th century, ultimately CSl. *obьtjo/*obьtjь 'surrounding' (associated by some with Lat. *ambitiō* 'going around', cf. обойти 'to go round', обиход 'use, practice', by others with обть = опть 'total', cf. óптом 'wholesale'), -šč- (from -tj-) being of ChSl. provenance.

ОБЪЕМ [ob''ëm] 'volume, capacity'. From ob- + CSl. *jęti 'to take, seize, grip' (cf. обнять 'to embrace'), patterned in similar fashion to Ger. *Umfang* 'circumference' from *umfangen* 'to encompass'.

ОБЯЗАТЬ [objazát'] 'to oblige'. 11th century обязати (-б- from earlier -бв-) 'to wind round, bandage', 14th century 'to tie to', subsequently (fig.) 'to bind, oblige' (cf., with restored -бв-, обвязáть 'to tie round').

ОВОЩ [óvošč] 'vegetable'. 10th century 'vegetable, fruit', perhaps from CSl. *ovotjь, with -šč- (from -tj-) of ChSl. origin, cf. Ukr. *овочі* 'vegetables', Pol. *owoce* 'fruit'. Possibly cognate with or from Gmc., cf. Goth. *wahsjan* 'to grow', OHG *wahsan*, id., Ger. *wachsen*, id., thus perhaps lit. 'that which grows' (cf. CSl. *voksti 'to grow', Gk. *aúxē* 'growth', Lat. *augeō* 'I increase'). Cf. also possible cognates MHG *obez* (OHG *obaz*) 'side dish, vegetables, preserves' (cf. Ger. *essen* 'to eat'), Ger. *Obst* 'fruit'.

ОВЦА [ovcá] 'sheep'. 11th century, from CSl. *ovьkā, subsequently *ovьca (root *ov- + suffix *-ьc(a)), whence also овчи́на 'sheepskin', овчáрка 'sheepdog', cf. too овéн 'ram (obs.), Aries, first sign of the Zodiac', and with cognates in Skr. *aviḥ* 'sheep', Gk. *óïs*, id. (ram or ewe), Lat. *ovis*, id., Lith. *ãvinas* 'ram', Sp. *oveja* 'sheep', Eng. *ewe*.

ОГОНЬ [ogón'] 'fire'. 11th century *огнь* 'fire, light', from CSl. *ognь/*ognis, IE *īgni 'fire', with cognates in Lith. *ugnìs*, id., Lat. *īgnis*, id. (whence Eng. *ignition*). Considered by some to be related to Skr. *aṅgarāka* 'coal'.

ОГОРОД [ogoród] 'kitchen-garden'. Through deaffixation from OR *огородити* 'to surround with a fence or wall' (cf. огородить 'to fence in'), thus properly 'enclosed place', subsequently 'kitchen-garden'. See город 'town' and cf. отгородить 'to partition off', перегородка 'partition', ограда 'fence, enclosure'.

ОГРОМНЫЙ [ogrómnyj] 'enormous'. Possibly from *огром 'area over which a clap of thunder is audible' (cf. гром 'thunder', *огромить* 'to deafen with a loud noise', Pol. *ogrom* 'mass'). For an analogous formation, see околоток (obs.) 'neighbourhood, ward'.

ОГУРЕЦ [oguréc] 'cucumber'. 16th century, from Byz. Gk. *aggoúrion*, id., cf. Gk. *áōros* 'unripe' (unripe cucumbers were prized for their taste, contrasting with that of melons, eaten when ripe), cf. (also from the Gk.) Late Lat. and Ital. *anguria* 'watermelon'.

ОДЕТЬ [odét'] 'to clothe'. 11th century, from o- + CSl. *děti 'to put', lit. 'to put round' (cf. надеть 'to put on'), with cognates in одежда 'clothing', which is based on CSl. *odědja, with -dj- to ChSl. -žd-, and одеяло 'blanket', with suffix -л(о), thus lit. 'what you cover yourself with'.

ОДИН [odín] 'one'. 11th century, from CSl. *jedinъ, probably a compound of *ed-, which is based on an intensifying pronominal form with root *e-, as in этот 'this' (for -d, cf. Lat. neut. *id* 'this') + *inъ (from IE *oinos 'one', cf. OR *иньıи* 'one, other', иной 'other' and cognates Gk. *oínē* 'the ace on dice', Lat. *unus* 'one', Ger. *eins*, id.).

ОДНАЖДЫ [odnáždy] 'once'. From один 'one', cf. analogous formation in дважды 'twice' (see два 'two').

ОДНАКО [odnáko] 'however'. From OR *одинако*, id., with

subsequent loss of unstressed -и- (cf. its retention in одина́ковый 'identical'), a derivative of оди́н 'one, alone' (cf. OR *одинакыи* 'unanimous', *одинокыи* 'standing separately'). Cf. also, for an analogous dual meaning, Ger. *allein* 'alone, however' and, for a form combining the meanings 'one' and 'restriction, concession', the Gk. adv. *mónōs* 'on one condition only'.

ОДНОСТОРО́ННИЙ [odnostorónnij] 'one-sided, uni-lateral'. Probably a calque of Ger. *einseitig*, id.

ОДУВА́НЧИК [oduváṅčik] 'dandelion'. Based on dial. *одуван*, id., о(б)дува́ть 'to blow round, away, off', from the tendency for the plant's seeds to be carried on the wind.

ОЖЕРЕ́ЛЬЕ [ožerél'je] 'necklace'. OR *ожерелие* 'opening for the throat in clothing, necklace', from о- 'around' + CSl. *žьrlo 'throat', with ESl. inter-consonantal -epe- (cf. dial./obs. *огорлие* 'necklace, collar', го́рло 'throat', жерло́ 'mouth, orifice, muzzle of gun').

ОЗОРНО́Й [ozornój] 'mischievous'. OR *озорьныи* 'coarse', perhaps initially also with connotations of 'spying, sneaking', cf. dial. *озо́р* 'spy, informer' (alongside dial. *озо́р* 'mischief-maker'), *озо́рить* 'to spy on' (also 'to brawl'). Cognate with зо́ркий 'keen-eyed', зреть (obs.) 'to see', etc. (cf. also OR *озрѣтися* 'to look round').

ОКНО́ [oknó] 'window'. 13th century, from CSl. *okъno, id., from *oko 'eye', applied metaphorically to the window as the 'eye' of the house (cf. ME *windoze*, ON *vindauga*, lit. 'wind-eye'), cognate with Lat. *oculus* 'eye', Lith. *akis*, id., Ger. *Auge*, id. Cf. also глаз 'eye', originally 'polished stone, bead', replacing о́ко 'eye' (now obs./poet.), initially in expressive speech, in the 16th-/17th centuries, and variously derived from гла́дкий 'smooth' and Gmc. *glasa- 'amber' (cf. Ger. *Glas* 'glass', IE *ghel- 'to gleam').

О́КОЛО [ókolo] 'near, approximately'. 11th century 'around' (adv. and prep., a meaning retained until the early 19th century), 16th century 'near', from о- 'around' + acc. of OR *коло* 'circle, arc, wheel', whence also колесо́ 'wheel', кольцо́ 'ring', колея́ 'track'.

ОКОЛО́ТОК [okolótok] (obs.) 'neighbourhood, ward'. 14th-/15th centuries, cf. колоти́ть 'to strike on', thus, perhaps, lit. 'area over which the watchman's rattle (колоту́шка) is heard', then 'ward guarded by a watchman', cf. similar derivation of огро́мный 'enormous' from гром 'thunder'. Alternatively, from *kolo 'circle' or OR околъ, id. The formation is similar to that of промежу́ток 'interval' (from меж- 'between').

ОКТЯ́БРЬ [oktjábr'] 'October'. 11th century (also октямбрь and октомъбрь), from Lat. *Octōber*, id., via Gk. *októbri(o)s*, id. and ChSl., lit. 'the eighth month' (the Roman year began on 1 March), medial -я- by analogy with сентя́брь 'September' and ноя́брь 'November'.

ОЛЕ́НЬ [olén'] 'deer'. 12th century, from CSl. *(j)elenь (IE *elənis, id.), possibly by association with OHG *gelo 'brown, yellow', a reference to the animal's colour, with (j)e- to ESl. o- before medial -e- (cf. Pol. *jeleń* 'stag, deer'). Cognates include Lith. *elnias* 'deer', *elnė* 'doe', Gk. *élaphos* 'deer', *ellós* 'fawn'. See also лань 'doe' and лось 'elk'.

ОПА́СНЫЙ [opásnyj] 'dangerous'. 12th century, originally 'meticulous', from опасъ 'caution, fear, safety' (also 'protection', cf. 15th-century опа́сная гра́мота 'safe conduct'), from the root of пасти́ 'to tend, guard'. Cf. опаса́ться 'to beware of'.

ОПЕ́КА [opéka] 'guardianship'. Recorded in dictionaries from the 18th century (cf. 14th-century опекание = опе́ка), from Pol. *opieka* 'guardianship', a calque of Lat. *prōcūrātiō* 'superintendence' (cf. Lat. *cūrō* 'I care for', пе́чься 'to take care of', see also печа́ль 'sadness').

О́ПЕРА [ópera] 'opera'. Late 17th century (opera and ballet became an established feature of the Russian court by the 1730s), from Ital. *opera* 'work, opera' (cf. Lat. *opera* 'effort, work').

ОПЛЕУ́ХА [opleúcha] 'slap in the face'. 18th century,

originally *оплевуха, then оплеу́ха (cf. omission of -в- in dial., e.g. де́ушка 'girl' alongside standard де́вушка, though in оплеу́ха -в- is omitted possibly under the influence of у́хо 'ear'). From оплева́ть 'to spit on', from the practice of spitting on one's hands (or maybe at an opponent) before striking.

ОПРЕДЕЛИ́ТЬ [opredelít'] 'to determine'. Lit. 'to set a limit', from преде́л 'limit'.

О́ПТОМ [óptom] 'wholesale'. Mid-18th century at latest, instr. sing. of *оптъ* 'total', cognate with о́бщий 'general, total', cf. adj. опто́вый 'wholesale' (recorded in dictionaries 1793).

ОПЯ́ТЬ [opját'] 'again'. 10th century 'back', 12th century 'again', probably from CSl. *pęta 'heel' (пята́/пя́тка, id.), thus properly 'retracing one's steps' (cf. пя́титься 'to move back'), possibly comprising prefix о- + acc. case of *пять 'heel' (a form lost in resolving homonymy with пять 'five'). Cf. analogous formations о́бок (coll.) 'close by', поо́даль 'at some distance' (obs./dial. о́даль, id.), stressed -я́- in опя́ть by analogy with вспять (obs.) 'backwards'.

ОРА́НЖЕВЫЙ [oránževyj] 'orange'. 1860s, from Fr. *orange* 'orange' (adj. and noun), via Sp. *naranja* 'orange' from Pers. *nārang* 'orange'/Ar. *naranj* 'bitter orange', with ultimate source in India.

ОРГА́Н [orgán] 'organ' (musical instrument). 12th century, with the development of Christianity, from Gk. *órganon* 'instrument, tool, musical instrument' (whence Lat. *organum* 'organ', the source of 'organ' in WEur. languages), possibly via MHG *organa*, id., from Lat. pl. *organa*, id.

О́РГАН [órgan] 'organ'. 18th century, probably from Fr. *organe* 'organ, agency' (cf. Fr. *orgue* 'organ' (musical instrument), via Pol. *organ* 'organ', ultimately Lat. *organum* 'instrument, engine', Gk. *órganon* 'instrument, organ of sense' (from *érgon* 'work').

ОРЁЛ [orël] 'eagle'. 11th century *орьлъ (cf. IE *oros 'eagle, hawk', *orneu- 'move, fly'), with cognates in Gk. *órnis* 'bird', Lith. *erelis* 'eagle', Goth *ara* 'eagle' (Ger. *Aar*, id. (poet.) alongside standard *Adler*). Possibly also associated with Gk. *ornúō* 'I dart, rush forward', *órō* = *anō* 'upwards', Lat. *orior* 'I rise'. For suffix, cf. осёл 'donkey'.

ОРЕХ [oréch] 'nut'. From CSl., o- perhaps originally a prefix, cf. Lith. *riešutas*, id. Dubious possibility of association with *rěšiti 'to detach' (cf. OR *рѣшити* 'to untie', *орѣшие* 'nut trees'), thus 'an easily picked fruit'. For prefix o- in the meaning 'riddance', however, cf. освободи́ть 'to liberate'.

ОРУДИЕ [orúdije] 'implement, gun'. 12th century 'work', 13th century 'court case', also 'implement', then (recorded 1782) 'artillery piece' (for analogous dual meaning, cf. OR *дѣло* 'gun', де́ло 'business', Pol. *działo* 'artillery piece', Cz. *dělo*, id.). Derives from CSl. *orǫdьje 'implement', with -ǫ- changing to ESl. -y-, also connected with CSl. *rędъ (ряд, as in снаря́д 'contrivance, missile'), and with Gk. *aráriskō* 'I furnish', Lat. *arma* 'implements, weapons'. The suffix -ие suggests ChSl. provenance. Cf. also сооруди́ть 'to construct', обору́довать 'to equip'.

ОРУЖИЕ [orúžije] 'weapons'. CSl. *orǫžьje, OR 'implement, armaments', based on the root *rǫg- (cognate with руга́ть 'to abuse', Bulg. *ръгам* 'I stab'), with -g- changing to -ž- before -j-. Derivative *ружье́* 'armaments' evolved in the 17th century, the meaning subsequently narrowing to 'shot-gun' (cf., however, под ружьём 'under arms', see ружьё).

ОСА [osá] 'wasp'. 11th century, from CSl. *vopsā/*vosa (-ps- simplifying to -s-, cf. Lith. *vapsva*, id., Lat. *vespa*, id.). Ultimately from IE *u̯obhsa 'wasp, weaving' (*u̯ebh- 'to weave'), from the wasp's skill in constructing web-like nests. For v-, cf. dial. *во́стрый* 'sharp', alongside standard о́стрый.

ОСЁЛ [osël] 'donkey'. 11th century *осьлъ*, from Goth. *asilus* 'ass' (Ger. *Esel*, id.), Lat. *asinus*, id. (itself seemingly from a language of Asia Minor). For ending -ёл, cf. козёл 'goat'. There is a possibility of contamination with Lat. dim. *asellus* 'little ass,

ass's colt'.

ОСЕНЬ [ósen'] 'autumn'. From CSl. *jesenь (IE *as̩i̯ō(n) 'harvest time, autumn'), with (j)e- changing to ESl. o- before medial -e- (cf. Pol. *jesień* 'autumn'). Cognate with Goth. *asans* 'harvest, summer', cf. analogous association between OHG *herbist* 'autumn' (Ger. *Herbst*, id.) and Eng. *harvest* (perhaps ultimately from IE *(s)ker- 'to cut').

ОСЕТР [osëtr] 'sturgeon'. 12th century (17th century осетри́на 'flesh of the sturgeon'), from CSl. *jesetrъ (cf. Pol. *jesiotr* 'sturgeon'), with close cognates in Gmc., cf. Ger. *Stör*, id. (whence стéрлядь 'sterlet'), also MLat. *sturio* 'sturgeon', Lith. *eršketas*, id. The R. form is possibly influenced by CSl. *ostrъ 'sharp'.

ОСКОЛОК [oskólok] 'splinter'. Cognate with колóть 'to prick, stab', cf. скалá 'cliff', Lith. *skelti* 'to split' and (with consonant mutation) щель 'crack'. Dim. of оскóл 'splinter' (Dal').

ОСНОВА [osnóva] 'basis'. From CSl., denoting the warp (the threads stretched in the loom to be crossed by the weft -- the cross-threads -- [утóк]), later generalized as 'basis, foundation'. Cf. also сновáть 'to stretch longitudinal threads, warp, dart hither and thither' (from the movements of a weaver).

ОСПА [óspa] 'smallpox'. 12th century *осъпьныи недугъ*, id., 15th century *осъпы* 'spotted disease', from CSl. *osъpa (*sъp- cognate with *sypati 'to sprinkle'), based on *obsъpti, cf. обсы́пать 'to sprinkle', сыпь 'rash', referring to the spread of smallpox pustules over the body.

ОСТРОВ [óstrov] 'island'. 11th century, from CSl. *ostrovъ/o(b)srovъ, lit. 'land washed by the current, island' (for prefix o-, cf. омы́ть 'to wash', of seas). Cf. IE *sreu- 'flow, stream', Lith. *srovė* 'current', Skr. *srava* 'flow'. For interconsonantal -t-, cf. Gmc. *strauma 'flowing water', струя́ 'stream'.

ОСТРЫЙ [óstryj] 'sharp'. 11th century, from CSl. *os- + *rъ, cf. Lat. *acus* 'needle', Gk. *akís* 'point', with subsequent interconsonantal -t-, cf. Lith. *aštrus* 'sharp'. Derivatives include поощря́ть 'to encourage', навостри́ть (coll.) 'to sharpen'.

ОСЬ [os'] 'axle, axis'. 14th century, from CSl. (IE *ak̂sis, id.), with cognates in Gk. *áxōn*, id., Lat. *axis*, id., Lith. *ašis*, id., and with -ks- simplifying to -s-. Perhaps cognate with Lat. *agō* 'I put in motion'.

ОТВА́ГА [otvága] 'daring'. 18th century, seemingly ante-dated by отва́житься 'to venture' and отва́жный 'daring', from Pol. *odwaga* 'daring', *odważyć się* 'to risk', cf. Pol. *odważyć* 'to weigh', a derivative of *ważyć* 'to weigh, weigh up, risk'. The correlation between 'weighing' and 'daring' is illustrated by Ger. *Waage* 'scale' and *wagen* 'to dare', esp. in the phrase *in die Waagschale werfen* 'to throw onto the scales, risk' and in dial. *отва́жить* 'to weigh out'/отва́житься 'to venture'.

ОТВЕ́РСТИЕ [otvérstije] 'opening'. 11th century, in origin a verbal noun from *отъвьрзти* 'to open' (-с- being of ChSl. provenance).

ОТЕ́Ц [otéc] 'father'. 11th century *отьць*, from CSl. *ot- (IE *atā- 'daddy') + suffix -ьсь (earlier *отькъ 'father'), a hypocoristic form (cf. Gk. *átta* (whence Attila) 'a salutation made to elders, father'), originally a child's form of address that subsequently replaced IE *pətēr in Slav. Cf. derivatives о́тчество 'patronymic', оте́чество 'fatherland', о́тчим 'stepfather'. Note also (non-IE) Turk. *ata* 'father, ancestor'.

ОТЧА́ЯТЬСЯ [otčájat'sja] 'to despair'. 11th century, from ChSl., cf. от- 'detached from', ча́ять 'to hope', thus 'to lose hope', cf. неча́янно 'inadvertently'.

ОФИЦЕ́Р [oficér] 'officer'. 17th century, becoming common in the reign of Peter I, from Sw. *officer*, id. or Ger. *Offizier*, id., ultimately Fr. *officier*, id., from MLat. *officiārius* 'functionary, officer', Lat. *officium* 'service, duty'. End stress casts doubt on any likelihood of Pol. provenance.

ОХОТА [ochóta] 'desire, hunt'. 14th century 'pleasure, joy' (mainly as *охвота*, esp. in older texts), 17th century 'hunt', replacing *ловъ*, pl. *ловы* 'hunting', perhaps as a tabooistic semantic extension (cf. Pol. *polować* 'to hunt', from *pole* 'field'). The meaning progresses from 'urge' to 'urge to acquire, catch, hunt', on the basis of CSl. *chotěti 'to want'. OR *охвота* possibly results from a contamination of *охота* and *хватати* 'to seize', cf., for analogous chv-/ch- alternations, Pol. *chory* 'sick' and хворь (coll.) 'ailment', Pol. *choina* 'pine tree' and хвóя 'needle(s) of conifer'.

ОЧЕНЬ [óčen'] 'very'. 17th century *очунь/очюнь* 'barely conscious' (cf. OR *очутие* 'consciousness', очу́хаться 'to come to'). Possibly from *очьнь, short form of OR *очьный*, from *око* 'eye' (cf. óчная ста́вка 'confrontation', очеви́дный 'obvious'), with -к- palatalizing to -ч- before -ь and semantic development from 'awake', 'with one's own eyes', 'definitely' to 'extremely'.

ОЧКИ [očkí] 'spectacles'. Early 17th century, from очкó 'point', dim. of óко 'eye', possibly under the influence of Lat. *oculārius* 'relating to the eyes' (Lat. *oculus* 'eye').

ОШЕЛОМИТЬ [ošelomít'] 'to stun'. From OR *шеломъ* 'helmet', cf. шлем, id., originally 'to strike on the helmet, head' (according to Šanskij, 'knock off the helmet'), then 'to render unconscious', finally 'to stun' (fig.).

ОШИБКА [ošíbka] 'mistake'. 17th-/18th centuries (15th century *ошибитися* 'to refrain, lag, be deprived, side-lined, secluded', with the meaning 'make a mistake' recorded in dictionaries 1731). Based on o- + CSl. root *šib- 'a blow', cf. pattern o- + root + -ка 'mistake' in опи́ска 'slip of the pen', etc.

П

ПАВА [páva] 'peahen'. 17th century, from Lat. *pāvŏ* 'peacock', Gk. *taŏs*, id. (cf. 15th-17th centuries *таусинный*, of red-blue shades), with initial p- under the influence of Lat. *paupulŏ* (onomatopoeic, of the peacock's cry). Possibly via OHG *pfawo*, id. (Ger. *Pfau*, id.), ultimately from an E. source (peacocks are said to have been scarce in W. countries until brought from India by Alexander of Macedonia).

ПАВЛИН [pavlín] 'peacock'. Recorded in dictionaries since 1704 (cf. 16th century *павъ*, id.), from Fr. *pavillon* 'pavilion, tent' (the bird thus being named from the similarity between its tail fan and a marquee), itself from Lat. *pāpiliŏ* 'butterfly'. Alternatively, from Lat. *pāvŏnīnus* 'peacock's', with dissimilation from n-n to l-n.

ПАДАТЬ [pádat'] 'to fall'. 11th century *падати*, ultimately from IE *pād 'fall', also cognate with IE radical *pod- 'foot, base', whence Gk. *poús*, gen. *podós* 'foot', Lat. *pēs*, gen. *pedis*, id., and with dial. *под* 'bottom, floor', под 'sole of furnace', 'under'. Cognates include пропасть 'chasm', запад 'west', Skr. *pad* 'fall', *patya* 'falling'.

ПАДЕЖ [padéž] 'case' (gram.). From ChSl. (cf. -ě- in cognate падёж 'cattle murrain', lit. 'falling disease'), a calque (like Lat. *cāsus* 'fall, case') of Gk. *ptŏsis*, id., cf. Ger. *Fall*, id.

ПАДЧЕРИЦА [pádčerica] 'step-daughter'. 13th century *падъщерица*, based on па- 'secondary' + CSl. *dъkti, acc. *dъkterь 'daughter', cf. Lith. *podukra* 'step-daughter'.

ПАЛАТКА [palátka] 'tent'. Early 18th century, from 11th century *полата/палата* 'house, palace, marquee', ultimately from Gk. *Palátion*, Lat. *palātium* 'the Palatine Hill' (residence of the Roman emperors since the time of Augustus) and, by meaning transfer, 'palace'. Unconnected with полотно 'canvas'.

ПАЛАЧ [paláč] 'executioner'. 16th century, from Tkc. (cf.

Turk. *pala* 'scimitar', also early 17th-century палаш 'broadsword', for agent suffix, cf. трубач 'trumpeter'). Alternative associations have been made with палка 'stick', палить 'to shoot' and полати 'high raised platform' (later peasant's sleeping bench), since executions were carried out on such platforms.

ПАЛЕЦ [pálec] 'finger'. 11th century пальць, id., seemingly also 'thumb', 16th-/17th centuries exclusively 'finger', from the CSl. root *pal- (whence беспалый 'lacking one or more fingers or toes'). Cognate with Lat. *pollex* 'thumb', possibly Bulg. *палам* (obs./reg.) 'I look for' (alongside standard *търся*, id.). An intriguing connection with Gk. *psalmós* 'song of the bowstring' is posited by Vasmer (with special reference to the role of the thumb in drawing a bow Mongol-style). See напёрсток 'thimble', перчатка 'glove', cf. Bulg. *палец* 'thumb', *пръст* 'finger'.

ПАЛКА [pálka] 'stick'. 11th century *палъка/палица* 'stick, staff', from CSl. *pala, cf. Pol. *pal* 'stake', *patka* 'club'. Possibly cognate with палить 'to burn' (thus 'what is burnt, firewood, branch burnt on fire', or 'piece of wood, device for making fire by friction'), also with OHG *spaltan* 'to chop' (Ger. *spalten*, id.). Less likely to be connected with OHG *pfal* 'stake' (Ger. *Pfahl*, id.), from Lat. *pālus* 'stake, wooden post'.

ПАЛОМНИК [palómnik] 'pilgrim'. 13th century, possibly from пальма 'palm' (Lat. *palma* 'palm, palm-tree'), properly 'traveller returning from distant holy lands with a palm branch' (in N. countries the palm was replaced by the верба 'willow' during the Easter ceremonial, hence вербное воскресенье 'Palm Sunday'). Perhaps some influence of псалом 'psalm', псаломщик 'psalm-reader'.

ПАЛУБА [páluba] 'deck'. CSl., probably from па- 'similarity' + луб 'bast, usually lime-bark for roofing', thus initially 'floor made of a material resembling bast'.

ПАМЯТЬ [pámjat'] 'memory'. 11th century, from CSl. *pamętь/*pomьntь (*po- 'consequence' + *mьntь 'thinking', thus properly 'the result of thinking'), with -ę- to ESl. -я-. Cf.

Lith. *mintis* 'thought', *atmintis* 'memory', Lat. *mens*, gen. *mentis* 'mind', also мнить 'to think, imagine', мнение 'opinion'.

ПАНИХИДА [panichída] 'requiem'. 14th century, from Byz. Gk. *pannychída* 'night service' (Gk. *pannychís*, gen. *pannychídos* 'vigil', from *pân* 'all', *nýx* 'night', also calqued as всенощная 'night service'), subsequently 'night vigil by the body of a deceased, requiem mass'.

ПАНЦЫРЬ [páncyr'] 'armour'. Late 15th-/mid-17th centuries *пансырь*, id. (-с- perhaps under the influence of OFr. *pancier*, id.), later пáнцырь, id., perhaps influenced by Pol. *pancerz* 'coat of mail'. Cf. also Ital. *panciera* 'cuirass', with -c- seemingly pronounced as -c- in N. Ital. dialect (Venice and line E. of Venice, cf. standard -č-). Via MHG *panzier* (Ger. *Panzer* 'armour-plating'), Pol. *pancerz* or Cz. *pancéř* 'armour', ultimately from OFr. *pancier*, Lat. *pantex* 'paunch', thus lit. 'that which covers the belly' (cf. Ital. *pancia* 'stomach', *panciera* 'cuirass').

ПАПИРОСА [papirósa] 'cigarette'. Mid-19th century, from Pol. *papieros*, id., hence *папирос* (1847) (-s on the pattern of Sp. pl. *cigarros* 'cigars'), from Pol. *papier* 'paper', a reference to the smoking of tobacco wrapped in paper, instead of in a pipe. Final -a perhaps under the influence of early 19th-century *цигá(р)ра*, then сигáра 'cigar' (initially also 'cigarette').

ПАПКА [pápka] 'file'. Early 19th century, from Ger. *Pappe* 'pasteboard', lit. 'pap' (from the thick layers of paste that held sheaves of paper together), ultimately from Lat. *pap(p)ō* 'I eat, eat pap', onomatopoeic *păpa/pappa* 'word with which infants call for food'.

ПАПОРОТНИК [páporotnik] 'fern'. 17th century, cf. OR *папороть* 'forest thicket', CSl. *pa 'similar to' + *portь 'wing' (IE *peros 'feather, wing'), so called from the wing-like appearance of fern fronds, cf. Lith. *sparnas* 'wing', *papartis* 'fern', Gk. *pterón* 'feather, wings, winged creature', *pterís* 'kind of fern', dial. *папороть* 'second joint of a bird's wing'. Cf. also Eng. *fern*, primary meaning 'feathery leaf'.

ПАР [par] 'steam'. 11th century *napa* 'steam, smoke', later пар, cognate with преть 'to rot, sweat, stew, become damp'.

ПАРИКМАХЕР [parikmácher] 'hairdresser'. First half of 18th century, from Ger. (cf. Ger. *Perückenmacher*, lit. 'wig-maker', 17th-/18th centuries *Parucke* 'wig'), form influenced by парик 'wig' (early 18th century), Fr. *perruque*, id. (Provençal *perucat* 'with a good hair-style', lit. 'like a parrot'). Парик possibly directly from D. (D. *pruik*, id.), ultimately from Lat. *pilus* 'hair', whence eventually Ital. *parrucca* 'wig' (according to Grimm, a distortion of Lat. *pilucca*, dim. of *pilus* 'hair').

ПАРОМ [paróm] 'ferry'. ChSl. *прамъ* (15th century), OR *поромъ* (recorded 1585), from CSl. *pormъ (IE *por- 'to bring over', *poros 'crossing, track' -- cf. Gk. *póros* 'means of passing a river, ford, ferry' -- *pormos 'progress, ferry'), with interconsonantal -opo- in ESl. (then -apo- through *akan'je*). Cognate with Ger. *fahren* 'to travel' (cf. also Ger. *Prahm* 'flat-bottomed boat', from Cz. *pram* 'ferry'), thus lit. 'what you travel on'.

ПАРТА [párta] 'school desk'. Mid-19th century, possibly from Fr. *à part* 'apart, separately', perhaps via Ger. *apart*, id., following the introduction of individual desks into schools, by contrast with communal benches.

ПАРТЕР [partér] 'stalls'. 18th century, from Fr. *parterre*, id., possibly via Ger. *Parterre*, id.

ПАРУС [párus] 'sail'. 15th century, from Gk. *pháros* 'sailcloth' (for ph:p correlation, cf. Gk. *Stéphanos* and Степан 'Stephen'). Possibly influenced by OR *n(ъ)ря* 'sail'.

ПАССАЖИР [passažír] 'passenger'. Early 18th century, from Fr. *passager*, id., via Ger. *Passagier*, id., D. *passagier*, id. or (perhaps less likely) Ital. *passeggiero*, id.

ПАСТИ [pastí] 'to tend'. 11th century, from CSl. *pasti (IE *pā̆- 'feed, guard', *pāskō 'feed, tend, protect'), cognate with Lat. *pāscō* 'I feed, tend', *pastor* 'shepherd' (perhaps also *pānis* 'bread', *pābulum* 'fodder'). Derivatives include пáстбище 'pasture' (from *nácmьба* 'tending' + -ище 'place').

ПАСХА [páscha] 'Easter', also 'a sweet cream-cheese dish eaten at Easter'. 11th century, of ChSl. provenance, from Gk. *Páscha* 'Passover or Paschal feast, Paschal lamb' (whence Lat. *pascha* 'feast of the Passover, Easter', Ital. *Pasqua* 'Easter'), ultimately Hebr. *pesah* 'passover', name of the festival commemorating the liberation of the Jews from Egyptian bondage and the flight from Egypt (involving the sacrifice of a lamb, to avoid God's slaughter of all the first-born in the land of Egypt, see *Exodus* 10-12), Christ later being equated with the Paschal lamb as a sacrifice of atonement, a symbolic significance not easily translatable, hence retention of the Hebrew word: Пácxa is seemingly the only festival in the Orthodox calendar with a foreign name. Adj. *пасхáльный* 'paschal' under the influence of Lat. *paschālis*, id.

ПАУК [paúk] 'spider'. 15th century 'hooked mark' (in music), 17th century 'spider', from CSl. *paǫkъ (*pa- 'similarity' + *ǫkъ (IE *onkos 'hook'), cognate with Gk. *ógkos* 'curve', *agkṓn* 'bend, elbow', Lat. *uncus* 'hook', thus lit. 'hook-like', of a spider's curved legs, or the hooks on its feet, with -ǫ- to ESl. -y. Note end stress (cf. пá- in пáлуба 'deck', пáдчерица 'stepdaughter'). 18th century паутúна 'web' (OR *паучина*, id.), perhaps through contamination with тянýть 'to stretch' or пýтать 'to tangle'.

ПАЧКА [páčka] 'packet'. From Pol. *paczka* 'small packet', dim. of *paka* 'pack, bale', from Ger. *Pack* 'packet', cf. паковáть 'to pack', possibly from Ger. *packen*, id., via Pol. *pakować*, id.

ПАЯТЬ [pajátʼ] 'to solder'. OR *паяти* 'to forge', possibly cognate with пойть 'to water' (cf. Pol. *spajać, spoić* 'to solder'), since early techniques of soldering involved 'drenching' hard metal with its molten counterpart.

ПЕЛЬМЕНИ [pelʼméni] 'pelmeni'. Early 19th century, from Komi (a Finno-Ugrian language), lit. 'ears of bread' (*pelʼ* 'ear', *ńań* 'bread'), from the shape of the small pastries that comprise the dish, with dissimilation from n-n to m-n, *пермени* being an erroneous form based on a false association with the city of Perm'.

ПЕРВЫЙ [pérvyj] 'first'. 11th century *пьрвыи* 'first, former', from CSl. (IE *prīmos 'first', *prīuos 'first, foremost'), possibly cognate with перед 'in front of', also with Skr. *pūrvya* 'former, ancient, first', Lith. *pirmas* 'first', Fr. *premier*, id.

ПЕРЕВОД [perevód] 'translation'. 16th century, calqued from Fr. *traduction*, id., Lat. *trăductio* 'removal, transfer of meaning'.

ПЕРЕВОРОТ [perevorót] 'coup d'état'. 18th century, a calque of Fr. *révolution*, Lat. *revolūtio* 'revolving, revolution'.

ПЕРЕПЕЛ [pérepel] 'quail'. 15th-/16th centuries at latest, originally, seemingly, *пелепелъ* (Dal'), from *pelpelъ, a reduplication of onomatopoeic *pel, partly from the bird's cry (described by S.T. Aksakov, however, as 'va-vva', then 'podьpolotь'), partly from the sound of its wings on take-off, with ESl. inter-consonantal -еле-, then -ере-, by dissimilation of л-л to р-л.

ПЕРЕЦ [pérec] 'pepper'. 16th century, from 12th century *пьпьрьць*, a derivative of OR *пьпьръ*, perhaps ultimately from Skr. *pippalī* '(long) pepper', via Lat. *piper* 'pepper' and Gk. *péperi*, id. (perhaps through Gmc. mediation -- pepper was used by the W. Goths), one syllable having been lost through haplology (i.e., пьпь- to пь-, then пе-, thus: пе́рец 'pepper' from *пьпьрьць*, in its turn from *пьпьръ*), cf. Pol. *pieprz*, id.

ПЕРИЛА [perila] 'railing'. Late 17th century, as the pl. of *перило, from CSl. *perti 'to press, lean on' (cf. пере́ть 'to push, press'), lit. 'what you lean on'. For -ил(а), cf. pl. agent words черни́ла 'ink', бели́ла 'whitewash'.

ПЕРО [peró] 'feather, pen'. 12th century 'wing', 15th century 'feather' (IE *peros 'feather, wing'), cognate with пари́ть 'to soar', Lith. *sparnas* 'wing', debatably with Gk. *pterón* 'feather, wings, winged creature'. See also пра́порщик 'ensign', па́поротник 'fern'.

ПЕ́РСИК [pérsik] 'peach'. Late 17th-/18th centuries, probably via MLG or D. (cf. D. *perzik*, id.), from MLat. *persica* 'Persian (fruit)', Lat. *Persicum mālum*, lit. 'Persian apple' (the peach is the fruit of the tree *Amygdalus persica*), whence OE *persoc* 'peach' (Lat. *mālum* 'apple' could denote any tree-fruit fleshy on the outside and having a kernel within, including the peach).

ПЕРСТ [perst] (obs.) 'finger'. 11th century, from CSl. *pьrstъ, with a cognate in Lith. *pirštas* 'finger'. See перча́тка 'glove', напёрсток 'thimble', па́лец 'finger'. Пе́рстень 'signet-ring' is a calque of Gk. *daktýlios*, id., from Gk. *dáktylos* 'finger'.

ПЕ́РХОТЬ [pérchot'] 'dandruff'. Recorded in dictionaries since 1847, though seemingly much older, from CSl., cf. IE *preus- 'sprinkle, spray', *pelsn- 'powder, dandruff'. Cognate with по́рох 'powder', прах 'ashes', порха́ть 'to flutter about'.

ПЕРЧА́ТКА [perčátka] 'glove'. Early 18th century, originally *пьрщатька* (also *перс(т)чатка*), lit. 'mitten with fingers', from перст 'finger', cf. рукави́ца 'mitten', ва́режка 'knitted or sewn mitten with thumb but no fingers'. See перст 'finger'.

ПЁС [pës] (coll.) 'dog'. 11th century *пьсъ/песъ*, possibly named after the colour of a particular breed, cf. *pьs(t)гь 'many-coloured, spotted' (пёстрый, id.), less plausibly associated with Lat. *pecus* 'cattle, head of cattle, animal' (the dog was the first domesticated animal), thus possibly 'guardian of cattle' (Vasmer cites *pecus servans* 'sheep dog'). Note also assumed connection with Lat. *speciō* 'I watch'. See соба́ка 'dog'.

ПЁСТРЫЙ [pëstryj] 'many-coloured'. 11th century, from CSl. *pьstrь, associated with CSl. *pьs-, the root of *pьsati 'to daub, make colourful' (cf. писа́ть 'to write') + suffix *-гь, with subsequent inter-consonantal -t- (cf. о́стрый 'sharp').

ПЕТРУ́ШКА I [petrúška] 'parsley'. 17th century, from Pol. *pietruszka*, id., possibly via Ger. *Petersilie*, id., from MLat.

petrosilium/petroselīnon, id., Gk. *petroselīnon*, id. (comprising *pétros* 'rock', *sélīnon* 'celery'). Alternatively, a reworking of the Gk./Lat. on the basis of Пётр 'Peter', cf. Gk. *Pétros* 'Peter', *pétros* 'rock'.

ПЕТРУШКА II [petrúška] 'Punch'. At the latest mid-18th century, possibly calqued from Ital. *Pulcinella*, id. (a comic figure in the Neapolitan *Commedia dell'arte*, associated through false etymology with *pulcino* 'chick', cf., from animal tales, Пётя-петушóк 'Pete the cockerel'), or based on Петрýха, a comic figure in popular prints of the 17th-/18th centuries.

ПЕТУХ [petúch] 'cockerel'. 17th century (16th century also as a nickname), from the root of петь 'to sing' (cf. OR *пѣтие* 'singing', пéние, id.). For suffix -ух, cf. пастýх 'shepherd'.

ПЕТЬ [pet'] 'to sing'. Usually associated with Gk. *paián* 'paeon' (choral hymn, mainly in honour of Apollo). Derivative *песнь* (obs.) 'song' was reshaped as пéсня, id., on the pattern of nouns in -ня, певéц/певíца 'singer' come from iterative певáть 'to sing'. Interpretation of the homonymy between пою 'I sing' (from петь) and пою 'I give to drink' (from поить 'to give to drink') by reference to the heathen rite of sacrificial libation, which includes ceremonies that involve drinking and extolling, has all the appearance of a false etymology.

ПЕХОТА [pechóta] 'infantry'. 17th century *пѣхомá*, id. (present stress in dictionary of 1704), from CSl. *pěš- 'foot' (IE *ped-), a root retained in пешехóд 'pedestrian', пéшка 'pawn', пешкóм 'on foot'. See ногá 'foot'.

ПЕЧАЛЬ [pečál'] 'sadness'. 11th century, from CSl. *pečalь, itself from *pekělь, based on *pekti 'to bake', with -k- to -č- before -ě- (first palatalization of velars) and -ě- to -a- after -č-. Thus lit. 'that which burns'. Alternatively, from *pekti sę (пéчься) 'to care for' (cf. OR *печися* 'to be concerned, grieve').

ПЕЧАТЬ [pečát'] 'print, press'. 10th century 'sign, sign cut in metal or stone for off-printing', from CSl. *pekěti (perhaps from *pekti 'to bake'), with -k- changing to -č- before -ě-, -ě- to -a-after -č-). Initially 'hot metal, printing mechanism', then (19th century, influenced by the appearance of the word пре́сса 'press' in the 1840s, according to Vasmer) 'print, press'. Ger. *Petschaft* 'seal', MHG *petschat*, id. are from Cz. *pečet*, id. (specifically the Bohemian Chancery in 13th-/14th centuries).

ПЕЧЕНЬ [péčen'] 'liver'. 15th century, through reaffixation from *печенъ*, past pass. part. of *печи* (печь 'to bake'), thus lit. 'something fried'. Cf. печёнка 'liver' (as food), Lith. *kepenis* 'liver' (with metathesis p-k(č)/k-p).

ПЕЧЬ I [peč'] 'to bake'. 11th century *печи*, from CSl. *pekti 'bake' (IE *pequ̯ō 'to cook, bake'), cf. Skr. *pakti* 'cooking', Lat. *coquō* 'I bake', Lith. *kepti* 'to bake' (with metathesis p-k/k-p).

ПЕЧЬ II [peč'] 'stove'. From CSl. *pektь, see печь I 'to bake'.

ПЕЩЕРА [peščéra] 'cave'. 11th century OR *печера* (-щ- from ChSl.), whence Пече́рский монасты́рь 'Cave Monastery' in Kiev and the Pečora river in the Dnieper basin (purportedly from the many caves in the lower reaches of its N. course). Based on *pektь 'stove' + -era (said to denote similarity), thus properly 'recess like a stove' (from the similarity of the entrance to a stove or the use of cave-like recesses as stoves). Probably no connection with Lat. *specus* 'cave'.

ПИВО [pívo] 'beer'. 11th century 'drink' (cf. IE *pīi̯ō 'drink', *pibō 'drink'), 14th century 'beer', through semantic narrowing. Cf. Eng. *beer* from Lat. *bibō* 'I drink'.

ПИДЖАК [pidžák] 'jacket'. 1840s/50s, from Eng. *pea-jacket* (sailor's short double-breasted overcoat of coarse woollen cloth), probably from D. *pijjakker* (MD *pij* 'flannelette jacket', D. *jekker* 'jacket'), perhaps with some influence of Fr. *jaque* 'type of jerkin'.

ПИКИ [píki] 'spades' (suit in cards). Seemingly appeared first quarter of the 19th century (replacing earlier *ви́ны* or *ви́ни*, id.), from Fr. *pique* 'pike', also 'spade(s)', cf. too Ger. *Pik* 'spades', Pol. *pik*, id., so called because the tip of a pike is depicted on this suit of cards. Пик 'mountain peak' is from Fr. *pic*, id. and пика 'pike' from Ital. *picca*, id., via Ger. or Fr.

ПИЛА [pilá] 'saw'. 11th century, probably from OHG *fila* 'file' (Ger. *Feile*, id.), perhaps cognate with Lith. *peilis* 'knife'. Cf. IE *peil- 'tool, file', напильник 'file'.

ПИЛЮЛЯ [piljúlja] 'pill'. 17th century, from Lat. *pilula*, id., the dim. of *pila* 'ball', via Fr. *pilule* 'pill'.

ПИР [pir] 'feast'. 11th century, from CSl. *piti 'to drink' + suffix -гъ, cf. дар 'gift' from дать 'to give', жир 'fat' from жить 'to live'.

ПИРОГ [piróg] 'pie'. 12th century, originally 'loaf made of sifted flour', maybe 'ceremonial wheaten loaf', from CSl. *pirъ 'feast', alternatively from OR *пыро* 'spelt' (wheat giving a fine flour, cf. IE *pyrós 'wheat, spelt', Gk. *pyrós* 'wheat'), with -ы- changing to -и- under the influence of пир 'feast'. For suffix, cf. творог 'cottage cheese'.

ПИСАТЬ [pisát'] 'to write, paint (artistically)'. 10th century *писати* 'to write, paint', from CSl. *pьsati (IE *peik- 'mark, paint, draw, write'), cognate with *pьstrъ (пёстрый 'many-coloured') and with Gk. *poikílos* 'many-coloured', Lat. *pingō* 'I paint, adorn', Lith. *piešti* 'to draw'. Originally 'to adorn, depict through carving or paints, make colourful' (cf. расписной 'decorated', Ukr. *писанка* 'decorated Easter egg').

ПИСЬМО [pis'mó] 'letter'. Initially 'writing' (see писать 'to write'), then 'letter', usually associated with Lith. *piešimas* 'drawing'. For suffix, cf. бельмо 'cataract'.

ПИТЬ [pit'] 'to drink'. 11th century *пити*, id., cf. IE *pīiō 'drink', *potos 'drink' (and root variants in поить 'to give to drink', пей! 'drink!'), cognate with Skr. *pā* 'drink', Gk. *pínō* 'I drink', Lat. *bibō*, id., *pōtus* 'drink, drunk'.

ПИЩА [píšča] 'food'. 11th century, from CSl. *pitja, via ChSl. (hence -šč- from -tj-, for ESl. reflex -č- cf. пичкать (coll.) 'to stuff, cram'). Cognate with питáть 'to feed'.

ПИЯ́ВКА [pijávka] 'leech'. OR *пиявица* (present form recorded in dictionaries 1793), lit. 'that which drinks', with -и- for expected -ь-, perhaps under the influence of пить 'to drink', note -ь-, however, in dial. *пья́вка* 'leech' and пья́ный 'drunk'.

ПЛА́КАТЬ [plákat'] 'to weep'. 11th century *плакати* (from CSl. *plakati, IE *plāg- 'beat, beat the breast, mourn'), properly 'to pummel oneself on the chest in grief', cf. Lith. *plakti* 'to flog', Lat. *plangō* 'I beat, beat in lamentation, lament'. Possibly cognate with Ger. *fluchen* 'to curse' (from Gmc. *flokan).

ПЛА́МЯ [plámja] 'flames'. 11th century, from ChSl. (hence inter-consonantal -ла-, cf. dial. *пóломя/пóлымя*, id.), ultimately CSl. *polmę/*polmen 'that which burns', from CSl. *polti 'to burn'. Cognates include пали́ть 'to burn', пе́пел 'ash', поле́но 'log'.

ПЛА́СТЫРЬ [plástyr'] 'plaster'. 11th century, via ChSl., and OHG *pflastar*, id. from Late Lat. (*plastrum francum* 'white lime plaster'), Gk. *émplastron* 'plaster', or via Pol. *plaster*, id.

ПЛА́ТА [pláta] 'payment'. Cognate with плат (obs.) 'kerchief, large piece of fabric', whence also пла́тье 'dress', earlier 'clothing' (hence платяна́я щётка 'clothes-brush'), cf. полотно́ 'linen' (with ESl. -оло-). The meaning 'payment' is said to derive from a 9th-/10th-century practice of using lengths of fabric for trade and the payment of tribute.

ПЛАТА́Н [platán] 'plane-tree'. 1860s, from Lat. *platanus* 'Oriental plane-tree', possibly via Fr. *platane* 'plane-tree', ultimately Gk. *plátanos*, id., from the breadth of the tree's flat leaves, or of its crown (Gk. *platýs* 'broad').

ПЛАЩ [plašč] 'raincoat'. 13th century *плащь*, usually associated with плат (obs.) 'piece of material', or with пло́ский 'flat' (cf. Pol. *płaski*, id.), perhaps therefore referring to a smooth fit, alternatively with roots denoting 'broad', from the appearance of the coat (cf. IE *platus 'broad').

ПЛЕВАТЬ [plevát'] 'to spit'. 11th century *плевати*, onomatopoeic, from CSl. *pjuti, with pj- changing to пл- and cognates in Lat. *spuō* 'I spit', Lith. *spiauti* 'to spit', Eng. *spew*.

ПЛЕМЯ [plémja] 'tribe'. 11th century, id., from CSl. *pledmen 'people', probably comprising *pled-/*plod- 'fruit' + *-men, resultant -dm- simplifying to -m- (cf. CSl. *věmь 'I know' from *vědmь) and -ę, subsequently -я, evolving from -en. Cf. also Gk. *plēthos* 'multitude', Lat. *plēbs* 'common people'. Derivatives include племя́нник 'nephew', племя́нница 'niece'.

ПЛЕСТИ [plestí] 'to braid, plait'. 11th century, from CSl. *pletti/*plesti, ultimately *plekti (assimilation of -kt- to -tt-, dissimilation of -tt- to -st-), cf. Gk. *plékō* 'I plait', Lat. *plectō*, id., Ger. *flechte*, id. Cf. also cognates плеть 'whip', плот 'raft'.

ПЛЕЧО [plečó] 'shoulder'. 11th century *плече*, from CSl. *pletje, perhaps based on IE *platus 'broad', *plātos 'flat object', and cognate with Gk. *ōmoplátē* 'shoulder-blade'. Подоплёка, initially 'shoulder lining of a shirt', then 'underlying cause', may be back-formed (-к- from -ч-), see фля́га 'flask'.

ПЛИТА [plitá] 'slab, stove, cooker'. 12th-/13th centuries 'stone, brick' (also OR плинтъ and плинфъ 'brick'), probably cognate with Gk. *plínthos* 'brick, tile, stone squared for building, plinth', the name given by Byz. builders to the smooth stone from which the buildings of ancient Kiev were constructed. Possibly also cognate with Eng. *flint*.

ПЛОД [plod] 'fruit'. 11th century, from CSl. *plodъ/*pledъ (which is associated with плéмя 'tribe'), thus perhaps lit. 'born', subsequently 'fruit', maybe based on IE *plō- 'full'.

ПЛОТ [plot] 'raft'. Cognate with плыть 'to swim, sail', cf. Gk. *plōtós* 'sailing, navigable', Ger. *Floβ* 'raft', alternatively with плести́ 'to braid' (плету́ 'I braid'), thus initially (11th century) 'wattle fencing, enclosure', then 'logs fastened together to form a raft' (hence пло́тник 'carpenter', lit. 'raft-maker, craftsman expert in securing beams'). Derivatives include плоти́на 'dam', probably initially 'large fence' (cf. домина 'large house').

ПЛОТНЫЙ [plótnyj] 'dense, solid'. Probably an extension of OR *плотьныи* 'bodily, material' (from плоть 'flesh') to the meaning 'compact'. Alternatively connected with плету 'I braid', thus lit. 'firmly woven together' (see плот 'raft').

ПЛОЩАДЬ [plóščad'] 'square'. OR 'square, street', from ChSl., based on Gk. *plateia (hodós* 'way' understood) 'street', lit. 'flat, broad way', alternatively from *ploskědь, cf. плóский 'flat', with -sk- palatalizing to -šč- before -ě-, thus 'flat area'.

ПЛЫТЬ [plyt'] 'to swim, float'. 11th century *плути, плавати* 'to sail' (IE *pleudos 'flow, float, swim'), 17th-/18th centuries плыть (however, prefixed derivatives appear much earlier). Cognates include пловец/пловчиха 'swimmer', плот 'raft', Gk. *pléō* 'I sail', Lith. *plauti* 'to rinse, wash', Ger. *Flut* 'flood'.

ПЛЮЩ [pljušč] 'ivy'. OR *блющь*, id., плющ recorded in dictionaries since 1762, with п- for б- possibly under the influence of plant names such as повилика 'dodder' (a twining parasitic plant) and повой (*Convolvulus arvensis*), or influenced by плюю 'I spit' (cf. блюю 'I vomit', and for б:п mutation cf. брызгать 'to splash', прыскать 'to sprinkle'). Ultimately from CSl. *bljuščь and cognate with блевать 'to vomit', from the expectorant effect of the plant's poisonous berries.

ПОБЕДА [pobéda] 'victory'. From ChSl., possibly CSl. *poboida, id., based on *boi- 'beat', -oi- changing to -ě- in OR/ChSl. Alternatively, from беда 'misfortune' (cf. *побѣда* 'a small misfortune, consequent on a major one' (Dal')). The coexistence of conflicting connotations in one word may be due to the sequence: по беде ('after the misfortune'), then победный 'victorious', also 'hapless' (Ušakov), backformed to победа 'victory, defeat' (e.g., in the 16th-century *Степенная книга* 'Book of Degrees'). The meaning 'defeat' is said to have been expunged after the victories of the early 18th century. For an analogous formation, cf. пособие 'assistance', and for opposite meanings invested in one word, cf. Lat. *sinister* 'left, favourable, unfavourable' (apparently depending on the direction in which the augurs faced, the Romans S., with the propitious E. on the left, the Gks. N.).

ПОВЕСТЬ [póvest'] 'tale'. Through deaffixation from OR *повѣстити* 'to recount', from CSl. *povědti/*povědĕti 'to communicate' (cf. повéдать 'to relate').

ПОГОДА [pogóda] 'weather'. 14th century, originally 'good weather' (hence непогóда 'bad weather'), then 'weather in general'. Cf. год 'year', originally 'good, convenient time'.

ПОДДАННЫЙ [póddannyj] 'subject'. 17th century, from Pol. *poddany*, id., a calque of Late Lat. *subditus*, id., pass. part. of *subdō* 'I place under, subject'.

ПОДЕЛОМ [podelóm] 'deservedly'. Recorded in dictionaries from 18th century, from *по* + *дѣломъ* (old dat. pl. of дéло 'deed'), thus 'according to one's deserts'.

ПОДКУЗЬМИТЬ [podkuz'mít'] 'to do someone a bad turn'. From the festival of Sts. Kuz'ma and Dem'jan (17th October, OS), at which deals were concluded and accounts settled between employer and employee, originally 'to dispel hopes connected with St. Kuz'ma's Day'. Cf. объегóрить 'to cheat', originally referring to the practice of reneging on similar deals struck before St. George's Day (Егóр(ий) from Геóргий, patron saint of agriculture), 26 November NS.

ПОДЛЕЖАЩЕЕ [podležáščeje] 'subject' (gram.). Lit. 'lying under', imprecise calque of Lat. *obiectum* 'object' (part. from *obiciō* 'I throw before'), Gk. *hypokeímenon* 'substance, external reality, logical subject', from *hypókeimai* 'to be subject to'.

ПОДЛИННЫЙ [pódlinnyj] 'genuine'. From the ancient practice of beating suspects during interrogation with long sticks, said to have been called пóдлинники, from длúнный 'long'.

ПОДНОГОТНАЯ [podnogótnaja] (coll.) 'the whole truth'. Adj. noun based on подногóтная тáйна, lit. 'under-nail secret' (cf. нóготь 'finger-nail'), from the medieval practice of forcing needles under the finger-nails of suspects to obtain evidence.

ПОДОБНЫЙ [podóbnyj] 'similar'. From OR *подоба* 'likeness' (seemingly a prefixed derivative of *доба* 'benefit, profit'). Initially 'suitable', cf. удóбный 'convenient'.

ПОДОЗРЕНИЕ [podozrénije] 'suspicion'. Calque based on под- 'surreptitious' and зреть 'to see', cf. analogous Lat. *suspicor* 'I suspect' (*sub-/sus-* 'under' + *spiciō* 'I see', cf. also подозревáть 'to suspect', подозрéть (obs.) 'to spy').

ПОДОШВА [podóšva] 'sole, foot (of slope)'. 14th century *подъшьва* 'sole', from под- 'under' + *šьv- 'sew' (for -в-, cf. шов 'seam'), thus lit. 'something sewn under'. Cf. пóчва 'soil'.

ПОДРАЖАТЬ [podražát'] 'to imitate'. From ChSl., recorded in R. since the 11th century (cf. also OR *подрагъ* 'likeness, imitation'), based on *по* + *драга* (дорóга) 'path', thus lit. 'to follow the same path'. Alternatively from 'assimilative' prefix под- (cf. поддéлываться под 'to assimilate to') + the root of *ражество*, *ражесть* 'quality, state', also 'valour, beauty, approval' (Dal'), thus lit. 'to assimilate to the quality of'.

ПОДРОБНЫЙ [podróbnyj] 'detailed'. From дробь 'fraction'.

ПОДУШКА [podúška] 'pillow, cushion'. Lit. 'something puffed up', cf. Pol. *duchna* 'pillow with down'. Alternatively, perhaps through a false etymology, from под ýшко 'under the ear' (cf. Fr. *oreiller* 'pillow', from *oreille* 'ear'). Final -a perhaps by analogy with пери́на 'feather-bed' or dims. in -ушка (cf. голóвушка, emotive dim. of головá 'head').

ПОЕДИНОК [poedínok] 'duel'. From Pol. *pojedynek*, id. (Pol. *jeden* 'one'), ChSl. provenance precluded by the meaning.

ПОЖАЛУЙСТА [požálujsta] 'please'. Recorded in dictionaries from first half of the 19th century (for 18th-century пожа́луй), from the sing. imper. or first pers. sing. of пожа́ловать 'to grant, bestow, confer' + particle -ста, which imparts a nuance of courtesy and is perhaps an abbreviation, via *-сда, of су́дарь (obs.) 'sir'.

ПОЗВОНО́К [pozvonók] 'vertebra'. Recorded in dictionaries from the first half of the 18th century, connected through e:o vowel mutation with звено́ 'link'.

ПОЗО́Р [pozór] 'shame'. 11th century 'spectacle', then 'laughing-stock, disgrace', cognate with зо́ркий 'keen-sighted', взор 'glance', зреть 'to see', cf. Pol. *pozór* 'appearance', Cz. *pozor!* 'attention, look out!'. The meanings 'spectacle' and 'shame' are combined in позо́рный столб 'pillory'.

ПОЙМА́ТЬ [pojmát'] 'to catch'. From prefix по- + OR *имати* 'to take, seize'. Cf. поня́ть 'to understand'.

ПОКА́ [poká] 'while'. A coalescence of по 'up to' (cf. по щи́колотку 'up to the ankle(s)', по 1 ма́я 'up to 1 May') + ка 'which' (neut. nom./acc. pl.), from *покаместа* (second half of 15th century) 'to which place(s), time(s)', used esp. in legal documents, then almost exclusively in temporal meaning from the second half of the 16th century (as *покамест,* in business, subsequently diplomatic, correspondence, cf. spatial куда́ 'where to', which replaced *покамест* by the early 17th century). Пока́ (from *покамест*) is sparsely represented in the 16th century but develops in the 17th century and is the norm from the early 18th century (cf. tendency of many conjunctions to be disyllabic).

ПОКО́Й [pokój] 'rest, peace'. 11th century, from CSl. *pokoj (IE *kuiea- 'rest', whence also Goth. *hweila* 'time', OHG *(h)wile* 'while, rest, pause', Lat. *quiēs* 'rest', *tranquillus* 'tranquil'). Possibly a deaffixed form from поко́ить (obs.) 'to tend, cherish', cognate with почи́ть 'to rest'.

ПОЛ I [pol] 'half, sex'. 11th century, from CSl. *polъ, possibly from IE *(s)p(h)el- 'to split', the meaning 'sex' having developed from 'half' in the OR period.

ПОЛ II [pol] 'floor'. 12th century *полъ* 'bottom, foundation', 15th century 'floor', possibly from CSl. *pod- 'bottom, foundation' + -lъ (cf. тыл 'rear', ýзел 'knot'), with subsequent simplification of -dlъ to -lъ. Alternatively, associated with Skr. *phalaka* 'board, plank' or пóлка 'shelf'.

ПОЛЕ [póle] 'field'. 11th century 'field, steppe', from CSl. *polje, IE *pel- 'broad, flat, to spread out', connected with пóлый 'hollow', dial. 'open' (as in пóлая водá 'expanse of flood water'), thus 'open, woodless (area)', cognate with Lat. *palam* 'openly', Ger. *Feld* 'field', *flach* 'flat', perhaps also *Westfalen* 'Westphalia' (and *Ostfalen* 'Eastphalia'). Cf. also поляки 'Poles', properly 'field-dwellers', Pol. *polować* 'to hunt' (perhaps tabooistic, properly 'roam the fields'). Cf. also OR *польскьıи* 'relating to fields, plains' and пóльский 'Polish'.

ПОЛК [polk] 'regiment'. 11th century 'host, detachment, campaign', from CSl. *пълкъ 'multitude, people' (IE *pulkos 'crowd', perhaps IE *pelu- 'many'). Maybe directly from Gmc. *fulka-, cf. Goth. *fulk(s) 'military detachment', OHG *folc* 'people, host', ON *folk* 'people, army, detachment'. Subsequently the meaning 'regiment' evolved, with cognates in Lith. *pulkas* (from OR) 'regiment, crowd', cf. also Ger. *Fußvolk* 'infantry' (also *Infanterie*). The Gmc. lexis is related to Lat. *plēbs* 'common people' and perhaps Gk. *plēthos* 'mass, the people'.

ПОЛКА [pólka] 'shelf'. In dictionaries since 1704, replacing *полúца*, cognate with or derived from пол 'floor', cognate with Skr. *phalaka* 'plank', OHG *spaltan* (Ger. *spalten* 'to split').

ПОЛКОВНИК [polkóvnik] 'colonel'. 17th century, from Pol. *pułkownik*, id., cf. полк 'regiment', Pol. *pułk*, id.

ПОЛНЫЙ [pólnyj] 'full'. 11th century, with cognates in Lith. *pilnas*, id., Lat. *plēnus*, id., Goth. *fulls*, id. (Ger. *voll*). Ultimately from IE *pol-, pl̥nos 'full'.

ПОЛОЖЕНИЕ [položénije] 'position'. 11th century 'burial',

18th century a calque of Fr. *position* 'position' (Fr. *poser* 'to place', положить, id.).

ПОЛОТНО [polotnó] 'linen'. OR 'linen fabric, web', from CSl. *poltьno, with inter-consonantal -оло- in ESl. Cognate with Skr. *paṭaḥ* 'piece of cloth', cf. dim. derivative полотéнце 'towel'.

ПОЛТОРА/ПОЛТОРЫ [poltorá/poltorý] 'one and a half'. Early 15th century, from *полъ вътора/въторы*, lit. 'half of the second' (cf. analogous Ger. *anderthalb*, id., from *ander* (obs.) 'second, next'), with -лъ вът- simplifying to -лт-. The only survivor in a series that continued *полъ третья/треты* 'two and a half', etc., i.e. *полъ* 'half' + gen. of short-form ordinal numerals.

ПОЛУОСТРОВ [poluóstrov] 'peninsula'. Calqued from Ger. *Halbinsel*, id., lit. 'half island', cf. more accurate Fr. calque *presqu-île* 'peninsula', from Lat. *paenīnsula*, id. (*paene* 'almost', *insula* 'island').

ПОЛЬЗА [pól'za] 'use, benefit'. 11th century, via ChSl., from *polьga (po + lьga 'freedom', perhaps 'permission', see нельзя 'one may not'), with ChSl. mutation of -g- to -z- after -ь- (third palatalization of velars), cf. soft -z- in cognate нельзя 'one may not'. Derivatives include пóльзоваться 'to use' (1627) and 11th-century *пользьныи* 'beneficial' (cf. полéзный 'useful'), cf. also льгóта 'privilege' and вольгóтный (coll.) 'free and easy'.

ПОЛЬКА [pól'ka] 'polka'. 1840s, based on a Cz. folk dance performed by circling pairs executing half-steps and hops, from Cz. *Polka* (the dance arose in Prague in 1831), perhaps initially from Cz. *půlka* 'half', *půlkrok* 'half step', the basic movement in the dance. Reinterpreted, following the brutally-suppressed Pol. rising of 1830, as a mark of solidarity with the Poles. For ending -ка, cf. венгéрка 'Hungarian dance', etc.

ПОЛЮС [póljus] 'pole'. 17th century (in the early 18th century supplanting *полъ*, id., which dominated in the second half of the 17th century, cf. also attempted calques оборóт 'rotation', верх 'summit'). Via Ukr. *полюс* 'pole' or WEur. languages, from Lat. *polus* 'pivot, axis, pole', Gk. *pólos* 'pivot, axis' (*poleúõ* 'I turn, go about'). Полярный 'polar' is from Lat. *polāris*, id.

ПОЛЯНА [poljána] 'glade'. OR 'field', suffixal derivative of по́ле 'field'.

ПОМЕЩИК [poméščik] 'landowner'. 17th century (when the поме́стье 'estate', emulating the во́тчина 'inherited estate', itself became hereditary), from поме́стье 'estate' (cf. ме́сто 'place'), with -ст- palatalizing to -щ-.

ПОМИДОР [pomidór] 'tomato'. Mid-19th century, from Ital. *pomi d'oro* 'tomatoes', lit. 'golden apples', from the red-gold colour of the fruit.

ПОМОЩЬ [pómošč'] 'help'. From ChSl., comprising *pomogti 'to help' + suffix -ть, with subsequent mutation to -šč- (cf., with ESl. -č-, помо́чь 'to help').

ПОНЕДЕЛЬНИК [ponedél'nik] 'Monday'. 11th century, lit. 'day after Sunday' (*po- 'after' + *nedělja 'Sunday'), possibly under the influence of MLat. *feria secunda* 'Monday', lit. 'second festival' (MLat., rejecting pagan names, used *feria* 'festival' to denote days of the week, thus *feria prima* 'Sunday' -- much rarer, however, than *dies domenicus*, id. -- *feria secunda* 'Monday', thus 'day after Sunday', etc., cf. Port. *segunda-feira* 'Monday', lit. 'second day'). See неде́ля 'week'.

ПОНЧИК [pónčik] 'doughnut'. Early 20th century, from Pol. 15th-century *pączek* 'pancake, doughnut', lit. 'small bud', cf. Pol. *pąk* 'bud'.

ПОНЯТЬ [ponját'] 'to understand'. 10th century 'to seize', cf. (with inserted consonant -н-), -(н)ять 'to take, seize', заня́ть 'to occupy'. Subsequently 'to grasp mentally, comprehend', cf. Eng. *comprehend*, from Lat. *comprehendō* 'I grasp, comprehend'.

ПООЩРИТЬ [pooščrít'] 'to encourage'. From ChSl., based on о́стрый 'sharp', with -ст-:-щ- mutation, the present meaning, recorded since the first half of the 18th century, being secondary and metaphorical to the obs. meaning 'to sharpen' (cf. заострить 'to sharpen').

ПОПУГАЙ [popugáj] 'parrot'. 16th century (also *папагай*, -у- possibly under the influence of пугать 'to frighten'). Probably via D. *papegaai*, id., MHG *papegan*, id. (Ger. *Papagei*, id.), from Fr. *papegai* (arch.) 'American parrot' (now 'popinjay', a cut-out model used for archery and cross-bow practice in the N. of France), via Sp. *papagayo* 'parrot', ultimately Ar. *babbaghā'*, id.

ПОРОК [porók] 'vice'. 11th century 'vice, censure, reproach', cognate with порицать 'to censure', with -к-:-ц- mutation (third palatalization of velars). Ultimately from CSl. *rekti 'to speak'. Cf. пророк 'prophet', etc., for -рок 'speech'.

ПОРОСЕНОК [porosënok] 'piglet'. 11th century *порося*, id., from CSl. *porsę, itself said to be from *porsent 'spotted', purportedly a reference to the speckled skin of the young of the wild pig (cf. IE *pŗks 'speckle, sprinkle'), with ESl. inter-consonantal -оро- and suffix -ёнок 'young of animals' (cf. IE *porĝos 'pig', *porkos 'hog, sow'). Cognates include Lat. *porcus* 'pig', Lith. *paršas*, id., Ger. *Ferkel* 'piglet'.

ПОРОХ [póroch] 'gunpowder'. 11th century 'dust', late 16th-/early 17th centuries 'gun-powder' (replacing *зелье* in this meaning, seemingly on the basis of Pol. *proch* 'dust, powder, gunpowder', from CSl. *porchъ 'dust', IE *pŗs 'sprinkle'). Cognates include перхоть 'dandruff', порхать 'to flutter' and its 18th-century derivative поршень 'piston', the two being linked by the concept of movement. Cf. also прах 'ashes' (of ChSl. origin).

ПОРТНОЙ [portnój] 'tailor'. 18th century, an adj. noun based on 16th-century *портнои мастеръ*, from OR *пъртъ* 'piece of coarse fabric', then 'clothes' (cf. *пърты*, subsequently replaced by одежда, id., of ChSl. origin). Cognate with портянка 'puttee', порты (coll.) 'trousers', perhaps пороть 'to rip'.

ПОСЕТИТЬ [posetít'] 'to visit'. 11th century, seemingly based on CSl. *sětь 'guest' (IE *se- 'self', thus perhaps lit. 'to become one of the family, feel at home', cf., based on свой 'one's own', освóиться 'to familiarize oneself, feel at home'). Cognates in Lith. *svečias* 'visitor', Gk. *hetaîros* 'companion'.

ПОСОБИЕ [posóbije] 'aid'. Based on OR *пособъ/пособь*, id. (cf. coll. пособи́ть 'to help'), from *по собѣ* 'after oneself' (possibly from the custom of donating money to the church in the hope of being remembered after death).

ПОСОЛ [posól] 'ambassador'. Based on *посълати* 'to send' (послáть, id.), cf. analogous Eng. *envoy*, ultimately from Fr. *envoyer* 'to send'.

ПОСТЕЛЬ [postél'] 'bed'. 11th century, from *постьлати* 'to spread' (cf. (по)стлáть, id., (по)стелю́ 'I (will) spread').

ПОТОК [potók] 'stream'. 11th century, cognate with течь 'to flow', ток 'electric current', притóк 'tributary', etc.

ПОТОЛОК [potolók] 'ceiling'. Recorded in dictionaries since 1704, based on OR *тьло* (mainly pl. *тьла*) 'floor, foundation' (cf. дотлá 'to the foundation, utterly'). Lit. 'equal to, level with the floor' (according to Šanskij, *по тьлу*). Has also been associated with Lith. *patalas* 'bed', Lat. *tellūs* 'the earth', Ger. *Diele* 'floor-board' and Lat. *palātum* 'vault of heaven, palate'. Cognate with при́толока 'lintel'.

ПОТОМ [potóm] 'afterwards'. Based on CSl. *po tomь 'after that'.

ПОТОМОК [potómok] 'descendant'. 14th century, derivative of потóм 'afterwards', thus lit. 'he who comes afterwards'.

ПОЧВА [póčva] 'soil'. Recorded in dictionaries as 'soil' since 1793, a reworking, perhaps based on allegro pronunciation (cf. -- from *подъшьва* -- *подшва,* an earlier variant of пóчва) of подóшва 'foot of a hill, base, sole of foot' (cf. dial. *пóчва* 'thick soling leather, sole'). The meaning 'soil' possibly developed from the connotation 'base, foundation'. See подóшва 'sole'.

ПОЧКА I [póčka] 'kidney'. A derivative of *pekti 'to bake', cf. пéчень 'liver'.

ПОЧКА II [póčka] 'bud'. From CSl. *pъtj-, cognate with Lith. *pusti* 'to swell' and dial. *пýкаться* 'to open, of buds', cf. also Pol. *pączek* 'bud'. Has been associated with пóчка 'kidney' through a supposed similarity in shape, cf. analogous rapprochement of Lat. *inguen* 'tumour' and Lith. *inskstas* 'bud'.

ПОЧТА [póčta] 'post-office, post, mail'. Known in 16th century, common in 17th century (when a postal relay system was established in the state of Muscovy with the assistance of Ger. commissioners). Originally also *пост* (cf. Ger. *Post*, id.) and *пошта*, id. (the pronunciation -č- was thought to be hypercorrect and pedantically artificial, perhaps a reaction against the pronunciation št- in, for example, что 'what', cf. also мáчта 'mast' for earlier *машта*). *Пошта*, considered as coll., was from Pol. *poszta*, now *poczta*, possibly under the reverse influence of пóчта. Пóчта derived ultimately, via Ital. *posta*, id., from MLat. *posita* (sc. *mansiō* 'stay' or *statiō* 'station, post') 'relay station' (lit. 'established halt'), where horses were changed during a journey, from Lat. *posita* 'situated', fem. part. from *pōnō* 'I set down'. Penultimate stress in the adj. почтóвый 'postal' suggests the possible influence of Pol. *pocztowy*, id. Cognates (-ч- for -s- by analogy with пóчта) include почтальóн 'postman', via Ger. and Fr. from Ital. *postiglione* 'postillion', and почтáмт 'main post office', from Ger. *Postamt*, id.

ПОЧТИ [počtí] 'almost'. Recorded in dictionaries from the first half of the 18th century, an adverbialization of the imper. sing. of *почьсти* 'to reckon' (cf. почéсть (obs.) 'to consider', used in meaning 'almost' in 19th century). Thus lit. 'reckon!', then 'as much as one can reckon, close to what is necessary, almost'.

ПРАВДА [právda] 'truth'. 11th century 'truth, justice, code of rules' (hence the Russian Law Code *Рýсская Прáвда*, dated c. 1282), later прáво 'law', under influence of Pol. *prawo*, id. From CSl. *pravъ 'right'. For suffix -да, cf. враждá 'enmity'.

ПРАВИЛО [právilo] 'rule'. Of ChSl. provenance (cf. OR *правило* 'rudder, helm', *пра́вило* 'rule'), based on *правити* 'to establish, carry out' + suffix -л(о), thus lit. 'what you act by'.

ПРАВОПИСАНИЕ [pravopisánije] 'orthography'. Calque of Gk. *orthografía*, id. (*orthós* 'correct', *gráphō* 'I write').

ПРАВОСЛАВИЕ [pravoslávije] 'orthodoxy' (rel.). From a ChSl. calque of Gk. *Orthodoxía*, id. (*orthós* 'correct', *dóxa* 'opinion').

ПРАЗДНИК [prázdnik] 'festival'. Of ChSl. provenance, ultimately from CSl. *porzdьnъ 'empty', with SSl. interconsonantal -ра- and cognates in пра́здный 'idle' and (with ESl. -оро-) поро́жний 'empty' (cf. поро́жний ход (tech.) 'idling').

ПРАПОРЩИК [práporščik] 'ensign'. Of ChSl. provenance, possibly a calque of Ger. *Fähnrich*, id. (cf. Ger. *Fahne* 'banner', *-rich* on the pattern of *Dietrich, Friedrich*, etc.). From *прапор* 'banner', lit. 'fluttering' (cf. CSl. reduplicated *porpor, whence *perǫ 'I fly'). Cognate with перо́ 'feather', пари́ть 'to soar'.

ПРАЧКА [práčka] 'laundress'. Recorded in dictionaries since 1762, based on 11th-century *пьрати* 'to wash' (13th century 'to press', cf. прать (obs.) 'to squeeze, beat'), from the practice of beating the damp out of washed clothes at the village stream with a *пра́льник* 'wooden roller'. Cf. пра́чечная 'laundry', Pol. *prać* 'to launder', Lith. *perti* 'to flog', *pirtis* 'bath'.

ПРЕГРАДА [pregráda] 'obstacle'. Based on ChSl. *прѣ-* 'across' and *градъ* 'town' (originally 'wall'). Cf., with ESl. flanking vowels, перегоро́дка 'partition'.

ПРЕДАТЬ [predát'] 'to betray'. From ChSl., fig. counterpart to переда́ть 'to hand over'.

ПРЕДВАРИТЕЛЬНЫЙ [predvarítel'nyj] 'preliminary'. Recorded in dictionaries from the 18th century, cf. предвари́ть (obs.) 'to forewarn', comprising ChSl. *прѣд-* and *вари́ть* 'to warn'. Cf. Eng. *preliminary* (Lat. *prae* 'before', *līmen* 'threshold').

ПРЕДЛОГ [predlóg] 'pretext, preposition'. 11th century 'fortification, cause', subsequently 'preposition', a calque of Gk. *próthesis* 'placing before, preposition', Lat. *praepositiō* (most prepositions 'appear before' the noun they govern).

ПРЕДМЕСТЬЕ [predmést'je] 'suburb'. An early 18th-century reshaping of Pol. *przedmieście*, id. (Pol. *miasto* 'town').

ПРЕДМЕТ [predmét] 'object'. First third of 18th century, modelled on Pol. *przedmiot* 'object', itself calqued from Lat. *obiectum*, past. part. of *obiciō* 'I throw towards, place in front of' (cf. пред- 'before', мет- 'throw').

ПРЕДОК [prédok] 'ancestor'. From ChSl., lit. 'one who lived before' (пред- 'before', cf. Eng. *ancestor*, from Lat. *antecēdō* 'I precede'). Cf. also прéжде 'before', from CSl. *perdje, with ChSl. -pe- and -dj- palatalizing to -žd-.

ПРЕДПОЛАГАТЬ [predpolagát'] 'to presuppose'. Calqued from Ger. *voraussetzen*, id., from Ger. philosophical lexis.

ПРЕДРАССУДОК [predrassúdok] 'prejudice'. Second half of the 18th century, calqued from Fr. *préjugé*, id., cf. пред- 'pre' + рассýдок 'reason'.

ПРЕДСЕДАТЕЛЬ [predsedátel'] 'chairman'. From OR *прѣдсѣдати* 'to occupy the first place', with agent suffix -тель.

ПРЕЗИРАТЬ [prezirát'] 'to despise'. From ChSl., perhaps lit. 'to look through, down on' (cf. Eng. *supercilious*, from *super* 'above' + Lat. *cilium* 'lower eyelid'). Cognate with зреть (obs.) 'to look', зрéние 'vision'.

ПРЕКРАСНЫЙ [prekrásnyj] 'magnificent'. From ChSl., comprising superlative prefix *прѣ*- and крáсный 'red' (earlier 'beautiful'). See крáсный 'red'.

ПРЕКРАТИТЬ [prekratít'] 'to cease'. From ChSl., possibly calqued from Ger. *abkürzen* 'to shorten, abbreviate' (cf. Ger. *kurz* 'short', крат- 'brief').

ПРЕЛЕСТЬ [prélest'] 'charm'. From ChSl., comprising *прѣ-* 'intensity' + *льсть* 'flattery' (cf. лесть, id.), initially 'temptation, illusion', then (late 18th century) 'charm'.

ПРЕНИЯ [prénija] 'debate'. 11th century *пьрѣние* 'argument', from *пьрѣтися* 'to argue'. Cognate with ра́спря 'quarrel, feud', спо́рить 'to argue'. Present meanings possibly secondary to 'pressure', cf. напира́ть 'to put pressure on', напо́р 'pressure' (запира́ть 'to lock' and отпира́ть 'to unlock' may also have had early connotations of 'pressure', cf. also Lith. *spirti* 'to press'). For analogous pl.-only noun, cf. перегово́ры 'negotiations'.

ПРЕПЯТСТВИЕ [prepjátstvije] 'obstacle'. From ChSl., based ultimately on *прѣпятыи*, past pass. part. of *прѣпяти* 'to stretch, strain, hinder', cognate with other lexis implying stretching or obstruction, e.g. за́понка 'stud', препо́на (obs.) 'impediment', распя́ть 'to crucify', препина́ние 'punctuation'.

ПРЕСЛОВУТЫЙ [preslovútyj] 'notorious'. From ChSl., comprising *прѣ-* + *словутыи* 'famous' (cf. OR *прѣсловьи* 'respected, renowned'), based on an obs. pres. act. part. from an earlier form of слыть (cf. CSl. *slūti* 'to have a reputation for'. For part. provenance, cf. ртуть 'mercury'.

ПРЕСТОЛ [prestól] 'throne'. 11th century, from ChSl., based on *столъ* 'chair, bench', cf. стлать 'to spread', стелю́ 'I spread'.

ПРИВЕТ [privét] 'greeting'. 11th century, cognate with отве́т 'answer', обе́т 'vow', etc. Cf. OR *вѣтовати* 'to speak'

ПРИВЫКАТЬ [privykát'] 'to get used to'. ESl., cognate with на́вык 'skill', обы́чай 'custom'. See нау́ка 'science'.

ПРИЗВАНИЕ [prizvánije] 'vocation'. 19th-century calque of

Ger. *Beruf* 'profession', a deaffixation of Ger. *berufen* 'to call, appeal', cf. призва́ть, id.

ПРИЗРАК [prízrak] 'spectre'. From ChSl., based on *зрак* (obs.) 'face, image', cognate with зреть (obs.) 'to look', cf. невзра́чный 'unprepossessing'.

ПРИКЛЮЧЕНИЕ [priključénije] 'adventure'. Based on past pass. part. in -ен + verbal noun suffix -ие. Ultimately from CSl. *ključiti 'to catch on, engage' (cognate with клюка́ 'walking-stick'), with reflexive meaning 'to occur, coincide'. Cf. OR *приключаи* 'chance', приключи́ть 'to connect up', приключи́ться 'to happen'.

ПРИЛИЧНЫЙ [priličnyj] 'decent'. From OR *приличьныи* 'similar, corresponding', subsequently 'worthy', adj. to *приликъ* 'facial similarity' (cf. прили́к, in pop. speech 'appearance, propriety'). Alternatively based on OR *прилика* 'example', thus 'exemplary, decent'.

ПРИСТАЛЬНЫЙ [prístal'nyj] 'intent'. Based on past act. part. *присталъ*, from 11th-century *пристати* 'to approach, attach oneself, pester' (cf. приста́ть, id.). Initially 'attached, persistent', then exclusively of glances.

ПРИСУТСТВОВАТЬ [prisútstvovat'] 'to be present'. 18th century, based ultimately on *суть* (obs.) 'they are', whence also, of part. origin, су́щий (obs.) 'existing, (coll.) real' and prefixal derivative прису́щий 'inherent'.

ПРИСЯГА [prisjága] 'oath'. 11th century, comprising при- 'slightly' + the root of *сяга́ть* (obs.) 'to reach, achieve', thus initially 'contact' (with the object on which the oath is taken). Cf. прися́жный 'juror' (following the 1864 law reform), досяга́емость 'range' and cognates осяза́ть 'to feel', осяза́ние 'touch', Pol. *sięgać* 'to stretch out one's hand, reach'.

ПРИТОЛОКА [prítoloka] 'lintel'. Cognate with потоло́к 'ceiling', при- denoting attachment. See потоло́к 'ceiling'.

ПРИЧАСТИЕ [pričástije] 'participle, communion'. 11th century, a calque of Lat. *participium* 'participation, participle' (a verb form that 'participates in', shares features of noun and verb). Alternatively from a ChSl. calque of Gk. *metochḗ* 'partaking of, communion' (i.e. participation in the Eucharist).

ПРИЧИНА [pričína] 'cause'. 15th century, originally 'beginning, initiative', a remodelling of Pol. *przyczyna* 'cause', based on чин 'sequence, rank', чинить 'to carry out'.

ПРИЮТ [prijút] 'shelter, refuge'. Late 18th-/early 19th centuries, by deaffixation from приютить 'to give shelter'. Ultimately comprises CSl. *pri- + *jǫtъ 'roof' (cognate with Latv. *jumts*, id.), whence also уют 'comfort', ютиться 'to take shelter'.

ПРИЯТЕЛЬ [prijátel'] 'friend'. 14th century, from CSl. *prijatelь, cognate with приязнь (obs.) 'good-will' (cf. IE *prii̯āi̯ō 'like, love, favour', *prīi̯ət 'friend', Skr. *priya* 'dear, beloved'), also with OHG *friudel* 'beloved, friend', MHG *vriedel* 'beloved, bridegroom, husband', Ger. *freien* 'to court' (from Gmc. *fri- 'to love, cherish').

ПРИЯТНЫЙ [prijátnyj] 'pleasant'. Based on the pass. part. of OR *прияти* 'to accept' + suffix -ьн-, lit. 'worthy of acceptance'.

ПРОБА [próba] 'trial, test'. 17th-/early 18th centuries, probably via Pol. *próba* 'experiment, trial' or Ger. *Probe*, id. (whence *probieren* 'to try, test, taste'), from Lat. *proba* 'proof', *probō* 'I try, test, inspect', with derivative пробовать 'to try, test, taste'.

ПРОБИРКА [probírka] 'test-tube'. Second half of the 19th century, based on Ger. *probieren* 'to try, test' (cf. obs. *Probierglas* 'test-tube', now *Reagenzglas*, id.), possibly via пробировать 'to test, assay'.

ПРОБКА [próbka] 'cork'. Early 18th century (earlier *проб/проп* 'stopper for a gun-muzzle', from D. (cf. D. *prop* 'plug, stopper'). **Пробка** is probably from LG (since corks used to be imported from Bremen and Oldenburg in N. Germany), cf. Ger. *Propfen* 'cork', from LG *propp(en)*. Final -ка possibly under the influence of затычка 'stopper', втулка 'bung'.

ПРОВОЛОКА [próvoloka] 'wire'. Early 17th century, by deaffixation from *проволочить* (obs.) 'to draw through', thus lit. 'an object made by drawing through' (a reference to wire-drawing), cf. волочильная доска 'draw-plate', волочить 'to drag', волочь (coll.), id.

ПРОЗОРЛИВЫЙ [prozorlívyj] 'perspicacious'. Cognate with прозреть 'to regain one's sight, come to understand, foresee', cf. *прозор* (obs.) 'foresight'. For the ending -(л)ивый, denoting a quality, cf. терпеливый 'patient'.

ПРОЗРАЧНЫЙ [prozráčnyj] 'transparent'. 11th century, from ChSl., comprising про- 'through' + -зрачный (cf. dial. *зрачный* 'visible'), based on *прозрак* (obs.) 'seeing through', from *зрак* (obs.) 'image', thus lit. 'which can be seen through'.

ПРОМЕЖУТОК [promežútok] 'interval'. Based on промеж (coll.) 'between, among'. Both меж 'between' (from OR *межи*, prep. sing. of *межа* 'boundary') and standard между 'between' (of ChSl. provenance, the prep. dual of *межда* 'boundary') derive from CSl. *medja, IE *medhi̯os 'middle'.

ПРОМЫШЛЕННОСТЬ [promýšlennost'] 'industry'. Late 18th century, calqued from Lat. *industria* 'industry, zeal', possibly via Fr. *industrie* 'industry' on the basis of промышленный 'industrial', in origin a part. from промыслить (coll.) 'to get, come by' (impf. промышлять also means 'to earn one's living, trade in'). Initially of any practical activity for the production of useful artefacts, subsequently exclusively of industry. According to Vasmer, Lat. *industria* derives from *endo* (old form of *in* 'in') + *struō* 'I fabricate'.

ПРОНИЦАТЕЛЬНЫЙ [pronicátel'nyj] 'penetrating, perspicacious'. Early 18th century, based on проницать (obs.) 'to penetrate' (cf. проникать, id.).

ПРОРОК [prorók] 'prophet'. 11th century, from ChSl., a calque of Gk. *prophḗtēs*, id. (*pro-* 'before', *phēmí* 'to say'), thus 'he who foretells', -рок from CSl. *rekti 'to speak'.

ПРОСТИТЬ [prostít'] 'to forgive'. OR 'to forgive, heal', from OR *простыи* 'free', probably initially 'to liberate' (from debts, sins, etc.), then 'to forgive'.

ПРОСТОЙ [prostój] 'simple'. 11th century *простыи* 'straight, standing, extending, simple', from CSl. *prostъ (possibly in its turn from *prostrъ 'spread out', cf. простóр 'expanse'). Alternatively, from *pro- + *-stъ (from *-stho) 'stand' (cf. IE *prosthos 'simple', radical *sthā- 'standing'), thus 'straight, standing straight', then 'simple'.

ПРОСТОР [prostór] 'expanse'. 11th century 'freedom, opportunity', 14th century 'expanse', from CSl. *prosterti 'to spread, stretch out' (cf. простерéть, id.), cognate with Skr. *prastara* 'flat surface, bedding', простирáться 'to stretch, extend' (cf. IE *ster- 'spread').

ПРОСТРАНСТВО [prostránstvo] 'space'. 11th century, of ChSl. provenance, cf. прострáнный 'broad, spacious, extensive', странá 'country'.

ПРОСТУДА [prostúda] 'cold'. See студи́ть 'to cool'

ПРОСТЫНЯ [prostynjá] 'sheet'. First half of the 18th century, possibly from простóй 'simple', thus properly 'simple, unsewn linen' (cf. 11th century *простыня* 'simplicity').

ПРОТИВОЯДИЕ [protivojádije] 'antidote'. A calque of Ger. *Gegengift*, id. or Fr. *contrepoison*, id., both based on Lat. *antidotum* 'remedy against poison', Gk. *antídoton* 'antidote' (*antí* 'against', *dotéos* 'to be given').

ПРОХЛАДА [prochláda] 'coolness'. From ChSl., by deaffixation from 11th-century *прохладити* 'to make cold' (cf. also OR *прохладъ/прохлада* 'pleasure'). See холóдный 'cold'.

ПРУД [prud] 'pond'. 12th century 'stream, pressure', 14th century 'dammed area', from CSl. *prǫdъ 'swift current' (cf. Pol. *prąd* 'current'), with -ǫ- changing to R. -y-. The meaning develops from 'swift current' to 'dam, weir', then 'dammed area, pond', cf. прудить 'to dam'. Purportedly also cognate with прядать (obs.) 'to jump, bound'.

ПРУЖИНА [pružína] 'spring'. 16th century 'snare', 17th century 'gun-spring'. Based ultimately on CSl. *prǫgъ 'clamp' (cf. dial. *пруга* 'spring', obs. пружиться 'to tense'), -ǫ- changing to -u- and -g- palatalizing to -ž- before -i-. Cognates include упругий 'resilient' and (from root variant пряг-) напрягать 'to stress', пряжка 'a buckle'.

ПРЯМОЙ [prjamój] 'straight, direct'. 13th century *прямьи* (прямо of earlier provenance), from IE *prom- 'forth, forward', with cognates in Gk. *prómos* 'foremost man', Norw. *fram* 'forward', also Ger. *fromm* 'pious'.

ПРЯМОУГОЛЬНЫЙ [prjamougól'nyj] 'rectangular'. Calque of Ger. *rechtwinklig*, id. or Fr. *rectangulaire*, id.

ПРЯНИК [prjánik] 'gingerbread'. 17th century, from OR *пряньи* 'spicy' (cf. пряный, id.), based on *пьпьр-* 'pepper' + adj. suffix *-ян-*, see перец, id. Cf. Ger. *Pfefferkuchen* 'gingerbread', lit. 'spicy cake'.

ПРЯТАТЬ [prjátat'] 'to hide'. CSl. *prętati, cf. 11th century *опрятати* 'to clear away, prepare for burial' (also dial. *опрятать*, id., прятать сор со двора 'to clear rubbish from the yard'). Perhaps also cognate with *prǫtъ (прут 'twig, switch' [used for binding]), thus lit. 'to twine round' (and thus conceal) or (Černych) 'mark with twigs'. Cf. also опрятный 'tidy'.

ПТИЦА [ptíca] 'bird'. 11th century *пъта, пътаха* (cf. ранняя пташка 'early bird'), *пътица*, id., from CSl. *пъta, id. + dim. suffix -ица. Seemingly cognate with IE *putros 'offspring, chick, cub', cf. Lat. *pullus* 'young animal', *pūtus* 'boy', and with words of flight such as Gk. *ptēnós* 'feathered, winged' (cf. птенец 'fledgeling'), *pterón* 'feather, winged creature' (cf. also IE *pterom 'wing', птеродактиль 'pterodactyl', from Gk. *pterón* 'wing' and *dáktylos* 'finger'). Apparently unconnected with IE *pet- 'fly', Gk. *pétomai* 'I fly'.

ПУГОВИЦА [púgovica] 'button'. Based on OR *пугы*, gen. *пугъве* 'circular ornament', *пугъва, пугъвица*, id., cf. CSl. *pǫgъ (Pol. *pąk* 'bud' perhaps from a button's similarity to a bud, cf. also OPol. *pągwica* 'button'). Cognate with Latv. *poga* 'button' (IE *pungos 'bulge, mass').

ПУЗЫРЬ [puzýr'] 'bubble, blister, bladder'. Early 17th century at latest, from пу́зо 'belly' or CSl. *pǫxurь (cf. Pol. *pęcherz* 'bladder, blister', Cz. *puchyř* 'blister', пу́хнуть 'to swell'), -з- perhaps under the influence of пу́зо. A proposed link with Gk. *physalís* 'bubble, bladder', *physárion*, dim. of *phýsa* 'bubble' is disputed.

ПУЛЯ [púlja] 'bullet'. End 16th century пу́лька, 1630s пу́ля, id. From Pol. *kula/kulka* 'ball, bullet', itself from MHG *kule/kugele*, id. (cf. Ger. *Kaule*, id., alongside standard *Kugel*, id.). K- was replaced by p- possibly under the influence of пали́ть 'to shoot' or пу́шка 'gun' (in OR also 'hand-launched shell'), or of Fr. *boule* 'ball'. Alternatively, пу́лька may come from Pol. *kulka* by dissimilation of k-k to p-k. Finally, пу́ля/пу́лька may be indigenous forms which evolved on the basis of IE *pŭ(k) 'swell, puff'.

ПУНЦОВЫЙ [puncóvyj] 'crimson'. Early 18th century *пунсовый*, mid-18th century пунцо́вый, possibly via Pol. *ponsowy*, id., from Fr. *ponceau* 'corn-poppy, red colour, flame-coloured'.

ПУСТОЙ [pustój] 'empty'. 11th century *пустыи* 'empty' ('uninhabited' 1396), whence пусты́ня 'desert', пу́ща 'impenetrable forest'. Cognate with пусти́ть, initially (as OR *пустити*) 'to free', subsequently 'to set in motion'.

ПУТЬ [put'] 'way'. 11th century, from CSl. *pǫtь (IE *pontos crossing, passage', cf. Gk. *Póntos* 'Black Sea'), with cognates in Lat. *pons*, gen. *pontis* 'bridge, path', Skr. *panthan* 'path'.

ПУХ [puch] 'down, fluff'. 14th century 'trimming on outer clothing' (cf. опу́шка 'trimming'), CSl. *puchъ, perhaps from onomatopoeic *pu- (cf. IE *p(h)ous- 'down, fluff'), cognate with пу́хнуть 'to puff up', пу́хлый 'plump', пыхте́ть 'to puff'.

ПУШКА [púška] 'gun, cannon'. 15th century 'shell', 16th century (mainly pl.) 'cannon' (artillery was introduced into Russia at the end of the 14th century). From MHG *bühse* 'box' (cf. OHG *buhsa*, id.), then, in the second half of the 14th century, 'firearm' (cf. Ger. *Büchse* 'box, rifle'). Probably via Cz. *puška* 'gun' (cf. Pol. *puszka* 'box, case'), ultimately Lat. *buxus* 'box-tree', Gk. *pýxos*, id. May also be connected with пуска́ть 'to throw, launch'. For 16th-century *дѣло* 'cannon', see ору́дие 'field-gun'.

ПЧЕЛА́ [pčelá] 'bee'. 11th century *бъчела*, id., 12th-/13th centuries *пъчела*, id., from CSl. *bъčela, based on onomatopoeic *bъk-/*bъč- (cf. IE *bhukiǭ 'hum, roar'), with б- devoicing to п- before -ч-, cf. dial. *бучать* 'to roar, buzz' and, also onomatopoeic, бука́шка 'small insect', бык 'bull', dial. *бу́чень* 'bumble-bee', Lat. *būbō* 'owl', also Lat. *fūcus* 'drone'.

ПШЕНО́ [pšenó] 'millet'. From CSl. *pьšeno, originally neut. short-form pass. part. from *pьchati/*pьchnǫti 'to grind, crush', thus lit. 'something ground', whence пшени́ца 'wheat' (as early as 11th century). For -ица, cf. грани́ца 'boundary' from грань 'edge'.

ПЫЛ [pyl] 'ardour'. From CSl. *pylъ (whence early 17th-century пыла́ть 'to blaze'), perhaps cognate with пла́мя 'flame', пали́ть 'to burn'. Ultimately from *polěti, id. (for analogous о:ы alternation, cf. нора́ 'den', ныря́ть 'to dive').

ПЫЛЬ [pyl'] 'dust'. 'Dust' seemingly a late meaning of пыл 'ardour', пыль being a phonetic variant. Perhaps cognate with пух 'fluff', Lith. *pūsti* 'to blow'. See пыл 'ardour'.

ПЬЯНЫЙ [p'jányj] 'drunk'. 11th century *пияньш*, id., from CSl. *pijanъ, pass. part. from *pijati, iterative of *piti 'to drink'. The river Пья́на 'P'jána', a left tributary of the Сура́ 'Surá', itself a tributary of the Volga, is said to owe its name to its meandering course, recalling the progress of a drunken man.

ПЯДЬ [pjad'] 'span' (former measure of length, distance between splayed thumb and index finger). 11th century, from CSl. *pędь, cf. *pęti 'to stretch', with -ę- changing to ESl. -я- and cognates in Lat. *pandō* 'I extend', Ger. *spannen* 'to stretch'. Cf. also запята́я 'comma', распя́ть 'to crucify', etc.

ПЯ́ТКА [pjátka] 'heel'. 11th century *пята* id. (пя́тка recorded in dictionaries since 1771), from CSl. *pęta, lit. 'stretched' (ę to я in ESl.), *pęti 'to stretch, press', possibly describing the movements of the heel. Cf. Pol. *pięta* 'heel', Lith. *pentinas* 'spur'. See also вспять (obs.) 'backwards', опя́ть 'again'.

ПЯ́ТЫЙ [pjátyj] 'fifth'. 11th century, from CSl. *pętъ, id., IE *penqutos, id., subsequently пять 'five' (IE *penque), following reinterpretation of the numeral as a cardinal, with -tъ softening to -tь and пять assuming the form of an i-stem noun (see шесть 'six', семь 'seven', etc.). Cf. Lith. *penki/penketas* 'five', Gk. *pénte*, id. Derivatives of пять 'five' include пя́тница 'Friday', пятна́дцать '15' (lit. '5 on 10'), пятьдеся́т '50' (lit. 'five tens'), пятьсо́т '500' (lit. 'five hundreds').

Р

РАБ [rab] 'slave'. 11th century 'slave, servant', probably from 9th/10th-century OBulg. *рабъ* (hence SSl. ра-, cf. хлебороб 'peasant engaged in arable farming', with ESl. по- -- but also Bulg. *роб* 'slave'). Ultimately from CSl. *orbъ, initially 'orphan', then 'slave' (possibly because orphans were often called upon to do most of the hard work in an adoptive household), from IE *orbh- 'deprived of'. Cognates include Lat. *orbus* 'parentless', *orba* 'orphan', Gk. *orphanós* 'orphaned'.

РАБОТА [rabóta] 'work'. 11th century *работа/робота* 'slavery, service, work', from CSl. *orbota, cognate with OHG *arabeit(i)* 'affliction, need' (cf. Ger. *Arbeit* 'work'). ChSl. па- derived from *or- (alternatively, работа, the exclusive form after the 17th century, could have resulted through *akan'je*). For the ending -ота, cf. беднота (coll.) 'poverty'. See раб 'slave', ребёнок 'child'.

РАВНОДУШНЫЙ [ravnodúšnyj] 'indifferent'. Probably via ChSl., calqued from Gk. *isópsychos*, id., cf. *ísos* 'equal', *psyché* 'soul' and Eng. *equanimity* (Lat. *aequus* 'equal', *animus* 'soul, mind').

РАДУГА [ráduga] 'rainbow'. Recorded in dictionaries from 1731 (cf. OR and dial. *дуга*, id.), based on рад 'glad' + дуга 'arc', with loss of one -д- through haplology (cf. будни 'weekdays'). Association with рай 'paradise' results from false etymology (cf. dial. *райдуга* 'rainbow').

РАЗ [raz] 'time, once'. Cognate with резать 'to cut' (for e:a mutation, cf. лезть/лазить 'to climb'), originally meaning 'blow', thus раз denoted 'one blow', then 'once' (cf. разить 'to strike').

РАЗВЕ [rázve] 'really, surely not'. From ChSl., based on CSl. *orzvě, perhaps originally the prep. sing. of *orzъ, (cf. кроме 'apart from', also based on a case form), ultimately from CSl. *orz- 'apart'.

РАЗВИТИЕ [razvítije] 'development'. 19th-century calque of Ger. *Entwicklung*, id. or Fr. *développement*, id., ultimately from Lat. *ēvolūtiō* 'unrolling' (cf. развить 'to unwind').

РАЗВЛЕЧЕНИЕ [razvlečénije] 'diversion'. 18th-century calque of Fr. *divertissement* 'amusement', cf. развлекать 'to divert', from Fr. *distraire*, id. (lit. 'draw apart', compound of *traire* 'to draw' (obs.), now 'to milk'), itself from Lat. *distrahō* 'I pull asunder'.

РАЗНЫЙ [ráznyj] 'various'. From ChSl., based on раз- 'apart' (cf., with ESl. роз-, рознь 'dissension', рóзничный 'retail', пóрознь 'separately').

РАЗУМ [rázum] 'reason'. Seemingly from ChSl., comprising раз- 'distribution, intensification' + ум 'mind' (cf. 12th-century *разумѣние* 'reason', 11th-century *разумѣти* 'to comprehend').

РАЙ [raj] 'paradise'. 11th century 'garden, paradise', probably from Indo-Iran., cf. Skr. *rayi* 'property, wealth, treasure'. Cognate with Lat. *rēs* 'cause, property'. Note раёк (obs.) 'gallery, gods' (theatr.), common in the 19th century, calqued from Fr. *paradis* 'paradise, gods' (theatr.).

РАК I [rak] 'crayfish'. OR 'crayfish, Cancer' (sign of Zodiac), possibly from CSl. *krakъ, itself from *karkъ, ultimately IE *karkəros 'tough', *kark- 'crab', *kar- 'hard' (whence also Ger. *hart* 'hard'). So called from the hardness of the crayfish's shell. Original kr-k to r-k through dissimilation or the influence of *raky 'casing, container' (cf. ра́ковина 'shell'). Cf. cognate Skr. *karka, karkaṭa* 'crab', *kārkaśya* 'roughness, hardness'.

РАК II [rak] 'cancer'. Recorded in dictionaries since the early 18th century, a semantic calque of Gk. *karkínos* 'crab, tongs, C(c)ancer' or of Lat. *cancer* 'crab, C(c)ancer' (originally *carcer, with dissimilation of r-r to n-r). Perhaps based on a comparison between the crayfish's habit of burrowing in river mud and the uncontrollably intrusive spread of cancer tissue, or from the similarity between the great veins that surround a cancerous growth and the claws of a crab, or, finally, from the popular belief in the presence of a crab within the body of one afflicted with cancer. Cf. Ger. *Krebs* 'crayfish, cancer'.

РАКОВИНА [rákovina] 'shell, wash-basin'. 16th century 'mother-of-pearl', from *raky, gen. *rakъve 'casing, container' (cf. Cz. *rakev* 'coffin', ра́ка 'shrine of a saint'). Ultimately from Lat. *arca* 'box' (*arceō* 'I enclose'), possibly via Goth. *arka* 'case' (Ger. *Arche* 'ark'). For formation, cf. морко́вь 'carrots', for suffix -ин(а), льди́на 'ice-floe'.

РАМА [ráma] 'frame'. 14th century at the latest (meaning 'ornamental ligatured script' = вязь, id.), first recorded in Novgorod. From OHG *rama* 'pillar, support' (Ger. *Rahmen* 'frame'), debatably via Pol. *rama*, id. (however, the Pol. word is said to be of later provenance and would in any case be unlikely to have found its way to Novgorod in the 14th century). Based ultimately on IE *rem- 'to rest, support'.

РАНЕЦ [ránec] 'haversack, satchel'. Recorded in dictionaries since 1731, from Ger. *Ranzen*, 'knapsack'. Introduced into Russia by Ger. mercenaries in the 17th century, the meaning 'school satchel' developing considerably later.

РАССЕЯННЫЙ [rasséjannyj] 'absent-minded'. In the meaning 'diffused', from an ChSl. past pass. part. (cf. рассе́ять 'to disperse'). In the meaning 'absent-minded', calqued from Fr. *distrait*, id. (probably via Ger. *zerstreut*, id.).

РАСТИ [rastí] 'to grow'. 11th century, from CSl. *orsti (originally *ordti 'to grow', cf. IE *ordh- 'to grow, growth', with -dt- assimilating to -tt-, -tt- dissimilating to -st-, and *or changing to pa- in ChSl.). Cf. derivative расте́ние 'plant' and, with ESl. po-, рост 'growth', ро́ща 'grove', etc. Cognates include Gk. *órnumi* 'to rouse, stir, call forth', Lat. *orior* 'I rise', *ortus* 'born, arising', *arduus* 'high, steep, arduous'.

РЕБЕНОК [rebĕnok] 'child'. OR *робя* (from CSl. *robę, whence subsequent -en-), later *робенок*, early 18th century *ребенок*, with o:e assimilating to e:e. For an analogous mutation, cf. тепéрь 'now', for initial ro-, cf. Cz. *robatko* 'baby'. Cognate with раб 'slave', рóбкий 'timid', Lat. *orba* 'orphan', Ger. *Erbe* 'heir, inheritance'.

РЕВÉНЬ [revén'] 'rhubarb'. Late 15th century, from Tkc. (cf. Turk. *ravent*, id.), ultimately of Pers. origin (Pers. *riwand*, id.).

РЕДИС/РЕДИСКА [redís/redíska] 'radish'. 18th-/19th centuries, probably from Fr. *radis*, id. (whence *рáдис*, id., recorded 1859, -e- perhaps under the influence of рéдька, id.), itself from Ital. *radice* 'root, horse-radish', Lat. *rădīx* 'root' (cf. Ital. *ravano* 'radish' and *Raphanus sativus*, botanical name for the domestic radish). Alternatively, via Ger. *Radies(chen)*, id., from D. *radijs*, id. (Pliny the Elder is said to have testified to the popularity of the radish among the Germans in the first century AD.) Рéдька, id., known since the 16th century at latest, is from MLG *redik* (Ger. *Rettich*, id.), and thought to be based on Lat. acc. *rădīcem* 'root' (final -a perhaps by analogy with свёкла 'beet', etc.).

РЕЗИНА [rezína] 'rubber'. 17th century, from Fr. *résine* 'resin', via Ital. *resina*, id., ultimately Lat. *rēsīna*, id., Gk. *rhētínē* 'pine resin'.

РЕКА [reká] 'river'. 11th century, from CSl., based on IE *rit- 'run, flow, move', perhaps also IE *rēi̯ō 'roam, stray', whence also рéять 'to soar, flutter', рой 'swarm', рúнуться 'to rush'. Cognates include Skr. *raya* 'current of a river', Lat. *rivus* 'brook', *Rhěnus* 'Rhine'.

РЕЛЬС [rel's] 'rail'. 1830s/1840s, coinciding with railway building in Russia, from Eng. *rails*, with misinterpretation of the Eng. pl. as a sing., cf. кекс 'fruit-cake' from Eng. *cake*. Eng. *rail* derives from OFr. *reille* 'iron rod', Lat. *rēgula* 'staff, rod'.

РЕМÉНЬ [remén'] 'strap'. 11th century, from CSl. *remy, gen. *remene (cf. кáмень 'stone', from *kamy, gen. *kamene), perhaps initially the strap on a cattle yoke or collar. Association with OHG *riomo* (Ger. *Riemen* 'strap') is disputed.

РЕМОНТ [remónt] 'repair'. Early 18th century, from Fr. *remonte*, originally 'supply of horses to the regiments' (*services chargés de fournir des chevaux*), cf. Fr. *remonter* 'to remount cavalry' (and 17th-century Eng. *remount* 'supply with fresh horses'), this being the task of the ремонтёр 'remount officer'. Ремóнт was later generalized to cover any kind of repair.

РЕСНИЦЫ [resnícy] 'eye-lashes'. OR *рясьнъ* 'fringe, decoration' (cf. 11th century *рясьно* 'eye-lash'). Ultimately from CSl. *ręsa 'pendant, fringe', cf. Pol. *rzęsa* 'eye-lash'. *Ряснíца*, id. appeared in the 18th century (cf. *рѣснíца*, id., lit. 'eye-fringe', recorded in dictionaries from 1771).

РЕЦЕНЗИЯ [recénzija] 'review'. 18th-/19th centuries, possibly via Ger. *Rezension*, id., from Lat. *recēnsiō* 'enumeration', *recēnseō* 'I review'.

РЕЧЬ [reč'] 'speech'. OR 'word, speech', from CSl. *rekъ, cognate with *rekti 'to speak' (cf. IE *rektis 'utterance'), -k- palatalizing to -č- before -ь. Cognates include отрéчься 'to abdicate', порóк 'vice', порицáть 'to censure', etc.

РЖА [rža] 'rust' (obs., cf. ржáвчина, id.). 11th century, from CSl. *rъdiā (cf. рдеть 'to glow red', IE *rudh- 'red'), with -dj- palatalizing to ESl. -ž- and cognates in рудá 'ore', Lith. *rudas* 'red, reddish', *rūda* 'ore', Eng. *rust* (from Gmc. *rud- 'red').

РИСОВАТЬ [risovát'] 'to draw'. Early 18th century, from Pol. *rysować*, id., a reshaping of OHG *rizan* 'to draw, write' (cognate with Eng. *write*). Cf. Ger. *reißen* 'to tear, draw', *Reißbrett* 'drawing board', *Riß* 'drawing'. For verb ending, cf. Pol. *rachować* 'to reckon', etc.

РИСУНОК [risúnok] 'drawing'. Late-17th/early 18th centuries, from Pol. *rysunek*, id., -unek from Ger. -ung, perhaps (in the absence of Ger. *Reißung) by analogy with nouns such as *rachunek* 'reckoning' from Ger. *Rechnung*, id.

РОВЕСНИК [rovésnik] 'person of the same age'. Recorded in dictionaries since 1704, from *rovo/*orvo, gen. *rovese/*orvese, cognate with ровный 'even', thus 'of even, equal age'. For -es-, cf. телесный 'corporal' from тело 'body', etc.

РОВНЫЙ [róvnyj] 'even'. 15th century 'equal' (cf. 11th century *равьныи* 'flat, smooth', from ChSl., whence равнина 'plain'). From CSl. *orvьnъ 'even, flat', said to be cognate with Lat. *rūs* 'lands, fields' (more tentatively with Lat. *arvum* 'arable field').

РОД [rod] 'family, kin, origin'. 11th century, from CSl. *rodъ 'origin, stock', based on *ordъ, which derives from *ordti 'to grow, be born' (cf. расти 'to grow', рост 'growth'), also the source of *roditi 'to bear' (cf. родить, id.), iterative *rodjati, whence рожать, id. (with ESl. -ж-) and рождать, id. (with SSl. -жд-). Cf. also рождение 'birth', Рождество 'Christmas'. Derivatives include родной 'native', народ 'people', уродить (coll.) 'to bring forth' (whence урожай 'harvest'). Род 'grammatical gender' is calqued from Gk. *génos* 'race, genus, grammatical gender'.

РОЖЬ [rož'] 'rye'. 12th century *ръжь*, id. (cf. IE *rughis, id.), with -ъ- vocalizing to -о- in nom./acc. case and instr. ржью but zero-reduced in gen./dat./prep. ржи, cf. ложь 'lie'. Cognates include Lith. *rugys* 'rye', Ger. *Roggen*, id.

РОМАШКА [romáška] 'camomile'. 1st half of 18th century, lit. 'Roman flower', based on *Anthemis rōmanā, Chamaemēlum rōmānum* (late Lat. *c(h)amomilla*), from Gk. *chamaímēlon*, lit. 'earth apple' (*chamaí* 'on the ground', *mēlon* 'apple, any tree fruit' -- from the apple-like scent of the plant). For -шка, cf. *роман* (also *романова трава*), found in pre-18th century herbaria, and ромашка 'camomile', and analogous Иван 'Ivan', dim. *Ивашка*. Seemingly directly via Pol. *rumianek* 'camomile' (from the pink tinge of the petals, cf. Pol. *rumiany* 'ruddy'), rather than from Fr. *camomille romaine (Anthemis nobilis)*, a plant whose leaves and flowerheads are used for medicinal purposes.

РОСКОШЬ [róskoš'] 'luxury'. From Cz. *rozkoš* 'pleasure, delight', cf. Cz. *kochati se* 'to enjoy something' (with ch:š alternation), thus 'that which is enjoyed' (cf. OR *роскошьница* 'lover of luxury'). Also said to be associated with коснýться 'to touch', perhaps a reference to tactile pleasure.

РОТ [rot] 'mouth'. 11th century *рътъ* 'mouth, prow', assumed to be cognate with CSl. *ryti 'to dig' (see рыть, id.), рыло 'snout' and рвать 'to tear, rend', thus perhaps initially 'something for digging or rending with' (cf. IE *rŭt 'digging', *rūi̯ō 'pluck, tear, uproot').

РОЯЛЬ [rojál'] 'piano, grand piano'. Early 19th century, from Fr. *royal* 'royal, magnificent'. Seemingly an ellipsis of *royal pianoforte* (cf., also from Fr., analogous formations *роялъ-папье* of a superior brand of paper, *роялъ-пунш* of a superior type of punch), referring to a de luxe model of piano designed and constructed in W. Europe.

РТУТЬ [rtut'] 'mercury'. 12th century, from CSl. *rьtǫtь, probably the pres. act. part. of *rьtti 'to roll' (cf. Lith. *ritinti*, id.), thus 'rolling' (of the movement of mercury). Alternatively, from Ar. *'uṭārid*, which denotes, however, only the *planet* Mercury (cf. contemporary Ar. *zi'baq* 'the metal mercury' and, for the planet -- and god -- R. Меркýрий).

РУБАШКА [rubáška] 'shirt'. 16th century, from рубáха, id., with -х-:-ш- mutation before suffix -(ь)ка, ultimately from *рубъ* 'rough clothing, working clothes, rags' + pejorative suffix -аха (cf. замарáха (coll.) 'sloven'). Cognate with рубить 'to cut', earlier also 'to hem' (cf. рубéц 'hem, seam'), thus originally, perhaps, 'a width of sewn linen, with seams', as opposed to простыня 'sheet' (Uspenskij). See простыня 'sheet'.

РУБИТЬ [rubít'] 'to chop, hack'. OR 'to build of wood', later 'chop', from CSl. *rǫbiti, *rǫbъ 'edge, piece of fabric', whence also рубáшка 'shirt', рýбище 'rags', рубéж 'boundary', прóрубь 'hole in the ice'.

РУБЛЬ [rubl'] 'rouble'. Known since the 12th or 13th centuries, maybe a Novgorod term adopted by Moscow when minting roubles began about 1450. Implies use of metal coinage, cf.

веверица, etc., based on furs. A derivative of рубить 'to chop, hack', first used in Novgorod in place of the гривна 'mark', a unit of currency, one ingot of which weighed 196 grams. Entered the unified monetary system of the Muscovite state in 1543, lit. 'a stump (обрубок) cut from a *grivna*' (cf. 13th century *рубль* 'stump', later 'piece of silver'), notwithstanding objections that roubles were *cast*, not 'cut off'. A possible association with Pers. *rúpiyah* 'rupee', Ar. *rub'iyyah* 'gold coin' has been disputed.

РУДА [rudá] 'ore'. 11th century, id., 12th century 'ore-mine' (now рудник, id.), based on CSl. *rudъ 'red', from the reddish hue of many iron and copper ores, cognate also with рыжий 'red-haired', русый 'light-brown', рдеть 'to glow red', Lith. *rudas* 'red', Lat. *rūfus* 'red, reddish', Gk. *éreuthos* 'redness' (cf. IE *roudhos 'red, russet').

РУЖЬЁ [ruž'ë] 'gun'. 17th century 'weapons, hand-held weapons', having evolved from *оружьё* 'gun, weapons' (individual light firearms were called карабин 'carbine', мушкет 'musket', пищаль 'arquebus', a portable gun supported on a tripod), with subsequent narrowing of meaning to 'gun', replacing пищаль 'arquebus'. Cf. old meaning 'weapons' in под ружьём 'under arms'.

РУКА [ruká] 'hand, arm'. 11th century, from CSl. *rǫka (-ǫ- to -y- in R.), cognate with Lith. *rinkti* 'to gather', *ranka* 'hand, arm', thus properly 'device for gathering in'. Derivative рукавá 'sleeves' is maybe a calque of Lat. *manicae* 'long sleeves, gloves', from *manus* 'hand'.

РУЛЬ [rul'] 'rudder, steering wheel'. Early 18th century (apparently also pronounced [rur]), from D. *roer* 'rudder', with dissimilation from r:r to r:l (cf. февраль 'February', ultimately from Lat. *Februārius*, id.).

РУПОР [rúpor] 'megaphone'. 18th century, from D. *roeper* (Vasmer), cf. *roepen* 'to shout'.

РУСЫЙ [rúsyj] 'light brown'. CSl. *rudsъ 'red-haired' (-ds- simplifying to -s-), cf. Lith. *rausvas* 'reddish, ruddy', Lat. *russus* 'red'. See руда́ 'ore'.

РУХЛЯДЬ [rúchljad'] 'junk'. 15th-/16th centuries 'movable property, belongings' (from *рухло* 'movable property', cf. CSl. *ruchъ 'movement'), 19th century 'lumber, junk', cognate with ру́шить 'to pull down'. For collective ending -ядь, cf. че́лядь (hist.) 'retainers',

РЫБА [rýba] 'fish'. 11th century, from CSl. *ryba, possibly cognate with late MHG *rup(p)e* 'caterpillar, grub' (Ger. *Raupe*, id., cf. also Ger. *Aalraupe* 'eel-pout, burbot'). A taboo for earlier *zъvь (cf. Lith. *žuvis* 'fish'), a word said to have been avoided by fishermen because of its similarity to звать 'to call' (to 'call' the fish would be unlucky, cf. не́вод 'sweep-net', lit. 'non-net'). A connection has also been proposed with рябо́й 'pock-marked', thus initially 'speckled fish' (e.g., a salmon).

РЫНОК [rýnok] 'market'. Early 18th century, from Pol. *rynek* 'market', a reshaping of MHG *rinc* 'ring, circle' (cf. Ger. *Ring* 'ring, association of dealers', Eng. *price-ring*).

РЫТЬ [ryt'] 'to dig'. OR *рыти*, from CSl. *ryti/*routi 'to dig', with stressed -y- changing to -o- before -j-, thus ро́ю 'I dig', and -ou- to -ov- before a vowel, thus ров 'ditch' (CSl. *rovъ, from *rouos). Seemingly cognate with рвать 'to tear, pick', perhaps from the dual action of digging and plucking out the roots of plants, cf. Lith. *rauti* 'to pull up'. Derivatives include ры́твина 'rut', рыло 'snout' (cf. 11th-century OR meaning 'spade, pick'). See рот 'mouth'.

РЮМКА [rjúmka] 'wine-glass'. 17th century, possibly via Ger. *Römer* 'large drinking glass' or D. *roemer* 'wine-glass' (D. *roemen* 'to extol'), in either case 'glass for drinking toasts', -ю- possibly under the influence of -ü- in Ger. *rühmen* 'to extol' (cf. Eng. *rummer* 'large wine-glass').

РЯД [rjad] 'row, series'. 11th century 'order, agreement', later 'row', from CSl. *rędъ 'row', associated by some with Lat. *ōrdō* 'row, series, order'.

С

САБЛЯ [sáblja] 'sabre'. From Hung. *szablya* 'chopper, sabre', cf. *szabás* 'a cut', *szabó* 'tailor'. Alternatively, *szablya* could be of Slav provenance, deriving initially from the language of the nomadic steppe horsemen who used this short curved sword as opposed to the long straight sword [меч] of Europe and Islam.

САВАН [sávan] 'shroud'. OR, from Gk. *sabánon* 'linen cloth or towel' (cf. Lat. *sabanum* 'linen cloth for wiping, wrapping'), itself from Ar. *sabaniyyah* 'black sash made in Saban near Baghdad'. Cf. also Sp. *sabana* 'bed sheet, altar cloth'.

САД [sad] 'garden, orchard'. 11th century 'plant, tree', 13th century 'garden', from CSl. *sadъ 'planting' (*saditi 'to plant', cf. сажáть/посадúть, id.). Cognate with Skr. *sadas* 'seat', сáжа 'soot'.

САЖА [sáža] 'soot'. From CSl. *sadja, cognate with сад 'garden', садúть 'to plant, place', lit. 'that which has settled', thus 'sediment, soot', cf. Gmc. *sotam (whence Eng. *soot*), lit. 'that which has settled'.

САЖЕНЬ [sážen'] '2.13 metres' (the span of both arms). 11th-/12th centuries, from CSl. sęžьnь (*sęg-, the root of *sęgati 'to reach', cf. *сягать* (obs.) 'to reach', Pol. *sięgać* 'to reach out for, attain'). Lit. 'what can be reached, encompassed by outstretched arms', cf. Eng. *fathom* 'six feet', OE *fæthm* 'embrace', OSax. pl. *fathmos* 'two arms outstretched'.

САЛАЗКИ [salázki] 'toboggan'. 19th century, from слáзить (coll.) 'to go, go down', са- possibly under the influence of сáни 'sledge'. Has also been associated with dial. *слúзкий* 'smooth, slippery' and Lat. *saliō* 'I jump.

САЛФЕТКА [salfétka] 'serviette'. Early 18th century, from Ital. *salvietta*, id. (*salvare* 'to save'), -ф- possibly under the influence of pronunciation [f] in Ger. *Serviette*, id.

САМОВАР [samovár] 'samovar'. From сам 'self', варить 'to boil', lit. 'that which boils (water) itself' (i.e. without a stove), cf. Lat. *authepsa* 'water boiler, urn' from Gk. *authépsēs*, id.

САМОДЕРЖЕЦ [samodéržec] 'autocrat'. Calqued from Gk. *autokrátōr* 'one's own master' (*autós* 'self', *krátos* 'power'). Taken as a title by Ivan IV after the conquest of Kazan' and Astrachan' in the 1550s. Самодержа́вие 'autocracy' was introduced soon after.

САНИ [sáni] 'sledge'. Pl. of OR *сань* 'snake', with semantic development perhaps based on the similarity of sledge tracks in the snow to snakes (cf. по́лоз 'grass-snake, sledge-runner').

САПОГИ [sapogí] 'boots'. Probably from Tkc. (cf. *sap, sapaq* 'stalk' in Čagataj lit. lang., Turk. *sap*, id.). Links have also been suggested with dial. *са́пить* 'to tie, hobble a horse' (purportedly referring, by extension, to the ancient Slav practice of tying boots at the ankle and under the sole), with *сопе́ть* 'to wheeze' (supposedly from the creaking sound made by boots) and *сопе́ль* 'iron tube through which a bellows pumps air into a furnace', also, more relevantly, 'one leg of trousers or *sharovary*', from the similarity of these objects to a boot-top (cf. Cz. *sopouch* 'flue, vent'), finally with Fr. *sabot* 'wooden shoe', Ital. *ciabatta* 'slipper'. For -ог, cf. остро́г 'gaol', etc.

САРАЙ [saráj] 'shed'. Early 17th century, from Tkc. (cf. Turk. *saray* 'palace' and, in various Tkc. dials., 'byre, stable, house'), ultimately from Pers. *sarāi* 'palace, harem', cf. сера́ль 'seraglio', from the same source, via Fr. *sérail*, id.

The town of Сара́й 'Saraj' was the capital of the Golden Horde on the left bank of the lower Volga, about 200 miles to the N. of Astrachan'. Founded in the 13th century, it was destroyed in 1460 by the Russians. Cf. also Бахчисара́й 'Bachčisaraj' in the Crimea, lit. 'palace in the garden', from бахча́ 'melon plantation'.

САРАНЧА [sarančá] 'locust'. 17th century (*пругъ*, id., being used 11th-15th centuries), from Tkc., seemingly based on *sary(y)* 'yellow' (cf. Turk. *sari*, id., *saryska* 'locust' in Tkc. dials.), from the insect's colour (considered by some a false etymology).

САРАФАН [sarafán] 'sarafan' (sleeveless dress worn by peasant women). First reference to sarafan as *female* wear was in the 17th century (hitherto it was apparently applied only to male clothing, esp. that of tsars and bojars). From Pers. *sarāpā* 'ceremonial dress', lit. 'from head to foot' (Pers. *sa* 'head', *pā* 'foot'), probably via Tkc. and reshaped under the influence of кафтáн 'kaftan'.

САХАР [sáchar] 'sugar'. From Gk. *sákchar*, id., itself from Skr. *śarkarā* 'sand, granulated sugar'. Cf., also ultimately from Gk., Eng. *saccharin* 'sugar substitute' (however, Eng. *sugar*, Sp. *azucar* 'sugar', etc. derive from Ar. *sukkar*, id.).

СВАДЬБА [svád'ba] 'wedding'. From *сватьба* 'fixing of a marriage, match-making' (cf. сватовствó, id.), with -т- subsequently voicing to -д- before -б-. Based on свáтать 'to marry off to', свáтаться 'to seek in marriage', from сват (fem. свáха) 'match-maker', originally father or relative of bride or groom in relation to their counterpart in the other family, perhaps lit. 'one's own' (IE *su̯ios 'one's own, kinsman').

СВЕКЛА [svëkla] 'beet'. 16-/17th centuries (earlier *севкла*, id., cf. 11th century *сеуклъ*), from Byz. Gk. *seûkla*, pl. of *seûklon* 'beet', reinterpreted in R. as a sing. (cf. скамья́ 'bench').

СВЕКРОВЬ [svekróv'] 'mother-in-law' (husband's mother). Originally the acc. sing. of 11th-century *свекры*, gen. *свекръве*, id., ultimately from IE *suekrūs, id., from *seu 'self'/*seu̯os 'one's own' + *-krū, which has been identified with *крꙑ* 'blood' (кровь, id.), possibly through a false etymology (cf. pop. interpretation of свекрóвь as *всех кровь* 'blood of all'). Cognate with Skr. *śvaśrūh̥* 'mother-in-law', Lat. *socrus*, id., OHG *swigar/swiger*, id. (Ger. *Schwiegermutter*, id.). Свёкор 'father-in-law' derives from CSl. *svekъrъ (IE *suekuros, id.) and is cognate with Skr. *śvaśurah̥*, id. and Ger. *Schwager*, id.

СВЕРЛО [sverló] 'drill'. CSl. *svьrdь + agent suffix -l(o), lit.

'what you drill with' (cf. сверлить 'to drill'). Has been variously associated with Ger. *Schwert* 'sword' (OHG/MHG *swert*), вертеть 'to twirl' and Ger. *Wirbel* 'vortex, whirl' (on the basis of assumed *svьrbdlo).

СВЕРСТНИК [svérstnik] 'person of same age'. From *sъ- 'shared' + CSl. *vьrsta 'age' (cf. OR *вьрста* 'age, maturity, person of same age', верста 'verst' -- 3,500 feet, originally a field measure 'a turn at regular intervals in ploughing', cognate with вертеть 'to turn round and round'). Cf. also верстать 'to rank with, compare with'.

СВЕТ [svet] 'light, world'. 11th century *свѣтъ* 'light' (CSl. *světъ, IE *k̂u̯oit- 'white, bright', *k̂u̯it- 'light, bright'). Derivatives include светить 'to shine', свеча 'candle' (with -tj- to -č- in ESl.), освещать 'to illuminate' (-tj- to -šč-, of ChSl. provenance). The secondary meaning 'world' evolved probably during the period of CSl. unity, only R. having retained the two meanings, cf. basic мир 'world'. See also цвет 'colour'.

СВИДЕТЕЛЬ [svidétel'] 'witness'. From ChSl., initially *съвѣдѣтель*, id., lit. 'he who knows' (cf. OR *съвѣдокъ*, id., ведать 'to know', Pol. *świadek* 'witness'), with -ѣ- in the first syllable changing to -и-, from a false etymology based on видеть 'to see'.

СВИНЬЯ [svin'já] 'pig'. 11th century, from CSl. *svinьja, IE *sū- 'pig' (and suffixes *-ino/*-ina, cf. Lat. *suinus* 'pig's'), cf. Lat. *sūs* 'pig', Ger. *Schwein*, id., *Sau* 'sow'. Possibly onomatopoeic, an association also being possible with Skr. *sū* 'beget', based on the pig's fecundity, or Lat. *sūcus* 'moisture', from its supposed liking for damp places.

СВОБОДА [svobóda] 'freedom'. 11th century, perhaps originally (with end stress) 'community, settlement' (ultimately from IE *su̯ebhi /*su̯obhi 'separate', based on *su̯eios/*su̯eios 'own'; for -ода, cf. господа 'masters', originally a collective), whence слобода 'settlement exempted from normal State obligations' (through dissimilation of labials: в-б to л-б), 'freedom' being a secondary connotation reflected in medial-stressed свобо́да, properly 'status of a (free) member of the clan'. Cognate with осо́ба 'individual', Ger. *Sippe* 'kin, kindred' and perhaps Ger. *Schwaben* 'Swabia', Lat. *Suēbi/Suēvi* 'a powerful people in the NE of Germany'. The Неме́цкая слобода́ 'German (i.e. Foreign) Settlement', a suburb built outside Moscow in the 17th century, played a significant role in the Europeanization of Russia.

СЕВЕР [séver] 'north'. 11th century 'north, north wind', from CSl. (cf. IE *(s)keuer(i)o 'north, north wind', whence Goth. *skura windis* 'storm-wind', eventually Ger. *Schauer* 'shower', cf. also IE *sk̂eur- 'downpour'). Cognate with Lith. *šiaurė* 'north', Lat. *Caurus/Cōrus* 'NW wind'. Cyganenko links CSl. *sěverъ 'north' with *sěu̯eros 'left' (since the N. was to the left of those who faced E. to pray).

СЕГОДНЯ [segódnja] 'today'. Early 18th century, from OR *сего дьне*, lit. 'of this day', subsequently сего́ дня under the influence of jo-stem nouns like конь, gen. коня 'horse' (день was originally a consonant-stem noun with genitive -e).

СЕДЛО [sedló] 'saddle'. CSl. *sedьlo/-ъlo, with cognates in сиде́ть 'to sit', Goth. *sitls* 'seat', Lat. *sella*, id., and with agent suffix -л(о), thus 'what you sit on'.

СЕДОЙ [sedój] 'grey-haired'. 11th century сѣдъи 'old', 17th century 'grey', cognate with се́рый, id., си́вый 'grey, greying'.

СЕЛЕЗЕНЬ [sélezen'] 'drake'. 15th century, possibly from the similarity of the bird's colouring to that of the (lilac-hued) spleen (cf. селезёнка 'spleen', OR *селезеня*, id.) or of the hollyhock (*Althaea rosa*), which is called слез in Serb. Alternatively onomatopoeic (cf., however, кря-кря 'quack-quack' and, of drakes in N. S. Leskov's novel *Соборя́не* 'Cathedral Folk' (1872), *заказа́л, заказа́л*).

СЕЛО [seló] 'village'. Seemingly from a merging of the homonyms *село* 'dwelling, settlement' (from *sedlo, based on IE *sed- 'to sit', with -dlo simplifying to -lo) and *село* 'field' (CSl. *selo 'ploughed field'), thus properly 'settlement on the land'.

Cognate with Lat. *solum* 'land, soil'.

СЕЛЬДЬ [sel'd'] 'herring'. Late 15th century, from OSc. *sild*, id., cf. Norw. *sild*, id.

СЕМЬ [sem'] 'seven'. 11th century, from CSl. ordinal *sedmъ 'seventh' (from *sebdmos, cf. IE *septm̩ 'seven', *sequdəmos 'seventh'), later reinterpreted (in the form *sedmь) as a cardinal and assigned to the category of i-stem nouns, with -dm- simplifying to -m- (cf. retention in седьмóй 'seventh'). For -pt- and -bd-, cf. Skr. *saptan* 'seven' (nom./acc. *sapta*), Lith. *septyni*, id., Gk. *heptá*, id., Lat. *septem*, id., and ordinals Gk. *hébdomos* 'seventh' (cf. *hebdomás* 'week', whence Fr. *hebdomadaire* 'weekly'), Lat. *septimus* 'seventh'.

СЕМЬЯ [sem'já] 'family'. 11th-/12th centuries 'retainers, family', a collective noun (cf. брáтья 'brothers') based on OR сѣминъ 'member of household' (also сѣмьянинъ, id.). Cognate with Lith. *šeima* 'family', Gk. *kṓmē* 'village, country town', Lat. *cīvis* 'citizen', Gmc. *haima (Ger. *Heim* 'home').

СЕМЯ [sémja] 'seed'. 11th century, from CSl. *sěmę, gen. *sěmene, IE *sēmn- 'that which is sown' (*sěti 'to sow'), cognate with Lat. *sēmen* 'seed' and Lith. *sėmenys* 'linseed'.

СЕНТЯБРЬ [sentjábr'] 'September'. 11th century (also *септябрь/семтябрь*, id.), originally *септямбрь*, id., abbreviating through transfer of -м- to a superscript ('tilde') above -п-, with -м- subsequently preceding, then replacing -п- and itself being replaced by -н-, thus finally сентябрь. A reshaping of Gk. *Septémbrios*, from Lat. *September*, September being the seventh month of the Roman calendar. *Септемврий*, from Late Gk., was still found in the early 18th century.

СЕРДЦЕ [sérdce] 'heart'. 11th century 'interior, heart, spirit, anger', from CSl. *sьrdьce 'heart', itself from *sьrdьko, comprising root *sьrdь (cf. IE *ḱerd-) and the seemingly dim. suffix -ko/-ce, cf. suffix-less root in сердобóльный (coll.) 'soft-hearted'. Lit. 'that which is at the centre' (from the central role played by the heart in the human organism). Cf., with ESl. inter-consonantal -ере-, середи́на 'middle'. Cognates include Lat. *cor*, gen. *cordis* 'heart', Lith. *širdis*, id., Gk. *kardía*, id. Cf. also серди́ть 'to anger' (IE *k̑r̥dii̯o 'to make angry, be angry'), perhaps originally 'to arouse any strong feeling', since the heart was considered to be the centre of emotions and mental states, cf. в сердца́х 'in a fit of temper'.

СЕРЕБРО [serebró] 'silver'. 11th century, from CSl. *sьrebro, based on a root exclusive to Balt./Slav./Gmc., with assimilation of liquid consonants (r-r) in Slav. (cf. Lith. *sidabras*, id., Goth. *silubr*, id.) and ESl. inter-consonantal -ере-. Perhaps originally an ancient loan from Asia Minor.

СЕРЕДИНА [seredína] 'middle'. OR *середа/середь*, id., середи́на having been recorded in dictionaries since 1771. Ultimately from CSl. *serd-, with ESl. inter-consonantal -ере-. Cognate with се́рдце 'heart', среда́ 'milieu, environment'.

СЕРП [serp] 'sickle'. From CSl. *sьrpъ (cf. IE *sr̄pos, id.), with cognates in Gk. *hárpē*, id., Lat. *sarpõ* 'I trim, prune', Ger. *scharf* 'sharp'.

СЕРЫЙ [séryj] 'grey'. OR *сѣрыи*, id. (initially with *вълкъ* 'wolf', an epithet popular in folk-lore, but in general use 15th-/16th centuries). Cognate with сия́ть 'to shine', Eng. *hoary*, Ger. *hehr* (itself related to *Herr* 'master') 'venerable' (IE *koiro- 'venerable', cf. Gmc. *heira- 'grey with age'), Lith. *šemas* 'ashy'. See седо́й 'grey-haired', си́вый 'grey(ing)'. Ultimately from IE *k̑aisros 'grey, hoary', *k̑as 'grey'.

СЕРЬГА [ser'gá] 'ear-ring'. Possibly from Tkc. (cf., in various dials., *syrga/syrgala* 'ear-rings' -- in some cases, perhaps, *from* R.), or from Goth. *ausihriggs* (whence OR *усерязь* 'ear-ring', itself eventually replaced by серьга́ id.), which is based on Goth. *auso* 'ear' and Gmc. *hringa 'circle'.

СЕСТРА [sestrá] 'sister'. 11th century, from CSl. *sesra (with subsequent -t- infix, cf. о́стрый 'sharp'), IE *swesr-/*swesōr, based on *su̯e- 'own by derivation', and perhaps *s(o)r 'woman', thus lit. 'one's own woman' (as opposed to daughters-in-law, etc., cf. IE *suo-sər 'own, wife, woman'). Cf. also Lat. *soror* 'sister', Skr. *svasṛi*, id. (*strī* 'woman'), Lith. *sesuo*, gen. *sesers* 'sister'.

СЕСТЬ [sest'] 'to sit down'. 11th century, from CSl. *sěsti, itself from *sědti (cf. Lat. *sedeō* 'I sit', Lith. *sėsti* 'to sit down', IE *sēdis/*sedos 'seat', *sědmi 'sit'). Сидеть 'to sit' evolved from variant *sid- (cf. Lat. *sīdō* 'I sit down'), while CSl. *sęd- (whence сяду 'I shall sit down') derived from root variant *sind- (-n- denotes 'commencement', according to Cyganenko). A further variant, *sad-, forms the basis of сад 'garden', садиться 'to sit down', осада 'siege' and, from iterative *sadjati, сажать 'to seat, plant' (with R. -ж-) and осаждать 'to besiege' (with ChSl. -жд-). The cognate roots appear in many derivatives, e.g. сосед 'neighbour' (lit. 'sitting beside'), сало 'lard, fat' (from CSl. *sadlo, with suffix -l(o), lit. 'that which is deposited, has settled', cf. Eng. *lard* 'a fatty deposit in the body's organism').

СЕЯТЬ [séjat'] 'to sow'. 11th century сѣяти, from CSl. (cf. IE *sēi̯ō 'sow'), cognate with семя 'seed', сито 'sieve', lit. 'what you sift with' (for agent suffix -то, cf. долото 'chisel'), Lith. *sėti* 'to sow', Ger. *säen*, id.

СИДЕТЬ [sidét'] 'to sit'. 11th century сѣдѣти (later си- by assimilation to ending -и- in conjugation, cf. сидишь 'you sit'), cognate with Lith. *sėdėti* 'to sit', Lat. *sedeō* 'I sit'.

СИНИЙ [sínij] 'dark blue'. 11th century, perhaps initially 'shining', cognate with сиять 'to shine', сизый 'dove-coloured', сивый 'grey(ing)'. Derivatives include синица 'blue-bird', синяк 'bruise'. Cf. IE *k̑ĭnis 'grey, blue'.

СИРЕНЬ [sirén'] 'lilac'. First half of 19th century (originally, apparently, as *сирена*). Cf. Eng. *syringa* 'lilac', first applied to the mock orange, whose stems were used to make reed pipes, later to the lilac, formerly called the 'pipe tree' (the plant has straight branches, from which a thick sap is squeezed to make a hollow pipe), hence the connection with Lat. *Syrinx* (also *Syringa*), gen. *Syringis* 'a nymph turned into a reed', Gk. *sŷrigx*, gen. *sŷriggos* 'shepherd's pipe, tube' (cf. Eng. *syringe*, also *syrinx* 'Pan-pipe, song-organ of birds', Ital. *siringa* 'syringa', *siringa di Pan* 'Pan-pipes'). Second-syllable -e- possibly by dissimilation from first-syllable -и-, or because the word may be a loan from Ger. dial. *Sirene* 'lilac' (Grimm), cf. also early form *сирéна* (the structure of the word is further variously said to have been influenced by сńний 'dark-blue', plant names like ясень 'ash-tree', and Gk. *Syría* 'Syria').

СИРОТА [sirotá] 'orphan'. 11th century, id. (cf. also *сирьιи* 'alone, abandoned, orphaned', from CSl. *sirъ 'without kin, homeless'), 14th century 'pauper'. Perhaps initially 'orphanhood' (for abstract suffix, cf. доброта́ 'kindness'). Cognates include Gk. *chêros* 'bereaved', Lat. *hêrês* 'heir'.

СКАЛА [skalá] 'rock, cliff'. 12th century, perhaps initially (Cyganenko) 'crevice', from CSl. *skala (IE *skel-/*skol- 'to divide', cf. Lith. *skelti* 'to split'), whence also оско́лок 'splinter', ска́лить 'to bare' (one's teeth), lit. 'form an aperture between the teeth', щель 'fissure', with -ск- palatalizing to -щ- before -e-. Cf. Ukr. *стрімка скеля* 'cliff'.

СКАМЬЯ [skam'já] 'bench'. OR *скамия*, from Byz. Gk. neut. pl. *skamnía*, reinterpreted as a sing. (cf. *рельс* 'rail'). Vlasto comments that R. end stress suggests an oral transmission, since spoken Gk. often had -iá for learned -ía. Cf. also Byz. Gk. pl. *skamna* 'small couch' (sing. *skamnon*, a reshaping of Lat. *scamnum* 'bench').

СКАТЕРТЬ [skátert'] 'table-cloth'. Mid-12th century, from *дъскотъртъ, comprising *дъска* 'board, table' + *търтъ 'rubbing' (тере́ть 'to rub', cf. dial. *рукотертъ* 'towel'). For loss of initial syllable, cf. стака́н 'glass', хорь 'pole-cat'. Alternatively, from ска́тывать/ската́ть 'to roll up', thus, perhaps, lit. 'something rolled ready for the table'.

СКВАЖИНА [skvážina] 'key-hole, bore-hole'. OR *скважьнь/сквожьнь* 'fissure, cave', сква́жина first half of 18th century, cognate with сквозь 'through', cf. сквозня́к 'draught'.

СКВОРЕЦ [skvoréc] 'starling'. CSl. *skvorьсь, based on

onomatopoeic *skvor-/*skver-, cognate with сверчо́к 'cricket', dial. *сверча́ть* (also onomatopoeic) 'to chirrup'.

СКОВОРОДА́ [skovorodá] 'frying-pan'. Ultimately from CSl. *skovorda and possibly cognate with dial. *скваpa* 'fire, burnt remnants', *шква́рить* 'to fry' (cf. Pol. *skwar* 'heat'), cf. also Arm. *skawaṙak* 'plate, disc', of Iran. origin.

СКОРБЬ [skorb'] 'grief'. 11th century *скърбь/скербь* (IE *skerb- 'cut, incise', thus perhaps lit. 'keen emotion', 'grief'), cognate with OHG *scirbi* 'earthenware vessel, shard' (Ger. *Scherbe*, id.). Perhaps also etymologically linked with ущéрб 'loss, detriment' (with ск- palatalizing to щ-, cf. щерба́тый 'chipped'), and with OE *sceorpan* 'to scrape'.

СКОРЛУПА́ [skorlupá] 'shell'. OR *скоролупля* 'fruit peel', from CSl. *skorupa (cf. Pol. *skorupa* 'shell'), based on *скора́* (obs.) 'bark, skin' (cf. скорня́к 'furrier'), -л- possibly under the influence of лупи́ть 'to peel', лущи́ть 'to shell'. See also шку́ра 'hide'.

СКО́РЫЙ [skóryj] 'quick'. 11th century, with cognates implying lively movement, thus Ger. *sich scheren* 'to hasten, make off', Lith. *skėrys* 'locust', Gk. *skaírō* 'I skip, dance, frisk', also я́щерица 'lizard' (-sk- palatalizing to -šč- before -e-).

СКОТ [skot] 'cattle'. 11th century 'cattle, property, money', corresponding to Gmc. *skatta- (originally 'cattle'), Ger. *Schatz* 'treasure'. For analogous correlations between cattle and money, cf. Lat. *pecus* 'cattle' (IE *peku 'small cattle', i.e. sheep, goats, pigs, *pek 'wool') and *pecūnia* 'money', Gk. *ktênos* 'piece of property, property in herds or flocks, cattle, fortune'. In antiquity cattle constituted a major source of wealth, thus words for cattle acquired monetary connotations as symbolic currency in the form of coins and notes began to be used in place of livestock, cf. Ger. *Vieh* 'cattle' from Goth. *faihu* 'money', OE *fēo* 'cattle', Eng. *fee* (an approximate homophone of *Vieh* 'cattle') 'inherited estate, sum payable to public officers', *scot-free* 'unpunished', from *scot* 'payment, contribution'. Gmc. may have borrowed from Slav., given that 'treasure' is more abstract than 'cattle' (the semantic progression being 'cattle', then 'property', then 'money') and thus probably a later development. On the other hand, there exist ancient words with monetary connotations (e.g. OIcel. *skattr* 'tax', Goth. *skatts* 'coin, money', OHG *skaz* 'coin, property'). The Slav. and Gmc. words may therefore derive from a third source.

СКРИПКА [skrípka] 'violin'. Onomatopoeic, from скрипе́ть 'to creak', cf. скрипа́ч 'violinist'.

СКРОМНЫЙ [skrómnyj] 'modest'. 17th century, from Pol. *skromny*, id., probably based on Pol. *kroma* 'edge, border', thus properly 'limited, confined'. Cognate with кремль 'Kremlin', кро́мка 'edge', кро́ме 'apart from'.

СКУКА [skúka] 'boredom'. Recorded in dictionaries since 1704, cognate with dial. ку́кать 'to pine, grieve' and onomatopoeic ку! (cf. ку́рица 'chicken', куку́шка 'cuckoo', dial. ску́чить 'to howl' (of a dog)). Cognate with доку́ка (obs.) 'tiresome request'. Perhaps originally 'agitation, anxiety'. Alternatively, related to Ger. *scheuchen* 'to scare away', *scheuen* 'to fear, shun'.

СЛАВА [sláva] 'glory'. 11th century 'glory, opinion', ultimately from IE *k̑lou̯ā 'rumour, glory', cognate with сло́во 'word', слыть 'to have the reputation' (first pers. sing. слыву́), слух 'hearing, rumour', слы́шать 'to hear', Gk. *kléos* 'glory', Lith. *šlovė*, id.

СЛАВЯНИН [slavjanín] 'Slav'. Recorded in dictionaries since the 18th century, ultimately from CSl. *slověninъ, with -a- for unstressed -o- through *akan'je* and -янин on the pattern of ethnonyms such as ри́млянин 'Roman', cf., however, non-ethnonym клича́нин (obs.) 'beater' (in hunting). Probably based on сло́во 'word, speech', thus lit. 'someone speaking comprehensibly' (cf. Albanian *shqip* 'in Albanian', *shqipoj* 'I understand'), by contrast with не́мцы, initially 'those who speak indistinctly', then 'Germans'. Alternatively, from the names of rivers (cf. *Словутич*, cited by Vasmer as an epithet used of the Dnieper) and other geographical features (cf. Pol. *Sława*, the name of a town on the Oder, of a village and of an upland region, also *Sławańskie jezioro* 'Lake Slawanskije'), less plausibly from personal names in -слав (Яросла́в 'Jaroslav', etc.). Association with сла́ва 'glory' is through false etymology.

СЛА́ДКИЙ [sládkij] 'sweet'. 11th century, from CSl. *soldъkъ 'sweet', IE *sal- 'salt, dirty-grey' (cf. соль 'salt' and, for -d/-t, Goth. *salt*, id.), -ла- being of ChSl. origin. Probably originally 'salty', then 'seasoned, tasty', finally 'sweet', cf. Lith. *saldus* 'sweet' and, with ESl. inter-consonantal -оло-, со́лод 'malt'.

СЛЕЗА́ [slezá] 'tear'. 11th century *сльза* 'tear, (pl.) weeping' (IE *slugos 'gulp, sob'), apparently cognate with слизь 'mucus', Ger. *schlickern* 'to slip, slide', *schlickerig* 'slimy', Lith. *šliaužti* 'to crawl'.

СЛЕ́САРЬ [slésar'] 'metal worker, locksmith'. Early 18th century, from Ger. *Schloßer*, id., with s- for Ger. š- by assimilation to medial -s- (rather than via Pol. *ślusarz*, id.), or under the influence of D. *slotenmaker*, id. Agent suffix -арь on the pattern of то́карь 'turner', etc.

СЛИ́ВА [slíva] 'plum'. 12th century, perhaps from the fruit's colour, cf. Lat. *līvor* 'bluish, leaden colour', *līvidus* 'blue, bluish', Eng. *sloe* 'small bluish-black wild plum, fruit of the blackthorn', Ger. *Schlehe* 'sloe, wild plum'.

СЛО́ВО [slóvo] 'word'. 11th century 'word, gift of speech, sense, homily', from CSl. *slovo, gen. *slovese (hence слове́сный 'verbal'), cf. IE *ḱleu̯os 'word, rumour, fame'. Cognate with сла́ва 'glory', слыть 'to have the reputation', слух 'hearing, rumour', Gk. *kléos* 'rumour, report'. Derivatives include предисло́вие 'foreword', посло́вица 'proverb', усло́вие 'condition'.

СЛОГ [slog] 'syllable'. Initially 'combination' (cf. сложи́ть 'to compile'), then specifically 'combination of letters, syllable'.

СЛОЙ [sloj] 'layer'. 14th century, cognate with слиться 'to flow together, merge', thus lit. 'what is fused together', cf. бой 'battle' from бить 'to strike'.

СЛОН [slon] 'elephant'. Perhaps a reshaping of a Tkc. word (cf. Turk. *aslan* 'lion' -- the names of exotic animals, known only through travellers' tales, sometimes became confused in people's minds, cf. верблюд 'camel', мамонт 'mammoth'). For loss of a-, cf. лошадь 'horse'. Also associated, presumably through false etymology, with прислоняться 'to lean on', from a medieval belief that the elephant could not bend at the knees and slept leaning against a tree or some other stable object.

СЛУГА [slugá] 'servant'. 11th century, assumed originally to have been a collective which meant 'retinue' (cf. прислуга 'domestic staff'), subsequently 'servant', with cognates in Balt. (Lith. *slaugyti* 'to tend') and Celtic (Ir. *sluag* 'crowd, detachment' Gael. *sluagh* 'people').

СЛУХ [sluch] 'hearing, rumour'. 11th century 'rumour, hearing, ear', from CSl. *sluchъ, IE *kleus 'hear', cognate with Lith. *klausyti* 'to listen', Gk. *kléōs* 'glory'. Слушать 'to listen' derives seemingly from *sluchěti, with -ch- changing to -š- before -ě- and -ě- to -a- after -š-.

СЛУЧАЙ [slúčaj] 'case, chance'. 11th century, seemingly from *sъlukjajь (-kj- to -č-), itself from *sъluka 'case' (cf. dial. слука, id.), purportedly a cognate of obs. *лукьш 'designated by fate' (Cyganenko).

СМЕРТЬ [smert'] 'death'. 11th century, from CSl. *sъmьrtь, root *mьr-, cf. IE *mor-/*mer-/*mr̥ 'die'. For prefix sъ- 'one's own, good', cf. Skr. *su* 'good' (much used as prefix *su-*, id.), *sva* 'own', thus lit. 'one's own, a natural, non-violent death', cf. умереть своей смертью 'to die a natural (lit. 'one's own') death'. For forms in m-, cf. мёртвый 'dead', Skr. *mṛita*, id., Lith. *mirtis* 'death', Lat. *mors*, id., Eng. *murder*, etc.

СМЕХ [smech] 'laughter'. 11th century (IE *smēi̯ō 'smile, blush'), probably onomatopoeic, cognate with Skr. *smi*, id. and (without s-) Gk. *meídēma* 'a smile' (cf. IE *smeid- 'smile, leer').

СМОРОДИНА [smoródina] 'currant(s)'. OR *смородъ* 'strong smell' (with ESl. inter-consonantal -oro-, from CSl. *smordъ) + -ина 'berries' (cf. малина 'raspberries'). From the fruit's pungent smell, cf. смрад 'stench', смердеть (obs.) 'to stink'.

СМОТРЕТЬ [smotrét'] 'to look'. 11th century, from CSl. *(sъ)motřeti 'to be cautious' (cf. смотри! 'watch out!'), assumed to be cognate with Lith. *matyti* 'to see', and possibly Gk. *mateúō* 'I seek'.

СНАРЯД [snarjád] 'artillery shell'. 17th century, originally deaffixed verbal noun from an earlier form of снарядить 'to equip', probably initially 'equipping, equipment', then 'artillery pieces', finally 'artillery shell'. Cf., for similar dual meanings, пушка 'cannon'.

СНЕГ [sneg] 'snow'. 11th century, from CSl. *sněgъ, IE *(s)neiguh- 'to snow', with Balto-Slav./Gmc. forms in sn-/šn- (Lith. *sniegas* 'snow', Goth. *snaiws*, id., Ger. *Schnee*, id.) running parallel to forms in n-, cf. Gk. *nípha*, id. (irreg. acc. of *niphás* 'snow-flake'), Lat. *nix* 'snow', Fr. *neige*, id., Gael. *sneachd*, id. Снегирь 'bull-finch' is probably so called because it is said to arrive in Russia with the first snow.

СНОВАТЬ [snovát'] 'to dart here and there'. CSl. *snovati, initially 'to warp' (stretch threads lengthwise on a loom, cf. IE *snūi̯ō- 'turn'), subsequently 'dart back and forth', from the movements of the weaver. See основа 'basis'.

СОБАКА [sobáka] 'dog'. 12th century at latest, probably from Median (an Iran. language) *spáka* 'dog', perhaps via the Scythians on the N. Black Sea littoral, eventually replacing пёс (coll.), id. Alternatively from Tkc. *köbäk*, id. (cf. Turk. *köpek*, id.).

СОБОЛЬ [sóbol'] 'sable'. Originally 'sable pelt', later 'sable', borrowed by other languages since the time of the Novgorod fur trade (e.g. Ger. *Zobel*, id., Ital. *zibellino*, id.), possibly (Černych) cognate with a Skr. root denoting 'many-coloured' (the prized Jenisej sable having a black muzzle and back, grey ears, brown neck and sides).

СОБОР [sobór] 'cathedral'. 11th century, from ChSl., originally 'a gathering', calqued from Gk. *synagogḗ* 'a gathering, place of assembly', cf. Gk. *synágō* 'I gather together'.

СОБСТВЕННЫЙ [sóbstvennyj] 'own'. 11th century 'personal', from *собьство* 'hypostasis (person of the Godhead), essence', CSl. *sobьstvo 'one's own, something personal', based on the pronominal noun *собь* 'essence' (from *собѣ* = себе́, cf. о́собь 'individual', from *о собѣ* '*per se*').

СОВА [sová] 'owl'. From CSl. *sova, possibly onomatopoeic (cf. IE *kaukō 'call, cry', Lith. *kaukti* 'to howl, hoot', *kovas* 'rook'). Cognates include MHG *hiulen* 'to howl' (Ger. *heulen*, id.), Ger. *Uhu* 'great horned owl'.

СОВЕСТЬ [sóvest'] 'conscience'. 11th century 'understanding, knowledge, conscience', calqued via ChSl. from Gk. *syneídēsis* 'joint knowledge, consciousness', then 'conscience', comprising *sýn-* 'with', *eídēsis* 'knowledge' (cf. CSl. *věstь from *vědtь, itself from *věděti 'to know', cf. ве́дать, id.).

СОВЕТ [sovét] 'council, advice'. 11th century 'agreement', a ChSl. calque of Gk. *symboúlion* 'advice, council', based on *sъ- 'community of action' + *vět- 'speaking' (cf. OR *вѣтовати* 'to speak'). The meaning 'organ of state power' arose in 1917 on the basis of Сове́т 'mass political organization of the R. working class', which originated in the revolution of 1905-07.

СОГЛАСНЫЙ [soglásnyj] 'agreeable (to), consonant'. Calqued via ChSl. from Lat. *consonans*, id. or Gk. *sýmphōnos* 'harmonious', cf. *sýn-*/со- 'together', *phōnḗ* 'sound'/глас (obs.) 'voice'.

СОЗДАТЬ [sozdát'] 'to create'. 11th century, from ChSl. (cf. *съ-* + *зьдати* 'to build', *зьдъ* 'clay'), subsequently misinterpreted as a compound of *дать* 'to give', after vocalization of -ъ- to -о- and the reduction of -ь-, thus создáть. Cf. здáние 'building'.

СОЛДАТ [soldát] 'soldier'. First third of 17th century, originally 'foreign mercenary', from Ital. *soldato* 'soldier', lit. 'salaried mercenary' (Ital. *soldo* 'salary'), via Fr. *soldat* 'soldier' (hence initial с-, pronounced [s]).

СОЛНЦЕ [sólnce] 'sun'. 11th century, from CSl. *sъlnьce, *sъln- (cf. dial. *солнопёк* 'sun-burn') + hypocoristic dim. -ьсе. Cf. IE *sāul-/*sau̯el- 'sun' and (with l-theme) Lith. *saulė*, id., Gk. *hēlios*, id., Lat. *sol*, id., (with n-theme) Ger. *Sonne*, id., both themes appearing in сóлнце, Pol. *słońce*, id., Bulg. *слънце*, id., perhaps through thematic contamination or, dubiously, from the influence of the CSl. root *ogn- 'fire'.

СОЛОВЕЙ [solovéj] 'nightingale'. 12th century *соловии*, id., from CSl. *solvijь, id., *solvъ 'grey, yellow-grey' (cf. солóвый 'light bay', of horses), with ESl. inter-consonantal -оло-, thus initially, perhaps, 'grey bird'. Cf. connection, possibly through a false etymology, with соловéть (coll.) 'to become drowsy', purportedly from the effect of the nightingale's song on listeners.

СОЛЬ [sol'] 'salt'. 11th century, from CSl. *solь (IE *sāl-, id., *sald- 'tasty, piquant'), with cognates in Gk. *háls* 'grain of salt' (pl. 'salt'), Lat. *sal* 'salt', etc. See слáдкий 'sweet'.

СОМНЕНИЕ [somnénije] 'doubt'. From ChSl., earlier су- 'incomplete, indeterminate' (cf. сýмрак 'twilight'), changing to со- by analogy with words such as сóвесть 'conscience'.

СОН [son] 'sleep'. 11th century 'sleep, dream', from CSl. *sъnъ, id., itself, through simplification (-pn to -n), from *sъpnъ (a derivative of *sъp-, cf. IE *supnos 'sleep, dream, drowsiness'). Cognate with Lith. *sapnas* 'dream', Gk. *hýpnos* 'sleep', Skr. *svapna*, id., Lat. *somnus*, id., *sopor* 'deep sleep'. The root *sъp- appears in impf. засыпáть 'to fall asleep', cf. *sъn- in pf. заснýть 'to fall asleep' (cf. also Gael. *suain* 'sleep').

СОПЕРНИК [sopérnik] 'rival'. Recorded in dictionaries since the 17th century, from ChSl., based on *s(o)- 'joint activity' and *perti 'to strike' (so- for original su-, cf. OR *супьрь* 'rival'). Cf. also прéния 'debate'.

СОРОК [sórok] 'forty'. 12th century, replacing *четыредесяте/четыридесяти*, id. (lit. 'four tens', cf. Pol. *czterdzieści*, id.). The meaning is assumed to have progressed from 'bag containing 40 sable or squirrel skins' (sufficient for a coat), perhaps originally in hunters' language, to 'forty', possibly on the pattern of OSc. *serkr* 'shirt' (cf. сорóчка, id.), 'a certain number of pelts'. For numerals based on objects, cf. Dan. *snes* 'a score', originally 'pole on which 20 fish were hung to dry', ON *skor* 'notch, tally, twenty'. Alternatively, from Gk. *tessarákonta* 'forty', or from Tkc. (cf. Turk. *kirk* 'forty', possibly with subsequent dissimilation of k-k to s-k).

СОСАТЬ [sosát] 'to suck'. 11th century 'to suck, breast-feed', from CSl. *sъsati, based on onomatopoeic IE *sūgō 'suck', cf. Lat. *sūgō* 'I suck', Fr. *sucer* 'to suck', Ger. *saugen*, id. Derivatives include сосóк 'nipple', сóска 'dummy'.

СОСЕД [soséd] 'neighbour'. CSl. *sǫsědъ 'sitting next to', cf. Skr. *samsad* 'assembly' (lit. 'sitting together'), Eng. *neighbour* (neigh- 'near', -bour, cf. Dan. *bo* 'to live').

СОСНА [sosná] 'pine-tree'. From CSl. *sopsnā/*sosna, possibly from the grey colour of the tree's bark (cf. IE *kasen- 'grey', OHG *haso*, id., whence *Hase* 'hare'). Alternatively, сосна́ may be cognate with Lat. *sapa* 'must, new wine boiled thick', thus lit. 'succulent, resinous tree', or with сопéть 'to breathe heavily', perhaps referring to sounds emanating from a hollow tree (сосна́ may originally have meant 'tree with a hollow', in the terminology of wild-honey farming).

СОСРЕДОТОЧИТЬ [sosredotóčit'] 'to concentrate'. 18th-century calque of Fr. *concentrer*, id.

СОСТОЯТЬ [sostoját'] 'to consist'. 19th-century calque of Ger. *bestehen*, id.

СОСТРАДАНИЕ [sostradánije] 'compassion'. Calqued, via ChSl., from Gk. *sympátheia*, id. (Gk. *sýn* 'together', *páthos* 'suffering').

СОСТЯЗАНИЕ [sostjazánije] 'contest'. Early 17th century, based on *съ-* 'together' + *тягати* 'to pull' (cf. тягáться 'to contend with'), with -g- changing to -z- after -ja- (third palatalization of velars).

СОЮЗ [sojúz] 'union'. From *съ-* 'joint' + (of ChSl. origin) -юз 'union', cognate with ýзы (fig.) 'bonds, ties'. In the grammatical meaning 'conjunction', a calque of Lat. *conjūnctiō*, id. or Gk. *sýndesmos* 'ligament, conjunction' (*desmós* 'bond'). Cf. also вязáть 'to tie'.

СПАСИБО [spasíbo] 'thank you'. Late 16th century, from OR *спаси Богъ* (спаси́ Бог, lit. 'may God save you'), with subsequent coalescence, and loss of final -г.

СПАТЬ [spat'] 'to sleep'. 11th century, from CSl. *sъpati, id., with cognate in Lat. *sōpiō* 'I lull'. See сон 'sleep'.

СПИНА [spiná] 'back'. Mid-16th century, possibly associated with Lat. *spīna* 'prickle, backbone, spine' (cf. позвонóчник 'spine').

СПИЦА [spíca] 'knitting needle, spoke'. Recorded in dictionaries since 1731, from CSl. *stъpica, OR *стъпица* 'stake', with -stp- simplifying to -sp- following the reduction of -ъ-. Cognates include Lith. *stipinas* 'spoke', Gk. *stýpos* 'stem, stick', Lat. *stipula* 'stalk, stem', probably стéбель, id. Cf. IE *sthip-/*stīpō 'steady, stiff'. A possible connection with Ger. *Spieß* 'spear', *spitz* 'pointed' is disputed.

СПИЧКА [spíčka] 'match'. 1820s at latest (the first R. match factory was opened in St. Petersburg in 1837), dim. of спи́ца 'spoke'.

СПОР [spor] 'argument'. From *съ-* 'joint activity' + the root of *perti (cf. перéть 'to push, press'), with -e-:-o- mutation. Cf.

сопе́рник 'rival', препира́ться (coll.) 'to squabble', ра́спря 'feud', Lith. *spirti* 'to kick, press', ultimately, perhaps, from IE *sporos 'impact, resistance'.

СПОСОБ [spósob] 'means'. A deaffixed form, cf. OR *съпособьникъ* 'assistant', посо́бствовать 'to foster', пособи́ть (coll.) 'to help', perhaps via Pol. *sposobić* 'to prepare', *sposób* 'means'.

СРЕДА [sredá] 'Wednesday'. 11th century *срѣда* (12th century *середа*, cf. Ukr. *середа*, id.), via ChSl. from CSl. *serda 'middle', среда́ 'Wednesday' being interpreted as the middle day of the week, cf. Ger. *Mittwoch*, id. Cognates include се́рдце 'heart', сре́дний 'middle', середи́на 'middle'.

СРОК [srok] 'time, period'. Originally 'agreement, pre-arranged time', ultimately from CSl. *sъrekti 'to agree', a compound of *rekti 'to speak'. A deaffixed form, with e:o mutation. See речь 'speech'.

СТАДО [stádo] 'herd'. 11th century, based on IE radical *sthā- 'standing', perhaps originally 'cattle-stall', then 'herd', possibly cognate with Ger. *Stute* 'mare', Eng. *stud, steed*. For -до, cf. чу́до 'miracle'.

СТАКАН [stakán] 'glass, tumbler'. Early 17th century at latest, possibly a truncation of 14th-century *достоканъ* 'glass' (of Tkc. origin, cf. Kirgh. *tostagan* 'small wooden cup', Čagataj *tostakan*, id.). Alternatively (since Tkc. may, conversely, have borrowed from R.), *достаканъ* may derive from *дъсканъ (cf. obs. до́скан 'box') and be cognate with чан 'vat' (from *дъщанъ 'made of boards', ultimately from доска́ 'board').

СТАЛЬ [stal'] 'steel'. Early 18th century, from Ger. *Stahl*, id. via Pol. *stal*, id., or possibly from LG (since early references were to steel produced in Hamburg).

СТАРЫЙ [stáryj] 'old'. 11th century, from CSl. *starъ, perhaps based on IE *sthā 'standing', thus lit. 'standing firm', and cognate with стоять 'to stand'. Other cognates, denoting apposite qualities (cf. IE *sthāros 'stiff, old, hardy, burly', *sther- 'firm, stiff'), include OIcel. *storr* 'strong, big, important, proud', Gk. *sterrós* 'firm, solid, stiff with age', Lith. *storas* 'fat, heavy', possibly Ger. *starr* 'stiff'.

СТАТЬ [stat'] 'to take up a standing position, stop'. From IE *sthă- 'standing', cf. Lith. *stoti*, id., Lat. *stō* 'I stand', with n-theme in стану 'I shall stand', станок 'lathe', Gk. *stěnai* 'to stand', OHG *stan*, id. (Ger. *stehen*, id.).

СТАЯ [stája] 'flock, pack'. From OR *стати* 'to stand'. Originally meant 'stall' (cf. dial. *стая* 'cattle-yard', also стадо 'herd').

СТВОЛ [stvol] 'tree-trunk, gun-barrel'. Possibly from assumed CSl. *stьbolъ, perhaps cognate with стебель 'stalk'.

СТЕКЛО [stekló] 'glass'. 11th century OR *стькло* 'crystal, glass', from CSl. *stьklo, Goth. *stikls* 'goblet, drinking-horn', seemingly from a Gmc. root meaning 'sharp' (cf. OHG *stihhil* 'thorn, point'), an apparent reference to the sharp point of the drinking-horn.

СТЕНА [stená] 'wall'. Cognate with Goth *stains* 'stone' (Ger. *Stein*, id.), and possibly Gk. *stíon*, dim. of *stía* 'pebble'. To Slavs, who built their dwellings of clay and wood, стена may have meant a *stone* wall, thus Дощатый забор не стена, а каменная ограда стена 'A wooden fence is not a wall, while a stone enclosure is' (Dal').

СТЕПЕНЬ [stépen'] 'degree'. 11th century, cognate with стопа 'foot', ступать 'to step', Ger. *Stufe* 'step'.

СТЕПЬ [step'] 'steppe'. Possibly from the language of nomad Pečenegs or Polovscy living in S. Russia, or associated with топтать 'to trample', стоптать (coll.), id., thus lit. 'trampled place, place devoid of trees'. Alternatively, linked with OR *сътепу*, from *сътети* 'to beat, hack', thus 'cleared area', or with words for feather grass (characteristic steppe vegetation) or other verdure, cf. Fr. *stipe* 'feather grass, stem' (whence 18th-century Eng. *stipe* 'footstalk'), from Lat. *stīpes* 'log, post', then 'stalk', Eng. *stipule* 'leaf-like appendage to leaf' (from Fr., or Lat. *stipula* 'straw'), *stipel* 'secondary stipule' (from Fr. *stipelle*, Lat. *stipella*), etc. Cf. also IE *stīpō 'stiffen', also said to be cognate with степь (also *stīpəlos 'stem, pole'). The word is said to have been borrowed by other Slav. languages after the defeat of the Swedes at Poltava in Ukraine in 1709 and by W. Eur. languages somewhat later.

СТЕРЕЧЬ [stereč'] 'to guard'. 11th century, from CSl. *stergti, id., with ESl. inter-consonantal -epe-, and -ч- by first palatalization of velars. Said to result from a contamination of the roots of Gk. *stérgō* 'I love', *stégō* 'I cover closely, fend off' and Lith. *sergėti* 'to guard'. Cf. сто́рож 'watchman' (IE *storg-, id.) and (with ChSl. -ра-) стра́жа 'guard, watch'.

СТИХ [stich] 'verse'. From Gk. *stíchos* 'file of soldiers, row of trees, line of verse or prose'. Стихи́ (used 11th-15th centuries) prevailed over ви́рши 'syllabic verses' (common in 17th century, from Lat. *versus* 'line') in the second quarter of the 18th century, due seemingly to the influence of V.K. Tredjakovskij and M.V. Lomonosov.

СТЛАТЬ [stlat'] 'to spread'. 11th century, with cognates in Gk. *stéllō* 'I arrange, furnish, equip', Lat. *lātus* 'broad' (cf. Lat. *stlāta* 'type of ship, merchant vessel', named for its breadth). Cognate with стол 'table', посте́ль 'bed', сте́лька 'insole'.

СТО [sto] 'hundred'. 11th century, ultimately from IE *(d)k̑m̥tóm, id., lit. 'ten tens' (cf. IE *dek̑m̥ 'ten'), whence also Gk. *hekatón* '100', Lat. *centum*, id., Skr. *śata*, id., Lith. *šimtas*, id., сто, id. (-m- is said to have been lost in allegro counting). Note: IE languages are classified into E./W. by the contrast, in certain words, including '100', of sibilants (E: Skr., Avestan, Arm., R., Lith.) as against velars (W: Gk., Lat., Ir., Goth.).

СТОЛ [stol] 'table'. 11th century 'bench, throne', subsequently acquiring the meanings 'pulpit' and 'table'. Probably cognate with стлать 'to spread' (first pers. sing. стелю́ 'I spread'), thus lit. 'something spread, that extends', with derivatives in престо́л 'throne', столи́ца 'capital', lit. 'seat of the throne', cf. also *сто́льный град* 'capital city' (and note OR *столъ* 'throne'). Alternatively, perhaps, from IE radical *sthā- 'standing', thus cognate with стоя́ть 'to stand' and lit. 'something placed standing, standing object'.

СТОРОНА́ [storoná] 'side'. From CSl. *storna 'space', IE *stor- 'to spread' (cf. Lat. *sternō* 'I spread out'), with cognates in просто́р 'expanse', простере́ть 'to extend', and with ESl. interconsonantal -оро- (cf. ChSl. -ра- in страна́ 'country', whence стра́нный 'strange', originally 'alien, from another land', страни́ца 'page'). Also related to Gk. *stórnymi* 'spread, spread out', and Ger. *Stirn* 'forehead' (originally 'extended surface', from IE *ster- 'to extend').

СТОЯ́ТЬ [stoját'] 'to stand'. 11th century, from CSl. *stojati, IE *sthā- 'standing', cognate with Lith. *stoti* 'to stand', Lat. *stō* 'I stand', Gk. *statós* 'standing'.

СТРАДА́ТЬ [stradát'] 'to suffer'. 11th century 'work, toil, suffer', 12th century 'endure', from CSl. *strad-, whence also (via *stradtь) страсть 'passion' (cf. Eng. *Passion* 'the sufferings of Christ on the Cross'). Assumed to derive from страда́ 'drudgery', cognate with Gk. *strēnés* 'rough, harsh, grating', Lat. *strēnuus* 'vigorous, strenuous'.

СТРА́УС [stráus] 'ostrich'. 18th century (*струс*, then *строус*, later стра́ус), from Ger. *Strauß*, id. (OHG *struz*), ultimately, via MLat. *strūthiō*, from Gk. *strouthós* 'bird, sparrow', *mégas strouthós* 'ostrich', lit. 'large bird' (also *strouthós katágaios*, lit. 'ground bird', so called because the ostrich runs rather than flies), later also Lat. *Strūthiō camēlus*/Gk. *stroutho-kámelos* 'ostrich', lit. 'cross between a sparrow and a camel', from the bird's camel-like neck.

СТРЕЛА́ [strelá] 'arrow'. 10th century *стрѣла* 'arrow, lightning', cognate with Lith. *strėlė* 'arrow', OHG *strala* 'arrow, lightning flash' (cf. Ger. *Strahl* 'beam'). Probably from IE *stre- 'to extend', thus lit. 'what is stretched, directed' (cf. also IE *strēlos 'arrow'). Стреля́ть 'to shoot', originally only of arrows, applied also to firearms from the 14th-/15th centuries (пали́ть, id., which it replaced, is retained in the imper. пали́! 'fire!').

СТРО́ГИЙ [strógij] 'strict'. Recorded in dictionaries since 1771, but known earlier, from CSl. *strogъ, possibly via Pol. *srogi* 'severe' and cognate with CSl. *storgъ 'guard' (see стере́чь 'to guard'), thus perhaps initially 'guarded, cautious', then 'demanding'. Alternatively, from IE *ster- 'stiff' and cognate with Ger. *Storch* 'stork' (from the bird's rigid gait, cf., however, а́ист, id., possibly from Tkc. on the basis of the stork's prominent beak, cf. Turk. *ağiz* 'mouth').

СТРОКА́ [stroká] 'line'. 11th century 'sign', 12th century 'point', 14th century 'line of words on a page', 16th century 'row of stitches' (cf. строчи́ть 'to stitch', стро́чка 'line, stitch'), from OR *стрѣкати* 'to prick, sting', perhaps also associated with dial. *стрека́ть* 'to sting, rush about' (thus стрекоза́ 'dragon-fly', дать стрекача́ (coll.) 'to take to one's heels').

СТРУНА́ [struná] 'string' (of instrument, racket). 12th century, perhaps closest to Ger. *Strieme* 'stripe, streak, weal', but also cognate with Lat. *struō* 'I arrange', thus lit. 'adjusted' (to an instrument or racket), cf. also IE *streugh- 'tighten; cord', *strōu̯- 'spread'.

СТРУЯ́ [strujá] 'jet, stream'. From CSl. *sreuja 'stream', IE *srou- 'to flow' (cf. Lith. *srautas* 'stream', Skr. *srava* 'flowing'), with subsequent -t- infix, cf. о́стров 'island'.

СТУДИ́ТЬ [studít'] 'to cool'. CSl. *studъ 'cold' (cf. OR *студъ* 'shame', стыд, id.), whence просту́да 'a cold', cf. стыть 'to get cold', purportedly also cognate with Gk. *Stýx* 'the Styx, river of the nether world', lit. 'the Hateful'. The part. derivative *студеный* (coll.) 'bitter, freezing' was the standard word for 'cold' until the 16th-/17th centuries, when it was replaced by холо́дный, id., cf. студёный, which has the meaning 'very cold'.

СТУЛ [stul] 'chair'. 16th century at latest, from OIcel. *stóll*, id. or N. Ger. *Stuhl* (s- pronounced [s]), cf. also D. *stoel*, id., rather than Ger. *Stuhl*, id. (s- pronounced [š]).

СТЫД [styd] 'shame'. 11th century *студъ* 'shame', a secondary, fig., meaning to 'cold', with -у-/-ы- mutation, perhaps under the influence of стыть 'to get cold' (cf. 15th-century *студити* 'to cool'). The dual meaning is said to have arisen from the twin (physical and moral) sensations experienced, for example, by an unclothed person. Note Serb. cognate *стидак* 'the last morsel everyone is ashamed to take'.

СУББОТА [subbóta] 'Saturday'. 11th century *субота* '6th day of the week' (also Jewish sabbath), probably, via ChSl., from MLat. *sabbata*, id., in its turn, via Gk. *Sábbaton* (also pl. *Sábbata*) 'the Hebrew Sabbath', from Hebrew *šabbat* 'rest, festive day', cognate with шабаш 'sabbath, knocking-off time' (also from Hebrew, via Pol. *szabas* 'sabbath' or Ger. *Schabbes*, id., Yiddish *shabes*, id.). R. -бб- evolved under the influence of -bb- in W. Eur. languages or in assimilation to the Lat./Gk. forms. Counterparts in -m- in other languages derive from medieval Gk. *sámbaton, pl. *sámbata (-mb- by dissimilation from -bb-), e.g. Ger. (S. Ger., Rheinland, Austria, Switzerland) *Samstag* 'Saturday' (cf. standard *Sonnabend*, id.), Rom. *sîmbătă*, id., Fr. *samedi*, id. (from Vulg. Lat. *sambati dies*).

СУГРОБ [sugrób] 'snow-drift'. 14th century *сугребъ* 'pile', cf. сгрести 'to rake together'. For -о-, cf. cognate гроб 'coffin'.

СУД [sud] 'judgement, court'. 11th century 'Day of Judgment', 12th century 'court, judgement, punishment'. From CSl. *sǫdъ 'judgement' (IE *som- 'together', *dhēmi 'say', thus properly 'joint investigation, resolution'). Cognates include Gk. *sýnthēma* 'agreement' (also Lith. *samda* 'hire').

СУДНО [súdno] 'vessel, ship, chamber-pot'. OR *судьно* 'vessel (container), ship'. Cf. derivation of Fr. *vaisseau* 'vessel (receptacle), ship', from Lat. *vasculum*, dim. of *vas* 'utensil, dish'.

СУМЕРКИ [súmerki] 'twilight'. Recorded in dictionaries from the early 18th century, from CSl. *sǫ- 'incomplete, indefinite' + *mьrk- 'to grow dim' (cf. OR *суморокъ* 'twilight' and, of ChSl. provenance, сýмрак, id.).

СУМКА [súmka] 'bag'. 16th-century dim. of сумá, id., deriving from OHG/MHG *soum* 'pack, load' (originally load that can be borne by a beast of burden, cf. Ger. *Saum* 'burden'), based on Vulg. Lat. *sauma/sagma*, from Gk. *ságma* 'pack saddle'.

СУНДУК [sundúk] 'trunk, chest'. 15th-/16th centuries, via Tkc. (cf. Turk. *sandik* 'box') and Ar. *ṣandūq* 'trunk, suitcase', from Byz. Gk. *syndocheion* (cf. Patristic Gk. *docheion* 'receptacle'). Perhaps ultimately from India.

СУПРУГ [suprúg] 'spouse, husband'. 11th century 'pair harnessed together, marital pair', from the root *pręgǫ (-прягý, whence спрягý, from спрячь 'to harness together'). Analogous to Lat. *coniūnx* 'spouse' (cf. Eng. *conjugal*), Gk. *sýzygos* 'yoked together (esp. wedded), wife, comrade'. Cf. also запрягáть 'to harness', пружúна 'spring'.

СУРОВЫЙ [suróvyj] 'severe'. OR 'raw, wild' (also 'damp'), perhaps initially of objects, then of personal qualities, thus 'stern, severe', cognate with сырóй 'raw', OHG *sur* 'sour'. Alternatively linked with CSl. *sěverъ 'north', Lat. *Caurus* 'NW wind'.

СУТКИ [sútki] '24-hour period'. OR *сътъкъ* 'collision' (*sъ- 'together' + *tъk- 'join'), 16th century *сутокъ* 'convergence, place where boundaries meet' (су- perhaps by analogy with nouns such as супрýг 'spouse'), early 18th century at latest сýтки 'day and night', lit. 'juncture of night and day'. Cf. стык 'join, junction', стыковáться 'to dock' (in space). For pl.-only nouns comprising two components, cf. очкú 'glasses'.

СУТЬ [sut'] 'essence'. In dictionaries from first half of 18th century in this meaning, a substantivization of суть 'they are' (CSl. *sǫtь, corresponding to Lat. *sunt*, id., Ger. *sind*, id.). Derivative сýщий 'real, absolute' (whence also существó 'essence') evolved from a ChSl. pres. act. part.

СЦЕНА [scéna] 'stage'. No later than the first half of the 18th century, via Ger. *Szene*, id. (cf. now standard *Bühne*, id.), from Lat. *scaena/scēna*, id., ultimately Gk. *skēnḗ*, initially 'tent, booth' (from Gk. *skiá* 'shade, shadow'), subsequently 'stage'.

СЧАСТЬЕ [ščást'je] 'happiness'. CSl. *sъčęstьje, id., comprising *sъ- (from *su 'good', cf. Skr. *su* 'good, well' -- mainly as a prefix) + *čęstь 'part' + suffix *-ьj-, thus lit. 'good part', i.e. 'happy lot'. Cf. ýчасть 'lot'.

СЪЕДОБНЫЙ [s''edóbnyj] 'edible'. Recorded in dictionaries from the 18th century, seemingly a blend of pass. part. *съедомый* (obs.) 'which can be, is eaten' (cf. ведóмый 'which is led') and удóбный 'convenient'.

СЫН [syn] 'son'. 11th century, from CSl. *synъ, IE *sūnus, id. (*su- 'to bear' + pass. *-nus, thus lit. 'born', cf. Skr. *sū* 'beget'). Cognate with Lith. *sūnus*, 'son', Goth. *sunus*, id.

СЫР [syr] 'cheese'. CSl. *syrъ, perhaps connected with *syrъ 'raw' (cf. сырóй, id.) and cognate with OHG *sur* 'sour' (Ger. *sauer*, id.). Cf. Lith. *sūris* 'cheese'. Сы́воротка 'whey, serum' evolved by metathesis from *сыровотка, which is based on *сыровать 'relating to cheese', perhaps 'containing clotted cream, cheese' (cf. Ukr. *сироватка* 'serum').

СЮДА [sjudá] 'here, hither'. Suffixal derivative of CSl. demonstrative pronoun *sь 'this', cf. кудá 'where to', тудá 'to there' (сю- under the influence of сей, сегó, etc. 'this').

Т

ТАБУН [tabún] 'herd' (of horses). First half of 17th century, of Tkc. origin, probably from Čagataj *tabun*, id.

ТАЗ I [taz] 'basin'. 15th-/16th centuries, of Tkc. origin, cf. Turk. *tas* 'cup, bowl', ultimately via Ar. *ṭăsah* 'round shallow metal drinking cup', from Pers. *tasht* 'bowl', whence also Fr. *tasse* 'cup', Ital. *tazza*, id., etc.

ТАЗ II [taz] 'pelvis'. Recorded in dictionaries since 1834, probably from the similarity of the broad pelvic bones with slightly concave base to a basin (see таз I), cf. Lat. *pelvis* 'basin' (Gk. *pélla* 'wooden bowl, drinking cup') and dual meanings in Fr. *bassin* 'basin, pelvis', Ital. *bacino*, id., Ger. *Becken*, id.

ТАЙГА [tajgá] 'taiga, Siberian coniferous forest'. In dictionaries from the mid-19th century, having *originally* gained currency through reports of scientific expeditions inaugurated in the 1730s. From a Tkc. source (perhaps via a Siberian dial.), cf. Turk. *daĝ* 'mountain, wild place', *dagbaş* 'wilds' ('forest' apparently being a secondary meaning). Cf. also Tkc. *taika* 'rocky, treeless mountains to the W. of the river Katun' (a branch of the Ob' in the Altaj mountains), cf. tree-covered mountains to the E.'. Alternatively, from a Jakut word meaning 'impenetrable forest'.

ТАЛАНТ [talánt] 'talent'. 11th century 'Gk./Roman weight, coin', via ChSl., from Gk. *tálanton* 'balance, weight, (pl.) scales, something weighed', subsequently 'talent' (commercial weight of 26.2 kg., sum of money represented by the equivalent weight in gold or silver). The fig. meaning developed from the use of the word in the Biblical parable of the slaves who invested the talents given them by their master, displaying 'talent' or acumen, by comparison with their idle colleague who buried the talent which had been entrusted to him (*Matthew* 25 : 14-30). The new meaning appeared in R. in the second half of the 18th century, via Fr. *talent*, id. Cf. (with -т-) талáнтливый 'talented', but бесталáнный 'untalented', the shape of the latter possibly influenced by талáн 'success, luck' (in folklore), of

Tkc. origin.

ТАМОЖНЯ [tamóžnja] 'custom-house'. First half of 17th century, from 14th-century *там(ъ)га* 'brand, seal', in Rus' a tax exacted by the Tatars, in Muscovy 'customs, duty'. From Tkc. **tamqa* 'brand, seal' (cf. Mong. *tamqa*, id., Turk. *damga* 'stamp, brand, hallmark'). For suffix -ня 'place', cf. колокóльня 'bell-tower'.

ТАНЕЦ [tánec] 'dance'. Mid-17th century at the latest, from MHG *tanz*, ultimately OFr. *danse*, via Pol. *taniec*, id. Reshaped on the pattern of words in -ец. Cf. indigenous пляска, id. (especially folk-dancing).

ТАРАКАН [tarakán] 'cockroach'. 15th-/16th centuries, from Tkc., with possible implications of running, scurrying (Vasmer quotes Čuvaš *tar-aqan* 'fugitive', cf. Uzb. *tez-yurmok* 'to run'). A suggested association with Ger. *Kakerlak* 'cockroach' from D. *kakkerlak*, id. assumes extensive consonant mutations.

ТАРЕЛКА [tarélka] 'plate'. Early 16th century *тарѣлъ*, id. (present form since the 17th century), from MHG *deller*, id. (cf. Ger. *Teller*, id.), through metathesis (l-r:r-l), + -ка (cf. вилка 'fork'). Probably via Pol. *talerz* 'plate', from Fr. *tailloir* (obs.) 'chopping board', Ital. *tagliere* 'board for cutting meat', *tagliare* 'to cut', Vulg. Lat. *taliō* 'I split'.

ТАСОВАТЬ [tasovát'] 'to shuffle'. Early 17th century, from Pol. *tasować*, id., a reshaping of Fr. *tasser* 'to heap up', *tas* 'heap' (cf., however, Fr. *battre* 'to shuffle' (cards)).

ТВОРОГ [tvoróg/tvórog] 'cottage cheese'. First reference seemingly 17th century, possibly associated with творить 'to create, give form to', cf. analogous derivation of Fr. *fromage* 'cheese', Ital. *formaggio*, id., from Vulg. Lat. **formaticum* 'what is made in a form/mould', cf. Lat. *formāre* 'to give shape'. Cf. also Ger. *Quark* 'curds' from Late MHG *twarc/quarc*, itself from Pol. *twaróg* 'cheese curds'. For -ог, cf. пиро́г 'pie'.

ТЕЗКА [tëzka] 'namesake'. OR *тезъ*, id., from **tь* 'that' +

particle *-zь (equivalent to -зи in Bulg. *онзи/този*, id.). Lit. 'the same, someone with the same name'.

ТЕЛО [télo] 'body'. 11th century 'body, depiction of the human body', 12th century 'idol'. Said to be derived from IE *sthā- 'standing', cf. Gk. *stélē* 'upright stone, boundary post', Ger. *stellen* 'to stand' (from IE *stel-, id.). The loss of s- is unexplained except by a less plausible connection with тень 'shadow', тло 'basis'. For -ло, cf. де́ло 'matter'.

ТЕМЯ [témja] 'crown of the head'. 12th century 'forehead', 14th century 'crown'. From CSl. *těmę, based on the root of *tenti 'to hack' (cf. OR *мяти*, id., *тьну* 'I hack') + *-men = *tenmen, -nm- simplifying to -m- and -en changing to -я. Lit. (Šanskij) 'what is hacked at', cf. Gk. *témnō* 'I cut', dial. *темяшить* 'to strike, beat with fists'. Cf. also supposed analogue in Ger. *Scheitel* 'crown of head' from *scheiden* 'to divide' (however, reference in *Scheitel* is to the hair parting down the centre of the skull, rather than 'split skull').

ТЕНЬ [ten'] 'shade, shadow'. Recorded in dictionaries since 1731 (cf. 11th-century сѣнь, стѣнь, later тѣня), probably from CSl. *тьпмть 'shade'. Cf., with -мн-, темнота́ 'darkness', and, with -м-, тьма, id. (also Skr. *tamas*, id., Lith. *temti* 'to grow dark', IE *tem- 'dark', *temos 'darkness'). Cognate also with Lat. *tenebrae*, id.

ТЕПЕРЬ [tepér'] 'now'. OR *топърво* (cf. dial. *топе́рво*, id., Pol. *dopiero* 'just now, but now'). Present form recorded, together with earlier *топерь*, in 1704. Ultimately from *то първо* 'now for the first time', then (15th-/16th centuries) *теперьво* 'only just', finally 'now', on the basis of CSl. *topьrvo (demonstrative pronoun *to + *pьrvo 'first'), -ь- subsequently vocalizing to -е- and те- evolving from то- through vowel assimilation (о-е to е-е), with loss of final unstressed -во.

ТЕПЛЫЙ [tëplyj] 'warm'. 11th century, from CSl. *teplъ, id., cognate with топи́ть 'to heat', Lat. *tepidus* 'tepid', Skr. *tapas* 'heat'. For suffix -л-, cf. кру́глый 'round', etc. Derivatives include тепли́ца 'greenhouse'.

ТЕРПЕТЬ [terpét'] 'to suffer, undergo'. Perhaps originally 'to go numb', with 'to endure' a secondary meaning (cf. Lat. *torpeō* 'I am numb', Eng. *torpor, torpid* and, with initial s-, *starve* (arch or dial.) 'die or suffer from cold', OHG *sterban* 'to go stiff' (cf. Ger. *sterben* 'to die', *starr* 'stiff'). Cf. also IE *terp- 'put through, pass through', *tr̥p- 'endure, experience'.

ТЕСНЫЙ [tésnyj] 'cramped'. 11th century 'narrow' (cf. Gk. *stenós*, id.), 'cramped', from CSl. *tĕsknъ (cognate with тискать/тиснуть 'to squeeze', cf. IE *tu̯īsk- 'press'), with -skn- simplifying to -sn-.

ТЕСТО [tésto] 'dough, pastry'. 11th century, from CSl. *tĕsto (IE *taistos 'dough, leaven', *deigh- 'knead, pastry', whence Ger. *Teig* 'pastry'). Cognate with тесный 'cramped', тиснуть 'to squeeze' and Gk. *staís* 'wheaten flour mixed and made into dough' (cf. also Ir. *taos* 'dough'). Lit. 'what is squeezed'.

ТЕСТЬ [test'] 'father-in-law' (wife's father). Possibly hypocoristic, and based on IE kinship root *tĕ (cf. Gk. *tétta* 'father', an address of youths to their elders, Lith. *tètè* 'dad'). From CSl. *tьtь (with suffix -tь, as in зять 'son-in-law'), -ttь dissimilating to -stь. See also тёща 'mother-in-law'.

ТЕТЕРЕВ [téterev] 'black grouse'. 12th century *тетерь*, 16th century *тетеревь* (IE *teteruos 'capercailzie'). Based on semi-reduplicated onomatopoeic *ter-, cf. similarly onomatopoeic Lith. *teterva* 'grey hen', Skr. *tittira* 'francolin partridge' (from 'titti', the bird's cry), Gk. *tétrax* 'pheasant', Lat. *tetrinniō* 'I quack', *turtur* 'turtle-dove'.

ТЕТРАДЬ [tetrád'] 'exercise book'. 11th century 'four sheets of parchment or paper sewn together, scroll', from Byz. Gk. *tetrádion* 'quarternion, sheet of parchment consisting of four parts or folded in four' (from Gk. *tetrás*, gen. *-ádos* 'the number four'), later applied to exercise books of all formats. Cf. Eng. *quarto* 'size of paper produced by folding a whole sheet twice so as to form four leaves' and, from Lat. *quaternio* 'fascicule of four sheets', Ital. *quaderno* 'exercise book', Fr. *cahier*, id.

ТЕТЯ [tëtja] 'aunt'. Still rare as late as 18th century (cf. 11th century *тета*, id., later *тетъка*). From childish prattling, cf. дя́дя 'uncle', Lith. *teta* 'aunt', etc. Cf. also Fr. *tante*, id. (ta + OFr. *ante*), from Lat. *amita* 'father's sister', an extension of hypocoristic *am(m)a 'mother'.

ТЕЧЬ [teč'] 'to flow'. 11th century *течи* 'to flow, run', from CSl. *tekti, IE *tek- id. (cf. предте́ча 'forerunner'), with -kt- palatalizing to ESl. -č-, cf. velar (-k-) in Lith. *tekèti* 'to flow'. Cf. also, with e:o mutation, ток 'current'.

ТЕЩА [tëšča] 'mother-in-law' (wife's mother). From CSl. *tьstja, derivative of тесть 'father-in-law'.

ТИСКИ [tiskí] 'vice' (tech.). 16th century, cf. ти́скать 'to squeeze', cognate with те́сный 'cramped'.

ТИХИЙ [tíchij] 'quiet'. 11th-/12th centuries, from CSl. *tichъ (IE *tāios 'secret, silence'), cognate with уте́шить 'to console' (with -ch- palatalizing to -š-)

ТКАТЬ [tkat'] 'to weave'. Said (like ты́кать/ткнуть 'to jab') to derive from IE *teuk- 'press, tip, point', thus perhaps initially 'to puncture, weaving with transverse threads', cf. Gk. *teúchō* 'I produce by work or art, make', Lat. *texō* 'I weave'. Ткань 'fabric', first recorded in 18th century, evolved through deaffixation from ткать (cf. дань 'tribute' from дать 'to give').

ТОВАРИЩ [tóváršč] 'comrade'. 14th century, from *товаръ* (originally 'camp, waggon train', then 'goods'). Of Tkc. origin, cf. Tkc. *tavar* 'property, goods, cattle, especially sheep' (possibly from Arm. *tavar* 'cattle', cf. also Turk. *davar* 'sheep, goat(s)') + Tkc. -iš 'friend' (-ищ possibly under the influence of OR *товарище* 'camp', where -ище means 'place' (cf. кла́дбище 'cemetery'). Cf. retention of -iš in Ukr. *товариш* 'comrade'. Thus initially 'trading partner'. In the Soviet period, a common form of address.

ТОГДА [togdá] 'then'. CSl., based on то 'that' + -гда, cf.

analogous когда́ 'when', всегда́ 'always'. According to one theory, based ultimately on *togo goda 'of that year, at that time' (the oldest meaning of CSl. *godъ was '(suitable) time', hence годи́ться 'to be good for', го́дный 'suitable').

ТОКАРЬ [tókar'] 'turner'. 16th century *такáрь* (perhaps through a:a vowel assimilation), later *токáрь*, finally то́карь. Cognate with точи́ть 'to grind' (for agent suffix and initial stress, cf. пе́карь 'baker').

ТОЛЬКО [tól'ko] 'only'. CSl. *toliko (pronoun *to + particle *li + suffix *-ko), with subsequent reduction of unstressed -i- (cf. ChSl. *толи* 'to that extent', ско́лько 'how much', сто́лько 'so much' and analogous -ko- in Gk. *tēlíkos* 'so great').

ТОНУТЬ [tonút'] 'to drown, sink' (intrans.). From CSl. *topnǫti, with -pn- simplifying to -n-. Cognate with топи́ть 'to drown, sink' (trans.).

ТОПЛИВО [tóplivo] 'fuel'. From *toplъ (a later variant of *teplъ 'warm', see тёплый, id.). For suffix, cf. огни́во 'steel for striking fire from a flint'.

ТОПОЛЬ [tópol'] 'poplar'. 11th-/12th centuries, seemingly derived from Lat. *pŏpulus* 'poplar', with dissimilation of plosives from p-p to t-p. Perhaps also cognate with Gk. *pteléa* 'elm'. Alternatively based on IE *pel- 'grey', from the colour of poplar bark.

ТОПОТ [tópot] 'clattering'. Onomatopoeic (IE *tap- 'tread, trample'). Cf. то́пать 'to stamp', Gk. *týptō* 'I strike', *týmpanon* 'kettle-drum'.

ТОРГОВЛЯ [torgóvlja] 'trade'. 14th century, from *търгъ* 'market-place, trade, market', perhaps ultimately from Ar. *tājir* 'merchant', *tijāra* 'trade' (with metathesis from j-r to r-g).

ТОРЖЕСТВО [toržestvó] 'celebration, triumph'. 11th century 'festival', based on торг (obs.) 'market', perhaps because celebrations were held on the market-square. From a ChSl.

calque of Gk. *panégyris* 'general, national or festive assembly' (*pân* 'all', *ágyris* 'a gathering', cf. *agorá* 'forum, place of assembly and business'). Alternatively, only *influenced* by the Gk.

ТОРМОЗ [tórmoz] 'brake'. From Gk. *tórmos* 'wheel-hub, socket into which a pin or peg is inserted'. Alternatively, from Tkc. (dial. *tormoš* = Crimean *torok* 'beam, chock').

ТОСКА [toská] 'melancholy'. From CSl. *tъska, orig. assumed to mean 'emptiness' (the precursor of melancholy) and cognate with тóщий 'emaciated' (originally 'empty', cf. натощáк 'on an empty stomach'), with -ск-:-щ- mutation. Cf. also тщéтный 'vain'.

ТОЧКА [tóčka] 'point, full stop'. Recorded in dictionaries since 1704, but used to denote a punctuation mark in the 15th-/16th centuries. From *tъk- (root of ткнуть 'to jab'), thus originally, perhaps, 'puncture mark'. Тóчка зрéния 'point of view' derives from Lat. *pūnctum vīsus*, id. (Lat. *pungō* 'I prick, puncture'), via Fr. *point de vue*, id..

ТРАВА [travá] 'grass'. 11th century, probably associated with травить 'to trample down, damage crops' (of cattle), and deriving from the infinitive by reaffixation.

ТРЕСКА [treská] 'cod'. Early 17th century in this meaning. Possibly from 11th-century meaning 'splinter', cf. earlier *рыбащéпка* 'cod', lit. 'splinter-fish', analogous to Ger. *Stockfisch* 'cod', lit. 'stick-fish'. Perhaps from the fish's tendency to shred into fibres, like wood, during the drying process (cf. трéскаться 'to crack'). Alternatively, cognate with Ger. *Dorsch* 'cod' (cf. Dan. *Torsk*, id.), from *dürr* 'dry, dried out' (*Dorsch* is properly *Dörrfisch* from *dörren* 'to dry, bake'), thus lit. 'dried smoked fish'. Cf. IE *ters- 'to rub, dry'.

ТРЕФЫ [tréfy] 'clubs' (cards). Second half of 18th century (originally *треф*, pl. трéфы), probably from Ger. *Treff*, id. (backformed from Swiss *Treffle*, -le having been misinterpreted as a dim.), Fr. *trèfle* 'clover, clubs', Lat. *trifolium* '3-leaved grass, trefoil', Gk. *tríphyllon* 'trefoil, clover'. For pl. number, cf. бу́бны 'diamonds', etc.

ТРИ [tri] 'three'. CSl. *trьje (masc.), *tri (fem./neut.), with cognates in Gk. *treis*, id., Lat. *trēs*, id., Ger. *drei*, id., etc. (cf. IE *treies, id.). Root variants account for трое 'three', трезво́нить 'to spread rumours' (originally to ring three times or three bells), трено́жить 'to hobble' (securing both a horse's front legs and one back), треуго́льник 'triangle', Тро́ица 'Trinity, Whitsun'. Derivatives include трина́дцать '13', три́дцать '30' and три́ста '300'. Три́жды 'three times' lit. means 'three moves', from *tri šьdy, nom. pl. of *šьdъ (whence also past act. part. ше́дший 'who was going'), a phonetic variant of *chodъ 'move' (with ch- palatalizing to š- before -ь-), š- subsequently voicing to ž- before -d- after the reduction of -ь- (cf. одна́жды, 'once', два́жды 'twice', четы́режды 'four times').

ТРОПА́ [tropá] 'path'. 12th century, by deaffixation from CSl. *tropati 'to trample' (IE *tremp- 'tread, trample'), cf. Lith. *trepsėti* 'to stamp one's feet', Gk. *atrapós* 'path'. Possibly cognate with Gk. *trapéō* 'I tread grapes', Ger. *traben* 'to trot', *Treppe* 'staircase'.

ТРОСТЬ [trost'] 'walking stick'. 11th century 'reed stem, stick', as 'walking stick' ostensibly calqued from Fr. *canne* 'reed, walking stick' in the mid-18th century (or perhaps *popularized* in this meaning, which was attested in the 11th century).

ТРУБА́ [trubá] 'pipe, chimney, trumpet'. Perhaps from OHG onomatopoeic *trumba* 'drum, trumpet' (cf. Ger. *Trommel* 'drum', *Trompete* 'trumpet', both ultimately from *trumba*, itself from MLat. *trumpa* 'trumpet').

ТРУС [trus] 'coward'. First written references in this meaning 16th century, but cf. earlier OR *трусъ* 'trembling, earthquake', from CSl. *tręs-/*trǫs- 'to tremble' (IE *trese- 'tremble'). Thus probably lit. 'he who trembles'. Cognate with трясти́ 'to shake', Pol. *truchleć*, id.

ТРУЩО́БА [truščóba] 'impenetrable place in a forest, slum'.

Recorded in dictionaries in the first meaning in the first half of the 19th century, perhaps from *трускъ* (obs.), verbal noun from трусить 'to strew', thus maybe 'forest strewn with brushwood, wind-fallen trees' (cf. also OR *трускъ* = треск 'sound of crackling'). 'Slum' is a fig. extension from the later 19th century.

ТУГОЙ [tugój] 'tight'. 11th century 'firm', cognate with тяга 'traction, pull' (CSl. *tǫg-/*tęg-) and тянуть 'to pull' (CSl. *tęg-/*tęgnǫti, id.), with nasal vowels -ę- and -ǫ- changing to ESl. -я-/-у-, thus perhaps lit. 'pulled tight'.

ТУЗ [tuz] 'ace' (in cards). Early 17th century, common from first half of 18th century. Derives, via Pol. *tuz*, id., late OHG *dus* (cf. Ger. *Daus* 'ace, two dice pips'), from SFr. *daus* '2 pips in card games', ultimately Lat. *duo*, acc. *duos* 'two' (seemingly the туз had two pips, later one, cf. ac 'ace', with only one). Cf. also Eng. *deuce* '2 on dice or (obs.) cards', from OFr. *deus*, Lat. acc. *duos*, also 'forty all' at tennis (with two consecutive points required for a win), and the imprecation *the deuce!* (because two aces at dice was said to be the worst throw).

ТУМАН [tumán] 'fog'. Of Tkc. provenance (cf. Turk. *duman* 'smoke, fog'), perhaps ultimately from Pers. (cf. Pers. *dūdeh* 'soot').

ТУНЕЯДЕЦ [tunejádec] 'sponger'. Late 14th century, from OR *туне* 'free of charge' (cf. втуне (obs.) 'in vain') + *jadьcь 'one who eats', thus lit. 'one who eats for nothing'. Cf. дармоед 'scrounger', даром 'for nothing', всеядный 'omnivorous'.

ТУПИК [tupík] 'cul-de-sac, deadlock'. From тупой 'blunt'.

ТЩАТЕЛЬНЫЙ [tščátel'nyj] 'thorough'. First half of the 18th century, based on OR *тъщатися* 'to hurry, strive'. Of ChSl. origin, ultimately from CSl. *tъsk-, probably cognate with тоска 'anguish' (with -sk-:-šč- mutation).

ТЩЕСЛАВИЕ [tščeslávije] 'vanity'. From ChSl. (cf. *тъщии* 'vain, insignificant', слава 'glory'), lit. 'vainglory'. Calqued in the 14th century, during the period of the second S. Slav influence, from Gk. *kenodoxía* 'vanity' (from *kenós* 'empty' -- whence Eng. *cenotaph*, lit. 'empty tomb'-- *dóxa* 'opinion').

ТЫКВА [týkva] 'pumpkin'. From OR *тыкы*, gen. *тыкъве* 'pumpkin', possibly associated with Gk. *síkuos* 'common gourd or cucumber', *sikúa* 'fruit like the cucumber or gourd but eaten ripe', cf. IE *tuk- 'fat'. Both Gk. and R. could be from a third source.

ТЫЛ [tyl] 'rear' (mil.). 11th century 'rear', also 'nape of the neck', 18th century 'posterior, nape of the neck'. Perhaps initially 'slight swelling' (cf. *тыти* (obs.) 'to swell', Gk. *týlos* 'lump', IE *tumō- 'swell'). Cf. also затылок 'nape of the neck'.

ТЫСЯЧА [týsjača] 'thousand'. 11th century, from CSl. *tysętja, id., comprising *ty- 'large, abundant' (cf. тук (obs.) 'fat', *тыти* 'to swell', Lith. *tukti* 'to grow fat') + *sęt- (from IE *k̂ṃtóm 'hundred'), thus тысяча '1,000' (ESl. -я- evolving from -ę-, -č- from -tj-) lit. means 'a fat hundred'. A Balt./Slav./Gmc. formation, cf. Lith. *tūkstantis* '1,000', Ger. *tausend*, id. (lit. 'many hundreds'), IE *tūksk̂ṃt-, id. (IE *tuk- 'fat').

ТЮЛЬПАН [tjul'pán] 'tulip'. 1731 *тулипан*, тюльпа́н in dictionaries since 1762, from OFr. *tulipan*, id. (cf. Fr. *tulipe*, id., Sp. *tulipan*, id.), from the flower's resemblance to a turban (c. 1554 Busbecq, Ferdinand I's ambassador to the Turkish sultan, reported that the Turks name the white tulip for its similarity to a turban). Cf., however, Turk. *sarik* 'turban' (*tülbent* 'gauze, muslin'), thus perhaps from Pers. *dulband* 'turban' (whence also тюрба́н, id.).

ТЮРЬМА [tjur'má] 'prison'. 16th-/17th centuries, possibly via Pol. *turma* 'dungeon, jail' (dated, however, as later than the R. by some), via Novgorod and Pskov territory from MHG *turn* (cf. Ger. *Turm* 'tower', pl. *Türme*). Ultimately from Lat. *turrim* (*turrem* a rarer form), acc. of *turris* 'tower'. Alternatively, from Tkc. *turmä* 'confinement, dungeon' (however, some Tkc. variants are *from* R.).

У

УВАЖАТЬ [uvažát'] 'to respect'. Seemingly unknown before mid-18th century, from Pol. *uważać* 'to observe, consider' (for meaning, cf. OR *уважити* 'to take into consideration', *уважить* 'to comply with'), a derivative of Pol. *uwaga* 'attention', ultimately CSl. *vaga, from OHG *waga* 'scales' (Ger. *Waage*, id., cf. OR *вага* 'weight', Pol. *waga*, id.). Thus lit. 'to give proper consideration, weight to'. Cf. ва́жный 'important'.

УГОЛ [úgol] 'corner, angle'. From CSl. *ǫgъlъ (ǫ- to у- in ESl.), cognate with Gk. *agkṓn* 'bend', Lat. *angulus* 'angle' (cf. IE *anktos 'bend, bent').

УГОЛОВНЫЙ [ugolóvnyj] 'criminal'. Early 18th century, originally 'relating to a murder victim', on the basis of OR *голова* 'head, murder victim' (cf. OR *головьникъ* 'murderer'). The word subsequently expanded its meaning, perhaps under the influence of Lat. *capitālis* 'punishable by death or the loss of civil rights', cf. Lat. *rēs capitālis* 'capital crime' (Lat. *caput* 'head'). Cf. also Ger. *Hauptverbrechen* 'capital offence' (from Ger. *Haupt* 'head').

УГОЛЬ [úgol'] 'coal'. 11th century, from CSl. *ǫglь (with ǫ- to ESl. y-), cf. Lith. *anglis*, id. Possibly also associated with Gk. *ánthrax* 'coal or charcoal' (whence Eng. *anthracite*).

УДОЧКА [údočka] 'fishing rod'. 11th century *уда*, from CSl. *ǫda or *onkda, cognate with Lat. *uncus* 'hook', thus lit. 'hooked rod'. Alternatively, based on CSl. *onk- + *děti 'put', lit. (Černych) 'hooked bait' ('bait placed on something').

УЖ [už] 'grass-snake'. 16th century, from CSl. *ǫžь, id., probably cognate with ýгорь 'eel' (IE *unguros 'reptile'). Cf. Lith. *angis* 'snake', Lat. *anguis*, id.

УЖИН [úžin] 'dinner, supper'. OR *ужина*, lit. 'south time' (i.e. 'midday', from CSl. *jugъ 'south', OR *угъ 'south, midday, southern countries'), originally 'midday meal', later (as masc.

ýжин, cf. зáвтрак 'breakfast', обéд 'lunch') 'evening meal' (since, in a city environment, people usually dined in the evenings, after work).

УЗЕЛ [úzel] 'knot'. Recorded in dictionaries since 1794 (cf. OR *узолъ* 'knot, sack'), from CSl. *vǫzьlъ 'knot', with subsequent loss of v- (cf. its retention in Pol. *węzeł*, id., вéнзель 'monogram'). Cognate with вязáть 'to tie', ýзы 'bonds', сою́з 'union'.

УЗКИЙ [úzkij] 'narrow'. 11th century, from CSl. *ǫzъkъ (IE *angh- 'restricted'), cognate with Lat. *angustus* 'narrow', Ger. *eng*, id., and possibly Gk. *ágchō* 'I press tight', Lat. *angō*, id.

УЗОР [uzór] 'pattern'. OR *узоръ*, cognate with зреть (obs.) 'to see' (cf. зреть/узрéть 'to behold'), thus perhaps initially 'what is looked at'. Cognates also include зóркий 'keen-eyed', взор 'glance'.

УКРОМНЫЙ [ukrómnyj] 'secluded'. Based on OR *укромъ* 'edge, limit' (cf. also OR *укромь* 'separately', *укромьствовати* 'to remain to one side'). Thus lit. 'on the periphery, marginalized'. Cf. крóме 'apart from', скрóмный 'modest'.

УКСУС [úksus] 'vinegar'. 12th century, a reshaping of Gk. *óxos* 'sour wine, vinegar', from *oxýs* 'keen, sharp'.

УЛЕЙ [úlej] 'bee-hive'. OR *улии* (cf. standard OR *бъртъ*, later бортъ 'hive of wild bees', especially in a tree or forest). From CSl. *ul- 'hollow, cavity', thus initially 'hollow in tree, home of bees', cognate with Gk. *aulós* 'hollow tube', Lat. *alveus* 'hollow, cavity, hive', Lith. *avilys* 'hive', Pol. *ul*, id.

УЛИТКА [ulítka] 'snail'. Recorded in dictionaries from 1731, from *улита* (1536, as a nickname) + -ка. Probably from adj. *ulitъ (CSl. *ul- 'hollow' + -it- 'endowed with', cf. имени́тый 'distinguished', lit. 'provided with a name'). Thus initially 'provided with a refuge, hollow', 'house-carrier' (cf. analogous Gk. *pheréoikos* (of Scythian nomads) 'carrying one's house', and (as adj. noun) 'snail'). Dal' suggests an alternative derivation from *уливáть* 'to drench', perhaps a reference to the damp trail left by snails or their damp body film.

УЛИЦА [úlica] 'street'. CSl. *ula (whence dial. *ýлка* 'road between houses') + -ica (cf. гранйца 'frontier' from грань 'verge'), OR *улица* 11th century 'street', 14th century 'square'. Cognate with *ýлей* 'bee-hive', Gk. *aulōn* 'ravine, hollow way, channel', *aulós* 'tube, pipe, groove'. For переýлок 'lane' and закоýлок 'back street', cf. dial. *ýлок* 'road between houses'.

УМ [um] 'mind, brain'. 11th century 'mind, soul, thought', probably ultimately from IE *āum- 'perception', with derivatives in рáзум 'reason', умéть 'to know how to', etc.

УНИЧТОЖАТЬ [uničtožát'] 'to annihilate'. Recorded in dictionaries from the second half of the 18th century, from OR *ничтоже* (comprising ничтó 'nothing' + particle же). Thus lit. 'to reduce to nothing', cf. Lat. *annihilō* 'I annihilate', from *nihil* 'nothing'.

УПОРНЫЙ [upórnyj] 'stubborn'. Cognate with перéть 'to push, press', thus lit. 'pressing' (cf. уперéть 'to prop up against'). See спор 'argument'.

УПРАЖНЯТЬСЯ [upražnját'sja] 'to practise'. 11th century (from ChSl.) 'to occupy oneself with, devote oneself to' (cf. 12th century *упражняти* 'to occupy', occasionally 'to abolish', perhaps originally, according to Černych, 'to fill a void'). Ultimately from CSl. *porz- and cognate with порóжний 'empty' and прáздный 'idle'. The meaning perhaps developed from 'to free oneself from work', 'to 'indulge in something at one's leisure', then 'to practise'.

УПРЁК [uprëk] 'reproach'. In dictionaries from the second half of the 18th century, through deaffixation from упрекáть 'to reproach'. Cf. cognates перéчить 'to contradict', поперёк 'athwart'.

УПРУГИЙ [uprúgij] 'elastic, resilient'. Recorded in dictionaries since 1771, from CSl. root *prǫgъ, cognate with пружи́на 'spring', у́пряжь 'harness'. Cf. also OR *упругъ*, assumed to mean 'mast' (from its resilience).

УРОЖАЙ [urožáj] 'harvest'. Recorded in dictionaries since 1782 (cf. 17th-century урожа́йный 'fertile'), a late derivative of OR *уродитися* 'to be born' (cf. уроди́ть (coll.) 'to bring forth', уроди́ться 'to ripen'). Thus lit. 'brought forth' (by the earth).

УРОК [urók] 'lesson'. 11th-/12th-century meanings 'rule, designation, condition' are succeeded by later meaning 'term, definite period' (i.e., for the completion of a task, cf. приуро́чить 'to time for'). Cognate with CSl. *rekti 'to speak'. The meaning 'school task, lesson' evolved no later than early 18th century.

УСТА [ustá] (obs./poet.) 'mouth, lips'. 11th century, id., also 'river mouth', from CSl. *usta. A pl. form, and not, as with пле́чи 'shoulders', у́ши 'ears', о́чи 'eyes', based on the dual number. Cognate with Lat. *ōs* 'mouth' (for -t-, cf. *ōstium* 'river mouth'), Skr. *ās* 'mouth'. Derivatives include у́стный 'oral', наизу́сть 'by heart'.

УСТРИЦА [ústrica] 'oyster'. Early 18th century (originally *устерсы* 'oysters'), from LG *uster* (cf. Ger. *Auster* 'oyster') or D. *oester*, id. Ultimately from Lat. *ostrea*, id., Gk. *óstreon*, id. Ending -ица under the influence of word-type карака́тица 'cuttle-fish'. Alternatively, directly from Ital. *ostrica* 'oyster'.

УСТЬЕ [úst'je] 'mouth of river'. 10th century (*устие*, *усть*, id.). Cognate with уста́ 'mouth', cf. Lat. *ōstium* 'river mouth'.

УТКА [útka] 'duck'. From CSl. *ǫty, id., OR *уты*, id. (IE *anǝtis, id.). Cf. Lat. *anas*, gen. *anatis*, id., Lith. *antis*, id. The meaning 'newspaper lie' is a semantic calque of Fr. *canard* 'duck, newspaper lie', cf. Ger. *Ente*, id.

УТРО [útro] 'morning'. 11th century *утро* 'dawn, morning, next day', *утрие* 'morning'. У́тро 'morning' possibly derives from the blending of two roots with similar meanings, firstly CSl. *jutro 'early hours, time of awakening' (cf. Lith. *jau* 'already'), in one interpretation 'time to harness' (cf. Lat. *iugum* 'yoke' and analogous Gk. concept *boulytós* 'time for *un*yoking oxen', thus 'evening'), and secondly CSl. *ustro 'dawn' (from *usro, with intrusive -t-, cf. о́стров 'island'), cognate with Lat. *aurora* 'dawn', Lith. *aušra*, id., Gk. *héōs* 'morning' (cf. IE *ausos 'morning red'). See also за́втра 'tomorrow'.

УТРОБА [utróba] 'womb'. 11th century 'heart, stomach', 15th century 'entrails', from CSl. *ǫtro 'intestines' (cf. нутро́ (coll.) 'interior'). Cognate with Gk. *énteron* 'piece of gut' (pl. 'intestines'), Skr. *antara* 'interior', Ger. *unter* 'among' (ultimately IE *antro- 'interior, hollow'). For -оба, cf. жа́лоба 'complaint'.

УТЮГ [utjúg] 'flat-iron'. Early 17th century, of Tkc. origin (Tkc. *ut* = *öt* 'to pass, pass across'), cf. Turk. *ütü* 'flat-iron'.

УХО [úcho] 'ear'. 11th century, from IE *ous- 'ear', with cognates in Lat. *auris*, id., Gk. *oûs*, id., Goth. *auso*, id. (Ger. *Ohr*, id.). У́ши 'ears' originally the dual number (-х- to -ш- before -и -- first palatalization of velars).

УЩЕЛЬЕ [uščél'je] 'ravine'. From щель 'crack, fissure'.

УЮТ [ujút] 'comfort'. Recorded in dictionaries since 1794, derivative of CSl. *jutъ 'roof', cf. юти́ться 'to take shelter', прию́т 'refuge', Latv. *jumts* 'roof'.

Ф

ФАБРИКА [fábrika] 'factory' (mainly for consumer goods, cf. завóд, id., mainly for heavy industry, producing machinery or processing farm produce). Early 18th century, from Ital. *fabbrica*, id. (possibly via Pol. *fabryka*, id.), *fabbricare* 'to manufacture'. Ultimately from Lat. *faber* 'workman', *fabrica* 'workshop, trade'. Фабрикáт 'finished product' is from Lat. *fabricātus*, part. from *fabricō* 'I manufacture'.

ФАРТУК [fártuk] 'apron'. Late 17th century, from MHG *vortuch*, id. (Grimm, which also refers to its use in Bavarian/Swabian/Austrian dial., cf. standard *Schürze*, id.), lit. 'fore-cloth', 15th century 'altar frontal'. For the change from -ch to -k, cf. гáлстук 'tie'. Фар- from vor- has been explained by association with Ger. *fahr-* 'travel'.

ФАСОЛЬ [fasól'] 'haricot bean, French bean'. Recorded in dictionaries since 1847 (earlier *фасули/фасоли*), via Pol. *fasola* 'kidney bean', from MHG *fasòl*, ultimately Lat. *phasēlus/-os* 'kidney bean', Gk. *phásēlos* 'bean(s)'.

ФЕВРАЛЬ [fevrál'] 'February'. 11th century *февруарь*, 12th century *феварь* (subsequently феврáль by dissimilation of p-p to p-л). Via ChSl. and Byz. Gk. *februorários*, id. (β was pronounced as [v] in Byz. Gk.), ultimately from Lat. *Februarius*, id., the last month in the pre-Julian year, lit. 'month of expiation' (in Ancient Rome the great feast of expiation and purification, *Februa* -- cf. *februa* 'expiatory rites, offerings for purification' -- was held on 15 February).

ФЕЛЬДШЕР [fél'dšer] 'surgeon's assistant'. Early 18th century, from Ger. (obs.) *Feldscher/Feldscherer*, initially 'field barber' (*Feld* 'field', *scheren* 'to cut, shear'), subsequently 'surgeon, surgeon's assistant'. For combination of activities as barber and surgeon, see also цирюльник (obs.) 'barber'.

ФЕРЗЬ [ferz'] 'queen' (chess). Via Turk. *vezir* 'vizier, queen at chess', from Pers. *firz* 'commander', in particular 'queen at chess' (in E. countries the main chess pieces were the king and the vizier).

ФИАЛКА [fiálka] 'violet'. 17th century *фьялка*, also *фиялок* (фиалка is recorded in dictionaries from 1704), via OPol. *fiałek*, id., 15th-century *fijałka*, id. (cf. Pol. *fiołek*, id.), from OHG *viola*, MHG *viel* id., itself from Lat. *viola*, id. Ending -ка possibly by analogy with flower-names незабу́дка 'forget-me-not', рома́шка 'camomile', гвозди́ка 'carnation', with dim. ending in Ger. *Veilchen* 'violet', or with Pol. -ek/-ka.

ФИНИК [fínik] 'date' (fruit). 11th century, from Gk. *phoînix* 'date-palm, date', lit. 'Phoenician', Phoenicia (*Финикия*, comprising modern Lebanon and parts of Israel and Syria) being the home of the date-palm, *Phoenix dactylifera*. Cf. also Gk. *phoînix/phoiníkeos* 'dark red' (shades from crimson to purple), a colour whose discovery is attributed to the Phoenicians. The date is thus named for its colour.

ФИТИЛЬ [fitíl'] 'wick'. Early 17th century, via Turk. *fitil*, id., ultimately Ar. *fitīlah*.

ФЛОТ [flot] 'fleet'. Late 17th century, probably from Fr. *flotte*, id. (OSc. *flotti*), with a cognate in Gk. *pléō* 'I sail, swim, float' (cf. IE *pleudos* 'to float, swim, flow').

ФЛЯГА [fljága] 'flask'. 16th century, purportedly back-formed from фля́жка, id. (cf. зонт 'umbrella' from зо́нтик), which is however attested only from the early 18th century (originally as *фля́шка*, subsequently фля́жка by analogy with доро́жка, dim. from доро́га 'road', -жка being homophonous with -шка), via Pol. *flasza/flaszka* 'bottle, flask', from Ger. *Flasche*, id. Alternatively, фля́га may derive from Fr. *flacon* 'small bottle, phial', Late Lat. *flascōnem* (acc. of *flascō* 'flask'), -яга perhaps under the influence of вла́га 'moisture'.

ФОНАРЬ [fonár'] 'lantern'. 14th century, from Byz. Gk. *phonárion* 'lamp', *phanós* 'lantern'.

ФОРТОЧКА [fórtočka] 'fortochka' (small hinged pane).

Фортка, recorded in dictionaries from early 19th century, later фо́рточка, is based on Pol. *forta/fortka* 'wicket, little gate'. Ultimately, via OHG *pforta* 'gate' (Ger. *Pforte*, id.), from Lat. *porta*, id.

ФРУКТ [frukt] 'fruit'. Late 17th century фру́кты, id., from Pol. *frukt* 'a fruit' (cf. standard *owoc*, id.), rather than Ger. *Frucht* 'fruit' or D. *vrucht*, id. Ultimately from Lat. *frūctus*, part. from *fruor* 'I enjoy', thus 'something enjoyed', also 'proceeds, produce, fruit'. Pl. perhaps by analogy with Pol. *owoce* 'fruit' or Ger. *Früchte* (as in *Früchte der Erde* 'fruits of the earth').

ФУРАЖКА [furážka] 'uniform cap'. First quarter of 19th century, perhaps based on фура́ж 'forage, fodder' or on фуражи́р 'fodder storeman, forager'. According to Cyganenko, фура́жка is a reshaping of Pol. *furażerka* (obs.) 'peaked cap', lit. 'headgear of a forager', thus perhaps the original R. form was **фуражирка* (cf. пило́тка 'forage cap' from пило́т 'pilot'). Ultimately from Fr. *fourrageur* 'forager', *fourrage* 'forage' (cf., also from the Fr., Ger. *furagieren* 'to forage').

X

ХАЛАТ [chalát] 'dressing-gown, oriental robe'. 17th century at the latest, via Tkc. (Radlov designates *khyl'at* as Turk.), from Ar. *khil'at* 'robe of honour'. (In some Asiatic societies such garments were presented by high-ranking dignitaries, as a mark of favour.) Derivatives include халáтный 'negligent'.

ХАМ [cham] 'boor'. From Ham, second of the three sons of Noah (Shem, Ham and Japheth), cursed by Noah through *his* son, Canaan, for mocking his father: 'And Noah began to be an husbandman, and he planted a vineyard: And he drank of the wine, and was drunken; and he was uncovered within his tent. And Ham, the father of Canaan, saw the nakedness of his father, and told his two brethren without ... And [Noah] said, Cursed be Canaan; a servant of servants shall he be unto his brethren'. (*Genesis* 9: 20-22, 25). Apparently originally used with reference to the low-born, but applied by 19th-century progressives to their reactionary contemporaries, according to N.I. Turgenev in 1818.

ХАНДРА [chandrá] 'depression'. 1820s, a reshaping of Lat. pl. *hypochondria* 'abdomen', itself from Gk. pl. *hypochóndria* 'the part of the abdomen below the ribs, containing liver and spleen' (*hypó* 'below', *chóndros* 'gristle, cartilage'), thought to be the seat of melancholy, hence initially a disease characterized by uneasiness in this vital area. Final stress perhaps by analogy with тоскá 'melancholy', -o- to -a- through *akan'je*. For truncation (loss of *hypó-*), cf. тýфли 'slippers' from Fr. *pantoufles* (or perhaps caused by dissimilation from ипохóндрия 'hypochondria', which appeared in the early 18th century).

ХВАСТАТЬ [chvástat'] 'to boast'. Recorded in dictionaries since 1704, perhaps onomatopoeic, maybe initially 'to chatter' (cf. Cz. *žvast* 'twaddle, foolish talk'), then 'chatter boastfully, brag'.

ХВАТАТЬ [chvatát'] 'to seize'. From CSl. *chvatati, id., also associated with the root *chyt-, cf. Cz. *chytati*, id., похи́тить 'to steal', хи́трый 'cunning' (probably initially 'agile in hunting'), хи́щник 'predator'.

ХИЖИНА [chížina] 'shack'. 12th century *хыжа/хижа* 'house' (could also mean 'monk's cell, marquee'), from CSl. **chyzъ/*chyza* 'house', Gmc. **husa-* (OHG *hus*, id.), maybe ultimately from IE **(s)keu-* 'to cover, shroud'.

ХЛЕБ [chleb] 'bread'. 11th century, from Goth. *hlaifs*, id. (cf. OE *hlāf* 'loaf', *hlæfdige* 'kneader of bread', whence ultimately Eng. *lady*). Perhaps also cognate with Lat. *lībum* 'cake, pancake', Ger. *Laib* 'loaf' (itself cognate with S. and W. Ger. *Lebkuchen* 'gingerbread'). Ger. *Laib* 'loaf' also derives, via OHG, from Goth. *hlaifs*, ultimately IE **kloibho-* 'bread baked in pans'.

ХЛОПАТЬ [chlópat'] 'to slam'. From onomatopoeic хлоп! (for -от, cf. гро́хот 'rumble'), whence also хло́поты 'trouble' (OR *хлопотъ* 'noise'). Cognates include клепа́ть 'to rivet' and шлёпать 'to smack'.

ХЛОПОК [chlópok] 'cotton'. First half of the 18th century 'produce ("flakes") of the cotton-plant', 1860s 'cotton, cotton-plant' (хлопча́тая бума́га (obs.) had been used to mean 'cotton, cotton-plant' since the 17th century). Perhaps based on CSl. **chlъръ* 'tuft' (cf. Cz. *chlup* 'hair'). Cognate with хло́пья 'flakes'.

ХОБОТ [chóbot] 'trunk, proboscis'. 12th century 'tail', 16th century 'trunk', from CSl., perhaps associated with Lith. *kabèti* 'to hang', thus lit. 'something hanging down' (х- possibly under the influence of хвост 'tail'). Alternatively, connected with *ха́битъ* (obs.) 'to seize', from the trunk's prehensile qualities.

ХОД [chod] 'move'. 14th century (11th century *ходити* 'to go, be going'), from CSl. **chodъ*, IE **sed-* 'sit', with s- changing to CSl. ch- after prefixes, thus **uchodъ*, etc., and **chodъ* subsequently evolving as an autonomous word, obviating homonymy with **sed-* 'sit', cf. the two root-meanings ('sit' and 'go') in Gk. cognates *hédos* 'seat', *hodós* 'path, entrance, approach', *hodeúō* 'I go, travel' (cf. also IE **sedos* 'seat', **sodos* 'way, manner, gait'). The affinity between the two concepts is demonstrated by the fact that words denoting 'sitting, resting', e.g. IE *nisdos/nizdos 'nest', whence гнездо́ 'nest', and words that denote 'going', e.g. е́здить 'to travel', derive from a common IE root *-sd-, a syncopated form of *sed- 'sit'. The meaning 'go' appears to have evolved from the root 'sit' as follows: 'to sit down near', 'to approach', 'to reach' (cf. Trubačev's interpretation of IE *sed- as 'moving along sitting in a carriage', subdividing into *sed- I 'sit' and *sed- II 'go').

ХОЗЯ́ИН [chozjáin] 'owner'. 15th century *хозя́* (in a non-R. context, Afanasij Nikitin's *Хожéние за три мо́ря* 'Journey Beyond Three Seas'), ultimately from Ar., via Pers. *khawājah* 'master'. Хозя́ин, id. (with singulative suffix -ин, cf. боя́рин 'bojar') evolved in the 16th-/early 17th centuries.

ХОЛО́ДНЫЙ [cholódnyj] 'cold'. Early 16th century, from CSl. *choldьnъjь, with ESl. inter-consonantal -оло- (cf. ChSl. *хла́дъ*, id., whence хладнокро́вие 'sang-froid', охлажда́ть 'to cool', etc.). Probably cognate with Goth. *kalds* 'cold' (Ger. *kalt*, id.), which is based on IE *gel- 'to cool, freeze' (cf. Lat. *gelidus* 'icy cold'), less plausibly with Lith. *šaltas* 'cold'. See коло́дец 'well' and студёный 'extremely cold'.

ХОЛОСТО́Й [cholostój] 'unmarried, blank (of cartridge)'. 12th century 'unmarried' (of men *and* women), from CSl. *cholstъ, perhaps originally 'castrated', cf. IE *(s)kel- 'to cut, split', вы́холостить 'to castrate', then 'impotent' (cf. dial. *холоста́я ры́ба* 'fish with no spawn', *холоста́я труба́* 'chimney through which no smoke has passed', холосто́й ход 'idling' (tech.), холосто́й патро́н 'blank cartridge'). Possibly cognate with шелуха́ 'pod' (thus, lit. 'barren'), less certainly with Lat. *sōlus* 'alone' and Goth. *halbs* 'half' (originally 'split'), thus 'devoid of the other half, single'. Cf. also Slovene *hlâst* 'bunch from which berries or grapes have been stripped'.

ХОЛСТ [cholst] 'canvas'. 15th century, from CSl., possibly a Gmc. loan, cf. OHG *hulla* 'cover', *hullan* 'to cover, conceal', Goth. *huljan*, id. (Ger. *hüllen*, id.), thus lit. 'covering'. Alternatively based on IE *(s)kel- 'to cut', thus perhaps referred originally to a piece of canvas shaped for a particular article (bag, mat, horse-cloth, etc.).

ХОРЕК [chorëk] 'ferret'. 14th century (acc. pl. *дхорь*), 15th century *дъхорь*, id., хорёк recorded in dictionaries from 1782. Ultimately from CSl. *дъchorь (IE *dhusəros 'ferret'), *дъch- 'smell', the animal thus being named for its pungent smell (cf. вонючка 'skunk', from вонять 'to stink', Fr. *putois* 'polecat' from *puer* 'to stink'), later *tъchorь, d- having devoiced to t- before -ch- following the reduction of -ъ-, and tch- subsequently simplifying to ch-. For suffix -ор(ь), cf. у́горь 'eel'. Cf. also cognate за́тхлый 'musty'.

ХОРОНИ́ТЬ [choronít'] 'to bury'. OR *хоронити* 'to conceal, preserve' (from CSl. *chorniti, id.), subsequently 'to bury' (cf. по́хороны 'funeral'). Cf. also, of ChSl. provenance (hence interconsonantal -ра-), храни́ть 'to preserve'. Lat. *servō* 'I preserve' is a disputed cognate.

ХОРО́ШИЙ [choróšij] 'good'. 14th century 'beautiful' (cf. хоро́ш собо́й 'handsome'), possibly from OR *хоробрь* 'strong, daring' (cf. хра́брый 'brave'), suffix -б- subsequently being replaced by hypocoristic -ш- (cf. Гри́ша 'Greg' from Григо́рий 'Gregory', etc.). The meaning 'good' derives perhaps from the value placed on courage in Slav. communities. For suffix -r(ъ)-, cf. CSl. *dobrъ. Cf. also nickname *Хорош* (1500), surname *Хорошевич* (1597). The place-name Хо́росино in Moscow Province may derive ultimately from Хорс, god of light and sun, equivalent of Apollo in the R. pagan pantheon and possibly an alternative source of хоро́ший.

ХОТЕ́ТЬ [chotét'] 'to want'. 10th century, perhaps associated with хвата́ть 'to seize' (for х-/хв- correlation, cf. охо́та 'hunting', NW dial. *охвота*, id.), less plausibly with Lith. *ketinti* 'to intend'. Perhaps cognate with Gk. *chatéō* 'I crave, need', *chatís* 'need'. Хотя́ 'although' originated as a pres. part. from хоте́ть, perhaps initially 'wanting (but unable) to'.

ХРА́БРЫЙ [chrábryj] 'brave'. Via ChSl. (hence interconsonantal -ра-, cf. 12th-century *хоробрыи* and see хоро́ший 'good'), from CSl. *chorbrъ 'brave'. An implausible link has been suggested with Gk. *kárcharos* 'sharp, biting'.

ХРЕБЕТ [chrebét] 'spinal column, mountain range, (coll.) back'. 11th century 'back, posterior, crest of wave', perhaps from a Slav. root meaning 'hill' (cf. CSl. *chrьbьtъ 'hill', Cz. *hřbet* 'spine, ridge'). Alternatively, if dubiously (disputed by Vasmer on phonetic grounds), a transformation of CSl. *gъrbъ 'back', cf. горб 'hump, (dial.) back', as in dial. *гнуть горб* 'to bend the back in toil'.

ХРУСТАЛЬ [chrustál'] 'cut glass'. An OR phonetic transformation of Gk. *krystállos* 'clear ice, rock crystal' (from *krúos* 'icy-cold', cf. Eng. *cryogenic* 'relating to very low temperatures') or Byz. Gk. *kroustálli* 'crystal cup, clear water', chr- replacing kr- perhaps under the influence of хрустéть 'to crunch' (which has an onomatopoeic base, like хру́пкий 'brittle'). Cf. also крест 'cross', dial. *хрест*, id. Криста́лл 'crystal' is also from the Gk., probably via Fr. *cristal* 'crystal, cut glass', the meanings of the R. words having become differentiated in the 18th century.

ХУДОЖНИК [chudóžnik] 'artist'. 11th century *худогыи* 'skilful, well-informed', *художьникъ* 'artist', from CSl. *chǫdogъ 'skilful'. Assimilated from Goth. **handags*, id. (Goth. *handus* 'hand'), with Gmc. -an- changing to CSl. -ǫ-, ESl. -y- (cf. Pol. *chędogi* 'neat, clean', *chędożyć* 'to clean').

Ц

ЦАПЛЯ [cáplja] 'heron'. Originally *чáпля*, id. (now dial., cf. Pol. *czapla*, id., Bulg. *чапла*, id., Cz. *čap* 'stork'), alongside цáпля, recorded since the early 17th century and dominant from the 18th. From CSl. **čapati* (*capati under the influence of N. dials.). For the meaning, cf. Ukr. *чапати* 'to squelch' (from the heron's movement through swamps) and цáпать 'to seize' (dial. *чáпать* 'to seize, scoop'), of the heron catching frogs, fish. All of onomatopoeic origin.

ЦАРЬ [car'] 'tsar'. 13th century 'Tatar khan', 15th century 'tsar' (a title assumed by Ivan IV at his coronation in 1547, supposedly reflecting the claim of the Grand Princes of Muscovy to be heirs to the Byz. Emperors). The word is a modification of OR *цесарь* (from *цѣсарь/цьсарь*, -рь by association with the suffix -арь), a reworking of Lat. *Caesar* (via Goth. *Kaisar*, cf. Ger. *Kaiser* 'Emperor'), the family name (*cōgnōmen*) of the Roman emperor Caius Julius Caesar, after whose death in 44 BC all Roman emperors bore this title (variously derived from Lat. *caesariēs* 'head of hair, locks' and *caedō* 'I cut, hew'). Apparently derivative place-names Царѝцын (Сталингрáд from 1925, Волгогрáд from 1961) and Цáрское Селó (presented to the tsaritsa by Peter I in 1708, after the October Revolution Солдáтское Селó, Дéтское Селó from 1918, Пýшкин from 1937) are said to result from false etymology, the first seemingly based on the ancient Tkc. name of the capital city of Chazaria, lit. 'yellowish, whitish', the second on a Finnic word meaning 'island' (Vasmer).

ЦВЕТ [cvet] 'colour, blossom'. 11th century 'flower', 14th century 'colour', from CSl. **květъ* (cf. Pol. *kwiat* 'flower'), with kv- to ESl. cv- before -ě-. Derivatives include цветóк 'flower', cf. pl. цветы́ 'flowers', цветá 'colours'. Cf. also цвестѝ 'to bloom' (from CSl. **kvisti, IE*k̑uietjō̄ 'shine').

ЦЕЛÉБНЫЙ [celébnyj] 'curative'. Of ChSl. origin, from *цѣльба* 'healing, medicine'. See цéлый 'whole'.

ЦЕЛИНА [celiná] 'virgin soil'. 14th-/15th centuries, from the root of цéлый 'whole', thus lit. 'uncultivated soil'.

ЦЕЛОВАТЬ [celovát'] 'to kiss'. 11th century 'to greet, kiss' (initially sacred objects in taking an oath), from CSl. *cělovati 'to wish good health, security, a safe return' (cf. *cělъ 'whole, health'), then 'kiss'. Probably a calque from Lat. *salūtō* 'I greet'. Cf. Eng. *salute* (arch.) 'to kiss' (especially at meeting or parting), здорóваться 'to greet' from здорóв 'healthy'.

ЦЕЛЫЙ [célyj] 'whole'. 11th century, cognate with Gmc. *haila- (Ger. *heil* 'sound, whole'). The meaning 'healthy, unscathed' is reflected in уцелéть 'to survive', its derivative meaning 'indivisible' in цéлое 'whole number'.

ЦЕЛЬ [cel'] 'aim, goal'. Recorded in dictionaries since 1731, from MHG *zil* (Ger. *Ziel*, id.), probably via Pol. *cel*, id. Derivatives include прицéлиться 'to take aim'.

ЦЕНА [cená] 'price'. 10th century, probably cognate with кáяться 'to repent' (from IE *kāi̯ō, id.), with IE -ai- to -ě- in CSl., and subsequently k- to c- before -ě- (second palatalization of velars). Initially, perhaps, 'retribution', 'recompense', then 'price'. Cognates include Lith. *kaina*, id., Gk. *poinḗ* 'redemption, recompense', Lat. *poena* 'recompense, penalty' (the apparent source of пéня 'fine').

ЦЕПЬ [cep'] 'chain'. OR *чепь* (deaffixed from CSl. *čěpiti 'to seize') and *цѣпь* (rarer, but standard after 17th century, ц- possibly under the influence of N. dials.), from OR *цѣпити*, originally 'to split, separate' (reflexive 'to be separated', cf. the link-structure of a chain), for later meaning 'to catch on', cf. цеплять (coll.) 'to clutch at', dial. *чепáть*, id. Derivatives include early 18th-century цéпкий 'tenacious'.

ЦЕРКОВЬ [cérkov'] 'church'. In origin the acc. case (*цьрквь*) of 11th-century *цьркы*, probably from late Gk. *kurikón* 'God's house', from earlier (4th century AD) adj. *kuriakón* 'the Lord's', which was substantivized as 'communion' (from *kuriakón deipnon*, id., lit. 'the Lord's meal') then 'church' (ellipsis for *to* (*dôma*) *kuriakón* 'House of the Lord'). Ultimately from Gk. *kúrios* 'lord' (*Kúrios* 'Christ'), with k- changing to ц- (for k- to ч- by first palatalization of velars, cf. Bulg. черква, alongside църква 'church'). Possibly via Goth. *kirikô, id. or OHG *kiricha*, id. (cf. Ger. *Kirche*, id.). Cf. also cognate куролéсить 'to play tricks'.

ЦИРКУЛЬ [církul'] 'compasses'. 17th century, via Pol. *cyrkiel*, id., or direct from Ger. *Zirkel*, id., with influence of Lat. *circulus* 'small circle' in the second syllable.

ЦИРЮЛЬНИК [cirjúl'nik] (obs.) 'barber'. From Pol. *cyrulik*, id., itself from Lat. *chīrurgus* 'surgeon', Gk. *cheirourgós* 'practising a handicraft' (*cheír* 'hand', *érgon* 'work'), substantivized as 'surgeon', with dissimilation of r-r to r-l in Slav. and reshaped in R. on the pattern of nouns in -ник. (From 17th to 19th centuries barbers also drew teeth and let blood, but цирюльник was distinguished from хирýрг 'surgeon' by 18th century, and replaced by парикмáхер 'hairdresser' 19th century, against the background of a fashion for wigs, cf. парúк 'wig'.)

ЦИФРА [cífra] 'figure'. Early 18th century (mainly in the meaning 'zero' -- meaning 'figure' mostly from the mid-18th century). From MLat. *cifra* 'zero', via Ital. *cifra* 'cipher' and Pol. *cyfra* 'number, cipher' or Ger. *Ziffer*, initially 'zero', then 'figure'. Ultimately from Ar. *ṣifr* 'zero', lit. 'empty place', denoting a gap in a numerical series. Cf. Eng. *cipher* 'arithmetical symbol (0) of no value in itself but used to occupy a vacant place in decimal etc. numeration'.

ЦЫПЛЕНОК [cyplënok] 'chick'. 15th-/16th centuries, as variants on names/nicknames, pl. цыпленки early 17th century (cf. modern standard цыплята 'chicks'). From assumed ципля 'chick' (cf. OR *теля* 'calf', телёнок, id.). Cf. also dial. цыпля, id., from цып-цып! (used in calling chickens).

ЦЫПОЧКИ [cýpočki] 'tip-toe'. Of onomatopoeic origin, possibly associated with MHG *zipfen* 'to mince, trot', *zippeltritt* 'mincing gait' (whence Ger. *Zipperlein* 'gout').

Ч

ЧАДО [čádo] (obs./jocular) 'child'. 11th century, via ChSl., from CSl. *čędo, ultimately IE *gen-/*ken- 'to beget' (with k- changing to CSl. č- before -ę- by the first palatalization of velars, cf. Gmc. *ken-, id., *kinda- 'begotten', OHG *kind* 'child', Ger. *Kind*, id.). Cognate with Gk. *kainós* 'new', Lat. *recēns* 'fresh, young, recent', зачáть 'to conceive', начáть 'to begin', thus lit. 'young, recently-born'. For -до, cf. стáдо 'herd'. Derivatives include исчáдие áда 'devil incarnate' and домочáдец 'member of household'.

ЧАЙ [čaj] 'tea'. Mid-17th century, by which time stable links had been formed with the Chinese Empire. Perhaps originally as a herbal remedy, from N. Chinese *č'a*, id., possibly via Tkc. (cf. Turk. *çay*, id.). (In 1638 R. ambassador Strakov presented sable furs to the Mongol khan and was given 200 packets of tea, which he passed on to the tsar. Tea caravans from N. China began in 1696. Tea was brought to Russia by caravan through C. Asia throughout the 18th and 19th centuries.) Cf., conveyed by sea routes, from S. Chinese (Amoy) and Malay *teh*, id., Eng. *tea*, Fr. *thé*, id., etc.

ЧАЙКА [čájka] 'seagull'. Early 18th century (cf. 12th-century *чаица* 'name of a bird'). Onomatopoeic, cf. Est. *kajak* 'seagull', Cz. *čejka* 'lapwing'.

ЧАС [čas] 'hour'. 10th-11th centuries 'time, appropriate time, period', from CSl. *časъ 'moment' (cf. сейчáс 'now'), subsequently 'time', then 'hour'. Possibly cognate with Serb. *касати* 'to run at a trot', Ger. *hasten* 'to hurry', or with чáять 'to expect'. The concept of час as one twenty-fourth part of a day, each hour divided into 6 10-minute periods called *часовец* and these into 10 1-minute periods called *часец*, was established in the 17th century. The pl.-only status of часы́ 'clock, watch' may be due to the fact that some early clocks were multi-dialled and extremely complex, cf. Kulibin's 18th-century pocket planetary watch, which indicated hour, minute, second, day of week and month, phase of moon, sunrise and sunset. Cf. analogous pl.-only весы́ 'scales'. See also мину́та 'minute', секу́нда 'second'.

ЧАСТЫЙ [částyj] 'frequent, dense'. From CSl. *čęstъ 'dense' (older form *kemstъ), cognate with Lith. *kimšti* 'to cram, stuff'.

ЧАСТЬ [čast'] 'part'. 11th century, from CSl. *čęstь, possibly associated with Lat. *scindō* 'I divide', Gk. *schízō* 'I split, separate', Lith. *skaidyti* 'to part, separate'. Alternatively, with CSl. *kǫsъ, cf. кусо́к 'piece', Lith. *kąsti* 'to bite'.

ЧАША [čáša] 'cup, bowl'. 11th century (14th century *чашька*, now ча́шка 'cup'), probably of Balto-Slav. origin, possibly associated with Lith. *kiaušas* 'skull' (early cups were made from skulls or fashioned in their likeness). Alternatively, from the Iran. group (whence also Arm. *čašak* 'goblet'), cf. Pers. *kāsah* 'bowl', cognate with Skr. *casakaḥ* 'drinking vessel'.

ЧЕЛОВЕК [čelovék] 'human being, person'. 11th century, from CSl. *čel- (cognate with че́лядь 'retainers', and possibly Lith. *kelti* 'to raise', *kilti* 'to be descended from') + *věkъ, which is cognate with Lith. *vaikas* 'child', thus lit. 'child of the clan'. Alternatively, from чело́, earlier 'peak', then 'forehead' + *vekъ 'strength' (cf. IE *u̯eik- 'force', dial. *обезвекнуть* 'to lose strength'), thus (a disputed etymology) 'man in his prime'. Finally, the meaning could be 'brain power', from чело́ 'forehead' + *vekъ 'strength'.

ЧЕЛЮСТЬ [čéljust'] 'jaw'. Possibly a blend of чело́ 'forehead' and уста́ 'mouth' (cf. Hung., *arc* 'face', seemingly a blend of *orr* 'nose' and *száj* 'mouth'). Alternatively, if controversially, 'bone of the mouth', based on *čel-, cognate with Skr. *kulya* 'repository for the bones of a burnt corpse', possibly *kulya- 'bone', or cognate with ска́лить 'to bare' (also щель 'crevice'), thus maybe 'mouth with bared teeth'.

ЧЕМОДАН [čemodán] 'suitcase'. 16th century, via Tkc. from Pers. *jāmahdān*, id. (*jāmah* 'clothes', whence *pyjamas*, + *dān* 'container').

ЧЕПУХА [čepuchá] 'nonsense'. Mid-18th century 'splinter' (cf. analogous вздор 'nonsense', originally 'litter', cognate with драть 'to tear'). Alternatively, a blend of щепá 'splinter' and чухá (obs., reg.) 'nonsense'. Unlikely to be associated with тщéтный 'futile'.

ЧЕРВЬ [červ'] 'worm'. 11th century, from CSl. *čьrvь, id., a parallel formation to *čьrmь 'red', from *kьrmь (cf. IE *kurmos 'creeper, crawler', Lith. *kirminas* 'worm'). For m:v mutation, cf. sub-standard gerunds of the type *евши/емши*, from есть 'to eat' (alternatively, -v- could have resulted from an analogy with CSl. *morvъ/*morvь 'ant'). For cognates with connotations of 'red' (червь/чьрвь 'worm' also meant 'red dye'), cf. OR *чьрмьньш* 'red', червлёный (obs.) 'dark red', Pol. *czerwony* 'red', *czerwiec* 'June', SW Bulg. dial. *чръвенъ* 'June, July', possibly because worms used for dyeing were collected in these months (or, given the Slavs' interest in bee-keeping, because this was the time when queen bees deposited their larvae (*чéрва*)).

ЧЕРДАК [čerdák] 'attic'. 16th century 'pergola', 18th century 'attic', via Tkc. (cf. Kar.-Balk. *čardak* 'balcony, turret', Turk. *čardak* 'arbour'). Ultimately said to come from a Pers./Ar. hybrid whose components denote, respectively, 'four' and 'vault/balcony'. Cf. чертóг (obs.) 'hall, mansion'.

ЧЕРЕМУХА [čerëmucha] 'bird cherry'. 15th century *черемъха* (implied by adj. *черемъховый*), with *-ъха subsequently changing to -уха by analogy with nouns of the type чернýха 'nutmeg flower', or to avoid confusion with cognate черемшá 'ransom, root of broad-leaved garlic'. Perhaps named after the dark colour of its berries, cf. dial. *черéмый* 'swarthy', or its distinctive reddish-brown wood (cf. dial. *черéмный* 'red'). Cognate with Lith. *šermukšnis* 'rowan' and Fr. *cormier*, a regional variant of *sorbier* 'sorb, service-tree', from Lat. *sorbus*, id. (similar to the rowan, but with cream-coloured flowers and round or pear-shaped fruit).

ЧЕРЕП [čérep] 'skull'. OR *чрепъ* 'shard', from CSl. *čerpъ 'shard, skull' (IE *(s)ker- 'to cut', cf. Lith. *kirpti*, id.), probably cognate with Skr. *karpara* 'shell' and (assumed, though unattested, meaning) 'skull', also with OHG *scirbi* 'shard', Ger. *Scherbe*, id. Derivatives include early 17th-century черепа́ха 'tortoise' (for ending -axa, cf. dial. *пта́ха* 'bird') and черепи́ца 'tile'.

ЧЕРЕШНЯ [čeréšnja] 'cherry-tree'. 12th century, from CSl. *čeršnia, id., cognate with *čьrnъ 'black' (cf. IE *k̑ēros 'dappled, marked with grey or black'), from the red-black colour of cherries. Formation of the word was influenced by Vulg. Lat. *ceresia* 'cherry-tree' (Lat. *cerasus*, id., Gk. *kerasós* 'cherry, cherry-tree'), whence also Fr. *cérise* 'cherry', Eng. *cherry* (a back formation based on a misinterpretation of ONFr. *cherise* as a pl., cf. Eng. pl. *cherries*). Ending -ня perhaps by analogy with ви́шня 'cherry'.

ЧЕРНИЛА [černíla] 'ink'. In origin the pl. of 11th-century чьрнило, id. (suffix -л(о), thus lit. 'blackening agent'), a semantic calque of Gk. *melánion*, dim. of *mélan* 'black dye, ink' (cf., also from Gk., меланхо́лия 'melancholy', lit. 'black bile'). For a pl.-only noun denoting a substance, cf. дро́жжи 'yeast'.

ЧЕРНЫЙ [čërnyj] 'black'. 11th century чьрньи, id., cf. IE *k̑ēros 'marked with grey or black', Lith. *keršas* 'black and white, piebald', also cognate with Skr. *kr̥ṣṇaḥ* 'black'.

ЧЕРТА [čertá] 'feature'. 11th century чьрта 'mark, line', from CSl. *čьrsti (IE *(s)ker- 'to cut'), cognate with Lith. *kirsti*, id., Lat. *cortex* 'bark, rind' (cut from a tree or fruit). Derivatives include 14th-century чьртежь 'mark, edge resulting from cutting' (cf. чертёж 'blueprint').

ЧЕСАТЬ [česát'] 'to scratch'. 11th century 'to rake up', 12th century 'to comb, scratch', from CSl. *česati (IE *kesō 'cut, chop, comb'). Cognate with чешуя́ 'scales' (zool.), lit. 'what can be scraped away' and with коса́ 'plait', Lith. *kasa* 'tress', *kasyti* 'to scratch', Gk. *xaínō* 'I scratch, comb', Gael. *cìr* 'comb', Ir. *cíor*, id.

ЧЕСНОК [česnók] 'garlic'. 16th century (cf. 14th century чесновитъкъ, id., чесновитьць, id.), lit. 'split into segments', from CSl. *česati 'to scrape, separate' (IE *kesn- 'garlic, onion, leek'), a reference to garlic's tendency to flake into sections, cf. Ger. *Knoblauch* 'garlic', lit. 'cleft leek', from Ger. *klieben* 'to cleave', *Lauch* 'leek'.

ЧЕТА [četá] 'couple, pair'. Early meanings 'military detachment' (cf. Cz. *četa* 'squad, platoon'), 'crowd', etc. were succeeded eventually by 'marital pair' (perhaps under the influence of *съчетатися* 'to unite'). Cognates include чёт 'even number', нéчет 'odd number', сочетáние 'combination', probably Lat. *catēna* 'chain', *caterva* 'crowd, detachment'. Perhaps ultimately from Turk. *çete* 'band of rebels', via SSl., cf. Serb. *чета* 'detachment, band, troop', *четник* 'chetnik, guerrilla fighter in the Balkans'.

ЧЕТВЕРГ [četvérg] 'Thursday'. 11th century *четвьртъкъ*, id. (from *четвьртъ* 'fourth' + -(ъ)къ), subsequently *четвьркъ* (recorded 1762), through loss of inter-consonantal -тъ-, then *четвьргъ* (recorded 1794). For the rare mutation from r-k to r-g, cf. *поперёг* (obs.) 'athwart' (CSl. *poperkъ, cf. поперёк, id.), still used in the early 19th century.

ЧЕТКИЙ [čëtkij] 'precise, legible'. From OR *чисти* 'to read, count', *чьту* 'I read, count', lit. 'legible', later broadening to mean 'precise'.

ЧЕТЫРЕ [četýre] 'four'. Ultimately from IE *ku̯etores/*ku̯etorə, id., cognate with Lith. *keturi*, id., Lat. *quattuor*, id., Skr. *catur*, id. (nom. masc. pl. *catvāras*).

ЧЕХАРДА [čechardá] 'leapfrog'. 18th century, originally 'unruly behaviour' (perhaps associated with groups or gangs, cf. dial. *ходить чехордóй* 'to go about in a gang', **У негó семья́ чехордá* 'His cottage is full of kids'). Possibly connected with dial. *чехóр* 'bully', alternatively with Pol. *czochrać* 'to tousle' (e.g. someone's hair in playing leapfrog), Cz. *čechrati*, id.

ЧЕШУЯ [češujá] 'scales' (zool.). See чесáть 'to scratch'.

ЧИН [čin] 'rank'. 11th century, probably based on CSl. *činъ 'order', thus originally 'established order', then (by extension of meaning from 'order' to 'sequence') 'service rank'. Derivatives include чи́нный 'orderly', чино́вник 'functionary', подчини́ть 'to subordinate'.

ЧИСЛО [čisló] 'number'. 11th century, from CSl. *čitslo, id., comprising *čit- 'to read, count' + agent suffix *-sl(o) (cf. весло́ 'oar'), lit. 'what you count with', with -tsl- subsequently simplifying to -sl-. Числи́тельное 'numeral' is a calque of Lat. *numerāle nomen*, id.

ЧИСТЫЙ [čístyj] 'clean'. 11th century, probably cognate with цеди́ть 'to strain, filter', perhaps lit. 'filtered', thus 'clean', also cognate with Lith. *skaidrus* 'limpid, clear', Lat. *scindō* 'I separate', Gk. *schízō*, id. Ultimately from IE *skei- 'separate, remove what is unnecessary'.

ЧИТАТЬ [čitát'] 'to read'. 11th century *чисти* (CSl. *čisti, iter. *čitati) 'to read, consider, esteem', with *-читати* found only in compounds, e.g. 11th-century *прочитати* (=проче́сть 'to read'). For meaning 'consider', cf. учи́тывать 'to take into consideration', for 'esteem', cf. почита́ть 'to revere', and for analogous root polysemy, cf. Lat. *legere* 'to gather, to read' and Ger. *lesen*, id. (*lesen* comes from OHG *lesan* 'to gather selectively', then 'report, narrate'), cf. IE *leĝō 'gather, pick out, read'.

ЧИХАТЬ [čichát'] 'to sneeze'. Onomatopoeic.

ЧЛЕН [člen] 'member'. 11th century 'limb', 18th century 'member' (initially of a court of law), via ChSl. from CSl. *čelnъ, with -el- to ChSl. -лѣ-. Cognate with коле́но 'knee', Lith. *kelis*, id., Gk. *kōlon* 'limb', less certainly with Gk. *skélos* 'leg'.

ЧУВСТВО [čúvstvo] 'feeling'. 11th century, ultimately from CSl. *čuvati, iterative of *čuti 'to hear, perceive' (cf. Bulg. *чувам* 'hear' and interjection чу 'hark' -- lit. 'did you hear?', originally the 2nd-/3rd-pers. sing. aorist (narrative past tense) of *чути* 'to hear'), чу́ять 'to scent, sense', чутьё 'sense', чу́ткий 'sensitive'.

ЧУГУН [čugún] 'cast iron'. 17th century (frequently in works on the history of peasant industry in Russia), from Tkc., cf. Tadž. *čujan* id., Kar.-Balk. *čojun*, id.

ЧУЖОЙ [čužój] 'alien, someone else's'. 11th century *чужии* 'someone else's, foreign', from CSl. *tjudjь (subsequently *tj- to ESl. č- and *-dj- to -ž-). Probably from Goth. *diuda* 'the people' (IE *teutos 'people, country, land', cf. Lith. *tauta* 'people'), the Goths' name for themselves, whence OHG *diutisc*, from *diot* 'people', Ger. *deutsch* 'German', properly 'popular, peculiar to the people'. In Slav., however, the word meant 'outsiders, aliens', with a cognate in Чудь, referring to Finnic tribes settled to the E. of Lake Onega along the rivers Onega and N. Dvina, hence Чудское озеро (more properly Чудско-Псковское озеро) 'Lake Čudskoje', lying partly in Pskov Province, partly in Estonia. Cf. (from ChSl., with SSl. -жд-) чуждый 'alien'.

ЧУЛОК [čulók] 'stocking'. Late 15th-/16th centuries 'soft footwear' (made of cloth or thin, e.g. morocco, leather), later 'stocking', possibly from Tkc., cf. Turk. *çul* 'coarse fabric, haircloth', Kirgh. *čulgō* 'socks or cloth puttees worn in the boot or shoe'. Alternatively, if somewhat implausibly, cognate with кутать 'to muffle, wrap'.

ЧУМА [čumá] 'plague'. Emerged during R.-Turk. Balkan War of 1768-74, first recorded in dictionaries 1771, the year of a plague in Moscow, possibly from Tkc. (cf. Ottoman Turk. *çuma*, however, the Tkc. words could be from Slav.). Alternatively, from Rom. *ciumă*, id. (the Turk. War took place partly in Moldavia and Wallachia, which united to form the principality of Romania much later, in 1859). Perhaps ultimately from Gk. *kûma* 'swell of the sea' (possibly used fig. of a plague epidemic).

Ш

ШАГ [šag] 'step'. Based on CSl. *sęg-, whence ESl. сяг-, the basis of *сягáть* (obs.) 'to attain', cf. dial. *сяг*, dim. *сяжóк* 'the distance you can stride'. Шаг is assumed to be a back formation from dim. шажóк 'small step', itself from *сяжóк* (ш-ж evolving from с-ж). For ша- from ся-, cf. also dial. *шабёр* 'neighbour', from *сябёр*, id.

ШАМПАНСКОЕ [šampánskoje] 'champagne'. 18th century, adj. noun based on шампáнское винó, from Fr. *vin de Champagne*, id. or Ger. *Champagner*, id. (alongside coll. *Sekt*, id.).

ШАПКА [šápka] 'cap'. Early 14th century (initially headgear of Grand Princes, later tsar's crown), perhaps via OHG *kappa* 'hooded cloak' or directly from OFr. *chape* 'cloak, cope' (possibly in connection with a high point in Fr.-R. cultural relations resulting from the marriage of Henri I to the daughter of Jaroslav Mudryj, Grand Prince of Kiev 1019-54). Ultimately from Late Lat. *cappa* 'hood, cape' (whence Fr. *chape* 'cloak, eccles. cope', cf. *chapeau* 'hat'). Ending -ка perhaps by analogy with similar nouns (cf. later кéпка 'cloth cap', ultimately from Fr. *képi* 'military cap'). Cognate with кáпор 'hood, bonnet' from D. *kaper* 'hood' and капюшóн 'hood' from Fr. *capuchon*, id.

ШАР [šar] 'sphere, globe'. Early 17th century. A proposed derivation from 11th century *шаръ* 'colour, paint' is disputed (cf. dial. *шар*, id.). However, the meaning 'sphere' perhaps referred initially to a round paint spot.

ШАРМАНКА [šarmánka] 'barrel-organ'. 18th-/early 19th centuries, perhaps originally **шармантка*, said to be based on the Ger. song *Scharmante Katharine* or the Fr. song *Charmante Gabrielle*, which was seemingly played on the barrel-organ by vagrant organ-grinders (some have disputed the existence of such a song, assuming the words referred to to have been the calling cry of organ-grinders, however a popular song, said to be from the Fr., is recorded, beginning Во всей дерéвне Катерúнка красáвицей слылá 'Catherine's beauty was famed throughout the village'). Alternatively, via Pol. *szarmant katrynka* or Fr. *charmante* 'charming' (Катерúнка-шармáнка was an alternative name for the barrel-organ), of the puppet shows that accompanied barrel-organ music (also, barrel-organs were often decorated with moving puppet figures), hence Pol. *katarynka* 'barrel-organ', perhaps based on a puppet-name. Cf., for dims. based on the names of dolls, мúшка 'Teddy bear', матрёшка 'nesting-doll'. See also Петрýшка 'Punch'.

ШАХМАТЫ [šáchmaty] 'chess'. Known in Rus' 11th century (according to the Novgorod birch-bark writs), ostensibly from Pers. *shāh mat* (probably via Iran. N. Black Sea tribes) and Ar. *šāh māt* 'the king is dead' (cf. Ar. *šaṭranǰ* 'chess'), rather than from MHG *schach unde mat* (cf. Ger. *schachmatt* 'checkmate'). However, 'the king has died' would be *māta l-malik* in Ar., *shah mord/mordeh ast* in Pers. The original may thus have been, in preference to the proposed hybrids, Ar. *al-shaykh mayt/mayyit* 'the chief/old man is dead' (Mattock).

ШАХТА [šáchta] 'mine' 16th century, from Ger., Germans being the supreme mining experts throughout the middle ages, cf. Ger. *Schacht* 'shaft, pit', ultimately MLG *schacht* 'vertical pit, mine', from Harz Mountains mining terminology, possibly via Pol. *szacht/szachta*, id. Шахтёр 'miner' is based on шáхта (cf. Ger. *Bergarbeiter*, id.).

ШАШЛЫК [šašlýk] 'kebab'. First half of 17th century, originally 'spit, skewer', then 'shashlyk', lit. 'food prepared on a skewer', from Tkc., cf. Tadž. *šašlik*, id. (however, some Tkc. forms are from R.).

ШВЕЙЦАР [švejcár] 'commissionaire'. 18th century, originally 'Swiss', later 'commissionaire' (cf. швейцáрец 'Swiss'). From Ger. *Schweizer* 'Swiss', then 'door-keeper in Catholic churches, member of Papal guard', probably via Pol. *szwajcar* 'Swiss, door-keeper'. From the custom among Fr. and Ger. dignitaries of employing Swiss mercenaries as bodyguards, cf. analogous meanings in Fr. *suisse* and Ital. *svizzero*.

ШЕЛК [šëlk] 'silk'. Perhaps via Gmc. (cf. OE *sioloc*, id.), a reshaping of Late Lat. *sēricum*, id., from Lat. *Sēricus* 'silken, Chinese', *Sēres* 'a people of E. Asia (the modern Chinese) famed for their silken fabrics' (silk was first obtained from China and passed through Slav. countries into the Baltic trade). Cf. Gk. *sēr* 'silkworm', *sērikós* 'silken', *Sēres* 'China, the Chinese' and, of Lat. origin, Fr. *serge* 'serge' (twilled worsted, etc., fabric).

ШЕЛУХА [šeluchá] 'peel, pod'. Recorded in dictionaries since 1731, probably cognate with холостóй 'unmarried, blank'. For ending -yxá, cf. требухá 'tripe', etc.

ШЕПОТ [šëpot] 'whisper'. Onomatopoeic. For -от, cf. тóпот 'clatter'.

ШЕРЕНГА [šerénga] 'file, column'. 17th century, via Pol. *szereg* 'row, file', from Hung. *sereg* 'host, flock, army'. Presumed ultimately to be from Tkc.

ШЕРСТЬ [šerst'] 'wool'. 13th century *сьрсть* 'wool', perhaps initially 'rough fabric', seemingly cognate with Lith. *šiurkštus* 'rough, coarse'. 14th century *шьрсть* 'hide, pelt', 15th century 'wool fabric', with с- changing to ш- possibly by dissimilation of sibilants (с-с to ш-с), or under the influence of шкýра 'skin, hide' or шершáвый 'rough'.

ШЕСТЬ [šest'] 'six'. 11th century, from CSl. *šestъ, originally *sesь (cf. IE *sueks/seks 'six', Goth. *saihs*, id., Lat. *sex*, id., Gk. *héx*, id.), then *šesь (š- by dissimilation of s-s to š-s, cf. Lith. *šeši*, id.). Finally *šestь, with -t- from ordinal *šestъ 'sixth' (cf. Lat. *sextus*, id., Lith. *šeštas*, id.), the cardinal numeral assuming the form of an i-stem noun. Derivatives include шестнáдцать 'sixteen', шестьдесят 'sixty', шестьсóт 'six hundred'.

ШЕЯ [šéja] 'neck'. 11th century *шия* (later шéя) 'neck, shoulders, back', from CSl. *šija, root *ši- (cf. за шúворот 'by the scruff of the neck', OR *воротъ* 'neck', which is cognate with вертéть 'to turn'). Шéя is cognate with шить 'to sew', and lit. means 'that which connects' (sc. the head to the torso). Cf. Cz.

vaz 'back of the neck, ligament' from *vazati* 'to bind'.

ШИНЕЛЬ [šinél'] 'greatcoat'. Mid-18th century 'morning-dress, dressing-gown', later 'greatcoat', from Fr. *chenille* 'caterpillar, kind of dressing-gown' (perhaps from the fluffy appearance of both), itself from Vulg. Lat. *canīcula* 'little dog'. The form of the word is said to have been influenced by полишинéль 'Punch(inello)', borrowed at about the same time and purportedly also meaning 'form of greatcoat', perhaps confused, through false etymology, with *полушинель* 'semi-greatcoat' (cf. полупальтó 'short coat', etc.).

ШИТЬ [šit'] 'to sew'. 12th century, id., from IE *sįū- 'to fasten together' (cognate with Lat. *suō* 'I sew together' and Lith. *siūti* 'to sew'). Derivatives include (with the agent-suffix -л(о)), шúло 'awl', lit. 'what you sew with', шов 'seam' and подóшва 'sole'.

ШИШКА [šíška] 'cone, lump'. 16th century 'cone', possibly from an IE root denoting 'container' (thus lit. 'fruit of the pine, containing seeds'), whence by extension early 18th-century 'lump'. Alternatively, from Tkc., via Turk. lexis denoting 'swelling, swollen'. The various meanings of шúшка possibly derive from different roots.

ШКАФ [škaf] 'cupboard'. Early 18th century шкаф and (arch. or dial.) шкап, id. The latter probably derives from Sc., cf. Norw. *skap*, id., ш- evolving possibly under the influence of *шаф* (arch.), id. (but cf. also šk- from sk- in analogous шквал from Eng. *squall*, шкатýлка 'box' from Ital. *scatola*, id.). *Шаф* derives from S. Ger. *Schaff* 'open vessel, tub, cupboard', which is also the source of шкаф (with -к- perhaps by analogy with the Sc.).

ШКОЛА [škóla] 'school'. Late 14th century (in W. of Russia, elsewhere 16th-/17th centuries, superseding учúлище, id.). Ultimately from Gk. *scholḗ* 'leisure, learned discussion', later 'school', via Lat. *schola* (whence схолáстика 'scholastics'), Pol. *szkoła*, id.

ШКУРА [škúra] 'hide, pelt'. 16th century (earlier *скора*), from

CSl. *skora, id., lit. 'that which is flayed, cut' (IE *(s)ker- 'to cut', *sk̃indh 'to flay'). Probably via Pol. *skóra* 'hide, skin' (cf. скорняк 'furrier', Pol. *skórnik* 'currier, leather dealer'), with cognates in корá 'bark' (which is flayed from trees), корь 'measles' (symptomized by peeling skin), Lat. *corium* 'skin, hide, leather', Lith. *skìrti* 'to separate, divide'. Initial ш- possibly under the influence of шерсть 'wool', cf. also шк- from sk- in шкаф 'cupboard', etc. Vowel -у- perhaps under the influence of words such as кожурá 'rind' (only attested, however, in mid-18th century) or Pol. -ó-.

ШЛЕМ [šlem] 'helmet'. Via ChSl. (hence -ле-), from CSl. *šelmъ (IE *kel- 'to conceal'), replacing ESl. *шеломъ* 'helmet', from W. Gmc. *helmaz (cf. also Goth. *hilms*, id., Ger. *Helm*, id.). Initial ш- by first palatalization of velars. See ошеломи́ть 'to stun'.

ШЛЯПА [šljápa] 'hat'. Late 16th century, from Ger., cf. Bavarian *Schlappe* 'cap', MHG *slappe* 'type of soft hat' (both cited by Vasmer), Ger. *Schlapphut* 'slouch hat', *schlapp* 'slack, flabby' (coll., from LG *slapp*, id.). For -ля- from -la-, cf. популя́рный 'popular'.

ШМЕЛЬ [šmel'] 'bumble-bee'. From CSl. *čmelь, onomatopoeic *čьm- (IE *kem- 'to buzz', *kemelos 'bumble bee'), cf. Cz. *čmelak*, id., Pol. *trzmiel*, id. (for correlation čm-/šm-, cf., e.g. pronunciation -čn- in коне́чный 'final' as against -šn- in коне́чно 'of course' (however, Černych assumes шмель derives from *щмель). Cognate with комáр 'gnat', Ger. *Hummel* 'bumble-bee' (OHG *humbal*, id.), Eng. *bumble-bee*, originally *humble-bee*, from *humble* (arch.) 'to rumble, mumble'.

ШНУР [šnur] 'cord, flex'. Early 17th century, via Pol. *sznur*, id., from Ger *Schnur* (OHG *snuor*). *Снур*, id., an early variant, is from Sc. -- the word was first used in the N., cf. Dan. *snor* 'cord, line, string'.

ШОКОЛАД [šokolád] 'chocolate'. Established mid-18th century (earlier *чекулат/чоколáд*, from Ital. *cioccolata*, id.), via Fr. *chocolat*, id. or Ger. *Schokolade*, id., ultimately from Sp. *choco-*

late, id., adapted from Nahuatl (an Aztec language) *chocolatl* 'food made from cocoa seeds'.

ШОССЕ [šossé] 'highway'. Early 19th century, from Fr. *chaussée*, id. (possibly via Ger. *Chaussee*, id.), based on Fr. *chausser* 'to provide with shoes', from Vulg. Lat. *calceō* 'I provide with shoes', whence *(via) calceāta* 'paved (lit. 'shod') road'. Alternatively, 'road paved with limestone' (Fr. *chaux* 'limestone', Lat. *calx*, id.).

ШПАЛА [špála] 'railway sleeper'. Second half of the 19th century, parallel with the development of the R. railway network, possibly from D. *spalk* 'splint, board' (perhaps via a R. dim. in *-ок, cf. Cz. *špalek* 'block, log'), or via Pol. dial. from Ger. *Spale* (rare, cited by Grimm with a reference from 1482) 'ladder-rung'. Implausibly, from Eng. *spall* 'chip, splinter'. In view of meaning discrepancies, perhaps indigenous and cognate with па́лка 'stick', поле́но 'log', ultimately IE *(s)p(h)el- 'to chop, split'.

ШПАРГАЛКА [špargálka] 'crib' (school slang). From *шпарга́лы* (obs./jocular) 'junk, bits and pieces', Pol. *szpargał* (pl. *szpargały*) 'waste paper'. Ultimately, seemingly via Late Lat. from Gk. *spárganon* 'band for swaddling infants'.

ШПИЛЬ [špil'] 'spire, capstan'. 18th century, from Ger. *Spill* 'capstan' or D. *spil* 'spindle' (cf. Ger. *Spille*, id.). 18th-century derivative шпи́лька 'hair-pin, hat-pin' is from Pol. *szpilka* 'pin'.

ШРАМ [šram] 'scar'. First half of 18th century, via Pol. *szrama* 'scratch, scar', from Ger. *Schramme*, id. (MHG *schram(me)* 'long wound'), cognate with Ger. *scheren* 'to cut', ultimately from IE *(s)ker-, id. Masc. gender possibly under the influence of рубе́ц 'scar', cf. also D. *schram* 'scratch'.

ШТАНЫ [štaný] 'trousers'. Early 17th century, perhaps originally *штоны, from Tkc. (cf. Uzb. *išton*, id.), alternatively based on dial. *стан* 'sewn widths of fabric without sleeves or collars' (e.g.. стан руба́хи 'shirt length'), from which trousers could also have been made. Initial š- from s-, rare in an indigenous word, perhaps by analogy with шаровáры 'wide trousers'.

ШТОПАТЬ [štópat'] 'to darn'. 18th century, from D. *stoppen* 'to darn, fill' (or LG *stoppen*), ultimately MLat. *stuppare* 'to caulk' (from Lat. *stūp(p)a* 'tow, oakum', Gk. *stýp(p)ē*, id.). Initial ш- possibly under the influence of Ger. *stopfen* 'to darn' (Ger. st- is pronounced št-).

ШТУКА [štúka] 'item'. First half of 17th century, possibly via Pol. *sztuka* 'piece, part', from MHG *stücke* 'item' (cf. Ger. *Stück*, id.).

ШТУКАТУР [štukatúr] 'plasterer'. 18th century, from Ital. *stuccatore* 'plasterer, stucco-worker' (possibly via Ger., cf. Ger. *Stukkateur*, id. *Stukkatur* 'plastering', *Stuck* 'plaster'), a derivative of Ital. *stucco* 'plaster, stucco', itself from OHG *stucki* 'fragment, crust'.

ШТЫК [štyk] 'bayonet'. Early 18th century (also *багинетъ*, id.), possibly from Pol. *sztych* 'stab, thrust, point', MHG *stich* 'stab, thrust' (Goth. *stiks*, IE *(s)teig- 'to prick, stab', cf. Ger. *Stichwaffe* 'pointed weapon'). Initially, perhaps *штыхъ*, subsequently штык under the influence of тыкать 'to jab' (cf. гáлстук 'tie', фáртук 'apron'). Cf. also Sw. *stickvapen* 'pointed weapon', but *bajonet* 'bayonet' (Peter I corresponded on the subject of Sw. weapons, Sweden being his main opponent in the Great N. War 1700-21).

ШУБА [šúba] 'fur coat'. 14th century, from Late MHG *schube/schaube* 'long loose outer garment' (cf. Ger. *Schaube* 'fur-lined mantle for men'), itself, via Ital. *giubba* 'coat, jacket', from Ar. *jubba* 'outer garment with long broad sleeves', whence also Fr. *jupe* 'skirt' (cf. юбка, id.).

ШУРЫ-МУРЫ [šúry-múry] 'love affairs'. A reshaping of Fr. *cher amour* 'precious love' (or its pl.), through adaptation of a Tkc. loan, cf. Čagataj *šuruš-muruš* 'indignation, revolt', whence LG *schurrmurr* 'muddle, confusion', N. Ger. *Schurrmurr*, id.

Щ

ЩЁГОЛЬ [ščëgol'] 'fop'. 18th century (16th century as nickname), probably from the fig. use of щегóл 'goldfinch' (cf. analogous ворóна 'crow, gawper', пáва 'peahen, proud beauty', etc.), with differentiating stress change and -л to -ль. CSl. *ščьglъ 'goldfinch' derived from onomatopoeic *skъg- + -lъ (for suffix, cf. орёл 'eagle'), with sk- palatalizing to šč- before -ь-. Alternatively, щёголь has been associated with Pol. *szczegól* 'detail', *szczególny* 'particular', perhaps referring to a dandy's individualism.

ЩЕКА [ščeká] 'cheek'. 17th century (cf. arch. лани́та, id., also poet.), possibly cognate with Icel. *skegg* 'beard', Norw. *skjegg*, id. Alternatively, from IE *skekō 'to jump', the cheek being one of the face's most mobile features, thus cognate with скакáть, id. Derivatives include пощёчина 'slap'.

ЩЕЛЬ [ščel'] 'slit'. Recorded early 17th century, from CSl. *ščelь, ultimately from IE *(s)kel- 'to cut, split', with sk- palatalizing to šč- before -e-. Cognate with скалá 'rock, cliff', оскóлок 'splinter', Lith. *skelti* 'to cleave'.

ЩЕНОК [ščenók] 'puppy'. 11th century щеня, from CSl. *ščenę (cf. Pol. *szczenię*, id.), probably (cf. чáдо 'child') from IE *ken- 'to beget' (with initial *s-, thus root *ščen- from *(s)ken-). Perhaps lit. 'new-born'. Cognate with зачáть 'to conceive', Gk. *kainós* 'new, fresh', Lat. *recēns* 'lately arisen'. A suggested link with Pol. *szczekać* 'to bark' is disputed.

ЩЕПЕТИЛЬНЫЙ [ščepetíl'nyj] 'punctilious'. 18th century *щепети́льные товáры* 'haberdashery' (later галантерéя, id.), from dial. *щепети́ть* 'to flaunt', cf. *щепети́нье* (obs.) 'knickknacks', *щепети́льник* (obs.) 'pedlar'. Apparently ultimately from щепá 'splinter', also (according to Vasmer) 'trifle'. Meaning changed from 'dealing in small articles' to 'attentive to small details'.

ЩЕТИНА [ščetína] 'bristle'. Recorded 17th century, though known earlier, ultimately from CSl. *ščetь (cf. dial. *щеть* 'coarse hair, bristle'), *ščetina. Щётка 'brush' also derives from *щеть* (with stressed -e- to -ё- before a hard consonant).

ЩИ [šči] 'cabbage soup'. From earlier *шти*, still common in dial. (with ingredients ranging from fish to groats, potatoes and carrots, sour cabbage and meat, cf. implication of meat content in the saying попа́сть как кур во́ щи 'to land up (lit. 'like a cockerel') in the soup'). From OR *сътъ* (pl. *с(ъ)ты*) 'honeycomb' (cf. соты 'honeycombs'), earlier (Černych) 'liquid sustenance (perhaps with vegetables), nourishing drink'. Cognate with сы́тый 'replete', соса́ть 'to suck', possibly сок 'juice', щи has also tentatively been associated with a truncated form of the pl. of борщ (борщи́) 'beetroot soup', also with Dan. *Sky* 'meat broth' and щаве́ль 'sorrel'.

ЩИТ [ščit] 'shield'. 10th century, from CSl. *ščitъ (originally *skitъ, cf. IE *skei- 'to divide, separate', with sk- palatalizing to šč- before -i-). Perhaps lit. 'that which separates'. Cf. cognates Goth. *skaidan* 'to separate' (Ger. *scheiden*, id.), Lat. *scūtum* 'shield', Ir. *sciat*, id., and derivative защи́та 'defence'.

ЩУКА [ščúka] 'pike' (fish). 15th century, possibly originally *щупка (cf. dial. *щупа́к*, id., Pol. *szczupak*, id.), with subsequent simplification of -pk- to -k-. Cognate with щу́плый 'frail' (from the elongated appearance of the fish). Alternatively, associated with скака́ть 'to jump', perhaps from the fish's speed or its swift leaps from the water, or with IE *skeuh(w)a)- 'shy', cf. MHG *schiuhen* 'to scare off' (Ger. *scheuchen*, id.), from the fish's awesome appearance and reputation.

ЩУПЛЫЙ [ščúplyj] 'puny'. From CSl. *ščuplъ, cognate with щу́пать 'to feel, grope' (cf. analogous до́хлый 'dead', до́хнуть 'to die'), perhaps 'so thin its bones can be felt' (possibly a false etymology). Cf. also cognate щу́пальце 'tentacle', dim. of *щу́пало* (with agent-suffix -л(о), lit. 'what you grope with').

Ю

ЮБКА [júbka] 'skirt'. From 16th-century *юпа* 'warm cloth jacket or gown' (as recorded by 18th-century historiographer N.M. Karamzin, cf. dial. *юбка* 'sleeveless jacket with shoulder-straps, worn by peasant-women'), *юбка* 'skirt' evolving instead of **юпка*, probably by analogy with nouns like трубка 'pipe' (since -бка is pronounced as -пка). Ultimately, from Ar. *jubba* 'outer garment of Moslems and Parsees' (whence also шуба 'fur-coat', зипун 'homespun coat'), via Pol. *jupka* 'juppon' or MHG *juppe/joppe* 'jacket, frock' (cf. Ger. *Joppe* 'man's jacket') and Romance languages, perhaps through Sicily (cf. Ital. *giubba* 'sleeveless garment', also Fr. *jupe* 'skirt', Sp. *aljuba* 'jibba(h), an ancient Moorish garment', *chupa* 'undercoat with sleeves').

ЮГ [jug] 'south'. 11th century *югъ*, id. (of ChSl. origin), *угъ* 'south, south wind, southern countries'. Cognate with Gk. *augé* 'bright light' (IE *augā 'light, gleam'), less certainly with Lat. *augeō* 'I increase', Lith. *augti* 'to grow'. See ужин 'dinner'.

ЮНЫЙ [júnyj] 'young'. 11th century (also *уньıи*, id., ю- from ChSl.), cognate with Lat. *juvenis*, id., Lith. *jaunas*, id., Ger. *jung*, id. Юнга 'ship's boy', an early 18th-century loan, derives from D. *jongen* 'boy', rather than Ger. *Junge*, id., with final -a under the influence of юноша 'youth'.

ЮРОДИВЫЙ [juródivyj] 'holy fool'. 11th century 'stupid' (from ChSl.), also 11th-century *уродивыи* 'stupid', 12th century 'holy fool', from у- 'defect' + род 'birth, origin', cf. урод 'monster'. Покровский собор 'Pokrovskij Cathedral' on Red Square, constructed 1555-60 in the reign of Ivan IV to mark the subjugation of the Kazan' khanate, is also known as Храм Василия Блаженного 'Church of Basil the Blessed', after the best-known of the holy fools, who were popularly credited with the gift of clairvoyance.

Я

ЯБЛОКО [jábloko] 'apple'. OR 'apple, globe, orb', from CSl. *ablъko (IE *abəlis 'apple'), cognate with Lith. *obuolys*, id., Ger. *Apfel*, id. Possibly a loan from the Celts on the Lower Danube (cf. also Gael. *ubhall*, id.), or connected with Lat. *Abella* (called *malifera* 'apple-bearing' in Vergil's *Aeneid*), a town in Campagna famed for growing fruit (alternatively, the place-name may come from the name of the fruit).

ЯГНЕНОК [jagnënok] 'lamb'. 11th century *агня* (= *ягня*), id., from CSl. *(j)agnę (IE *agunos, id.). According to one theory connected with CSl. *ognь 'fire', thus originally 'burnt offering'. Cognate with Lat. *agnus* 'lamb', Eng. *yean* 'to bring forth' (a lamb or kid). Cf., from ChSl., áгнец (eccles.) 'lamb'.

ЯГОДА [jágoda] 'berry'. OR, id. (mainly of grapes). For CSl. roots *(j)agъ/*(j)aga (cf. IE *akīnos 'berry'), cf. Croat. *vinjaga* 'wild grapes' and *vinjag* 'bunch of wild grapes'. Suffix -од(а) corresponds to the formant in Gk. *lampádos*, gen. of *lampás* 'lamp'. Cognate with Lith. *uoga* 'berry', debatably with Lat. *augeõ* 'I increase'.

ЯД [jad] 'poison'. Euphemistic, developing from the meaning 'food', then probably (initially in emotive speech) 'bad food', 'poisoned food', 'poison'. Cf. 11th-century *ядь* 'food', *ѣдь*, id., *ѣдъ* 'food, poison', *ядъ* 'poison', and analogous Fr. *poison* 'poison' from Lat. *põtiõ* 'drink, poisonous draught', OHG *gift* 'gift, poison', Ger. *Gift* 'poison', травá 'grass' and cognate отрáва 'poison'. Cognates also include яства 'victuals', ясли 'manger', éдкий 'acrid' ('edible' in OR), всеядный 'omnivorous', тунеядец 'parasite'.

ЯДРО [jadró] 'kernel, core'. 11th century (mainly in pl.) 'depths', 12th century 'womb'. From CSl. *jędro, possibly cognate with Gk. *hadrós* 'strong' or IE *dəru 'tree' (a metaphor for strength), cf. ядрёный 'healthy, vigorous', ядерный 'nuclear'.

ЯЗЫК [jazýk] 'tongue, language'. Known since the 10th

century, 11th century 'tongue, speech, language, people, interpreter'. Seemingly cognate with OPr. *insuwis*, Lat. *lingua* 'tongue, language' (from **dingua*, cf. IE **dn̥ĝuhā* 'tongue', l- perhaps by analogy with *lingō* 'I lick'), and Lith. *liežuvis* 'tongue' (l- perhaps by analogy with *laižyti* 'to lick'). According to one theory, from IE **anghō* 'narrow', thus lit. 'narrow strip of skin or tissue', then 'tongue'. Alternatively, associated with CSl. **vęzati* 'to bind', thus 'speech, what binds people together, a people'.

ЯЙЦО [jajcó] 'egg'. 11th century *аице*, id., 14th century *яице*, later яйцó, id., with -e to -o in stressed position after -ц-, cf. лицó 'face'. From CSl. **(j)ajьce* (dim. of **(j)aje*, cf. Pol. *jaje/jajko* 'egg'), assumed to have developed from IE **ōu̯i̯om* 'egg', whence also Gk. *ō(i)ón*, id., Lat. *ovum*, id., Ger. *Ei*, id.

ЯКОРЬ [jákor'] 'anchor'. First reference 10th century, from Byz. Gk. or Sc. (the trade route 'from the Varangians to the Greeks' was being developed at the time). Possibly from OSw. *ankari*, id., Lat. *ancora*, id., ultimately from Gk. *ágkȳra*, id. (named after its curved shape, cf. Gk. *ágkos* 'bend', also IE **ankos*, id.).

ЯМА [jáma] 'hole'. 11th century, from CSl. **jama* (IE **i̯ōmā* 'cave'), perhaps cognate with Gk. *ámē* 'spade' (also 'bucket', whence Lat. *hama*, id.). Perhaps lit. 'what is dug with a spade'.

ЯНВАРЬ [janvár'] 'January'. 12th century *генварь* (still used in standard, especially bureaucratic, language till 19th century), also *геньварь, генуарь*, subsequently янвáрь, from Lat. *Iānuārius*, id., via Gk. *genouári(o)s*, after Janus, god of gates and beginnings, depicted with faces on the front and back of his head, looking into the past and the coming year (cf. Lat. *jānua* 'door').

ЯНТАРЬ [jantár'] 'amber'. Mid-16th century (originally with initial e-), probably from Lith. *gintaras*, id.

ЯРКИЙ [járkij] 'bright'. From OR *яръ, ярьи* 'spring' (adj.), cf. IE **iēros* 'period, year', whence also Goth *jer* 'year' (Ger. *Jahr*, id.), the Gmc. root probably meaning 'course of the sun'.

Cf. also Gk. *ōra* 'blooming season, spring, summer', яровой 'spring' (adj.), ярка 'young ewe' (up to first lambing), ярый 'bright (obs.), vehement' (whence ярость 'rage').

ЯРМАРКА [jármarka] 'trade fair'. Early 17th century, from MHG (cf. Ger. *Jahrmarkt*, id.), directly from the Ger. territories with which Greater Novgorod traded, or via Pol. *jarmark*, id.

ЯСНЫЙ [jásnyj] 'clear'. 11th century 'bright', 14th century 'clear', from CSl. **jasnъ*, based either on **ja(v)snъ* (**javs-* 'manifest, visible' + *-nъ*), cf. явный 'obvious', with -vs- simplifying to -s-, but more probably from **(j)ĕsknъ* (with -skn- simplifying to -sn-). Variants of root **ĕsk-* are found in искра 'spark', Pol. *jaskrawy* 'dazzling'. Cf. also Lith. *aiškus* 'clear, lucid'.

ЯСТРЕБ [jástreb] 'hawk'. CSl. **jastrębъ* (possibly **jastrebъ*, for suffix, cf. CSl. **golǫbь* 'dove'). From **astrъ* 'swift' (IE **ōḱus*, id.), the bird being named for its speed of flight or vision, cf. Gk. *ōkýs*, id., *ōkypétēs* 'swift-flying', Lat. *accipiter* 'hawk'.

ЯЧМЕНЬ [jačmén'] 'barley'. Based on the oblique cases of CSl. **jęčьmy*, gen. **jęčmene* (cf. Pol. *jęczmień*, id.), related to IE **onkos* 'hook' or **anktos* 'bend' (cf. Lat. *uncus* 'hooked') -- when ripening, barley inclines its ears to the soil. Cf. Cz. *ječmen je v hačku* (*háčkuje*), lit. 'the barley is "in hook"', i.e. ripening.

ЯЩЕРИЦА [jáščerica] 'lizard'. 14th century ящеръ, 16th century ящерица. Probably cognate with скорый 'fast' and named for its speed of movement, cf. Gk. *skaírō* 'I dance, bound', *(a)skarízō* 'I jump, palpitate', Ger. *sich scheren* 'to clear off', Lith. *skėrys* 'locust' (IE **skəros* 'swift, sudden'). Alternatively, if debatably, cognate with скора (arch.) 'skin', from the lizard's propensity to slough.

ЯЩИК [jáščik] 'box, drawer'. 14th-/15th centuries аскъ, then яскъ 'basket', possibly of Gmc. origin, cf. OIcel. *askr* 'ash-tree, wooden vessel' (the ash was much prized in wood carving), cf. OHG *asc* 'dish', earlier 'boat', probably of ash-wood.

BIBLIOGRAPHY

Russian Etymological Dictionaries

Cyganenko, G.P., *Этимологический словарь русского языка*, Kiev, 1970
Černych, P. Ja., *Историко-этимологический словарь русского языка*, 2 vols., Moscow, 1993
Preobraženskij, A.G., *Этимологический словарь русского языка*, 2 vols., Moscow, 1959
Šanskij, N.M., *Этимологический словарь русского языка*, A-K, 2 vols. in 8 books, Moscow, 1963-82
Šanskij, N.M., V.V. Ivanov, T.V. Šanskaja, *Краткий этимологический словарь русского языка*, Moscow, 1961
Uspenkij, L., *Почему не иначе?*, Moscow, 1967
Vasmer, M., *Этимологический словарь русского языка*, 4 vols., translated from German, with additions, by O.N. Trubačev, Moscow, 1964-73

Other Etymological and Historical Dictionaries

Alekseev, P., *Церковный словарь*, five parts in two books, Hildesheim/New York, 1976. Reprint of St. Petersburg edition of 1817
Berneker, E., *Slavisches Etymologisches Wörterbuch*, 2 vols., Heidelberg, 1924
Bloch, O., W. von Wartburg, *Dictionnaire étymologique de la langue française*, Paris, 1932
Brückner, A., *Słownik etymologiczny języka polskiego*, Warsaw, 1957
Corominas, J., *Breve Diccionario Etimológico*, Madrid, 1961
Dauzat, A., *Dictionnaire étymologique de la langue française*, Paris, 1954
de Vries, J., *Nederlands Etymologisch Woordenboek*, Leiden, 1971
Gloger, Z., *Encyklopedia staropolska*, 4 vols., Warsaw, 1989
Kluge, F., *Etymologisches Wörterbuch der deutschen Sprache*, Berlin, 1963
MacBain, A. *An Etymological Dictionary of the Gaelic*

Language, Glasgow, 1982. Reprint of 1911 edition.
Mann, S.E., *An Indo-European Comparative Dictionary*, Hamburg, 1984-87
Mladenov, S., *Етимологически и правописенъ речникъ на българския книжовенъ езикъ*, Sofia, 1941
Onions, C.T. (ed.), *Dictionary of English Etymology*, Oxford, 1978
Sevortjan, E.V., *Этимологический словарь тюркских языков*, Moscow, 1978-80
Sreznevskij, I.I., *Материалы для словаря древнерусского языка по письменным памятникам*, 3 vols., Graz, 1955-56
Wasserzieher, E., *Kleines etymologisches Wörterbuch der deutschen Sprache*, Leipzig, 1977

Standard Dictionaries

Alderson, A.D., Fahir Iz, *The Concise Oxford Turkish Dictionary*, Oxford, 1959
Atanassova, T., *et al.*, English-Bulgarian Dictionary, 1994
Bertel's, E.E., ed., *Русско-таджикский словарь*, Stalinabad, 1949
Boyce, E.J., *Glossary of Words from the Greek*, London, 1878
Civil, M. *et al.*, eds., *The Assyrian Dictionary of the Oriental Institute of the University of Chicago*, 21 vols., Chicago/Glückstadt, 1961-89
Corten, I.H., *Vocabulary of Soviet Society and Culture*, London, 1992
Cowan, J.M., ed., *Arabic-English Dictionary*, New York, 1976
Černyšev, V.I., *et al.*, *Словарь современного русского языка*, 17 vols., Moscow, 1950-65
Dal', V., *Толковый словарь живого великорусского языка*, 4 vols., Moscow, 1956
Doroszewski, W., *Słownik poprawnej polszczyzny*, Warsaw, 1973
D'jačenko, G., *Полный церковнославянский словарь*, Moscow, 1993
Endzelins, J., K. Mühlenbach, *Latviešu Valodas Vārdnīca*, Riga, 1923-25
Feist, S., *Wörterbuch der gotischen Sprache*, Halle, 1909
Filin, F.P., *Словарь русских народных говоров*, 15 books *A* to *Первачок*, Moscow/Leningrad, 1965-90

Grimm, J. and W. Grimm, *Deutsches Wörterbuch*, 33 vols., Munich, 1984. Reprint of original Leipzig edition.
Hannay, M., *Handwoordenboek Nederlands-Engels*, Utrecht/Antwerp, 1994
Havránek, B., ed., *Slovník spisovného jazyka českého*, 3 vols., Prague, 1960-66
Hazon, M., *Dizionario Inglese-Italiano/Italiano-Inglese*, 2 vols., Milan, 1967
Jockin-la-Bastide, J.A., G. van Kooten, *English-Dutch/Dutch-English Dictionary*, London, 1985
Koščanov, M.K., ed., *Русско-узбекский словарь*, 2 vols., Taškent, 1983-84
Kotnik, J., *Slovensko-Angelški Slovar*, Ljubljana, 1952
Lambertz, M., *Albanisch-Deutsches Wörterbuch*, Berlin, 1954
Larin, B.A., *Русско-английский словарь-дневник Ричарда Джемса (1618-19)*, Leningrad, 1959
Latham, R.E., *Revised Medieval Latin Wordlist*, Oxford, 1965
Lewis, C.T., C. Short, *A Latin Dictionary*, Oxford, 1951
Lexer, M., *Mittelhochdeutsches Handwörterbuch*, 3 vols., Leipzig, 1978
Liddell, H.G., R. Scott, *Greek-English Lexicon*, 2 vols., Oxford, 1951
Macdonell, A.A., *A Sanskrit-English Dictionary*, London, 1893
Mac Mathúna, S., A. Ó Corráin, *Irish Dictionary*, Glasgow, 1995
Magnussen, J. et al., *Engelsk-Dansk/Dansk-Engelsk Ordbog*, 2 vols., Copenhagen, 1937/1944
Martínez Amador, E.M., *Diccionario inglés-español y español-inglés*, Oxford/Barcelona, 1953
Meyer Myklestad, J., H. Søraas, *Engelsk-Norsk/Norsk-Engelsk Lommeordbok*, Oslo, 1955
Nadeljaev, V.M., et al., *Древнетюркский словарь*, Leningrad, 1969
Niemeyer, J.F., *Mediae Latinitatis Lexicon Minus*, Leiden, 1976
Ožegov, S.I., ed. N. Ju. Švedova, *Словарь русского языка*, Moscow, 1987
Piesarskas, B., B. Svecevičius, *Lietuvių-Anglų Kalbų Žodynas*, USA, 1991
Podvesko, M.L., *English-Ukrainian Dictionary*, Kiev, 1948
Prochazka, J., *English-Czech and Czech-English Dictionary*,

London, 1952
Prochorov, A.M. *et al.*, eds., *Советский энциклопедический словарь*, Moscow, 1980
Radlov, V.V., *Versuch eines Wörterbuches der Türk-dialecte*, 4 vols., 's Gravenhage, 1960
Rey, A., J. Rey-Debove, *Le Petit Robert. Dictionnaire de la langue française*, Paris, 1992
Roty, M., *Dictionnaire russe-français des termes en usage dans l'église russe*, Paris, 1980
Sal'nova, A.V., *Карманный новогреческо-русский словарь*, Moscow, 1992
Skorupka, St., *Słownik frazeologiczny języka polskiego*, 2 vols., Warsaw, 1974
Smith, W., revised by E.H. Blakeney and J. Warrington, *Everyman's Smaller Classical Dictionary*, London/New York, 1952
Sophocles, E.A., *Greek Lexicon of the Roman and Byzantine Periods BC 146-AD 1100*, Boston, 1870
Souter, A., *A Glossary of Later Latin to 600 AD*, Oxford, 1949
Sujunčev, Ch. I., I. Ch. Urusbiev, *Русско-карачаево--балкарский словарь*, Moscow, 1965
Steingass, F., *A Comprehensive Persian-English Dictionary*, London, 1892
Tangl, E., *Hrvatski-Njemački i Njemački-Hrvatski*, Berlin, undated
Tolstoj, I.I., *Сербскохорватско-русский словарь*, Moscow, 1970
Torikashvili, J.J., *Georgian-English/English-Georgian Dictionary*, New York, 1992
Trešnikov, A.F., ed., *Географический энциклопедический словарь*, Moscow, 1983
Troxel, D.A., *Mongolian Vocabulary*, Washington, 1953
Ušakov, D.N., ed., *Толковый словарь русского языка*, 4 vols., Moscow, 1935-40
Wahrig, G., *Deutsches Wörterbuch*, Mosaik Verlag, 1980
Wells, J.C., *Althochdeutsches Glossenwörterbuch*, Heidelberg, 1990
Wheeler, M., *The Oxford Russian-English Dictionary*, Oxford, 1972
Wilkinson, R.J., ed., *A Malay-English Dictionary*, 2 parts,

London/New York, 1957
Williams, M., *A Sanskrit-English Dictionary*, Oxford, 1872
Yacoubian, A.N., *English-Armenian and Armenian-English Dictionary*, Los Angeles, 1944
Zingarelli, N., *Il Nuovo Zingarelli*, Bologna, 1986

History of Language and Linguistics

Aitchison, J., *Linguistics*, London/Sydney/Auckland, 1992
Anikin, A.E. et al., *Из истории русских слов*, Moscow, 1993
Barfield, O., *History in English Words*, London, 1953
Chambers, W.W., J.R. Wilkie, *A Short History of the German Language*, London, 1970
Charčenkova, L., *По одежде встечают.Секреты русского костюма*, St. Petersburg, 1994
Černych, P. Ja., *Историческая грамматика русского языка*, Moscow, 1962
Entwistle, W.J., W.A. Morison, *Russian and the Slavonic Languages*, London, 1949
Gudzij, N.K., compiler, *Хрестоматия по древней русской литературе XI-XVII веков*, Moscow, 1962
Günther-Hielscher, K. et al., *Real- und Sachwörterbuch zum Altrussischen*, Neuried, 1985
Ivanov, V.V., *Историческая грамматика русского языка*, Moscow, 1964
Lehmann, W.P., *Historical Linguistics*, London/New York, 1992
Lord, R., *Comparative Linguistics*, London, 1966
Matthews, W.K., *Russian Historical Grammar*, London, 1960
Otkupščikov, *К истокам слова*, Leningrad, 1968
Potter, S., *Language in the Modern World*, London, 1975
Vlasto, A.P., *A Linguistic History of Russia*, Oxford, 1988

Linguistic Glossaries

Pei, M.A. and F. Gaynor, *Dictionary of Linguistics*, London, 1960
Steible, D., *Concise Handbook of Linguistics*, London, 1967